European Yearbook of International Economic Law

EYIEL Monographs - Studies in European and International Economic Law

Volume 23

Series Editors

Marc Bungenberg, Saarbrücken, Germany
Christoph Herrmann, Passau, Germany
Markus Krajewski, Erlangen, Germany
Jörg Philipp Terhechte, Lüneburg, Germany
Andreas R. Ziegler, Lausanne, Switzerland

EYIEL Monographs is a subseries of the European Yearbook of International Economic Law (EYIEL). It contains scholarly works in the fields of European and international economic law, in particular WTO law, international investment law, international monetary law, law of regional economic integration, external trade law of the EU and EU internal market law. The series does not include edited volumes. EYIEL Monographs are peer-reviewed by the series editors and external reviewers.

More information about this subseries at https://link.springer.com/bookseries/15744

Patricia Trapp

The European Union's Trade Defence Modernisation Package

A Missed Opportunity at Reconciling Trade and Competition?

 Springer

Patricia Trapp
Düsseldorf, Germany

ISSN 2364-8392 ISSN 2364-8406 (electronic)
European Yearbook of International Economic Law
ISSN 2524-6658 ISSN 2524-6666 (electronic)
EYIEL Monographs - Studies in European and International Economic Law
ISBN 978-3-030-91362-5 ISBN 978-3-030-91363-2 (eBook)
https://doi.org/10.1007/978-3-030-91363-2

This Springer imprint is published by the registered company Springer Nature Switzerland AG.
The registered company address is: Gewerbestrasse 11, 6330 Cham, Switzerland

Acknowledgments

This book was submitted as a PhD thesis at the University of Passau in February 2021. I wish to express my sincere gratitude to my supervisor, Professor Dr. Christoph Herrmann, LL.M., for his support during the entire PhD process. I benefitted immensely from his academic guidance and profound knowledge in EU trade defence law. I am also very thankful to Prof. Dr. Till Müller-Ibold for kindly agreeing to be the second examiner. Being an internationally recognized expert both in EU trade defence law and EU competition law, his comments on my work were extremely valuable.

As part of my PhD project, I was able to spend two months working in the *Cabinet* of Judge Ian S. Forrester at the General Court in Luxembourg. I am deeply grateful for this opportunity to pursue my PhD project at the very place where EU law is shaped and to benefit from the inspiring environment there.

I would further like to express my gratitude to the *Studienstiftung des deutschen Volkes e.V.* for funding my PhD thesis.

Pursuing a PhD can sometimes be quite a challenge, and it is easier to face this challenge if one does not have to do it on one's own. Therefore, I would like to thank Kara, Simon G., Chris, Gideon, Mareike, Simon M., Sebiha and all other members of the Chair for two wonderful years (and the many cups of coffee we had together).

Lastly, on a personal note, I would like to thank my family and my friends for their support and understanding. They have been at my side and encouraged me throughout this project. This, of course, also applies to you, Philip—thank you for being my emotional support system, for always believing in me and for being endlessly patient and understanding.

Contents

Abbreviations

AAC	Average avoidable cost
ADA	Agreement on Implementation of Article VI GATT: Anti-Dumping Agreement
AIC	Average incremental cost
ASCM	Agreement on Subsidies and Countervailing Measures
ATC	Average total cost
AVC	Average variable cost
BADR	Basic anti-dumping regulation
BASR	Basic anti-subsidy regulation
CCP	Common commercial policy
CETA	Comprehensive Economic and Trade Agreement
Charter	Charter of Fundamental Rights of the European Union
CJEU	Court of Justice of the European Union
Constitutional Treaty	Treaty establishing a Constitution for Europe
DSB	Dispute Settlement Body
EBA	Everything but arms
ECA	European Court of Auditors
ECHR	European Convention on Human Rights
ECSC Treaty	Treaty of Paris establishing the European Coal and Steel Community
ECSC	European Coal and Steel Community
EEC Treaty	Treaty of Rome establishing the European Economic Community
EEC	European Economic Community
ETS	Emissions Trading Scheme
EU	European Union
GSP	Generalised Scheme of Preferences
ILO	International Labour Organization
IMF	International Monetary Fund
LRAIC	Long-run average incremental cost

MEA	Multilateral environmental agreements
OECD	Organization for Economic Co-operation and Development
R&D	Research and development
SEA	Single European Act
SG&A	Selling, general and administrative expenses
SSNIP	Small but significant and non-transitory increase in price
TBR	Trade Barriers Regulation
TDIs	Trade Defence Instruments
TEU	Treaty on European Union
TFEU	Treaty on the Functioning of the European Union
TSD	Trade and Sustainable Development
VCLT	Vienna Convention on the Law of Treaties
WTO	World Trade Organization

Chapter 1
Introduction

1.1 The Changing Landscape of International Trade

In the summer of 2018, on the event of the entry into force of the European Union's (EU) reformed trade defence instruments, then President of the European Commission (Commission) *Jean-Claude Juncker* announced:

> The EU believes in open and fair trade but we are not naïve free traders. We have shown our teeth when we had to by adopting anti-dumping and anti-subsidy measures. And now we have new and improved trade defence rules in our arsenal to face down some of today's challenges in global trade. Make no mistake – we will do whatever it takes to defend European producers and workers when others distort the market or don't play by the rules.[1]

To those following current developments in world politics, it is hardly breaking news that international trade policy is operating in an increasingly hostile climate, with a variety of actors questioning the benefits of the existing international trade system. The declining significance of the World Trade Organization (WTO), favoured by the failure of the last WTO negotiating rounds, and accelerated by the blockade of the WTO Appellate Body, is an expression of the changes the world trading order is currently undergoing.

At the same time, States are resorting to ever more aggressive rhetoric when identifying the negative effects of free trade to their own domestic industries, as evidenced *inter alia* by the statement of Commission President *Juncker*. This growing scepticism does not only express itself in words: the WTO Trade Statistical Review of 2019 shows that trade flows are being hit by new trade restrictions at a historically high level.[2]

---

[1] European Commission, *EU trade defence: stronger and more effective rules enter into force* (2018).

[2] World Trade Organization, 'World Trade Statistical Review 2019' 68, available at <https://www.wto.org/english/res_e/statis_e/wts2019_e/wts2019_e.pdf>.

© The Author(s), under exclusive license to Springer Nature Switzerland AG 2022
P. Trapp, *The European Union's Trade Defence Modernisation Package*, EYIEL Monographs - Studies in European and International Economic Law 23, https://doi.org/10.1007/978-3-030-91363-2_1

The EU, the world's largest trading block, is not immune to these changes to the perception of international trade. The current Commission headed by *Ursula von der Leyen* as well as its predecessor under the *Juncker* presidency have placed the issue of an international level playing field at the centre of the bloc's policy priorities.[3] In June 2020, the Commission presented its White Paper on levelling the playing field as regards foreign subsidies,[4] which was followed by legislative proposals addressing the competition-distorting effects of subsidies granted by third States within the internal market in May 2021. The EU's efforts at ensuring a level playing field on the international plane include *inter alia* its attempts at reviving the WTO Appellate Body, proposals to amend the WTO rulebook with the objective of increasing members' compliance with their notification requirements under the Agreement on Subsidies and Countervailing Measures (ASCM)[5] and the Commission's International Public Procurement Initiative to help improve EU companies' access to global procurement markets.[6]

Most importantly, however, the EU has reformed its basic anti-dumping regulation (BADR)[7] and its basic anti-subsidy regulation (BASR)[8] through the Trade Defence Modernisation Package. The package comprises two Regulations, Regulation (EU) 2017/2321[9] and Regulation (EU) 2018/825,[10] which entered into force in December 2017 and June 2018 respectively. Among the considerations underlying the reform was the desire to make the EU's anti-subsidy and anti-dumping rules more effective and to improve enforcement.[11]

Rules on action that may be taken against imports of dumped or subsidised products form the two central pillars of the EU's trade defence arsenal. Another element of said arsenal are the so-called safeguard measures. Safeguard measures are

---

[3]Ursula von der Leyen, *Political Guidelines for the Next European Commission 2019–2024: A Union that strives for more – my agenda for Europe* (2019) 17.

[4]European Commission, 'White Paper on levelling the playing field as regards foreign subsidies (COM(2020) 253 final)' (Brussels 17 June 2020). For a first assessment of the Commission proposals cf. Trapp (2020), p. 964.

[5]On both aspects cf. e.g. European Commission, 'Concept Paper on WTO Reform' (July 2018).

[6]For more information on the matter cf. European Parliament, *Briefing: EU international procurement instrument* (2020).

[7]Regulation (EU) 2016/1036 of the European Parliament and of the Council of 8 June 2016 on protection against dumped imports from countries not members of the European Union.

[8]Regulation (EU) 2016/1037 of the European Parliament and of the Council of 8 June 2016 on protection against subsidised imports from countries not members of the European Union.

[9]Regulation (EU) 2017/2321 of the European Parliament and of the Council of 12 December 2017 amending Regulation (EU) 2016/1036 on protection against dumped imports from countries not members of the European Union and Regulation (EU) 2016/1037 on protection against subsidised imports from countries not members of the European Union.

[10]Regulation (EU) 2018/825 of the European Parliament and of the Council of 30 May 2018 amending Regulation (EU) 2016/1036 on protection against dumped imports from countries not members of the European Union and Regulation (EU) 2016/1037 on protection against subsidised imports from countries not members of the European Union.

[11]Recital 3 of Regulation (EU) 2018/825 (n 10).

used to limit the volume of imports where there is an increase in imports that could not have been reasonably foreseen and that has resulted in injury for the domestic industry producing competing goods.[12] Conversely, under anti-dumping and anti-subsidy measures, States will not regulate the volume of the imported goods, but the price at which the goods may be imported with the objective of countering trading practices that are considered unfair. The circumstances under which a WTO member may resort to the use of trade defence instruments are specified in WTO law.

While it was initially left undefined what exactly was to be subsumed under the term 'subsidy', Article 1 of the Agreement on Subsidies and Countervailing Measures (ASCM)[13] defines the term as the financial contribution by a government or any public body within the territory of a member or any form of price support in the sense of Article XVI of the GATT 1994 by which a benefit is conferred.[14]

Already the GATT 1947 contained rules addressing the issue of subsidisation, albeit only rudimentary ones. Under Article XVI GATT 1947, members were required to notify and consult on subsidies, and Article VI GATT 1947 allowed for the imposition of countervailing measures. The Tokyo Round Subsidies Code of 1979 presented first attempts at a more detailed regulation of the issue, as it provided for a separate treatment of export subsidies, which were prohibited in respect of industrial products, and 'other than export' subsidies. The Uruguay Round Agreement of 1994 resulted in the adoption of the ASCM, which is the most important benchmark for assessing the legality of countervailing measures under WTO law today.

The notion of dumping is used to describe price discrimination between national markets.[15] This is also the starting point of the definition employed in Article 2.1 Anti-Dumping Agreement (ADA),[16] which defines dumping as the introduction of a good into the commerce of another country at less than normal value. The term 'normal value' denotes the comparable price, in the ordinary course of trade, for the like product when destined for consumption in the exporting country.[17] Scholars differentiate between various forms of dumping, such as 'predatory dumping', 'market opening dumping', 'cyclical dumping' and 'State trading dumping'.[18]

Just as it had been the case for rules on anti-subsidy measures, already Article VI GATT 1947 provided for rules on the imposition of anti-dumping measures. However, its broad wording was deemed insufficient to regulate the matter

---

[12] Mavroidis (2016), p. 313.

[13] 'Agreement on Subsidies and Countervailing Measures: Marrakesh Agreement Establishing the World Trade Organization, Annex 1A' (1869 U.N.T.S. 14).

[14] Article 1 ASCM.

[15] Viner (1923), p. 3.

[16] 'Agreement on Implementation of Article VI of the General Agreement on Tariffs and Trade 1994: Marrakesh Agreement Establishing the World Trade Organization, Annex 1A' (1868 U.N.T.S. 201).

[17] Article 2.1 ADA.

[18] Hoffmeister (2018), paras. 8–16.

satisfactorily.[19] This led to the adoption of the Kennedy Round Code in 1968, the Tokyo Round Code in 1979, and eventually the ADA as one of the agreements annexed to the Uruguay Round Agreement of 1994. The ADA sets out the circumstances under which members are authorised to impose a specific anti-dumping duty on imports in goods from a particular source, in excess of bound rates.[20]

Then as now, the use of trade defence instruments is considered pivotal in averting injury to one's own domestic industry caused by imports. In the event of safeguard measures, it is the volume of imports that gives cause for concern. Conversely, it is the perception that foreign importers resort, to the detriment of one's own industry, to trading practices that are considered unfair, namely by practicing dumping or by receiving subsidisation from their home State, which is one of the rationales underlying the imposition of anti-dumping or anti-subsidy measures.[21]

This shows that, at least historically, competition concerns are at the heart of the use of anti-dumping and anti-subsidy instruments. Consequently, a frequently advanced reason for the imposition of anti-dumping or anti-subsidy measures is the necessity to offset the negative effects on competition caused by imports benefitting from unfair competitive advantages and to provide for a 'level playing field' also in international trade.[22]

Competition concerns may have been central in justifying the imposition of anti-subsidy and anti-dumping measures, and they still figure in the rhetoric employed by those who advocate the use of trade defence instruments. It must however be taken into account that their use may itself produce restrictive effects on competition. These include increases in the prices of imported goods, reducing the contestability of markets, and creating incentives for anti-competitive behaviour such as price coordination.[23] Another issue that is intrinsically linked to the issue of avoiding market foreclosure effects caused by the imposition of trade defence measures is whether and under which circumstances anti-dumping or anti-subsidy measures are used not to offset any genuine comparative disadvantages suffered by one's own domestic industry as a result of unfair trading practices, but for protectionist reasons.

---

[19] Bourgeois (2008), para. 7.

[20] Cf. Article II (2) lit. b) GATT 1994: '*Nothing in this Article shall prevent any contracting party from imposing at any time on the importation of any product any anti-dumping or countervailing duty applied consistently with the provisions of Article VI.*'

[21] The accuracy of this assessment is often questioned however, cf. e.g. Macrory et al. (2005), pp. 489–491.

[22] Cf. e.g. the statement made by former Commissioner for Trade Phil Hogan regarding the 2019 trade defence report published by the Directorate General for Trade: '*A strong and effective trade defence is of key importance to protect our companies and jobs against unfair trading practices and to ensure diversity of supply. (. . .) While imports offer more choice at a competitive price for our consumers and businesses, we need to make sure they come to Europe on fair terms, not dumped or subsidised*', European Commission, *Trade defence report: restoring the level playing field for European producers* (2020).

[23] On the effects of anti-dumping measures cf. Tavares de Araujo Jr. (2002), pp. 159, 166.

Protectionism is commonly defined as the doctrine that domestic industries should be protected from foreign competition by the imposition of duties, quotas, etc. on foreign goods.[24] The issue is as old as the use of trade defence legislation itself, with some scholars going as far as condemning the use of anti-dumping legislation altogether, holding that *'antidumping is the fox put in charge of the henhouse – ordinary protection with a good public relations program'*.[25]

While the intersection between trade and competition has long been recognised, scholarly interest in the effect of trade defence on competition and the interactions between the two areas of law peaked around the noughties.[26] This was triggered by the adoption of a resolution by the Singapore WTO Ministerial Conference of 1997 to establish a working group studying the relationship between trade and competition policy,[27] with the possible outcome of concluding an agreement on competition policy within the framework of the WTO. Accordingly, the feasibility of a multilateral solution to the matter under the auspices of the WTO was frequently the focus of the contributions on the subject published at that point in time.[28]

However, after the WTO General Council decided that the interaction between trade and competition policy would not form part of the Work Programme set out in the Doha Ministerial Declaration,[29] academic interest in the subject subsided.

With all attempts at regulating the relationship between trade and competition on a multilateral level having failed so far, it remains largely at the discretion of the users of anti-dumping and anti-subsidy legislation to decide whether and to what extent they choose to address the restrictive effects on competition caused by the imposition of measures, both within the design of their anti-dumping and anti-subsidy instruments and their application.

This also applies to the EU's legal framework governing the use of anti-dumping and anti-subsidy measures. The basic anti-dumping and the basic anti-subsidy regulation include various provisions intended to strike a balance between protecting the interests of the import-competing EU industry and avoiding undue restrictions to competition within the European Union. In particular, the EU's attempts at limiting the anti-competitive effects caused by the imposition of measures by applying the

---

[24] Oxford Dictionary of English (2010), *protectionism*, Oxford University Press.

[25] Finger (1992), p. 121.

[26] Cf. e.g. Sacher (2004); Boscheck (2000), p. 282; Cadot et al. (2000), p. 1; Pierce (2000), p. 725; Davidow (1999), p. 681; Zäch and Correa (1999); Hindley and Messerlin (1996).

[27] 'Singapore WTO Ministerial 1996: Ministerial Declaration (WT/MIN(96)/DEC)' (13 December 1996) para. 20.

[28] Boscheck (2000). Arguing against the conclusion of such an agreement Matsushita (2009), p. 665.

[29] 'Decision Adopted by the General Council on 1 August 2004: Doha Work Programme (WT/L/579)' (2 August 2004) n. 1 lit. g).

so-called lesser duty rule[30] and the inclusion of a public interest analysis in its basic regulations[31] must be noted here.

This study examines the relationship between trade defence and competition as defined by the EU legal framework, with an emphasis on the impact of the Trade Defence Modernisation Package. This focus on the EU is appropriate since, historically, it is one of the most active[32] and established[33] users of trade defence instruments. Moreover, due to its leading role in international trade and its often-voiced commitment to the promotion of international trade, other users of trade defence instruments may choose to emulate the EU's practices in this field. For this reason, the effect of the Trade Defence Modernisation Package may go well beyond the EU's own commercial policy.

EU competition law has been the subject of a large number of publications, examining at length its procedural law, its substantive design and—more recently—the challenges competition law is facing regarding its application in digital markets.[34] Likewise, the EU's trade defence instruments have been examined thoroughly, also pertaining to their WTO compatibility.[35] Yet, these publications usually deal with the two areas of law separately, without putting them into context. Conducting an in-depth comparative analysis of the two areas of law has been attempted far less often. As indicated, the effect of the use of trade defence instruments on competition and the interactions between the two areas of law were the subject of several publications around the noughties.[36] Said publications did identify some linkages between the two areas of law and developed possible avenues

---

[30] On the lesser duty rule cf. below pp. 192 et seq.

[31] On the so-called 'Union interest analysis' as prescribed by Article 21 of Regulation (EU) 2016/1036 and Article 31 of Regulation (EU) 2016/1037 cf. below pp. 224 et seq.

[32] At the end of 2020, the EU had 150 trade defence measures in force, cf. *European Commission*, 39th Annual Report from the Commission to the Council and the European Parliament on the EU's Anti-Dumping, Anti-Subsidy and Safeguard activities and the Use of trade defence instruments by Third Countries targeting the EU in 2020 (COM(2021) 496 final) 3. Among the WTO members to use anti-dumping measures, the EU ranks in sixth place, with the United States as the most frequent user of anti-dumping measures having a whopping 398 measures in place as of June 2020, cf. World Trade Organization, 'Report (2020) of the Committee on Anti-Dumping Practices (G/L/1366; G/ADP27)' (28 October 2020) Annex C. Regarding anti-subsidy measures, the EU ranks in third place, with the United States, again being the most frequent user of the trade remedy, having 135 measures in place, cf. World Trade Organization, 'Report (2020) of the Committee on Subsidies and Countervailing Measures (G/L/1368; G/SCM/157)' (27 October 2020) Annex H.

[33] The EU first adopted trade defence legislation in 1968 when the EU (then the European Economic Community) became a signatory of the first GATT Anti-Dumping Code: Regulation (EEC) No 459/68 of the Council of 5 April 1968 on protection against dumping or the granting of bounties or subsidies by countries which are not members of the European Economic Community.

[34] Cf. e.g. Bailey and John (2018); Ibáñez Colomo (2018); Whish and Bailey (2018). On the challenges for EU competition law in digital markets cf. e.g. Reyna (2019), p. 1 or Filistrucchi et al. (2014), p. 293.

[35] Cf. e.g. Vermulst and Dion Sud (2020), van Bael and Bellis (2019), Bungenberg et al. (2018) and Müller (2017).

[36] Cf. the sources cited above, n 26.

of limiting the negative effects to competition caused by the imposition of trade defence measures. Due to the vast majority of contributions on the issue having been published around two decades ago, they are outdated in that they do not address changes in the practice of the Commission over the last two decades. Most importantly, however, the EU's trade defence regime has undergone major reform, amending the basic anti-dumping regulation and the basic anti-subsidy regulation to a significant extent. Some of the most notable modifications to the substantive provisions of the basic regulations include the introduction of a new methodology for calculating normal value in anti-dumping investigations, limitations to the scope of application of the lesser duty rule or new rules in calculating the injury margin. All of the above parts of an anti-dumping or an anti-subsidy investigation are key factors in limiting or aggravating the anti-competitive effects of the EU's trade defence instruments. The present thesis thus aims to assess to what extent the findings made in the already existing body of literature are still valid and in how far these findings must be updated in light of the amendments introduced by the Trade Defence Modernisation Package.

1.2 Research Question

On an abstract level, the aim of the study is to examine the relationship between competition law and the EU's provisions regulating the imposition of anti-dumping and anti-subsidy measures within the legal framework of the EU. Starting from the premise that restrictive effects on competition resulting from their application should be avoided, the book builds on the already existing literature on the subject and addresses the concrete question of the extent to which the modifications introduced by the Trade Defence Modernisation Package affect the relationship between the two areas of law. In doing so, the work further draws on the Commission practice and documents published under the modified basic regulations.

The study is intended to shed light on the extent to which conflicts between competition and the trade defence instruments, which had already been identified in the past, have been resolved or conversely intensified by the modernisation of the basic regulations. In addition, the work will also evaluate to what degree the design and application of the reformed basic regulations have a negative impact on competition within the Union.

1.3 Scope

At the outset, some limitations to the subject of the study must be made. First, it restricts itself to the EU-dimension of the subject. This is due to the reasons set out above and because a wider analysis of the relationship between trade defence and competition would exceed the scope of this work. The questions on the relationship between competition and trade defence instruments arise mainly in relation to the use of anti-dumping and anti-subsidy measures. At the same time, owing to the structural similarities between the BASR and the BADR, the reasoning put forward in the thesis can frequently be applied both to anti-dumping and to anti-subsidy measures adopted under the basic regulations. As anti-dumping measures are much more relevant in practice than anti-subsidy measures,[37] the thesis will place a focus on measures adopted under the BADR. Conversely, due to their differences from anti-dumping measures and anti-subsidy measures in terms of their rationale and the manner in which they are applied, the thesis will not discuss safeguard measures. Thus, where it makes mention of trade defence instruments, the term is used to denote anti-dumping and anti-subsidy measures, except where indicated otherwise.

Moreover, in examining the reform of the basic regulations, the analysis will be limited to the key features of the Trade Defence Modernisation Package which, in the view of the author, are most liable to have an impact on the competitive situation on the internal market. This concerns primarily changes to the substantive rules of the basic regulations. While it is acknowledged that procedural fairness is a key element in ensuring that the basic regulations operate properly for all parties involved, the provisions on procedure contained in the basic regulations did not undergo substantive changes in the course of the reform.[38] For this reason, they will mostly be excluded from the study.

To date, all attempts at restructuring the relationship between trade defence and competition in a comprehensive manner—such as the above-mentioned conclusion of an agreement on competition within the framework of the WTO, substituting trade defence provisions for international rules on competition altogether,[39] replacing trade defence instruments with far-reaching provisions on market integration (including rules on competition) in free trade agreements,[40] or re-aligning anti-dumping laws with competition concepts[41]—have failed. Nor can any political aspirations on an EU level at changing this situation be discerned at present. Consequently, the thesis will only advance proposals on how to better accommodate competition concerns within the already existing framework of the basic regulations as it has developed over the last decades.

---

[37] van Bael and Bellis (2019), § 1.05–§ 1.09. This can also be derived from the statistics provided in the annual reports published by the WTO Committee on Anti-Dumping Practices and the Committee on Anti-Subsidy Practices, n 32.

[38] The changes to the procedural rules include *inter alia* the shortening of deadlines within which measures have to be adopted, the reimbursement of duties collected during an expiry review that results in the repeal of measures and the introduction of a pre-disclosure period. For an analysis cf. Müller (2018), pp. 54–55.

[39] Boscheck (2001), p. 41.

[40] van Vaerenbergh (2018), p. 217; for an overview on the subject cf. also Müller-Ibold (2018).

[41] Matsushita (2015), p. 406.

1.4   Structure

As just indicated, it is the main objective of this work to conduct a comprehensive analysis of the effects on the relationship between trade and competition in the EU brought about by the Trade Defence Modernisation Package. It follows that, before embarking on such a study, it must be established what role the EU Treaties assign to these two policy areas and how the Treaties intend for conflicts between them to be resolved. These preliminary questions are addressed in Chap. 2. After having laid the necessary groundwork, Chap. 3 provides an overview of the current legal framework governing the EU's competition law and its use of trade defence instruments. As becomes apparent from Chaps. 2 and 3, *prima facie*, the two areas of law exhibit a number of similarities, in particular owing to their common historical roots. This extends to the objectives they pursue and certain concepts that are central to both areas of law. Chapters 4 and 5 are dedicated to a more detailed examination of these shared features. They reveal that any historical commonalities hardly find any expression in the objectives currently pursued by EU competition and trade defence policy or in the design and application of the legal framework within which they operate. Instead, trade defence and competition law have diverged significantly, both as regards their respective objectives and the precise content of concepts such as market definition or price discrimination.

Following the abstract analysis regarding the relationship between trade and competition provided in the first part of the thesis, the second part of this study assesses the impact the Trade Defence Modernisation Package has had on the relationship between trade defence and competition within the EU legal framework *in concreto*. Differentiating between concrete conflicts with EU competition law provisions and general restrictions to competition, Chap. 6 will be devoted to inspecting the circumstances under which the reformed trade defence instruments might be used for practices that infringe Articles 101, 102 of the Treaty on the Functioning of the European Union (TFEU), whereas Chap. 7 is dedicated to examining the balance between protection and protectionism struck under the amended basic regulations. Another novelty of the reformed basic regulations lies in their inclusion of social and environmental concerns during the investigation. Chapter 8 evaluates these amendments with a view to first, their protectionist potential, second, whether the EU Treaties provide a legal basis for this, and third, their compatibility with the overall approach pursued by the EU in promoting non-commercial objectives through its common commercial policy. Given the paramount importance of WTO law for the EU's trade defence regime, Chap. 9 provides the reader with an overview over select issues surrounding the WTO compatibility of the reformed basic regulations. Chapter 10 concludes.

References[42]

Bailey D, John LE (eds) (2018) European Union law of competition, 5th edn. Oxford University Press

Boscheck R (2000) Trade, competition and antidumping-Breaking the impasse!?, Intereconomics 35(6):282

Boscheck R (2001) The governance of global market relations: the case of substituting antitrust for antidumping. World Compet 24(1):41

Bourgeois J (2008) Article 1 ADA. In: Wolfrum R, Stoll P-T, Koebele M (eds) WTO – trade remedies. Martinus Nijhoff Publishers

Bungenberg M et al (eds) (2018) The future of trade defence instruments – global policy trends and legal challenges. Springer

Cadot O, Grether J-M, de Melo J (2000) Trade and competition policy: where do we stand? J World Trade 34(3):1

Davidow J (1999) Antitrust issues arising out of actual or potential enforcement of trade laws. J Int Econ Law 2(4):681

Filistrucchi L et al and others (2014) Market definition in two-sided markets: theory and practice. J Compet Law Econ 10(2):293

Finger JM (1992) Dumping and antidumping: the rhetoric and the reality of protection in industrial countries. World Bank Res Observer 7(2):121

Hindley B, Messerlin PA (1996) Antidumping industrial policy: legalized protectionism in the WTO and what to do about it. American Enterprise Institute for Public Policy Research

Hoffmeister F (2018) AD-GVO 2016 vor Art. 1 [Erwägungsgründe]. In: Krenzler HG, Herrmann C, Niestedt M (eds) EU-Außenwirtschafts- und Zollrecht. C.H. Beck

Ibáñez Colomo P (2018) The shaping of EU competition law. Cambridge University Press

Macrory P, Appleton A, Plummer M (eds) (2005) The World Trade Organization: legal, economic and political analysis, vol I. Springer Science and Business Media

Matsushita M (2009) Trade and competition policy. In: Bethlehem D and others (eds) The Oxford handbook of international trade law. Oxford University Press

Matsushita M and others (2015) The World Trade Organization: law, practice, and policy, 3rd edn. Oxford University Press

Mavroidis PC (2016) The regulation of international trade: vol II: the WTO Agreements on trade in goods. MIT Press

Müller W (2017) The EU's trade defence instruments: recent judicial and policy developments. In: Bungenberg M and others (eds) European yearbook of international economic law 2017. Springer

Müller W (2018) The EU's new trade defence laws: a two steps approach. In: Bungenberg M and others (eds) The future of trade defence instruments – global policy trends and legal challenges. Springer

Müller-Ibold T (2018) EU trade defence instruments and free trade agreements. In: Bungenberg M and others (eds) The future of trade defence instruments – global policy trends and legal challenges. Springer

Pierce RJ (2000) Antidumping law as means of facilitating cartelization. Anti Law J 67(3):725

Reyna A (2019) The shaping of a European consumer welfare standard for the digital age. J Eur Compet Law Pract 10(1):1

Sacher S (2004) Trade Barriers and Antitrust Analysis. Available at <https://papers.ssrn.com/sol3/papers.cfm?abstract_id=1967684>

Tavares de Araujo Jr. J (2002) Legal and economic interfaces between antidumping and competition policy. World Compet 25(2):159

---

[42] All online sources were last accessed on 8 September 2021.

Trapp P (2020) Das Weißbuch der Kommission zur Gewährleistung fairer Wettbewerbsbedingungen bei Subventionen aus Drittstaaten. Zeitschrift für europäisches Wirtschaftsrecht (EuZW) 964

van Bael I, Bellis J-F (2019) EU anti-dumping and other trade defence instruments, 6th edn. Kluwer Law International

van Vaerenbergh P (2018) The role of trade defence instruments in EU trade agreements: theory versus practice. Zeitschrift für Europäische Studien (ZEUS) 21(2):217

Vermulst E, Dion Sud J (2020) Are the EU's trade defence instruments WTO compliant?. In: Weiß W, Furculita C (eds) Global politics and EU trade policy: facing the challenges to a multilateral approach. Springer

Viner J (1923) Dumping: a problem in international trade (re-print 1996). Kelley

Whish R, Bailey D (2018) Competition law, 9th edn. Oxford University Press

Zäch R, Correa CM (eds) (1999) Towards WTO competition rules: key issues and comments on the WTO Report (1998) on Trade and Competition. Stämpfli

Chapter 2
Competition and Commercial Policy in the European Treaties

2.1 Introduction

One central aspect discussed in the academic literature on the relationship between competition law and trade defence law are the possible anti-competitive effects caused by the imposition of trade defence measures. This presupposes that such anti-competitive effects are undesirable; hence, that the objective of undistorted competition should take precedence over possible beneficial effects brought about by the use of trade defence instruments.

Chapter 2 attempts to analyse whether this hypothesis regarding the basis of the relationship between competition law and trade defence law can indeed by derived from the provisions of the EU Treaties. To this end, the chapter will subject the European Treaties to an in-depth examination with regard to the role and relevance ascribed to the respective policy field in the course of the historical process of European integration.

2.2 The Treaty of Paris

2.2.1 Competition Policy in the Treaty of Paris

While it is argued that it was the 1957 Treaty of Rome that laid the formal basis for today's European competition policy,[1] a full account of the role of competition policy in the European integration process can only be given when also considering

---

[1] 'Treaty establishing the European Economic Community (Treaty of Rome)' (25 March 1957). Statement by Patel and Schweitzer (2012), p. 5.

© The Author(s), under exclusive license to Springer Nature Switzerland AG 2022
P. Trapp, *The European Union's Trade Defence Modernisation Package*, EYIEL Monographs - Studies in European and International Economic Law 23, https://doi.org/10.1007/978-3-030-91363-2_2

the Treaty of Paris establishing the European Coal and Steel Community of 1951[2] (ECSC Treaty). The Treaty included provisions on competition outlawing agreements between undertakings, decisions by associations of undertakings and concerted practices (Article 65), the abuse of a dominant position for purposes contrary to the objectives of the Treaty (Article 66). Moreover, it provided for the control of concentrations (Article 66). Its provisions also showed that the drafters of the Treaty regarded competition as essential for the realisation of the Community's overarching task of establishing a common market for coal and steel:[3,4] Article 3 ECSC Treaty listed a number of policy objectives the ECSC was to pursue, such as the maintenance of conditions under which undertakings have the incentive to expand and improve their production potential and under which natural resources are used rationally.[5]

Note should further be taken of the now famous declaration made by *Robert Schuman* (Schuman Declaration), which laid the ground for the creation of the ECSC. *Inter alia*, it emphasized that the organisation was intended to clearly distance itself from protectionist '*international cartels*' by ensuring the fusion of markets and expanding production.[6] Hence, the founding fathers were aware of the issue of international cartelisation and intended to counter it via the establishment of the ECSC.[7]

2.2.2 Trade Policy in the Treaty of Paris

Commercial policy forms the historical nucleus of the EU's external relations powers. Already the ECSC Treaty included a set of provisions on commercial policy in its Articles 71 to 75, albeit fairly narrow ones. Even though neither the Preamble nor Article 2 ECSC Treaty on the tasks of the Community mentioned commercial policy, Article 3 lit. f) ECSC Treaty listed furthering the development of international trade as a policy objective of the Community. The inclusion of provisions on commercial policy shows that the founders of the ECSC recognised that the common

---

[2] 'Treaty establishing the European Coal and Steel Community (Treaty of Paris)' (18 April 1951).
[3] Article 2 ECSC Treaty.
[4] Nazzini (2011), p. 122.
[5] Article 3 lit. d) ECSC Treaty reads: '*The institutions of the Community shall, within the limits of their respective powers, in the common interest (. . .) ensure the maintenance of conditions which will encourage undertakings to expand and improve their production potential and to promote a policy of using natural resources rationally and avoiding their unconsidered exhaustion, (. . .).*'
[6] Robert Schuman, 'La Déclaration Schuman' (9 May 1950) 2, available at <https://europa.eu/european-union/about-eu/symbols/europe-day/schuman-declaration_de>. The original text goes as follows : '*A l'opposé d'un cartel international tendant à la répartation et à l'exploitation des marchés nationaux par des pratiques restrictives et le maintien de profits élevés, l'organisation projetée assurera la fusion des marchés et l'expansion de la production*'.
[7] Chiriță (2014), p. 286.

market for coal and steel also possessed an external dimension. This external dimension was expressed in the basic rules addressing the Member States' commercial policy towards third States, even though the powers in matters of trade policy generally remained with the Member States—a truly 'common' commercial policy was yet to be developed.

The powers attributed to the ECSC, specifically to its High Authority, were limited to the economic areas covered by the Treaty, as well as being limited in nature.[8] Article 72 ECSC Treaty laid the ground for what would later on become the common customs tariff. According to the provision, the Council, acting upon the proposal of the High Authority, could fix minimum and maximum rates on the customs duties on coal and steel levied by the Member States *vis-à-vis* third States. It should be noted that despite the Community's commercial policy powers only being rudimentary, Article 74 ECSC Treaty empowered the High Authority to take measures in a number of circumstances that are in essence the same warranting the EU making use of its trade defence instruments today.[9] The ECSC hence placed trade defence at the core of the Community's commercial policy.

Consequently, a multi-dimensional link between trade and competition as an essential element of the common market for coal and steel was visible in the beginning of the European integration process: first, the founders of the ECSC had realised that the common market for the coal and steel sector required, to some extent, the coordination of the Member States' policies towards third States. This resulted in the ECSC Treaty already containing the predecessors of what would later become the rules on a common commercial policy (CCP). Among those rudimental provisions on the ECSC's commercial policy were provisions relating to the use of trade defence instruments, placing the international 'level playing field' at the centre of the Community's commercial policy. It is thus fitting that it was in the context of anti-dumping proceedings in the sixties that the ECSC first assumed its role as a foreign representative for the Member States.[10] This focus on free and fair trade persisting in its trade relations with third States was further visible in the Schuman Declaration and the reference to international cartels contained therein. At the same time, while intended to alleviate fears of market foreclosure effects arising as the result of the foundation of the ECSC, it is evidence to the fact that the founders of the ECSC were aware of the impact the ECSC's establishment would have on international trade and *vice versa*.

---

[8] Leal-Arcas (2007), p. 310.

[9] Such circumstances included dumping by third State exporters (Article 74 (1) subpara. 1 ECSC Treaty), differences in quotations between undertakings outside and inside the Community due to the fact that that those of the former are based on conditions of competition contrary to the ECSC Treaty (Article 74 (1) subpara. 2 ECSC Treaty) and increases in imports to the EU causing serious injury to Community production (Article 74 (1) subpara. 3 ECSC Treaty). Today's equivalents of these constellations are the three main pillars of the EU's trade defence instruments: anti-dumping measures, countervailing measures and safeguard measures.

[10] Alter and Steinberg (2007), p. 91.

2.3　The Treaty of Rome

2.3.1　Competition Policy in the Treaty of Rome

This interplay between trade and competition continued to be expressed in the Treaty of Rome of 1957 establishing the European Economic Community (EEC Treaty). While some go so far as to call competition the *'motive force of the economic revolution'*,[11] the consensus was that competition was not an end in itself, but subordinated to the purpose of establishing a common market.[12]

As it already had been the case in the ECSC Treaty, Article 2 EEC Treaty named the establishment of a common market as an aim of the Community.[13] Likewise, Article 3 lit. f) EEC Treaty prescribed that for the purposes set out in Article 2 EEC Treaty, the activities in the Community were to include, *inter alia*, the institution of a system ensuring that competition in the common market is not distorted and, *a fortiori*, not eliminated.[14]

The substantive instruments of Community competition policy consisted of rules concerning restrictive agreements (Article 85 EEC Treaty), the abuse of dominance (Article 86 EEC Treaty) as well as rules on privileged undertakings such as State monopolies (Articles 37 and 90 EEC Treaty) and State aid (Articles 92 to 94 EEC Treaty). An agreement between undertakings under Article 85 EEC Treaty, or an abuse of a dominant position under Article 86 EEC Treaty, were prohibited as 'incompatible with the common market', highlighting the link between the Community's competition policy and the common market objective contained in Article 2 EEC Treaty.[15]

The connection between competition policy and the objective of market integration is also reflected in a series of judgments issued by the Court of Justice of the European Union[16] (CJEU) in the sixties, in which it adopted a teleological approach

---

[11] Spaak and Jaeger (1961), p. 487.

[12] Ibid. Under the EEC Treaty, negative integration, or completion of the internal market through application of the four basic freedoms and competition policy, was at the heart of the Community's priorities; cf. Sauter (1997), p. 3.

[13] It is important to note, though, that the common market was not an end in itself but a means to reach the Community's tasks listed in Article 2 EEC Treaty, namely the promotion of a harmonious development of economic activities, of continuous and balanced expansion, an accelerated standard of living and closer relations between the States belonging to the Community, cf. Kaupa (2016), p. 27.

[14] *Europemballage Corporation and Continental Can Company Inc. v Commission of the European Communities* (21 February 1973) C-6/72 24 (European Court of Justice); cf. further Bailey (2018) para. 1.023.

[15] This wording is still in place today, although the phrase 'common market' has been replaced by 'internal market'.

[16] At the time, the institution was named 'European Court of Justice', only to be renamed into 'Court of Justice of the European Union' by the Treaty of Lisbon. However, for better readability, this work will use the term 'Court of Justice of the European Union' or 'CJEU' through the entire thesis to denote the judicial organ of the EU. For identical reasons, the first instance of the EU judicial

towards the interpretation of the provisions of competition law, putting them in the context of the objectives of the Treaty.[17] In its *Société Technique Minière* judgment, the Court held that in assessing an agreement's potential effect on trade between Member States under Article 85 (1) EEC Treaty, it would be

> necessary to consider in particular whether it is capable of bringing about a partitioning of the market in certain products between Member States and thus rendering more difficult the interpenetration of trade which the [T]reaty is intended to create.[18]

The Court thereby effectively made the Community's objective of market integration a direct objective of Article 85 (1) EEC Treaty.[19] Similarly, in its 1976 *Walt Wilhelm* judgment,[20] the Court explicitly considered the creation of a single market to be the predominant objective of EEC competition law.[21] One year later, the Court once more ruled that the requirement contained in the EEC Treaty that competition shall not be distorted implies the existence of workable competition on the market, that is to say the degree of competition necessary to ensure the attainment of the objectives of the Treaty, in particular the creation of a single market.[22] Thus, the Court applied competition law in the light of the overarching goal of the EEC; namely the establishment of a common market as set out in Article 2 EEC Treaty.[23]

The competition necessary to create said common market was thought to be found inside the European Community. Competition from the world market was to be regulated by the common customs tariff and through the Community's commercial policy.[24]

Interestingly, Article 91 EEC Treaty contained rules on intra-communal dumping during the transitional period. By including the provision in the section on competition law, the Treaty's drafters emphasised that intra-communal dumping would jeopardise a system of undistorted competition, causing deflections of trade and ultimately endangering the success of the common market. At the same time, Article 91 EEC Treaty also was a testimony to the central differences between distortions to competition emanating from firms' behaviour on the common market and distortions caused by third country producers exporting to the EU. While intra-communal dumping was considered to pose a threat to the realisation of the common market,

---

system will be referred to as the 'General Court', even though it bore the name 'Court of First Instance' until the entry into force of the Treaty of Lisbon.

[17] Ramírez Pérez and van de Scheur (2012), p. 38.

[18] *Société Technique Minière (STM)* (30 June 1966) 56/65 249 (European Court of Justice).

[19] Ramírez Pérez and van de Scheur (2012), p. 40.

[20] *Walt Wilhelm* (13 February 1969) 14/68 (European Court of Justice).

[21] Ramírez Pérez and van de Scheur (2012).

[22] *Metro SB-Großmärkte GmbH & Co. KG v Commission* (25 October 1977) 26/76 20 (European Court of Justice).

[23] Ramírez Pérez and van de Scheur (2012), p. 43, cf. also the Court's reasoning already in *Europemballage Corporation and Continental Can Company Inc. v Commission of the European Communities* (Chap. 1, n 14) 24.

[24] Bourgeois (1993), p. 117.

this was—and is—not the case for extra-communal dumping. Even though dumping by foreign producers could be considered indirectly detrimental to the common market project by causing distortions of competition between the market actors, opposite to the behaviour of firms operating within the common market, it does not entail a separation of the EU Member States' respective national markets. Furthermore, Article 91 EEC Treaty tackled the root cause of the problem of intra-communal dumping by directly prohibiting practices aiming at a partition of the common market. This, however, is not possible for measures directed against extra-communal dumping. These only address the negative consequences on competition caused by the presence of the dumped imports on the internal market.

2.3.2 Trade Policy in the Treaty of Rome

The relevance of commercial policy increased with the EEC Treaty and the concomitant expansion of the common market from a sectoral one for coal and steel to a general one. This was already reflected in the Treaty's preamble, according to which the founders of the EEC desired to contribute, by means of a common commercial policy, to the progressive abolition of restrictions on international trade. Likewise, Article 3 lit. b) EEC Treaty named the establishment of a common customs tariff and of a common commercial policy towards third countries as an activity of the Community. By listing the customs tariff and the common commercial policy as one activity instead of two separate ones, the Treaty accentuated the connection between the customs union, which formed the basis of the Community,[25] and the CCP.

The external dimension of the customs union found expression in various provisions of the Treaty. One example for this is Article 29 lit. a) EEC Treaty, which called upon the Commission to be guided by the need to promote trade between Member States and third countries in setting up the customs union. Similarly, Article 110 (1) EEC Treaty stated that by establishing a customs union between themselves, Member States aimed to contribute to the development of world trade, the progressive abolition of restrictions on international trade and the lowering of customs barriers. Thus, from the beginning of European integration, the drafters of the Treaties intended for the liberalisation of intra-communal trade to also have a liberalising effect on extra-EEC trade. Despite this focus on trade liberalisation, Article 113 (1) EEC Treaty still permitted the imposition trade defence measures such as those taken against dumping or subsidies against imports originating in third States.

---

[25] Article 9 (1) EEC Treaty read: *'The Community shall be based upon a customs union which shall cover all trade in goods and which shall involve the prohibition between Member States of customs duties on imports and exports and of all charges having equivalent effect, and the adoption of a common customs tariff in their relations with third countries.'*

Moreover, a common commercial policy, based on uniform principles, had also become necessary in order to ensure the functioning of the common market.[26] With the launch of a customs union between the Member States, a common customs tariff was established for all goods coming from third countries. Accordingly, the unity of the common market would be endangered if Member States were to pursue their individual trade policies, as this would result in possible distortions of competition and trade deflections.[27] The principle of uniformity was expressed in Article 113 (1) EEC Treaty. It applied *inter alia* to tariff rates, the conclusion of tariff and trade agreements, measures of liberalisation and trade defence measures. Regarding the use of trade defence instruments, it is important to note that the link between the CCP and the common market did not imply that the application of the principle of uniformity required for the CCP to adhere to the same objectives that existed in the common market, such as non-discrimination and the elimination of all trade barriers.[28] Hence, the use of trade-restrictive measures was still permissible when taking into account the principle of uniformity, just as it was from the perspective of trade liberalisation.

The necessity of a harmonisation of the Member States' commercial policy was further visible in Article 112 (1) EEC Treaty, which mandated the harmonisation of export subsidies granted by the Member States to the extent required to ensure that competition between undertakings of the Community is not distorted. The CJEU's Opinion in *Local Cost Standard* provided further insights regarding the relationship between trade and competition in the EC Treaty. In the Opinion, the Court addressed the question of the compatibility of the Member States' export aid with a uniform CCP. After stating that the conception of the common commercial policy was incompatible with a concurrent competence of the Member States, the Court went on to declare that any unilateral action on part of the Member States would lead to distortions of competition between undertakings of the various Member States in external markets. Such distortions could be eliminated only by means of a strict uniformity of credit conditions granted to undertakings in the Community, whatever their nationality.[29] While the statement concerned competition between undertakings abroad,[30] one can nevertheless infer from it that the concept of undistorted competition also had to be observed during the implementation of the common commercial policy. It follows that if competition between Community undertakings competing in third States was not to be affected by commercial policy measures, this must certainly extend to competition in the common market. One of the Court's later

---

[26] Pescatore (1987), p. 10.

[27] Steenbergen (1980), p. 229. It has to be noted that uniformity of the CCP was required only in areas of the internal market that had been fully harmonised, Dimopoulos (2010), p. 155.

[28] *Faust v Commission of the European Communities* (28 October 1982) C-52/81 25 (European Court of Justice); Dimopoulos (2010), p. 155.

[29] *Local Cost Standard* (11 November 1975) Opinion 1/75 (European Court of Justice), ECR 1975 01355-1364.

[30] Sprung (1959), p. 215.

judgments supports this conclusion. It adjudged that even if aid granted by a Member State to an undertaking was regarded as export aid in the sense of Article 112 (1) EEC Treaty, its legality could still be measured against the Community's State aid rules contained in Articles 92 to 94 EEC Treaty.[31] Hereby, the Court clarified that commercial policy measures could not only be measured against the Community CCP rules, but that they would also have to comply with the rules on Community competition policy. Where a particular measure had come under scrutiny due to its potentially distortive effect on competition abroad, this would be even more so if the measure distorted competition in the common market. Article 112 EEC Treaty therefore not only exemplified the Community's general commitment to ensuring that competition was not distorted in the common market, but also that commercial policy measures must abide by the Community competition rules.

Article 115 EEC Treaty, which allowed for trade defence measures to be taken by the Member States under certain circumstances, was an example of the more general interface between the common market and the common commercial policy, as the Court repeatedly held that its application depended on the non-existence or failure to implement a common commercial policy in certain sectors.[32] A weak or non-existing CCP would thus lead to the authorisation of measures under Article 115 EEC Treaty—which included import restrictions between the Member States—and hence derogations from the principle of free movement as a corner stone of the internal market.

Article 116 EEC Treaty was another one of the Treaty's provisions which revealed the Community's CCP to be focussed on the needs of the common market. The provision prescribed for the Member States to act by common action within the framework of international organisations of an economic character, if the matter concerned was of particular interest to the common market. This nexus was further affirmed in the jurisprudence of the Court, including the *Donckerwolcke* judgment. Herein, the Court adjudged that the incompleteness of the common commercial policy was capable of affecting the free movement of goods within the Community.[33] Likewise, in its *Opinion 1/78*, the Court held that the interpretation of the concept of common commercial policy also depended on the effects the interpretation might have on intra-community trade,[34] once more accentuating the link between the needs of the common market and the common commercial policy.[35]

Ultimately, at this point of European integration, the view on the Community's commercial policy thus was an instrumental one, as it was perceived to be based on

---

[31] *Kingdom of Belgium v Commission of the European Communities* (21 March 1990) C-142/87 32 (European Court of Justice).

[32] *Donckerwolcke* (15 December 1976) C-41/76 (European Court of Justice) 24; *Kaufhof AG v Commission of the European Communities* (8 April 1976) C-29/75 (European Court of Justice) 5.

[33] *Donckerwolcke* (n 32) 27–28.

[34] *International Agreement on Natural Rubber* (4 October 1979) Opinion 1/78 45 (European Court of Justice). In a similar vein, the Commission had argued in favour of a wide interpretation of Article 113 EC Treaty in order to avoid barriers and distortions to intra-Community trade, ibid 38.

[35] Cremona (2002), p. 355.

the needs of the internal market.[36] The drafters of the EEC Treaty acknowledged that a liberal trade policy would generally benefit the economic operators in the Member States, while uniformity was required in order to prevent the Member States from securing themselves advantages in their trade relations with third States, which ultimately would undermine the customs union and endanger the existence of fair competition in the common market. The instrumental view on the CCP is particularly evident in Article 115 EEC Treaty which, as explained above, constituted an exception to the uniformity of the Community's commercial policy itself. However, the Court held that the norm was to be interpreted restrictively, mainly due to its negative impact on the common market.[37] It is precisely for this reason that the provision was already to be repealed by the Treaty of Maastricht[38]—and not because it countered the objective of a uniform commercial policy *vis-à-vis* third States.[39]

At Community level, the first anti-dumping regulation was adopted in 1968.[40] It essentially translated the 1967 GATT Anti-Dumping Code into Union law and divided the responsibilities for its implementation between the Community organs.[41] The trade defence instruments reflected the instrumental understanding of the CCP: their use was considered essential in defending the common market from exogenous influences considered harmful to it. From this perspective, trade defence instruments could be regarded as constituting an early external complement to the internal competition and State aid policy of the Community. While the latter is aimed at guaranteeing a fair and level playing field within the EU, the former combats any outside interference with, or abuse of, this level playing field,[42] thereby ensuring the economic success of the internal market.

---

[36] Ibid 355, 392.

[37] *Donckerwolcke* (n 32); *Kaufhof AG v Commission of the European Communities* (n 32).

[38] van Bael and Bellis (2019) § 1.03.

[39] This is particularly astonishing as the number of applications to the Commission under Article 115 (1) EEC Treaty had risen to an average of 286 applications per year since 1980 and was threatening to lead to the collapse of the CCP, cf. Schuknecht (1991), p. 40.

[40] Regulation (EEC) No 459/68 of the Council of 5 April 1968 on protection against dumping or the granting of bounties or subsidies by countries which are not members of the European Economic Community (Chap. 1, n 33).

[41] van Bael and Bellis (2019) § 2.02; Stanbrook and Bentley (1996), p. 15.

[42] Larik (2011), pp. 19–20.

2.4   The Treaty of Lisbon

2.4.1   Competition Policy in the Treaty of Lisbon

2.4.1.1   The Amendments to Competition Policy Introduced by the Treaty of Maastricht

Of the Treaties following the Treaty of Rome, it was the 1992 Treaty of Maastricht[43] that devoted most attention to the Community's competition law provisions. Competition remained at the heart of the reformed EC Treaty: there now were repeated references to the principle of competition in the Treaty. As it had already been the case in the EEC Treaty,[44] Article 3 lit. g) EC Treaty on the activities of the European Community included, for the purposes set out in Article 2 EC Treaty, the establishment of a system 'ensuring that competition in the internal market is not distorted'. Additionally, the new Article 3a (1) EC Treaty as well as the provisions of the new Title VI on economic and monetary policy called for the adoption of an economic policy as an activity of the Community and the Member States, which was to be conducted 'in accordance with the principle of an open market economy with free competition'. The same applied with regard to the new Title XIII on the Community industry policy, which was to be carried out in accordance with a system of open and competitive markets.[45]

The increased visibility of the principle of competition in the Treaty could lead one to assume that competition policy as such was awarded greater significance. Indeed, in particular the new Article 3a EC Treaty was regarded an example of the Community's choice in favour of a specific socio-economic order. *Mestmäcker* argued that '*[t]he outlined development of Community law may be interpreted as the implementation of an economic order based upon markets and undistorted competition*'.[46] Nonetheless, due to the broad set of other policy objectives set out in Article 3 EC Treaty and the large number of 'non-market objectives' contained in the provision as well as the increased importance of industrial policy, *Mestmäcker*'s conclusion regarding the existence of a specific economic order based upon markets and undistorted competition in the European Treaties must be contested. Rather, the character of the European economic constitution remained an open one,[47] with competition remaining essential for the market integration objective but far from being the only relevant consideration in the application of other aspects of European economic policy.

---

[43] 'Treaty on European Union (Treaty of Maastricht) (OJ C 191/1)' (29 July 1992).

[44] Article 3 lit. f) EEC Treaty.

[45] Article 130 (1) EC Treaty.

[46] Mestmäcker (1994), p. 633.

[47] Kaupa (2016); Maduro (1998), p. 159.

2.4.1.2 The Repeal of Article 3 (1) lit. g) EC Treaty

Neither the Treaty of Amsterdam (1997)[48] nor the Treaty of Nice (2001)[49] touched upon the status of competition in the European Treaties. However, due to the amendments made by the Treaty of Amsterdam, what was formerly Article 3 lit. g) EC Treaty became Article 3 (1) lit. g) EC Treaty and Article 3a EC Treaty was renumbered to become Article 4 EC Treaty. Therefore, the next step in the European integration process which addressed said topic was the 2007 Treaty of Lisbon.[50] As is well known, its beginnings lie in the European Council Declaration on the Future of the European Union of 2001 (Laeken Declaration).[51] In 2002 and 2003, the Laeken Declaration was followed up by the European Convention, which drafted the Treaty establishing a Constitution for Europe (Constitutional Treaty), followed by an Intergovernmental Conference. Due to the negative outcome of two referenda on the Constitutional Treaty held in France and the Netherlands in 2005, the Constitutional Treaty never entered into force.

While the Treaty of Lisbon left the substantive content of the Community's competition law provisions largely unchanged,[52] its entry into force nonetheless incited considerable debate among scholars regarding the role competition policy was to play under the reformed EU Treaty framework. One of the reasons for this lies in the exclusion of competition policy from Article 3 TEU: under both the EEC Treaty and the EC Treaty, the provision setting out the activities of the EU had referred to a system of undistorted competition. Instead, the substantive content of what formerly was Article 3 (1) lit. g) EC Treaty was removed from the TEU itself, and is now contained in Protocol No. 27 on the Internal Market and Competition, which reads that 'the internal market (...) includes a system ensuring that competition is not distorted'.

A related aspect of the debate revolved around the issue of whether the Lisbon Treaty did indeed downgrade the protection of undistorted competition in the European Treaties. Under Article I-3 of the Constitutional Treaty on the basic objectives of the European Union, an economic system based on competition would have become a central objective to the EU, closely linked to the goal of

---

[48] 'Treaty of Amsterdam amending the Treaty on European Union, the Treaties establishing the European Communities and certain related acts (OJ 1997 C 340/01)' (2 October 1997).

[49] 'Treaty of Nice amending the Treaty on European Union, the Treaties establishing the European Communities and certain related acts (OJ 2001 C 80/1)' (10 March 2001).

[50] 'Treaty of Lisbon amending the Treaty on European Union and the Treaty establishing the European Community (OJ 2007 C 306/1)' (13 December 2007).

[51] Office for Official Publications of the European Communities, 'Presidency Conclusions of the Laeken European Council: Laeken Declaration on the future of the European Union' (Luxembourg 15 December 2001).

[52] The Treaty did include some terminological modifications, such as the replacement of the phrase 'common market' with the one of 'internal market'. Apart from that, the Lisbon Treaty replicated the majority of the EC Treaty's competition provisions.

market integration[53] and its importance further elevated by the inclusion of the substantive competition law provisions in the chapter on the internal market.[54] While these changes regarding a potential upgrade of the status of competition policy never materialised, commentators had observed that in its case law before the entry into force of the Treaty of Lisbon, the Court had relied heavily on Article 3 (1) lit. g) EC Treaty.[55] Already in 1973, the CJEU had stressed the vital importance of Article 3 (1) lit. g) EC Treaty.[56] In its subsequent decisions, the Court frequently referred to the provision, and even held that the protection of free competition constituted a *'fundamental objective'* of the European Community.[57] Scholars thus argued that the removal of Article 3 (1) lit. g) EC Treaty could potentially lead to a change in the interpretation and application of EU competition law.[58]

Even though the case law of the CJEU undoubtedly highlights the importance of competition within the European Treaties, one cannot infer from it that competition was an objective of the European Treaties in the technical sense before the Lisbon Treaty entered into force. In particular, one has to take into account that the references to the status of competition as an objective of the EU frequently concerned the protection of competition within the internal market, thereby again connecting competition with the central internal market objective.[59] The references by the CJEU are hence rather to be interpreted as highlighting that the provisions on competition, like the provisions on free movement, are fundamental provisions of the EU legal order, without attributing them the status of an objective of the European Treaties *strictu sensu.*[60]

Instead of debating whether competition is or indeed ever was an objective of the European Union, the question thus rather has to be whether the Treaty of Lisbon changed the status of competition within the European economic constitution. Article 51 TEU ascribes the Protocol the same rank as the Treaties within the EU legal order. One can therefore not deduce a lesser significance of competition from the relocation, despite the decrease in visibility in the TEU. The link between competition and the internal market objective is still discernible in the wording of Protocol No. 27. While reproducing the substantive content of Article 3 (1) lit. g) EC Treaty, it does not strictly adhere to its phrasing. Instead, the link between

---

[53] Nowak (2004), p. 70.

[54] Lianos (2012), p. 257.

[55] Petit and Neyrinck (2010), p. 3.

[56] *Europemballage Corporation and Continental Can Company Inc. v Commission of the European Communities* (Chap. 1, n 14).

[57] *Raiffeisen Zentralbank Österreich AG and others v Commission of the European Communities* (14 December 2006) joined cases T-259/02 to T-264/02 and T-271/02 255 (European Court of Justice); *Showa Denko KK v Commission of the European Communities* (29 June 2006) C-289/04 P 55 (European Court of Justice). For an overview of the Courts' decisional practice with regard to Article 3 (1) lit. g) EC Treaty cf. van Rompuy (2011).

[58] Cf. e.g. Drexl (2009), p. 913.

[59] Cf. e.g. *Showa Denko KK v Commission of the European Communities* (n 57).

[60] Buendia Sierra (2012), p. 358; van Rompuy (2011), p. 5.

competition and the internal market is strengthened even further by the Protocol explicitly declaring that the internal market—as an objective of the European Union—includes a system ensuring that competition is not distorted. Hereby, the Protocol clearly states that despite the entry into force of the Lisbon Treaty, the legal situation with regard to the status of competition remains unchanged.[61]

The decisional practice of the CJEU supports this finding, as both the General Court and the Court of Justice continue to refer to Protocol No. 27 in conjunction with Article 3 (3) TEU as though there is no difference to Article 3 (1) lit. g) EC Treaty.[62] Indeed, in *Timab*, the General Court expressly held that Article 3 TEU read in conjunction with Protocol No. 27 has changed neither the purpose of Article 101 TFEU nor the rules for the imposition of fines.[63]

2.4.1.3   The Repeal of Article 4 EC Treaty

Another point of concern regarding the role of competition in the European Treaties was the repeal of Article 4 EC Treaty.[64] Under the Treaty of Lisbon, reference to the 'principle of an open market economy with free competition' is first made in Article 119 TFEU, the first provision on the EU's economic and monetary policy. Even before the Treaty of Lisbon, the legal relevance of Article 4 EC Treaty was disputed. In particular, the Court considered Article 4 EC Treaty to be non-judiciable, as it did not impose sufficiently clear and unconditional obligations on the Member States.[65] In line with its limited utilisation of Article 4 EC Treaty under the old Treaty framework, the relocation of the provision to Title VIII on the EU's economic and monetary policy has not proven significant for the interpretation and application of the EU's competition law provisions by the CJEU or the Commission.

2.4.1.4   The Inclusion of the Term 'Social Market Economy'

It was mainly the French president *Nicolas Sarkozy* who wanted the objective of undistorted competition excluded from Article 3 TEU. He furthermore pushed for the inclusion of the term of a social market economy in Article 3 (3) TEU, both in

---

[61] Drexl (2009), p. 910.

[62] *European Commission v Kingdom of Spain* (11 December 2012) C-610/10 126 (European Court of Justice); *Slovak Telekom a.s. v European Commission* (22 March 2012) joined cases T-458/09 and T-171/10 36 (European Court of Justice); *Commission v Italian Republic* (17 November 2011) C-496/09 60 (European Court of Justice); *Konkurrensverket v TeliaSonera Sverige AB* (17 February 2011) C-52/09 20 (European Court of Justice).

[63] *Timab Industries and CFPR v European Commission* (20 May 2015) T-456/10 211–212 (European Court of Justice).

[64] Cf. Drexl (2009), p. 910 et seq.

[65] *Échirolles Distribution SA v Association du Dauphiné and others* (3 October 2000) C-9/99 25 (European Court of Justice).

order to prevent the impression of the EU being a *'neo-liberalist, elitist project'*.[66,67] The concept of a social market economy is rooted in the German political philosophy of ordo-liberalism. The school's most influential leaders, *Walter Eucken, Franz Böhm, Wilhelm Röpke, Alexander Rüstow* and *Alfred Müller-Armack* coined the term as *'market freedoms capable of achieving social objectives'*.[68] The exact characteristics of the concept depend on the context in which it is interpreted and applied. Nevertheless, the core requirements of a social market economy are conventionally identified as being a regulatory policy aimed at addressing market failures and as corrective policies limiting the inequalities that arise from the market system itself.[69] Article 3 (3) TEU leaves the expression undefined. The question of the precise content of the notion has however long been part of political discussions within the EU institutions.[70] Also on the European level, while lacking a detailed definition, the 'social market economy' encompasses a system combining a strong body of competition law preventing market actors from destroying economic freedom[71] with social protection agreements.[72]

In spite of—or maybe because of—the lack of a precise definition, the introduction of the 'social market economy' together with a number of broader horizontal integration provisions led some scholars to assume that the interpretation of competition law provisions was to change in favour of a more *'holistic approach'*, in particular in order to assure the attainment of other objectives and public policies.[73] These projections, though, have not proven to be correct, as the reforms of the Lisbon Treaty have not led to broader public interest concerns being assigned more importance than before. Instead, the case law and the discussion regarding the intersection between competition law and social objectives follow the same lines as before.[74]

---

[66] Terhechte (2009), p. 193.

[67] On the event of the signing of the Lisbon Treaty, Mr. Sarkozy declared: *'La concurrence n'est plus un objectif de l'Union ou une fin en soi, mais un moyen au service du marché intérieur. Un protocole confirme que les questions de concurrence relèvent de l'organisation du marché intérieur, c'est un point majeur'*, Nicolas Sarkozy, *Conférence de presse finale sur le contenu de l'accord des 27 pays membres de l'Union européenne concernant le Traité européen simplifié* (2007).

[68] Sally (1996), p. 233.

[69] With further references Ferri and Cortese (2019), p. 6.

[70] Cf. the speech given by Commissioner for Competition Mario Monti, *Competition in a Social Market Economy: Speech at the Conference of the European Parliament and the European Commission on "Reform of European Competition Law"* (2000) 3.

[71] Heinemann (2019), p. 127.

[72] Claassen et al. (2019), p. 7. The 'social' aspect of the social market economy is to be interpreted rather broadly, as revealed by the social principles enumerated in subparagraph 2 of Article 3 (3) TEU; Sommermann (2013) para. 35.

[73] Lianos (2013), p. 40; Lianos (2012), p. 260.

[74] Heinemann (2019), p. 139.

To conclude, *prima facie,* many of the changes introduced by the Treaty of Lisbon give rise to questions regarding the role of competition policy within the Treaties. Upon closer examination, it however becomes evident that no fundamental re-conceptualisation of competition within the Treaty framework has occurred. Competition remains an activity of the European Union, and of central importance to the realisation of the internal market objective as evidenced by Protocol No. 27. While the insertion of the term 'social market economy' in Article 3 (3) TEU accentuates the need to have regard to social policy considerations in implementing the EU's policies, it has not resulted in the examination of competition law cases following entirely new paradigms. Similarly, the relocation of the 'principle of an open market economy with free competition' from Article 4 EC Treaty to Article 119 TFEU has not had any discernible effects on the interpretation and application of EU competition law.

2.4.2   Trade Policy in the Treaty of Lisbon

Just as it was the case for competition policy, none of the Treaties concluded in the decades following the entry into force of the Treaty of Rome touched upon the status of the common commercial policy as an activity of the European Community. Concerning the external relations of the then-EEC, the Single European Act[75] introduced provisions on European co-cooperation in the sphere of foreign policy, the forerunner of what would later become the European Union's Common Foreign and Security Policy (CFSP).[76] However, the rules at the heart of the Community's external action, the substantive provisions on its common commercial policy, were left unchanged.

The Maastricht Treaty built on the foundations laid by the Single European Act regarding the development of a European common foreign and security policy, which was contained in its Title V. Herein, the Member States and the Union pledged to define and implement a common foreign and security policy. The common commercial policy still occupied a prominent place among the activities of the Community. It was listed in Article 3 lit. b) of the reformed EC Treaty, which enumerated the tasks of the Community, second only to the internal elimination of customs duties and quantitative restrictions on the import and export of goods. The substantive content of the Treaty's section on commercial policy did not undergo any significant changes.[77] However, Articles 111, 114 and 116 EC Treaty were repealed, as they were all addressed at the transitional period set out in the Single European Act or, in the case of Article 116 EC Treaty, were integrated into other

---

[75]'Single European Act (OJ 1987 L 169/1)' (29 June 1987).

[76]Article 30 of the Single European Act.

[77]This led commentators to criticise the Maastricht Treaty as *'disappointing'*, cf. Maresceau (1993).

provisions[78] Article 115 EC Treaty now required the Member States to obtain prior authorisation of the Commission before implementing any protective measure.[79] The 1997 Treaty of Amsterdam amended the EC Treaty as well as the Treaty on European Union. It provided for a renumbering of the Articles of the EC Treaty, which led to the provisions on the Community's commercial policy being relocated to Articles 131 to 134 EC Treaty. The amendments to the EC Treaty by the Treaty of Amsterdam focussed on Article 133 EC Treaty,[80] enabling the Council to extend the application of paragraphs one to four to international negotiations and agreements on services and intellectual property.

In a similar vein, the amendments to the common commercial policy introduced by the Treaty of Nice of 2001[81] centered around Article 133 EC Treaty. It added paragraphs five to seven and introduced a second sentence into subparagraph one as well as subparagraph two of paragraph three. Due to their complexity and incoherence,[82] the alterations received a significant amount of criticism by legal scholars.[83] While the scope of the common commercial policy and the division of competences between the Community and the Member States was a hotly debated topic throughout the Treaty revisions, none of the reforms touched upon the status of commercial policy as an activity of the Community.

The magnitude of the changes introduced by the Treaty of Lisbon is reflected in the law governing the external relations of the European Union, with commentators announcing it to have caused a '*shift of paradigms*' regarding the CCP.[84] Under the TFEU, the substantive content of the CCP is now contained in two provisions, namely Articles 206 and 207 TFEU (ex-Articles 131 and 133 EC Treaty).[85] The inclusion of trade in services, commercial aspects of intellectual property and foreign direct investment in Article 207 (1) TFEU on the principles of the CCP settled some

---

[78]The substance of Article 116 EEC Treaty concerning the Member States' policies in international organisations was now included in Article J.2 of the Maastricht Treaty.

[79]Before the Maastricht Treaty, the Member States could adopt the protective measure before informing the Commission about it, which could then decide on authorising the measure or prohibit it from being carried out further.

[80]Ex-Article 113 EC Treaty.

[81]Treaty of Nice (n 49).

[82]Pescatore went so far as to call the alterations '*legal bricolage*', meaning '*a patchwork of incoherent additions to the provisions of the EU and EC Treaties*', cf. Pescatore (2001), p. 265.

[83]Cf. e.g. Cremona (2002), p. 370; Herrmann (2002), p. 7; Krenzler and Pitschas (2001), p. 291.

[84]Bungenberg (2010), p. 151. On the actors shaping the EU's CCP Dederer (2013).

[85]Furthermore, the Lisbon Treaty finally repealed Article 134 EC Treaty on the possible authorisation of protective measures by the Member States, which had already become obsolete with the completion of the internal market and which, for this reason, had not been used since 1993. The last measure authorised under Article 134 EC Treaty elapsed on 30 June 1993, cf. Commission Decision of 29 April 1993 authorizing the French Republic to apply safeguard measures to the importation of bananas originating in the African, Caribbean and Pacific (ACP) States (92/236/EEC). The continued application of Article 115 EEC Treaty for bananas after the date of 31 December 1992 was of an exceptional nature and was caused by a lack of agreement regarding a common market for bananas, cf. Eeckhout (1994), p. 245.

old controversies[86] and sparked new ones.[87] However, trade defence instruments remain at the core of the Union's commercial policy and are explicitly listed as parts of the EU's commercial policy instruments in Article 207 (1) TFEU—just as it has been the case since the 1957 Treaty of Rome.[88]

The Treaty of Lisbon differed significantly from its predecessors in that it incorporated the provisions governing the EU's external relations—and thus also the norms on the common commercial policy—into the wider framework of the TFEU and the TEU. In particular, the Treaty of Lisbon introduced a number of rules governing all aspects of the Union's external action, including the common commercial policy.[89] The first one of said provisions is Article 3 (5) TEU. Article 3 TEU contains the main objectives of the European Union.[90] It is however clear from its wording that it does not stipulate the external action to be one of the EU's objectives in itself. Rather, it sets out the guiding principles the Union is to adhere to in its external relations. The enumeration in Article 3 (5) TEU reveals that these guiding principles for the EU's external action shall, *mutatis mutandis,* be the same ones as for its internal relations. In accordance with its commitment to liberalising trade on an internal level, Article 3 (5) TEU prescribes that the Union shall, in its relations with the wider world, *inter alia* contribute to free and fair trade.[91] Article 21 TEU concretises the guiding principles set out in Article 3 (5) TEU. The parallelism between the EU's internal and its external policy objectives is further apparent in Article 21 (1) TEU, which prescribes that the EU's action on the international scene shall be guided by the principles which have inspired its own creation, development and enlargement, and which it seeks to advance in the wider world. Article 21 (2) TEU lists a number of policy objectives the EU is to pursue in all aspects of its external relation. As another novelty, the list includes a number of

---

[86] One achievement of the Lisbon Treaty lies in the simplification of the rules on the division of competencies between the Member States and the European Union, which after the amendments made by the Treaty of Nice was considered *'unreadable, unsystematic and complex'*, cf. Bungenberg (2010), p. 131.

[87] The question whether the Union's newly acquired competence only covers foreign direct investments or also portfolio investments was only answered by the Court in 2017, cf. *Free Trade Agreement with Singapore* (16 May 2017) Opinion 2/15 (European Court of Justice) and was at the centre of academic debate before the judgment, cf. e.g. Kübek and Kleimann (2016).

[88] The character of the EU's trade defence instruments as *'measures to protect trade'* within the meaning of Article 207 (1) TFEU was explicitly recognised by the Court, cf. *Free Trade Agreement with Singapore* (n 87) 42–43.

[89] The applicability of Article 3 TEU follows from its location in Part One on the Treaty's 'Common Provisions'. The applicability of Article 21 TEU can be derived from Article 205 TFEU, stating that *'[t]he Union's action on the international scene, (. . .), shall be guided by the objectives and be conducted in accordance with the general provisions laid down in Chapter 1 of Title V of the Treaty on European Union'*, as well as from the wording of Article 21 (3) TEU itself.

[90] Sommermann (2013) para. 1.

[91] The precise content of the objective of 'free and fair trade' will be examined extensively below in the section on the objectives of the European Union's trade defence instruments, cf. below p. 77 et seq.

non-commercial policy objectives, such as improving the quality of the environment and the sustainable management of global natural resources.[92] Thus, while gradual trade liberalisation continues to be a central policy objective of the EU's common commercial policy, it now also is to be guided by the non-commercial policy objectives contained in Articles 3 (5) TEU and 21 TEU.[93]

To conclude, the Lisbon Treaty did not change the formal status of commercial policy as an activity of the European Union, as none of the Treaties before it did. However, to some extent, it did away with the special status of the EU's external relations policy, as the Treaty integrated it into the framework of the TFEU and the TEU, hereby stressing the parallelism in the values and principles guiding the EU's action both internally and abroad.[94]

Further, the European Union has to ensure consistency between its policies. This is mandated by various provisions of the TEU and the TFEU,[95] and reiterated in Article 21 (3) subpara. 2 TEU. The provision *inter alia* sets out an obligation of horizontal coherence by prescribing that the European Union is to ensure inter-policy coherence both between its internal and its external policies.[96] When viewed together with the integration of the CCP in the wider plane of the EU' external policies, the provision is another element expressing the relevance of non-commercial policy objectives for the EU's CCP under the Treaty of Lisbon. Similarly, due to its reference to the EU's internal policies, the norm ensures that the EU's external action does not contravene its internal policies, which includes the EU's competition policy.

The structural equivalence of the Union's internal policies and its external actions is also discernible in liberalisation as one of the two core principles of the CCP.[97] Just as trade was to be liberalised between the Member States, impediments to trade with third States were also to be abolished. In this regard, trade defence instruments constitute an exception from the principle of liberalisation. However, at the same time, they are an expression of the common commercial policy once more serving the needs of the internal market, as one main rationale behind their application lies in ensuring a 'level playing field' for European companies at home and protecting them from 'unfair competition' on the internal market.[98] Lastly, the primacy of EU competition law can also be derived from the hierarchy of norms, as the EU rules

---

[92] Article 21 (2) lit. h) TEU.

[93] Kaddous (2016), p. 441, calling Article 21 TEU the *'spinal column'* of EU action on the international scene; Krajewski (2012), p. 297; Cremona (2003), p. 1363. For an overview cf. also Fernández-Pons (2021).

[94] Regelsberger and Kugelmann (2018) para. 2.

[95] Cf. e.g. Article 7 TFEU.

[96] Cremona (2008), pp. 19, 30; cf. also Müller-Graff (2008), p. 194.

[97] The other one being 'uniformity', cf. Cremona (2002).

[98] On the rationale of the use of trade defence instruments cf. below p. 89 et seq.

on competition are enshrined in the Treaties—and hence primary law—whereas its trade defence instruments are contained in secondary legislation.[99]

One can thus deduce from the Treaties as well as from the jurisprudence of the Court that, while the common commercial policy constitutes an essential activity for realising the success of economic integration between the Member States, it is precisely because of its close connection to the internal policies of the European Union that it may not run counter to them.

2.5   Chapter Conclusions

From the beginning of the European integration process, the drafters of the Treaties were aware of the existing interface between competition and trade, and more specifically, competition and trade defence. This is first apparent in the Schuman Declaration, which combined aspects of trade and competition policy. At this point, note should further be taken of the Spaak Report,[100] which laid the groundwork for the later conclusion of the Treaty of Rome, and which included anti-dumping policies *vis-à-vis* third States in the section on competition as well as in the section on the unification of trade policy. It thus considered dumping by firms from third States to also be a 'competition issue', albeit a different set of rules was applied to tackle it.[101]

But how did the drafters of the Treaties intend possible conflicts between the two policies resulting from this interface to be resolved? An examination of the provisions addressing the respective field of policy reveals that there is quite a number of similarities between them: formally, both are—using the terminology of the EC Treaty—activities of the European Union, but not objectives in themselves. Furthermore, competition and commercial policy have each been at the heart of the European Treaties, historically and regarding their importance for ensuring the success of European integration. Just as the competition rules were deemed of such paramount importance for the realisation of the internal market that without them, numerous provisions would be pointless,[102] the common commercial policy formed the necessary external corollary to the establishment of the internal market. It could even be said that the competition rules were aimed at ensuring the operability of the internal market 'on the inside' while the rules on the CCP were aimed at ensuring its operability 'on the outside'. One key argument supporting the

---

[99] Eeckhout (2011), p. 10.

[100] Comité intergouvernemental crée par la conférence de Messine, 'Rapport des chefs de délégation aux ministres des Affaires étrangères: ("Spaak Report")' (Brussels 21 April 1956).

[101] On the different treatment of 'unfair competition' by companies from abroad and by companies on the internal market cf. Bourgeois (1993), p. 116.

[102] *Europemballage Corporation and Continental Can Company Inc. v Commission of the European Communities* (Chap. 1, n 14).

hypothesis that trade policy measures may not distort competition thus already follows from the principle of uniformity, which forms one of the basic principles underlying the CCP. As shown above, a uniform commercial policy was necessary following the establishment of a common market, since its operability could only be ensured if there were no deflections of trade or distortions of competition in the common market caused by the individual commercial policies of the Member States. Hence, if the main rationale behind the common commercial policy was to *avoid* deflections of competition caused by diverging commercial policies of the Member States, it would be illogical if its application could lead to distortions of competition itself.[103] This conclusion is supported by the jurisprudence of the CJEU in *Local Cost Standard* and *Belgium v Commission* as presented above, with the reasoning of the Court indicating that commercial policy measures must not distort competition within the internal market. It thus follows from the history of the Union's common commercial policy as well as from its substantive provisions that the CCP may not run counter to the internal policies of the European Union, especially not to the needs of the common market. This includes the competition rules. In today's Treaty framework, this can be inferred from the hierarchy of norms and the obligation of the EU institutions to ensure the coherence of its common commercial policy measures with the EU's internal policies as mandated by Article 21 (3) subpara. 2 TEU. Therefore, the use of trade defence instruments may well be intended to offset the distortions of competition caused by dumping and subsidies. At the same time, their use must be restricted to what is necessary to achieve this aim and hence must not occur in a protectionist manner, as this would constitute a distortion of competition in itself. The hypothesis described at the outset, according to which the Treateis require for anti-competitive effects stemming from commercial policy measures and particularly trade defence measures to be avoided has thus proven to be correct.

References[104]

Alter KJ, Steinberg D (2007) The theory and reality of the European coal and steel community. In: Meunier S, McNamara KR (eds) Making history: European integration and institutional change at fifty. Oxford University Press

Bailey D (2018) Competition law and policy in the EU. In: Bailey D, John LE (eds) European Union law of competition, 5th edn. Oxford University Press

Bourgeois J (1993) Competition policy and commercial policy. In: Maresceau M (ed) The European Community's commercial policy after 1992: the legal dimension. Martinus Nijhoff Publishers

---

[103] Making a similar argument regarding possible anti-competitive effects of the EC-Japan arrangement on the importation of Japanese cars cf. Eeckhout (1994), p. 222.

[104] All online sources were last accessed on 8 September 2021.

Buendia Sierra JL (2012) Writing straight with crooked lines: competition policy and services of general economic interest in the treaty of Lisbon. In: Biondi A, Eeckhout P, Ripley S (eds) EU law after Lisbon. Oxford University Press

Bungenberg M (2010) Going global? The EU common commercial policy after Lisbon. In: Herrmann C, Terhechte JP (eds) European yearbook of international economic law 2010. Springer

Chiriţă AD (2014) A legal-historical review of the EU competition rules. Int Comp Law Q (ICLQ) 63(2):281

Claassen R et al (2019) Rethinking the European social market economy: introduction to the special issue. J Common Mark Stud 57(1):3

Cremona M (2002) The external dimension of the single market: building (on) the foundations. In: Barnard C, Scott J (eds) The law of the single European market: unpacking the premises. Hart

Cremona M (2003) The draft constitutional treaty: external relations and external action. Common Mark Law Rev 40(6):1347

Cremona M (2008) Coherence through law: what difference will the treaty of Lisbon make? Hamburg Rev Soc Sci 3(1):11

Dederer H-G (2013) The common commercial policy under the influence of commission, council, high representative and European External Action Service. In: Bungenberg M, Herrmann C (eds) Common commercial policy after Lisbon. Springer

Dimopoulos A (2010) The effects of the Lisbon treaty on the principles and objectives of the common commercial policy. Eur Foreign Aff Rev 15(2):153

Drexl J (2009) Wettbewerbsverfassung. In: von Bogdandy A, Bast J (eds) Europäisches Verfassungsrecht: Theoretische und dogmatische Grundzüge, 2nd edn. Springer

Eeckhout P (1994) The European internal market and international trade: a legal analysis. Clarendon Press

Eeckhout P (2011) Administrative Procedures in EU External Trade Law. Note Prepared for the Directorate-General of Internal Policies of the European Parliament. Available at <https://www.europarl.europa.eu/RegData/etudes/note/join/2011/432758/IPOL-JURI_NT(2011)432758_EN.pdf>

Fernández-Pons X (2021) The role of the EU in the promotion of sustainable development through multilateral trade. In: Eritja MC (ed) The European Union and global environmental protection: transforming influence into action. Routledge

Ferri D, Cortese F (2019) The social market economy in the European Union: theoretical perspectives and practical challenges. In: Ferri D, Cortese F (eds) The EU social market economy and the law. Routledge

Heinemann A (2019) Social considerations in EU competition law: the protection of competition as a cornerstone of the social market economy. In: Ferri D, Cortese F (eds) The EU social market economy and the law. Routledge

Herrmann C (2002) Common commercial policy after Nice: Sisyphus would have done a better job. Common Mark Law Rev 39(1):7

Kaddous C (2016) The transformation of the EU common commercial policy. In: Eeckhout P, López-Escudero M (eds) The European Union's external action in times of crisis. Hart

Kaupa C (2016) The pluralist character of the European economic constitution. Hart

Krajewski M (2012) The reform of the common commercial policy. In: Biondi A, Eeckhout P, Ripley S (eds) EU law after Lisbon. Oxford University Press

Krenzler HG, Pitschas C (2001) Progress or stagnation?: the common commercial policy after Nice. Eur Foreign Aff Rev 6(3):291

Kübek G, Kleimann D (2016) The Signing, Provisional Application, and Conclusion of Trade and Investment Agreements in the EU: The Case of CETA and Opinion 2/15. EUI Working Papers. Available at <https://cadmus.eui.eu/bitstream/handle/1814/51706/Kleimann_2018_LEIE_45.pdf?sequence=2&isAllowed=y>

Larik J (2011) Much more than trade: the common commercial policy in a global context. In: Evans MD, Koutrakos P (eds) Beyond the established legal orders: policy interconnections between the EU and the rest of the world. Hart

Leal-Arcas R (2007) Is EC trade policy up to par? a legal analysis over time – Rome, Marrakesh, Amsterdam, Nice and the constitutional treaty. Columbia J Eur Law 13(2):305

Lianos I (2012) Competition law in the European Union after the Treaty of Lisbon. In: Ashiagbor D, Countouris N, Lianos I (eds) The European Union after the treaty of Lisbon. Cambridge University Press

Lianos I (2013) Some Reflections on the Question of the Goals of EU Competition Law. CLES Working Paper Series. Available at <https://papers.ssrn.com/sol3/papers.cfm?abstract_id=2235875>

Maduro MP (1998) We the court: the European Court of Justice and the European economic constitution. Hart

Maresceau M (1993) The difficult road to Maastricht. In: Maresceau M (ed) The European community's commercial policy after 1992: the legal dimension. Martinus Nijhoff Publishers

Mestmäcker E-J (1994) On the legitimacy of European law. Rabels Zeitschrift für ausländisches und internationales Privatrecht 58(4):615

Müller-Graff P-C (2008) The common commercial policy enhanced by the reform treaty of Lisbon. In: Dashwood A, Maresceau M (eds) Law and practice of EU external relations: salient features of a changing landscape. Cambridge University Press

Nazzini R (2011) The foundations of European competition law: the objectives and principles of Article 102. Oxford University Press

Nowak C (2004) Wirtschaftsgrundrechte und Wirtschaftsverfassung in Deutschland und in der Europäischen Union. In: Bruha T, Nowak C, Petzold HA (eds) Grundrechtsschutz für Unternehmen im europäischen Binnenmarkt. Nomos

Patel K, Schweitzer H (2012) Introduction. In: Schweitzer H, Patel KK (eds) The historical foundations of EU competition law. Oxford University Press

Pescatore P (1987) Some critical remarks on the "Single European Act". Common Mark Law Rev 24:9

Pescatore P (2001) Guest editorial: Nice – aftermath. Common Mark Law Rev 38(2):265

Petit N, Neyrinck N (2010) A review of the competition law implications of the treaty on the functioning of the European Union. Compet Policy Int J 2:1–14

Ramírez Pérez SM, van de Scheur S (2012) The evolution of the law on Articles 85 and 86 EEC [Articles 101 and 102 TFEU]: ordoliberalism and its Keynesian challenge. In: Schweitzer H, Patel KK (eds) The historical foundations of EU competition law. Oxford University Press

Regelsberger E, Kugelmann D (2018) Artikel 3 EUV. In: Streinz R (ed) EUV/AEUV, 3rd edn. C.H. Beck

Sally R (1996) Ordoliberalism and the social market: classical political economy from Germany. New Polit Econ 1(2):233

Sauter W (1997) Competition law and industrial policy in the EU. Clarendon Press

Schuknecht L (1991) The political economy of EC protectionism: National protectionism based on Article 115, Treaty of Rome. Public Choice 72(1):37

Sommermann K-P (2013) Art. 3 TEU. In: Blanke H-J, Mangiameli S (eds) Treaty on European Union (TEU): a commentary. Springer

Spaak F, Jaeger J (1961) The rules of competition within the European common market. Law Contemp Probl 26(3):485

Sprung R (1959) Die Bestimmungen über die Beseitigung von Verzerrungen des Wettbewerbs im Vertrag über die EWG. Finanz Archiv/Public Financ Anal 20(2):201

Stanbrook C, Bentley P (1996) Dumping and subsidies: the law and procedures governing the imposition of anti-dumping and countervailing duties in the European Community, 3rd edn. Kluwer Law International

Steenbergen J (1980) The common commercial policy. Common Mark Law Rev 17(2):229

Terhechte JP (2009) Wandlungen der europäischen Wettbewerbsverfassung. In: Fastenrath U, Nowak C (eds) Tübinger Schriften zum internationalen und europäischen Recht. Duncker & Humblot

van Bael I, Bellis J-F (2019) EU anti-dumping and other trade defence instruments, 6th edn. Kluwer Law International

van Rompuy B (2011) The impact of the Lisbon treaty on EU competition law: a review of recent case law of the EU courts. CPI Antitrust Chronicle

Chapter 3
The Legal Framework Governing EU Competition and Trade Defence Law

3.1 Introduction

While the first chapter focused on outlining the historical and conceptual background of the relationship between competition law and trade defence law according to the European Treaties, the second chapter provides an overview of the legal framework governing the EU's competition policy and the use of its trade defence instruments as well as their institutional set-up. As there is a large body of literature on both EU competition law and its trade defence regime, the chapter does not attempt to examine each area of law in its entirety. Instead, it only seeks to present the necessary background information on the legal regime governing the two areas of law, which will then be used in the ensuing chapters.

3.2 Competition Law

3.2.1 Institutional Structure

Pursuant to Article 3 (1) lit. b) TFEU, the EU is exclusively competent in establishing the competition rules necessary for the functioning of the internal market. Consequently, the EU legislative organs are also exclusively competent in designing the EU's competition law framework. Among the EU organs, the EU Commission occupies a central role in defining and implementing EU competition policy:[1] *inter alia,* it is responsible for carrying out investigations regarding possible

---

[1] Article 17 (1) TEU: '*The Commission shall promote the general interest of the Union and take appropriate initiatives to that end. It shall ensure the application of the Treaties, and of measures adopted by the institutions pursuant to them. It shall oversee the application of Union law under the*

© The Author(s), under exclusive license to Springer Nature Switzerland AG 2022
P. Trapp, *The European Union's Trade Defence Modernisation Package*, EYIEL
Monographs - Studies in European and International Economic Law 23,
https://doi.org/10.1007/978-3-030-91363-2_3

infringements of EU competition provisions and for assessing the compatibility of mergers with the EU competition framework. Within the Commission, the Directorate-General for Competition (DG COMP) is the Directorate specifically responsible for competition policy. The competition authorities of the Member States or national courts may also scrutinise undertakings' behaviour under Articles 101 and 102 TFEU. The relationship between the different enforcers of EU competition law is governed by Regulation (EU) 1/2003.[2] While national competition authorities and courts may assess whether an undertaking's behaviour conforms with Articles 101, 102 TFEU, the Commission is exclusively competent in assessing mergers falling within the scope of application of EU merger control law.[3]

3.2.2   Article 101 TFEU: Prohibition of Agreements Between Undertakings Restricting Competition

3.2.2.1   The Elements of Article 101 (1) TFEU

3.2.2.1.1   Undertakings as Addressees

Both Article 101 TFEU and Article 102 TFEU are concerned with the behaviour of undertakings. It is therefore necessary to establish what exactly is encompassed by the concept of 'undertaking' in order to determine the *ratione personae* of the competition rules.[4] The term itself is not defined in the TFEU. The CJEU has adopted a functional approach in defining the notion, according to which the nature of the activity carried out by an entity is decisive in determining whether it is to be regarded as an undertaking within the meaning of EU competition law. It thus encompasses every entity engaged in economic activity, regardless of the legal status of the entity and the way in which it is financed.[5]

---

control of the Court of Justice of the European Union'; cf. also *Masterfoods Ltd. and others* (14 December 2000) C-344/98 46 (European Court of Justice).

[2] Council Regulation (EC) No 1/2003 of 16 December 2002 on the implementation of the rules on competition laid down in Articles 81 and 82 of the Treaty.

[3] Boyce and Lyle-Smythe (2018), para. 8.066.

[4] *Albany International BV v Stichting Bedrijfspensioenfonds Textielindustrie* (21 September 1999) C-67/96 206 (European Court of Justice).

[5] C.f. e.g. *Pavel Pavlov and others v Stichting Pensioenfonds Medische Specialisten* (12 September 2000) C-180/98 to C-184/98 74 (European Court of Justice); *SAT Fluggesellschaft mbH v Eurocontrol* (19 January 1994) C-364/92 18 (European Court of Justice); *Klaus Höfner and Fritz Elser v Macrotron GmbH* (23 April 1991) C-41/90 21 (European Court of Justice).

3.2.2.1.2 Agreement, Decision and Concerted Practice

While the terms 'agreement', 'decision' and 'concerted practice' are distinguishable from each other by their intensity and the forms in which they manifest, they overlap and it is irrelevant for finding an infringement of Article 101 (1) TFEU whether a certain behaviour is considered an agreement, a decision or a concerted practice.[6]

In general, the provision is concerned with joint conduct resulting from some form of collusion between independent undertakings. If this is not the case, the behaviour is not caught by Article 101 (1) TFEU.[7]

3.2.2.1.3 Object or Effect of the Prevention, Restriction or Distortion of Competition

The conduct in question needs to have as its object or effect the prevention, restriction or distortion of competition. 'Object or effect' is to be read disjunctively, as these are alternative requirements for finding an infringement of Article 101 (1) TFEU.[8] In order to establish whether competition is distorted, restricted or prevented, the conditions of competition with and without the conduct in question are compared.[9]

'By object' restrictions are prohibited under Article 101 (1) TFEU regardless of the actual result of the conduct, meaning that no concrete restriction of competition by the agreement has to be proven, as the coordination itself reveals a sufficient degree of harm to competition.[10] The distinction between infringements 'by object' and infringements 'by effect' thus arises from the fact that certain forms of collusion between undertakings can be regarded, by their very nature, as being injurious to the proper functioning of normal competition.[11] Conversely, even where the conduct does not have it as its object to restrict competition, the prohibition applies if its effect is a restriction of competition. This is the case if the conduct is liable to have an appreciable adverse impact on the parameters of competition, such as the price, the quality and quantity of the goods or services.[12] In determining whether there is indeed an actual or a potential detrimental effect on competition, it is necessary to

---

[6] Jones et al. (2019), p. 165.

[7] Khan and Suh (2015), para. 20.

[8] *Société Technique Minière (STM)* (n 18 in Chap. 2) 249.

[9] With further references cf. Schroeder et al. (2018), paras. 120–124.

[10] Khan and Suh (2015), para. 28 citing *Allianz Hungária and others* (14 March 2013) C-32/11 (European Court of Justice); *T-Mobile Netherlands and others* (4 June 2009) C-8/08 (European Court of Justice).

[11] *Beef Industry Development Society* (20 November 2008) C-209/07 17 (European Court of Justice).

[12] *MasterCard Inc. v European Commission* (11 September 2014) C-382/12 93 (European Court of Justice); the intention to distort competition can be taken into account, but is not necessary for finding an infringement of Article 101 (1) TFEU, cf. *T-Mobile Netherlands and others* (n 10) 27.

establish a 'counterfactual', that is to consider what the situation would have been like in absence of the conduct in question.[13] To this end, the actual or potential effect on competition caused by the conduct must be demonstrated.[14]

3.2.2.1.4   The *de minimis* Doctrine

In order to fall within the scope of Article 101 (1) TFEU, the agreement, decision or concerted practice in question must affect trade between Member States and the free play of competition to an appreciable extent.[15]

3.2.2.1.4.1   *Appreciable Effect on Trade Between the Member States*

Article 101 TFEU only protects competition in trade between Member States. Agreements, decisions or concerted practices restricting competition within a single Member State do not trigger the scope of application of EU competition law.[16] Similarly, conduct concerning third States is not caught by Article 101 TFEU unless it produces an effect on the internal market.[17]

The impact on trade must further be appreciable. Such an appreciable impact exists where

> it is possible to foresee with a sufficient degree of probability (. . .) that the agreement in question may have a direct or indirect, actual or potential influence on the pattern of trade between Member States in such a way that it might hinder the attainment of the objectives of a single market between States.[18]

3.2.2.1.4.2   *Appreciable Effect on Competition*

In addition, the agreement needs to have an appreciable effect on the free play of competition.[19] This does not apply to 'by object' restrictions, as they constitute, by

---

[13] *O2 (Germany) v Commission* (2 May 2006) T-328/03 108 et seq. (Court of First Instance).

[14] *John Deere v Commission* (28 May 1998) C-7/95 P 77 (European Court of Justice).

[15] *Béguelin Import Co. v S.A.G.L. Import Export* (25 November 1971) C-22/71 16 (European Court of Justice).

[16] *Consten and Grundig v Commission* (13 July 1966) joined cases C-56 and 58/64 330, 341 (European Court of Justice).

[17] *Javico International v Yves Saint Laurent Parfums* (28 April 1998) C-306/96 15–21 (European Court of Justice).

[18] *Voelk v Verwaecke* (9 July 1969) C-5/69 295, 302 (European Court of Justice). Regarding the criteria used by the Commission in determining whether an agreement is likely to appreciably affect inter-State trade cf. European Commission, 'Guidelines on the effect on trade concept contained in Articles 81 and 82 of the Treaty (2004/C 101/07)'.

[19] *Voelk v Verwaecke* (n 18); cf. the Commission's *De Minimis* Notice which provides certain market share thresholds below which the agreement is unlikely to restrict competition appreciably European Commission, 'Notice on agreements of minor importance which do not appreciably

their nature and independently of any concrete effect they may have, an appreciable effect on competition.[20]

3.2.2.2 Nullity According to Article 101 (2) TFEU

According to Article 101 (2) TFEU, any agreement or decision prohibited pursuant to this Article is automatically void. The agreement or decision is unenforceable as a whole, unless the elements which fall under Article 101 (1) TFEU and which are not saved by Article 101 (3) TFEU can be separated from the remainder. If this is the case, only the restrictive elements are void and unenforceable.[21]

3.2.2.3 The Exception Contained in Article 101 (3) TFEU

Article 101 (3) TFEU provides that the provisions of Article 101 (1) TFEU may be declared inapplicable if the conduct in question fulfils all four preconditions set out in Article 101 (3) TFEU are fulfilled.

There is a considerable debate regarding the scope of Article 101 (3) TFEU,[22] in particular as to the circumstances under which a benefit under Article 101 (3) TFEU can justify a restriction of competition under Article 101 (1) TFEU. The proponents of a narrow interpretation of Article 101 (3) TFEU propose that the provision applies exclusively to agreements that would bring about improvements in economic efficiency.[23] Other policy objectives, such as industry, employment or culture will not

---

restrict competition under Article 101(1) of the Treaty on the Functioning of the European Union: De Minimis Notice' (OJ 2014 C 291/1).

[20] *Expedia Inc. v Autorité de la concurrence and others* (13 December 2012) C-226/11 37 (European Court of Justice). This change in the jurisprudence of the CJEU is also reflected in the revised *De Minimis* Notice of the Commission, cf. European Commission, 'Notice on agreements of minor importance which do not appreciably restrict competition under Article 101(1) of the Treaty on the Functioning of the European Union' (n 19) para. 2. However, also under 'by object' restrictions, the practice must at least be capable of restricting competition, cf. Opinion of Advocate General Kokott in *Generics (UK) Ltd. and others v Competition and Markets* Authority, C-307/18 57 (22 January 2020).

[21] Faull et al. (2014), para. 3.442.

[22] For an overview cf. Brook (2019), p. 121.

[23] Whish and Bailey (2018), p. 163; Jones et al. (2019), p. 264; Faull et al. (2014), para. 3.460; cf. also European Commission, 'White Paper on Modernisation of the Rules implementing Articles 85 and 86 of the EC Treaty (1999/C 132/01)' paras. 72, 74 and European Commission, 'Guidelines on the application of Article 81(3) of the Treaty (2004/C 101/08)' para. 57, which describes the purpose of Article 85 (3) EC Treaty '*to provide a legal framework for the economic assessment of restrictive practices and not to allow application of the competition rules to be set aside because of political considerations.*'

be considered as 'efficiencies' under Article 101 (3) TFEU.[24] This interpretation is supported by the wording of Article 101 (3) TFEU and the Commission's use of economic analysis in assessing possible infringements of the EU competition rules.[25] Allowing for non-economic efficiencies, which are inherently hard to quantify, to be included in the Article 101 (3) TFEU-analysis would sit uneasy with this approach.

3.2.3 Article 102 TFEU: Abuse of a Dominant Position

Article 102 TFEU is the second key competition law provision in the European Treaties. Article 101 TFEU and Article 102 TFEU are not mutually exclusive. Instead, both may apply to the same behaviour.[26] According to the settled jurisprudence of the CJEU, Article 102 TFEU does not prohibit the creation or possession of a dominant position[27] but only the 'abuse' of such a position. The application of Article 102 TFEU thus hinges not only on whether an undertaking holds a dominant position on a certain market, but also on whether it has abused said dominant position.

3.2.3.1 Dominant Undertakings as Addressees

The definition of 'undertaking' is identical for both Article 101 and 102 TFEU. Thus, reference can be made to the definition provided above.[28] As indicated, in order for the behaviour of an undertaking to be measured against Article 102 TFEU, it has to occupy a dominant position on the market. The concept of dominance relates to a position of economic strength, which enables an undertaking to prevent effective competition being maintained on the relevant market by allowing it to act to an appreciable extent independently of its competitors, customers and ultimately of

---

[24] The past practice of the Commission contains isolated examples of the Commission including e.g. environmental benefits in its assessment under Article 101 (3) TFEU, cf. e.g. Commission Decision of 24 January 1999 relating to a proceeding under Article 81 of the EC Treaty and Article 53 of the EEA Agreement (CECED) (2000/475/EC) recitals 52–57; Commission Decision of 23 December 1992 relating to a proceeding pursuant to Article 85 of the EEEC Treaty (Ford/Volkswagen) (93/49/EEC) recital 26; Commission Decision of 4 July 1984 relating to a proceeding under Article 85 of the EEC Treaty (Synthetic Fibres) (84/380/EEC) recital 37 (on the social effects of the restructuring occurring in the industry).

[25] Heide-Jorgensen (2013), p. 109.

[26] *Hoffmann-La Roche v Commission* (13 February 1979) C-85/76 116 (European Court of Justice).

[27] *Konkurrensverket v TeliaSonera Sverige AB* (n 62 in Chap. 2) 26; *NV Nederlandsche Banden Industrie Michelin v Commission (Michelin I)* (9 November 1983) C-322/81 57 (European Court of Justice).

[28] Cf. the sources cited above, n 5.

its consumers.[29] In order to determine whether an undertaking is dominant on a given market, the relevant market has to be defined.[30]

3.2.3.2 Market Definition

Market definition is necessary in order to identify and define the boundaries of competition between firms. The objective of defining a market is to determine who the actual competitors of the undertakings involved in antitrust investigations are, who are capable of constraining these undertakings' behaviour[31] and of preventing them from behaving independently of competitive pressure.[32] Market definition plays a role in all aspects of EU competition law.[33] It is necessary for the purposes of applying Article 101 TFEU when considering whether an agreement has an appreciable effect on competition[34] or on trade between Member States,[35] when assessing whether an agreement would substantially eliminate competition under Article 101 (3) lit. b) TFEU[36] and in determining whether it falls under one of the block exemptions containing market share tests.[37] A definition of the market further has to be undertaken when evaluating a concentration under the EU Merger Regulation.[38] Lastly, market definition is of central relevance for the purposes of applying Article 102 TFEU, which is why it is presented in this section.

---

[29] *Hoffmann-La Roche v Commission* (n 26) 38; *United Brands Company v Commission* (14 February 1978) C-27/76 65 (European Court of Justice).

[30] *Europemballage Corporation and Continental Can Company Inc. v Commission of the European Communities* (n 14 in Chap. 2) 32.

[31] In general, companies are subject to three main sources of competitive constraints: demand substitutability, supply substitutability and potential competition.

[32] European Commission, 'Commission Notice on the definition of relevant market for the purposes of Community competition law' (OJ 1997 C 372/5) para. 2.

[33] On the changing role of market definition in EU competition law Podszun (2016), p. 121; Zimmer (2016), p. 133.

[34] European Commission, 'Notice on agreements of minor importance which do not appreciably restrict competition under Article 101(1) of the Treaty on the Functioning of the European Union' (n 19).

[35] European Commission, 'Guidelines on the effect on trade concept contained in Articles 81 and 82 of the Treaty' (n 18).

[36] European Commission, 'Guidelines on the application of Article 81(3) of the Treaty' (n 23) paras. 107–116.

[37] Cf. e.g. Commission Regulation (EU) 330/2010 of 20 April 2010 on the application of Article 101(3) of the Treaty on the Functioning of the European Union to categories of vertical agreements and concerted practices; Commission Regulation (EU) 1217/2010 of 14 December 2010 on the application of Article 101(3) of the Treaty on the Functioning of the European Union to certain categories of research and development agreements.

[38] On the EU system of merger control cf. below p. 49. Cf. also *French Republic and Société commerciale des potasses et de l'azote (SCPA) and Entreprise minière et chimique (EMC) v Commission of the European Communities (Kali and Salz)* (31 March 1998) joined cases C-68/

3.2.3.2.1   The Relevant Product Market

Defining the product market is of paramount importance in market definition. In essence, it can be considered a question of interchangeability: where goods or services can be regarded as interchangeable, they are in the same product market.[39] Here, the demand substitutability poses the most effective criterion in assessing the existence of competitive restraints,[40] while supply substitutability is usually considered a question of determining the market power an undertaking possesses rather than of delineating the market itself.[41] In determining the substitutability of two products, the physical and technical characteristics, uses and the price of the products are assessed.[42] In addition, other parameters such as the competitive conditions and the structure of supply and demand on the market are to be taken into account.[43] One prominent test for evaluating the competitive structure on a market is the so-called 'SSNIP' (small but significant and non-transitory increase in price) or 'hypothetical monopolist' test. This test is central for evaluating the demand substitutability of products, and thus in determining the scope of a certain market.[44] It evaluates whether a small increase in the price of a product would lead to consumers switching to another product. If this is the case, both products belong to the same market.[45]

---

94 and C-30/95 13 (European Court of Justice): '*[A] proper definition of the relevant market is a necessary precondition for any assessment of the effect of a concentration on competition.*'

[39] Whish and Bailey (2018), p. 29.

[40] *Easyjet v Commission* (4 July 2006) T-177/04 99 (Court of First Instance).

[41] In some instances, however, supply substitutability may also form part of the assessment of the relevant market, cf. European Commission, 'Commission Notice on the definition of relevant market for the purposes of Community competition law (97/C 372/03)' (n 32), para. 20 and European Commission, 'Commission Decision of 26 July 1988 relating to a proceeding under Articles 85 and 86 of the EEC Treaty (Tetra Pak I) (88/501/EEC)' recitals 30, 36–38.

[42] Jung (2015), para. 38.

[43] *Tetra Pak International SA v Commission (Tetra Pak II)* (14 November 1996) C-333/94 P 10, 13 (European Court of Justice); *NV Nederlandsche Banden Industrie Michelin v Commission (Michelin I)* (n 27) 37.

[44] European Commission, 'Commission Notice on the definition of relevant market for the purposes of Community competition law (97/C 372/03)' (n 32) para. 15.

[45] Faull et al. (2014), paras. 1.147–1.152. However, the application of this test runs into difficulties in a number of situations, e.g. in markets where the price is not the decisive criterion for consumers' purchasing decision, such as the pharmaceutical sector, Jung (2015), para. 42, or where an undertaking is charging unreasonably high prices because of a dominant position it holds on a certain market (so-called 'cellophane fallacy'), European Commission, 'Commission Notice on the definition of relevant market for the purposes of Community competition law (97/C 372/03)' (n 32) para. 19; Peeperkorn and Verouden (2014), para. 1.152.

3.2.3.2.2 The Relevant Geographic Market

Moreover, a correct definition of the geographic market is important in assessing whether a firm or firms have market power, as it too helps to indicate which other firms impose a competitive constraint on the one(s) under investigation.[46] In accordance with the Commission's notice on market definition and the jurisprudence of the CJEU, it is regularly defined as

> the area in which the undertakings concerned are involved in the supply and demand of products or services, in which the conditions of competition are sufficiently homogeneous and which can be distinguished from neighbouring areas because the conditions of competition are appreciably different in those areas.[47]

The Commission also uses the SSNIP test in order to identify the companies in other locations which can be considered to constitute alternative sources of supply. However, in the case of geographic market definition, the question is whether, if faced with an increase in price, consumers located in a particular area would switch their purchases to suppliers further away.[48] While the SSNIP test relates to demand substitutability (and hence focuses on the consumers' perspective), the supply substitutability in defining the relevant geographic market can be determined by identifying the possibility of suppliers located outside a certain geographic area to start supplying into that area.[49]

3.2.3.2.3 The Temporal Market

On rare occasions, the definition of the relevant temporal market may be warranted. For example, this may be required in instances where consumer demand changes with the seasons or where a product's availability is drastically reduced for a certain period of time.[50]

---

[46] Peeperkorn and Verouden (2014), para. 1.169; *United Brands Company v Commission* (n 29) 10–11.

[47] European Commission, 'Commission Notice on the definition of relevant market for the purposes of Community competition law (97/C 372/03)' (n 32) para. 8; *United Brands Company v Commission* (n 29) 10–11.

[48] European Commission, 'Commission Notice on the definition of relevant market for the purposes of Community competition law (97/C 372/03)' (n 32) para. 29.

[49] Peeperkorn and Verouden (2014), para. 1.172.

[50] *United Brands Company v Commission* (n 29) 32–35; European Commission, 'Commission Decision of 19 April 1977 relating to a proceeding under Article 86 of the EEC Treaty (ABG Oil Companies) (77/327/EEC)' recitals 3–8.

3.2.3.3   Dominant Position

A finding of dominance has to take competitive restraints on the undertaking imposed by its actual and potential competitors as well as constraints imposed by the bargaining strength of the undertaking's customers (countervailing buyer power) into account. In assessing the position of a firm *via-à-vis* its competitors, market shares may serve as a first indicator in assessing the undertaking's position on a certain market.[51] Nonetheless, market shares are not necessarily decisive, as they may vary and the importance of market shares in general may differ from market to market according to the respective market structure.[52] There is no formal 'safe harbour' below which a firm is never found to be dominant.[53] However, the larger the market share, the likelier is a finding of dominance. If the market share lies at 50%, there is a rebuttable presumption of dominance absent other exceptional circumstances pointing the other way.[54] The Commission requires a market share of 75% for an undertaking to be found dominant without any additional inquiries into the market structure.[55]

According to its wording, Article 102 TFEU applies to '*[a]ny abuse by one or more undertakings of a dominant position*'. Hence, the provision also covers cases where the dominant position is held by legally and economically independent firms if they are considered to hold a 'collective dominant position', without each being dominant individually.[56] Such a 'collective dominant position' exists where the legally independent undertakings present themselves or act together on a particular market as a collective entity.[57]

Finally, as prescribed by Article 102 TFEU, once a finding of dominance has been made, the dominant position must also be held in the entire internal market or in

---

[51] European Commission, 'Communication from the Commission: Guidance on the Commission's enforcement priorities in applying Article 82 of the Treaty to abusive exclusionary conduct by dominant undertakings (2009/C 45/02)' para. 13.

[52] *Hoffmann-La Roche v Commission* (n 26) 40.

[53] However, market shares below 30% in a correctly defined market would not be evidence of a dominant position save in wholly exceptional circumstances, Thompson et al. (2018), para. 10.028.

[54] *AKZO Chemie BV v Commission* (3 July 1991) C-62/86 60 (European Court of Justice); in *AstraZeneca,* the General Court furthermore pointed out the '*importance that had to be attached to [AstraZeneca's] very large market share*', *AstraZeneca v Commission* (1 July 2010) T-321/05 245 (General Court).

[55] Cf. with further references Jung (2015), para. 92.

[56] *Compagnie Maritime Belge Transports and others v Commission* (16 March 2000) C-395/96 P 60 (European Court of Justice); *Società Italiana Vetro SpA and others v Commission (Italian Flat Glass)* (10 March 1992) T-68/89 358 (Court of First Instance).

[57] *Compagnie Maritime Belge Transports and others v Commission* (n 56) 36; *Piau v Commission* (26 January 2005) T-193/02 110 (Court of First Instance). The question of whether multiple entities are collectively dominant is to be separated from the question whether two or more legally separate entities form a single undertaking so that their market shares should be aggregated in order to establish whether that single undertaking is dominant, *Irish Sugar plc v Commission* (7 October 1999) T-228/97 46–49 (Court of First Instance).

a substantial part of it. Neither the CJEU nor the Commission have laid down that any particular percentage of the internal market as a whole is critical in determining what constitutes a 'substantial part' of it.[58] In the past, already parts of a Member State were considered to form such a 'substantial part',[59] as well as individual facilities.[60]

3.2.3.4   Abuse

Once it has been established that an undertaking—or a group of undertakings—is indeed dominant on a certain market, one has to assess whether the undertaking abused its dominant position.

While it is settled that the concept of abuse is an objective one[61] and that no intent on the undertaking's side is necessary for a finding of abuse,[62] there is no clear-cut definition concerning the scope of actions that are considered abusive under Article 102 TFEU.

Article 102 TFEU contains a non-exhaustive list of practices that may be deemed abusive.[63] Traditionally, the two most important categories are exploitative and exclusionary[64] abuses.[65] As a general rule, it does not have to be shown that the conduct—whether exclusionary or exploitative—produces an actual anticompetitive effect.[66] However, the behaviour must at least tend to restrict competition or be capable of doing so.[67]

---

[58] Whish and Bailey (2018), p. 196.

[59] *Suiker Unie and others v Commission* (16 December 1975) joined cases C-40/73 etc. 371–375 (European Court of Justice).

[60] *Portuguese Republic v Commission (Portuguese Airports)* (29 March 2001) C-163/99 63–66 (European Court of Justice); *Corsica Ferries* (17 May 1994) C-18/93 40 (European Court of Justice).

[61] Khan and Suh (2015), para. 12, settled case law of the Court since *Hoffmann-La Roche v Commission* (n 26) 91.

[62] *Tomra Systems ASA and others v Commission* (19 April 2012) C-549/10 P 20–21 (European Court of Justice).

[63] *Compagnie Maritime Belge Transports and others v Commission* (n 56) 112; *Europemballage Corporation and Continental Can Company Inc. v Commission of the European Communities* (n 14 in Chap. 2) 12; *Tetra Pak International SA v Commission (Tetra Pak II)* (n 43) 37.

[64] The fact that Article 102 TFEU also covers exclusionary abuses was confirmed by the Court of Justice in *Europemballage Corporation and Continental Can Company Inc. v Commission of the European Communities* (n 14 in Chap. 2).

[65] Discriminatory abuses are frequently considered to constitute a third category of abuse. Discriminatory abuses are such where competition is harmed by discriminatory prices or trading conditions charged or applied by the dominant undertaking on an intermediate market with the effect of placing certain suppliers or customers of the dominant undertaking at a competitive disadvantage, de La Mano et al. (2014), para. 4.253; cf. also the wording of Article 102 lit. c) TFEU.

[66] Kellerbauer (2019), para. 55.

[67] *Generics (UK) Ltd. and others* (30 January 2020) C-307/18 154 (European Court of Justice).

As indicated, there is no clear test as to when a firm's conduct can be regarded abusive. In its *Hoffmann-La Roche* judgment, a case which concerned exclusionary abuses, the Court defined the concept as follows:

> The concept of abuse is an objective concept relating to the behaviour of an undertaking in a dominant position which is such as to influence the market structure where, as a result of the very presence of the undertaking in question, the degree of competition is weakened and which, through recourse to methods different from those which condition normal competition in products or services on the basis of the transactions of commercial operators, has the effect of hindering the maintenance of the degree of competition still existing in the market or the growth of that competition.[68]

While the concept of 'normal competition' or 'competition on the merits'[69] remains an elusive one, in general, behaviour can be considered to go beyond competition on the merits when it restricts competition by means other than behaviour based on efficiency or if the behaviour is inconsistent with the normal profit-maximising strategies of a non-dominant undertaking.[70] A number of tests based on economic principles are utilised by the competition authorities to aid the identification of competition on the merits.[71] However, ultimately, what is and is not competition on the merits has to be determined on a case-to-case basis, in relation to the form, purpose and effect of the conduct under review in each individual case.[72]

Article 102 TFEU has been interpreted as covering both exclusionary and exploitative abuses. Examples for exploitative abuses are contained in Article 102 lit. a), b) TFEU, namely imposing unfair purchase or selling prices or limiting the production, markets or technical development to the prejudice of consumers. Excessive pricing as prohibited by Article 102 lit. a) TFEU is the classic form of an exploitative abuse.[73]

3.2.3.5 Defence

Even though the wording of the provision does not contain a justification for infringements of Article 102 TFEU, conduct that amounts to a *prima facie* abuse

---

[68] *Hoffmann-La Roche v Commission* (n 26) 91.

[69] The term 'competition on the merits' is an alternative formulation used to denote 'normal competition', cf. e.g. *Post Danmark AS v Konkurrencerådet* (27 March 2012) C-209/10 25 (European Court of Justice); *France Télécom SA v Commission (Wanadoo)* (2 April 2009) C-202/07 P 106 (European Court of Justice).

[70] Nazzini (2011), p. 170. Similarly, Dolmans and Lin regard price competition as legitimate where it is justified on the basis of economic efficiency, Dolmans and Lin (2017), pp. 4, 12.

[71] These include *inter alia* the 'profit sacrifice'-test, the 'no economic sense'-test or the 'as efficient competitor'-test, cf. de La Mano et al. (2014), para. 4.265.

[72] Nazzini (2011), p. 171. Cf. also European Commission, 'Communication from the Commission: Guidance on the Commission's enforcement priorities in applying Article 82 of the Treaty to abusive exclusionary conduct by dominant undertakings' (n 51).

[73] Gal (2013), p. 386.

can be objectively justified. The possible defences include objective necessity[74] and efficiencies.[75]

3.2.3.6 Effect on Trade Between the Member States

Lastly, the abusive behaviour has to be capable of producing a distortion of trade between Member States, just as it is the case for Article 101 TFEU.[76] A hindrance of the objective of the creation of a uniform market between Member States only has to be possible.[77]

3.2.4 Merger Control

Merger control is the third central component of EU competition law. The EU Merger Regulation (EUMR) generally applies to all forms of concentrations with a Union dimension,[78] with a concentration being deemed to exist whenever a change of control on a lasting basis occurs.[79] While most mergers do not give rise to competitive concerns, there are cases where a potential merger could change the structure of the market in ways that provide the merged entity with both the incentive and the ability to exercise market power.[80] Under the EU merger regime, such a concentration that would significantly impede effective competition in the common market or in a substantial part of it, in particular as a result of the creation or strengthening of a dominant position,[81] will be declared incompatible with the internal market.[82] As mentioned, the definition of the relevant market thus plays a

---

[74] Examples of legitimate objectives justifying *prima facie* abusive conduct under Article 102 TFEU include e.g. safety concerns, cf. *Hilti AG v Commission* (12 December 1991) T-30/89 98 (Court of First Instance); Nazzini (2011), pp. 217–230.

[75] *Post Danmark AS v Konkurrencerådet* (n 69) 40–42; *Konkurrensverket v TeliaSonera Sverige AB* (n 62 in Chap. 2) 76; *British Airways v Commission* (15 March 2007) C-95/04 P 68 (European Court of Justice).

[76] Khan and Suh (2015), para. 16.

[77] Ibid.

[78] Article 1 (1) of Council Regulation (EC) No 139/2004 of 20 January 2004 on the control of concentrations between undertakings. The EUMR uses the term 'community' dimension. However, post-Lisbon, the term 'Union' dimension is more fitting.

[79] Article 3 (1) of Council Regulation (EC) No 139/2004 of 20 January 2004 on the control of concentrations between undertakings (n 78).

[80] Whish and Bailey (2018), p. 838.

[81] The concept of 'dominance' is identical for the purposes of the EUMR and Article 102 TFEU, Peeperkorn and Verouden (2014), para. 1.190.

[82] Article 2 (2) of Council Regulation (EC) No 139/2004 of 20 January 2004 on the control of concentrations between undertakings (n 78). While the regulation still speaks of a concentration to be incompatible with the 'common' market, the Commission has adapted its terminology and

central role in merger control, as the relevant market outlines the arena of competition in which to apply the competitive assessment.[83]

3.3 Law of Trade Defence Instruments

3.3.1 Introduction

Anti-dumping and anti-subsidy law form the two principal pillars of the EU's trade defence instruments. Both instruments intend to avert injurious effects of dumped or subsidised imports to the European industry. Their basis in primary law can be found in Article 207 (1) TFEU. Article 207 (2) TFEU in turn calls upon the European Parliament and the Council to adopt the measures defining the framework for implementing the EU's common commercial policy by means of regulations. For this reason, the EU legislation governing the use of trade defence instruments is contained in secondary legislation, most importantly the Regulation on protection against dumped imports from countries not members of the European Union (basic anti-dumping regulation or BADR) and the Regulation on protection against subsidised imports from countries not members of the European Union (basic anti-subsidy regulation or BASR).[84] The EU's trade defence law further includes two regulations laying down the ground rules for safeguard measures.[85] Under these regulations, the Commission may restrict the volume of imports. Lastly, the so-called trade barriers regulation (TBR) sets out procedures enabling EU industry and Member States to submit a complaint to EU institutions concerning alleged trade barriers put in place by third States that are contrary to international trade rules.[86] Of

---

declares a concentration as incompatible with the 'internal market' in its post-Lisbon decisions, cf. e.g. Commission Decision of 6 February 2019 declaring a concentration to be incompatible with the internal market and the functioning of the EEA Agreement (Case M.8677 Siemens/Alstom) (C (2019) 921 final) Article 1.

[83] Bengtsson et al. (2014), para. 5.587.

[84] Regulation (EU) 2016/1036 of the European Parliament and of the Council of 8 June 2016 on protection against dumped imports from countries not members of the European Union (n 7 in Chap. 1) (BADR); Regulation (EU) 2016/1037 of the European Parliament and of the Council of 8 June 2016 on protection against subsidised imports from countries not members of the European Union (BASR) (n 8 in Chap. 1).

[85] Regulation (EU) 2015/478 of the European Parliament and of the Council of 11 March 2015 on common rules for imports; Regulation (EU) 2015/755 of the European Parliament and of the Council of 29 April 2015 on common rules for imports from certain third countries.

[86] Regulation (EU) 2015/1843 of the European Parliament and of the Council of 6 October 2015 laying down Union procedures in the field of the common commercial policy in order to ensure the exercise of the Union's rights under international trade rules, in particular those established under the auspices of the World Trade Organization.

these instruments, anti-dumping measures are the most frequently used.[87] As mentioned in the introductory chapter, until 1994, the imposition of anti-dumping and
countervailing measures was regulated by the same regulation. This explains the
similarities still borne by the procedural and substantive provisions of the BADR and
the BASR today.[88] For this reason and due to the practical relevance of anti-dumping
measures, the main part of this section will be devoted to presenting the EU's anti-
dumping legislation and refer to the respective parts of this chapter when presenting
the basic anti-subsidy regulation whenever possible and appropriate.

3.3.2   Institutional Structure

The EU is exclusively competent in adopting the legislation governing the use of its
trade defence instruments.[89] As a rule, it is the Member States that are tasked with
enforcing EU law, as prescribed by Article 291 (1) TFEU. In the area of trade
defence, however, since the Treaty of Lisbon, it is upon the Commission to ensure
compliance with the requirements of EU law, as the implementation of the basic
regulations requires uniform conditions for the adoption of measures, and for the
termination of an investigation without measures. Hence, the Commission is the
competent authority for imposing trade defence measures through implementing
regulations, for carrying out investigations, and for the initiation and termination of
proceedings.[90] The Council—and through it the Member States—are involved in the
imposition of trade defence measures within the scope provided for by Regulation
(EU) 182/2011, which is based on Article 291 (3) TFEU.[91] In brief, Commission
proposals for the imposition of anti-dumping and countervailing duties will be
adopted unless Member States oppose the measures under the examination procedure set out in Article 5 Regulation (EU) 182/2011. However, the instances where
this has been the case have been extremely rare, with Commission proposals having
faced opposition from the Member States only on two occasions.[92]

---

[87] Cf. the official statistics provided in European Commission, 'Anti-Dumping, Anti-Subsidy,
Safeguard Statistics covering 2018' (Brussels December 2018).

[88] van Bael and Bellis (2019), § 1.01.

[89] Article 3 (1) lit. e) TFEU; *Free Trade Agreement with Singapore* (n 87 in Chap. 2) 42–43,
explicitly naming the EU's trade defence instruments a part of its commercial policy.

[90] van Bael and Bellis (2019), § 1.04 [A].

[91] Regulation (EU) No 182/2011 of the European Parliament and of the Council of 16 February
2011 laying down the rules and general principles concerning mechanisms for control by Member
States of the Commission's exercise of implementing powers.

[92] van Bael and Bellis (2019), § 1.04 [B] [3].

3.3.3   The Basic Anti-dumping Regulation

According to Article 1 (1) BADR, an anti-dumping duty may be imposed on any dumped product whose release for free circulation in the Union causes injury. Article 21 BADR further prescribes that measures under the basic anti-dumping regulation may only be taken if it cannot clearly be concluded that the imposition of anti-dumping measures would not be in the Union's interest. Thus, the four conditions that have to be met in order for measures to be taken under the BADR are dumping, injury, a causal link between the dumping and the injury sustained, and the fulfilment of the Union interest-test requirement as set out under Article 21 BADR.

3.3.3.1   Dumping

Article 1 (2) BADR sets out that a product is considered to be dumped if its export price to the Union is less than a comparable price for a like product, in the ordinary course of trade, as established for the exporting country (normal value). Additionally, when determining the normal value of the product exported to the EU, a comparison has to be made with the products sold by the foreign producer itself in its home country. This is provided for by Article 2 (1) subpara. 2, (6) BADR, which requires the product sold on the home market and the product exported to be 'like' products.[93]

3.3.3.1.1   Normal Value

Unless the exporter in the exporting country does not produce or does not sell the like product, the normal value is based on the prices paid or payable, in the ordinary course of trade, by independent customers in the exporting countries.[94] In a number of situations, this may not be possible, for example if there are no sufficient sales of the like product in the ordinary course of trade. If this is the case, alternative methods for calculating the normal value are used, such as the prices of other sellers or producers or the cost of production.[95]

Before the European Union's methodology in calculating dumping margins was overhauled by the Regulation (EU) 2017/2321, Article 2 (7) BADR foresaw a separate method of determining the normal value for non-market economies that are WTO members. If the allegedly dumped product originated in a country falling into this category, the normal value was to be calculated on the basis of the price or

---

[93] As determining the 'likeness' of products is also relevant in determining the injury sustained by the Union industry, the issue of product definition will be dealt with in the section on 'injury' below, p. 58.

[94] Article 2 (1) BADR.

[95] Article 2 (1) subpara. 2 BADR, Article 2 (3) BADR.

constructed value in a market economy third country, or the price from such a third country to other countries, including the EU, or, where this is not possible, on any other reasonable basis, including the price actually paid or payable in the Union for the like product. This so-called 'analogue country' method is still used under the modernised basic anti-dumping regulation, but only for imports from countries that are not members of the WTO and that are listed in Annex I to Regulation (EU) 2015/755.[96] A formal distinction between market economy countries and non-market economies is no longer made. Instead, according to the new Article 2 (6a) BADR, when it is determined that it is not appropriate to use domestic prices and costs in the exporting country due to the existence of significant distortions in that country, normal value shall be constructed exclusively on the basis of costs of production and sale reflecting undistorted prices or benchmarks. Significant distortions exist where the reported prices or costs are not the result of free market forces because they are affected by substantial government intervention.[97] The details of the so-called new methodology will be presented below, with a special focus on their impact on the relationship between trade defence and competition.[98]

3.3.3.1.2 Export Price

The second step in a dumping investigation involves the determination of the export price. The export price shall be the price actually paid or payable for the product when sold for export from the exporting country to the Union, Article 2 (8) BADR. In case this is not appropriate, the export price may be constructed on the basis of alternative calculation methods contained in Article 2 (9) BADR.

3.3.3.1.3 Comparison

Lastly, a 'fair comparison' between the export price and the normal value must be made. The general rule concerning the comparison between the export price and the normal value is set out in Article 2 (10) BADR. Usually, the comparison has to be conducted at the same level of trade and at as closely as possible the same time.[99] Where the normal value and the export price are not on such a comparable basis, due

---

[96] Regulation (EU) 2015/755 of the European Parliament and of the Council of 29 April 2015 on common rules for imports from certain third countries (n 85). Annex I to the Regulation lists Azerbaijan, Belarus, Kazakhstan, North Korea, Turkmenistan and Uzbekistan. Of these countries, only Kazakhstan is a member of the WTO.

[97] Article 2 (6a) lit. b) BADR.

[98] Cf. below pp. 174 et seq.

[99] Cf. Article 2 (10) BADR and van Bael and Bellis (2019), § 3.18.

allowance for factors affecting price comparability is to be made in the form of adjustments.[100]

3.3.3.1.4 Dumping Margin

According to Article 2 (12) BADR, the dumping margin shall be the amount by which the normal value exceeds the export price. At this point, it is important to distinguish between the dumping amount and the dumping margin. The comparison of the normal value with the export price, both on a comparable basis and after adjustments pursuant to Article 2 (10) BADR, will give the dumping amount by subtracting the export price from the normal value.[101] The dumping margin is the dumping amount as a percentage of the value of the CIF export price (duty unpaid) at the EU frontier.[102]

3.3.3.2 Determination of Injury to the Union Industry

In order to adopt anti-dumping measures under the BADR, injury to the Union industry needs to be proven. The rules governing the determination of injury are contained in Article 3 BADR. In a first step, the 'like product' analysis has to be carried out in order to establish that the product—or products—under investigation and the products produced by the Union industry are 'like'. Second, it must be evaluated whether domestic producers of the like product constitute a Union industry within the sense of Article 4 BADR and third, it must be determined whether the Union industry is experiencing 'injury' within the sense of Article 3 BADR.[103]

3.3.3.2.1 Product Definition

The first step in proving injury to the Union industry aims at establishing that the products produced by the Union industry and the products which are considered as being dumped (so-called 'product concerned' or 'product under consideration')[104] are 'like'. Pursuant to Article 1 (4) BADR, for the purposes of the BADR, 'like product' means a product which is identical, that is to say, alike in all respects, to the product under consideration, or in the absence of such a product, another product which, although not alike in all respects, has characteristics closely resembling those

---

[100] Cf. Article 2 (10) lit. a)–k) BADR, which contains a list of factors affecting price comparability.

[101] Mueller et al. (2009), para. 2.321.

[102] Krzeminska-Vamvaka (2012), para. 654.

[103] van Bael and Bellis (2019), § 4.01.

[104] *Portmeirion Group UK Ltd. v Commissioners for Her Majesty's Revenue & Customs* (17 March 2016) C-232/14 38–39 (European Court of Justice).

of the product under consideration. Lastly, it should be noted that the criteria set out below to identify the 'product concerned' can also be used in determining whether the exported product and the product sold on the exporter's home market are like.[105]

3.3.3.2.1.1 The 'Product Concerned' Analysis

Hence, the 'like product' analysis is twofold. In a first step, the product concerned (i.e. the product possibly covered by the anti-dumping investigation) has to be defined in order to determine the scope of the investigation. Here, it is important to note that also products which are not identical may be grouped together under the same definition of the product concerned.[106]

To determine whether the products are sufficiently alike, it needs to be assessed, *inter alia*, whether they share the same physical, technical and chemical characteristics, their use, interchangeability, consumer perception, distribution channels, manufacturing process, costs of production and quality.[107] These criteria are merely indicative and the Commission is not obliged to make use of all of them, as not all may be relevant in the case at hand.[108]

In practice, the Commission's examination focusses on the first factor, namely whether there is a common denominator between the various product types in that they share the same basic physical, chemical and/or technical qualities (physical characteristics).[109] While they do not necessarily have priority over other criteria used in distinguishing the product concerned,[110] the physical characteristics of the product are usually at the centre of the Commission's product definition. In order for products to fall within the category of the product concerned, it is only required that they share the same basic physical characteristics; minor differences in the physical characteristics of various product types do not preclude their being one product.[111]

---

[105] Hoffmeister (2018), para. 29.

[106] *Portmeirion Group UK Ltd. v Commissioners for Her Majesty's Revenue & Customs* (n 104) 42.

[107] *Steinel Vertrieb GmbH v Hauptzollamt Bielefeld* (18 April 2013) C-595/11 44 (European Court of Justice); *Whirlpool Europe Srl v Council* (13 September 2010) T-314/06 138 (General Court).

[108] Cf. e.g. *Brosmann Footwear (HK) Ltd. and others v Council* (4 March 2010) T-401/06 131–137 (General Court), where the product concerned was only defined by having recourse to its physical characteristics, its main use and consumer perception; Council Implementing Regulation (EU) 1238/2013 of 2 December 2013 imposing a definitive anti-dumping duty and collecting definitively the provisional duty imposed on imports of crystalline silicon photovoltaic modules and key components (i.e. cells) originating in or consigned from the People's Republic of China recital 44.

[109] Mueller et al. (2009), para. 1.27.

[110] *Photo USA Electronic Graphic, Inc. v Council* (18 November 2014) T-394/13 41 (General Court).

[111] Council Regulation (EC) No 954/2006 of 27 June 2006 imposing definitive anti-dumping duty on imports of certain seamless pipes and tubes, of iron or steel originating in Croatia, Romania, Russia and Ukraine recitals 21–26; Council Regulation (EEC) No 541/91 of 4 March 1991 imposing a definitive anti-dumping duty on imports of barium chloride originating in the People's Republic of China recitals 6–9.

Differences in the physical characteristics are also relevant if they are not reflected in consumer perception.[112] Different qualities of the products are irrelevant as long as they share the same basic characteristics and as long as the differences in quality do not lead to them being put to different uses.[113]

Another factor are the main uses and applications of the product or 'absence of significant differences in the uses' of the various product types.[114] In past cases, the Commission has distinguished products having identical essential physical characteristics on the basis of their final use.[115] Related to the question of the main use of the products under investigation is the degree of interchangeability between products. The interchangeability of the products and the fact that certain products are directly competing with each other might support and reinforce the result the investigating authority has arrived at on the basis of the physical characteristics of a product, but they cannot serve independently as a justification for considering various products as one single product.[116] Likewise, a lack in interchangeability may lead the Commission to arrive at a finding of goods not constituting a single product.[117]

As already touched upon above, consumer perception also plays a role in defining the product concerned. According to the jurisprudence of the General Court, consumer perception must be assessed at the finished product stage.[118] The practice of the EU institutions indicates that consumer perception may reinforce a finding of products either falling within the same category of products or not,[119] but it is not sufficient in itself to justify the in- or exclusion of a certain product from the definition of the 'product concerned'.

---

[112] *Photo USA Electronic Graphic, Inc. v Council* (n 110) 41, referring to *Whirlpool Europe Srl v Council* (n 107) 141.

[113] Hoffmeister (2018), para. 41.

[114] Commission Regulation (EC) No 940/96 of 23 May 1996 imposing a provisional anti-dumping duty on imports of polyester textured filament yarn originating in Indonesia and Thailand recital 9.

[115] van Bael and Bellis (2019), § 4.02 [A] [2].

[116] Mueller et al. (2009), para. 1.35.

[117] Cf. e.g. Commission Implementing Regulation (EU) 2017/141 of 26 January 2017 imposing definitive anti-dumping duties on imports of certain stainless steel tube and pipe butt-welding fittings, whether or not finished, originating in the People's Republic of China and Taiwan recital 65.

[118] *Photo USA Electronic Graphic, Inc. v Council* (n 110) 41.

[119] Cf. e.g. '*The exclusion [of special technology athletic footwear] was based on the fact that such type of footwear has different basic physical and technical characteristics, is sold via different sales channels, and has a different end use and consumer perception*', Council Regulation (EC) No 1472/2006 of 5 October 2006 imposing a definitive anti-dumping duty and collecting definitively the provisional duty imposed on imports of certain footwear with uppers of leather originating in the People's Republic of China and Vietnam recital 12.

3.3.3.2.1.2   The 'Like Product' Analysis

After the product concerned has been identified, it has to be examined whether the product concerned and the product(s) produced and sold by the Union industry are 'like products'. In this respect, the 'like' product forms the corollary to the 'product concerned'. In essence, the criteria used to define whether the goods produced by the Union industry and the product under consideration are 'like' are identical to the ones used when examining whether or not the products concerned form one single product.[120]

3.3.3.2.2   Union Industry

In assessing whether the Union industry did sustain injury as a result of the dumping, it has to be established what is encompassed by the notion 'Union industry'. Article 4 (1) BADR defines the term for the purposes of the regulation as 'referring to the Union producers as a whole of the like products or to those of them whose collective output of the products constitutes a major proportion of the total Union production'.[121] In turn, the extent of the Union production must be determined and the market share of the Union production held by the producers claiming to belong to the Union industry quantified.[122]

Usually, all products manufactured in the Union fall within the definition of Union production. Likewise, as a matter of principle, all producers of the product concerned located in the EU are taken into account to determine the Union industry. However, in the event of producers being related to the exporters or being importers of the allegedly dumped product themselves, these producers may be excluded from the Union industry according to Article 4 (1) lit. a) BADR.

As mentioned, the term 'Union industry' refers to those producers whose collective output of the products amounts to the whole Union production of the like products or to a major proportion of those products, Article 4 (1) BADR. Concerning the choice between the two ways of defining the Union industry, the Commission enjoys a broad discretion.[123] There is no clear benchmark as to when an output is considered a 'major proportion'; this is to be decided on a case-by-case basis.[124] In

---

[120] Mueller et al. (2009), para. 1.46. Hoffmeister (2018), paras. 52–56.

[121] Cf. also *Marine Harvest Norway v Council* (21 March 2012) T-113/06 47–48 (General Court).

[122] van Bael and Bellis (2019), § 4.04.

[123] Ibid.

[124] Rados (2018), para. 9. Under the old BADR and the reference to Article 5 (4) BADR contained in Article 4 (1) BADR, the Commission interpreted the term '*major proportion*' as a minimum threshold of 25%. However, the WTO Appellate Body has held that linking the '*major proportion*'-requirement of Article 4 (1) BADR to the benchmark contained in Article 5 (4) BADR violated the ADA, leading to the reference in Article 4 (1) BADR being deleted from the provision in 2018, *European Communities – Definitive Anti-Dumping Measures on Certain Iron or Steel Fasteners from China* (15 July 2011) WT/DS397/AB/R paras. 426–430 (Appellate Body Report).

addition to this quantitative element, the notion of 'major proportion' also possesses a qualitative connotation, as it has to be ensured that the domestic producers that are included in the 'domestic industry' are representative of the total domestic production.[125]

3.3.3.2.3 Injury

After the first two analyses have been conducted, it is to be examined whether the Union industry was injured as a result of the presence of dumped products on the internal market. Article 3 (1) BADR defines the term 'injury' as material injury to the Union industry, threat of material injury to the Union industry or material retardation of the establishment of such an industry.

Neither the jurisprudence of the CJEU nor the basic anti-dumping regulation give a definition of the notion of 'material injury'. Article 3 (2) BADR prescribes for the assessment on whether material injury exists to be based on positive evidence and to involve the objective examination of the volume of dumped imports, the effect of the dumped imports on prices in the Union market for like products and the ensuing impact of the dumped imports on the Union industry. In practice, material injury will be found if the injury is widespread in the industry concerned and the injury stems from significant volume and/or price effects with a consequent significant impact on the Union industry.[126] The opposite of material injury is negligible injury, which is defined in Article 9 (3) BADR. According to the provision, injury will normally be regarded as negligible where the imports concerned represent less than the volumes set out in Article 5 (7) BADR, i.e. less than 1% or less than 3% of Community consumption, depending on the circumstances of the case.[127]

The second alternative for a finding of injury is the 'threat of material injury'. It should be noted that this is a different test from that of material injury; in particular, the Union institutions may not simply fall back on it in cases where material injury could not be established. The basic requirement remains injury, which cannot be circumvented by invoking a threat of material injury.[128] The Union institutions may not base their assessment concerning the existence of a threat of material injury on a mere hypothesis.[129] Instead, the analysis must be based on concrete facts.[130]

---

[125] van Bael and Bellis (2019), § 4.06.

[126] Mueller et al. (2009), para. 3.10; cf. e.g. *Sanyo Electric v Council* (10 March 1992) C-177/87 34 (European Court of Justice).

[127] Mueller et al. (2009), para. 3.09.

[128] Ibid para. 3.150.

[129] *NTN Corporation and Koyo Seiko Co. Ltd. v Council* (2 May 1995) joined cases T-163/94 and T-165/94 106 (Court of First Instance).

[130] Kuplewatzky and Rusche (2018), para. 19. These two requirements can also be derived from Article 3 (9) BADR.

The third alternative for a finding of injury concerns the material retardation of the establishment of a Union industry. In *DRAMs from Japan*, the Union institutions based their finding of injury in the form of material retardation *inter alia* on the fact that during the investigation period, complainant companies had made serious commitments to start production of the product concerned in the Union, but the dumped imports had delayed the start of mass production by the claimant companies. Another factor taken into consideration were the heavy financial losses incurred by the Union industry.[131]

3.3.3.3   Causality

Following a finding of injury, the next step of an anti-dumping investigation involves an inquiry pertaining to the existence of a causal link between dumping and injury. Article 3 (6) BADR explicitly states that it must be demonstrated that it is the dumped imports that are causing injury within the meaning of the basic anti-dumping regulation. It does not require for the injury to be caused by the effects of dumping, instead, it is sufficient for the Union institutions to demonstrate that the volume and/or price levels of the dumped imports have an impact on the Union industry that may be classified as material, even though there may be more significant causes of injury to the Union industry than dumping.[132]

Conversely, it is also to be demonstrated that the harmful effect is not caused by factors other than the imports under consideration.[133] Such factors include the volume and prices of imports not sold at dumping prices, restrictive trade practices of, and competition between, third country and Union producers as well as developments in technology and the export performance and productivity of the Union industry.[134]

3.3.3.4   Union Interest

The imposition of measures must not run counter to the Union interest, Article 21 BADR. In making this determination, all interests at stake are identified before the various interests involved are weighed against each other, that is the interests of the Union industry on the one hand, and those of importers and other

---

[131] Commission Regulation (EEC) No 165/90 of 23 January 1990 imposing a provisional anti-dumping duty on imports of certain types of electronic microcircuits known as DRAMs (dynamic random access memories) originating in Japan.

[132] van Bael and Bellis (2019), § 4.20.

[133] Article 3 (7) BADR; cf. also *Extramet Industrie v Council* (11 June 1992) C-358/89 16 (European Court of Justice).

[134] Cf. also on a later judgment on the then Community organs' obligation to take into account whether the injury was not caused by practices restricting competition resorted to by the Community industry: Temple Lang (2002), p. 633.

parties on the other hand.[135] In such an examination, the need to eliminate the trade distorting effects of injurious dumping and to restore effective competition shall be given special consideration.[136]

3.3.3.5   Relief

Once it has been established that the four preconditions for measures to be taken under the basic anti-dumping regulation are fulfilled (dumping, injury, causality and Union interest), relief can be provided in the form of anti-dumping duties or undertakings.

3.3.3.5.1   Anti-dumping Duties

Pursuant to Article 14 (1) BADR, provisional and definitive anti-dumping duties may only be imposed by regulation.[137] They are applied on a Union-wide basis[138] and are usually only levied on products released for free circulation in the Union after the entry into force of the regulation imposing the duties.[139]

As a general rule, the amount of the duty may never exceed the dumping margin. However, the amount of the duty should be less than the dumping margin if a lesser duty would be adequate to remove the injury of the Union industry.[140] This principle is called the 'lesser duty rule'. Its objective is to prevent the anti-dumping duty from going beyond what is necessary to remove the injury caused by the dumped imports.[141]

Since the introduction of a new Article 7 (2b) BADR by Regulation (EU) 2018/825, the lesser duty rule is not applied if there are distortions on raw materials with regard to the product concerned, such as dual pricing schemes or export taxes, and the Commission can clearly conclude that it is in the Union's interest to base the amount of the duty on the dumping margin.[142] The lesser duty rule may also not be applied *vis-à-vis* companies that are considered to be non-cooperating.[143]

---

[135] Mueller et al. (2009), para. 21.03.

[136] Article 21 (1) BADR.

[137] On the information that has to be contained in the regulation cf. Article 9 (4), (5) BADR.

[138] van Bael and Bellis (2019), § 7.05.

[139] Article 10 (1) BADR. In certain circumstances, the duties may also be applied retroactively, Article 10 (4) BADR.

[140] Article 9 (4) BADR (for definitive anti-dumping duties) and Article 7 (2) BADR (for provisional anti-dumping duties).

[141] *Crown Equipment (Suzhou) Co. Ltd. and Crown Gabelstapler GmbH & Co. KG v Council* (18 October 2016) T-351/13 49–50 (General Court).

[142] Article 7 (2a) and (2b) BADR.

[143] Article 7 (2b) BADR.

Article 9 (3) BADR sets out a *de minimis* rule, according to which the proceeding shall be terminated immediately where it is determined that the margin of dumping is less than 2%, expressed as a percentage of the export price. Since the reform of the basic anti-dumping regulation, exporting producers who obtained a 0% anti-dumping duty in the original investigation may not be subject of a subsequent review investigation.[144]

3.3.3.5.2   Undertakings

Instead of imposing duties, in cases where an affirmative determination of dumping and injury has been made, the Commission may also accept voluntary undertaking offers submitted by any exporter to revise its prices (price undertaking) or to cease exports at dumped prices (quantitative undertaking), if the injurious effect of the dumping is thereby eliminated, Article 8 BADR. Following a decision by the WTO DSB outlawing quantitative undertakings under WTO law,[145] the Commission no longer accepts 'pure' quantitative undertakings.[146] In general, the frequency with which the Commission accepts undertakings has decreased over the last years.[147]

As it is the case for anti-dumping duties, the price increase under the undertaking may not be higher than necessary to eliminate the margin of dumping and it shall be less than the margin if such increase would be sufficient to remove the injury of the Union industry.[148] The rules concerning raw material distortions and the inapplicability of the lesser duty rule apply accordingly.[149]

There is no obligation for an exporter to offer or enter into an undertaking, and the fact they do not do so should in no way prejudice the consideration of the case.[150]

The Commission may not accept an undertaking if it considers it impractical. As provided for by the reformed Article 8 (3) BADR,[151] the instances where this may be

---

[144] Article 9 (3) BADR.

[145] *European Communities – Anti-Dumping Duties on Malleable Cast Iron Tube or Pipe Fittings from Brazil* (22 July 2003) WT/DS219/AB/R para. 7.78 (Appellate Body Report).

[146] European Commission, 'Eighteenth annual report from the Commission to the European Parliament on the Community's anti-dumping and anti-subsidy activities (1999) (COM/2000/0440 final)' (Brussels 11 July 2000) 94. However, mixed undertakings, i.e. price undertakings up to an annual volume threshold, remain permissible, cf. e.g. Commission Implementing Decision (EU) 2019/245 of 11 February 2019 accepting undertaking offers following the imposition of definitive countervailing duties on imports of biodiesel originating in Argentina.

[147] Cf. e.g. European Commission, '36th Annual Report from the Commission to the Council and the European Parliament on the EU's Anti-Dumping, Anti-Subsidy and Safeguard activities (2017) (COM (2018) 561 final)' (Brussels 31 July 2018) 2.2. Mainly as a result of the investigation into Chinese solar panels, 102 undertakings were in force at the beginning of 2017.

[148] Article 8 (1) subpara. 3 BADR.

[149] Article 8 (1) subpara. 4 BADR.

[150] Article 8 (2) BADR.

[151] Article 8 BADR was reformed by Article 1 (5) of Regulation (EU) 2018/825 (n 10 in Chap. 1).

the case include investigations where the number of actual or potential exporters is too great. Other reasons for the rejection of undertaking offers include competition considerations.[152] Since the modernisation of the BADR, the reasons of general policy for which an undertaking offer may be rejected explicitly include the principles and obligations set out in multilateral environmental agreements and conventions of the International Labour Organization (ILO).[153]

The acceptance of an undertaking leads to the non-application of the provisional or definitive anti-dumping duties to the imports of the product concerned manufactured by the companies mentioned in the Commission decision accepting undertakings.[154]

3.3.4 The Basic Anti-subsidy Regulation

Just like the basic anti-dumping regulation, the basic anti-subsidy regulation is concerned with unfair trading practices. While the EU's anti-dumping legislation addresses the unfair behaviour of undertakings, the anti-subsidy regulation seeks to offset unfair competitive advantages caused by the subsidisation of undertakings by third States. As mentioned above, the structure of an anti-dumping and an anti-subsidy investigation are comparable. Pursuant to Article 1 (1) BASR, countervailing measures may be imposed to offset any subsidy granted, directly or indirectly, for the manufacture, production, export or transport of any product whose release for free circulation in the Union causes industry. Parallel to the anti-dumping regulation, a countervailing duty may only be levied if this does not contravene the Union interest, Article 31 BASR.

3.3.4.1 Subsidised Product

According to Article 2 lit. a) BASR, a product is considered to be subsidised if it benefits from a countervailable subsidy. Such subsidy may be granted by the government of the country of origin of the imported product, or by the government of an intermediate country from which the product is exported to the Union.

---

[152]Cf. e.g. Council Regulation (EC) No 221/2008 of 10 March 2008 imposing a definitive anti-dumping duty and collecting definitively the provisional duty imposed on imports of certain manganese dioxides originating in South Africa recital 68. On possible conflicts between undertakings and competition law cf. in detail below pp. 148 et seq.

[153]Article 8 (3) BADR.

[154]Article 8 (1) BADR.

3.3.4.1.1 Subsidisation

The first precondition for a finding of subsidisation is the existence of a financial contribution by the government. Article 3 (1) lit. a) BASR lists a number of circumstances under which the Commission will conclude that a financial contribution has been made, such as the direct transfer of funds or instances in which government revenue that is otherwise due is foregone or not collected. A subsidy is likewise considered to exist where there is any form of income or price support within the meaning of Article XVI of the GATT 1994.[155] The financial contribution or the price/income support furthermore has to confer a benefit, Article 3 (2) BASR.

3.3.4.1.2 Countervailability

Under EU trade defence law, subsidies will only lead to the imposition of measures if they are specific. This requirement flows from the need to limit the broad range of possibly countervailable subsidies to those subsidies which affect normal conditions of competition by selectively benefiting certain enterprises or industry sectors.[156]

The types of subsidies listed in Article 4 (4) BASR—namely export subsidies and domestic content subsidies—will automatically be deemed specific and hence countervailable. Subsidies other than those have to fulfil certain criteria set out in Article 4 (2) and (3) BASR in order to be considered 'specific'.

3.3.4.1.3 Determination of the Amount of Subsidisation

Following the conclusion that a third State has indeed granted countervailable subsidies, the amount of subsidisation has to be determined. According to Article 5 BASR, the amount of countervailable subsidies shall be calculated in terms of the benefit conferred on the recipient which is found to exist during the investigation period. The rules concerning the calculation of the benefit conferred to the recipient are contained in Article 6 BASR.

3.3.4.2 Determination of Injury to the Union Industry and Causality

After a countervailable subsidy has been found to exist and its value has been determined, the Commission has to establish whether the release of the subsided product for free circulation in the Union causes injury. Under the BASR, the concept of 'injury' is governed by Articles 3 and 8 BASR. The concept itself as well as the methods used in determining the existence of injury are comparable to those in the

---

[155] Article 3 (1) lit. b) BASR.
[156] van Bael and Bellis (2019), § 11.05.

BADR. In another parallel to the BADR, the Commission has to establish that the injury was caused by the subsidised imports. Hence, reference can be made to the corresponding sections above.[157]

3.3.4.3   Union Interest

Article 31 BASR prescribes that measures may only be taken if it can be determined whether the Union's interest calls for intervention. Accordingly, one can again refer to the above section on the Union interest test in investigations carried out under the BADR.[158]

3.3.4.4   Relief

Once it has been established that the criteria set out above—subsidisation, injury, causation and Union interest—are fulfilled, relief can be provided in the form of a countervailing duty or an undertaking.

3.3.4.4.1   Countervailing Duties

Duties may only be imposed by way of regulation. However, there is one important variation concerning the height of the countervailing duty. While the amount of the countervailing duty may not exceed the amount of countervailable subsidies, the lesser duty rule will only be applied if the Commission, on the basis of all the information submitted, can clearly conclude that it is *not* in the Union's interest to impose the duty based on the amount of the countervailable subsidies.[159] Only if this is the case, the level of the duty will be based on the injury sustained by the Union industry. In all other instances, the duty will be based on the amount of the countervailable subsidies. As opposed to the BADR, the lesser duty rule thus does not apply by default.

3.3.4.4.2   Undertakings

Pursuant to Article 13 BASR, the Commission may also accept undertakings under which the country of origin and/or export agrees to eliminate or limit the subsidy or

---

[157] Cf. above p. 58. Specifically on product definition in the context of anti-subsidy proceedings cf. Adamantopoulos and Pereyra (2007), paras. 6.029 et seq.

[158] Cf. above pp. 59 et seq.

[159] This applies to provisional and definitive countervailing duties, cf. Article 12 (1) lit. d) BASR and Article 15 (1) BASR.

take other measures concerning its effects or any exporter undertakes to revise his prices or to cease exports to the area in question as long as such exports benefit from countervailable subsidies, if the injurious effect of the subsidies is thereby eliminated. The price increases under such undertakings may not exceed the level necessary to offset the amount of countervailable subsidies. As it is the case for countervailing duties, the price increase is only limited to the amount necessary to offset the level of injury suffered by the Union industry if the Commission can clearly conclude that it is not in the Union's interest to base it on the amount of countervailable subsidies. In subsidy cases, undertakings only play a minor role. The most recent undertaking to be accepted by the Commission concerned *Argentinian Biodiesel*. It was the only undertaking to be accepted in the last 10 years.[160]

3.3.5 The Trade Defence Modernisation Package

Attempts at reforming the EU's trade defence instruments date back to 2006, when Trade Commissioner *Peter Mandelson* initiated a public debate on the subject.[161] The project was later abandoned due to a lack of support in the EU institutions, particularly the European Parliament and the Council.[162] The matter resurfaced in 2013, with a first formal legislative proposal being made by the Commission. The proposal was supported by four draft guidelines on core issues during trade defence investigations such as the injury margin calculation or the Union interest test.[163] Nonetheless, it was not until November 2016 that the reform efforts yielded actual outcomes: Commissioner for Trade *Cecilia Malmström* proposed to adapt the basic anti-dumping regulation to provide for a new non-standard methodology for calculating normal value where there are significant distortions in an exporting country which is a WTO member.[164] The EU legislative organs supported the approach

---

[160]Commission Implementing Decision (EU) 2019/245 of 11 February 2019 accepting undertaking offers following the imposition of definitive countervailing duties on imports of biodiesel originating in Argentina (n 146).

[161]European Commission, 'Communication from the Commission: Global Europe – Europe's trade defence instruments in a changing global economy: A green paper for public consultation (COM (2006) 763 final)' (6 December 2006).

[162]For details cf. Graafsma and Cornelis (2007), p. 255.

[163]European Commission, 'Proposal for a Regulation of the European Parliament and of the Council amending Council Regulation (EC) No 1225/2009 on protection against dumped imports from countries not members of the European Community and Council Regulation (EC) No 597/2009 on protection against subsidised imports from countries not members of the European Community (COM(2013) 192 final)' (Brussels 10 April 2013). For details cf. Hoffmeister (2015).

[164]Hoffmeister (2020), p. 213. This political impetus was provided by the impending expiry of Article 15 lit. d) of the Chinese Protocol of Accession to the WTO, which had permitted the use of alternative methodologies in calculating the normal value during anti-dumping investigations concerning products originating in China for a period of 15 years. This period elapsed in December

proposed by the Commission, and Regulation (EU) 2017/2321 entered into force on 20 December 2017.

The second part of what is commonly referred to as the Trade Defence Modernisation Package is Regulation (EU) 2018/825, which entered into force on 8 June 2018. In December 2016, parallel to the ongoing attempts at reforming the dumping calculation methodology in the basic anti-dumping regulation, the Slovak Council Presidency received a mandate to work on a more comprehensive attempt at modernising the EU's trade defence instruments.[165] The main objectives of the reform were declared as being first, to improve transparency and predictability of the EU's trade defence instruments, second, to provide effective measures to fight against retaliation by third countries, third, to improve effectiveness and enforcement, and fourth, to optimise review practice.[166] Furthermore, the reforms addressed a number of inconsistencies between the EU's trade defence legislation and the requirements of WTO law that had arisen as a result of recent jurisprudence of the WTO adjudicative organs.[167]

Hoffmeister argues that when viewing the outcome of the two processes together, a certain balance between the interests of the EU industry and those of other interest groups, such as importers, was achieved. He contends that the Union maintained '*its basic approach to keep the [anti-dumping] instrument as a quasi-judicial and proportionate remedy against unfair trade practices*'.[168] The analysis of the amendments introduced by the Trade Defence Modernisation Package undertaken in the following chapters will examine whether this overall positive assessment of the reform holds true, and to what extent the amendments contribute to the attainment of the reform's declared objectives.

References[169]

Adamantopoulos K, Pereyra MJ (2007) EU anti-subsidy law and practice, 2nd edn. Sweet & Maxwell

Bengtsson C, Carpi Badia JM, Kadar M (2014) Mergers. In: Faull J, Nikpay A (eds) The EU law of competition, 3rd edn. Oxford University Press

Boyce J, Lyle-Smythe A (2018) Merger control. In: Bailey D, John LE (eds) European Union law of competition, 5th edn. Oxford University Press

---

2016, cf. World Trade Organization, 'Accession of the People's Republic of China (WT/L/432)' (23 November 2001).

[165] Müller (2018), p. 47.

[166] Recital 3 of Regulation (EU) 2018/825 (n 10 in Chap. 1).

[167] Cf. recitals 14–16 of Regulation (EU) 2018/825 (n 10 in Chap. 1), which take account of the Appellate Body's findings in *Mexico – Beef and Rice* (29 November 2005) WT/DS295/AB/R (Appellate Body Report).

[168] Hoffmeister (2020), p. 214.

[169] All online sources were last accessed on 8 September 2021.

Brook O (2019) Struggling with Article 101(3) TFEU: diverging approaches of the commission, EU Courts, and five competition authorities. Common Mark Law Rev 56(1):121

de La Mano M, Nazzini R, Zenger H (2014) Article 102 TFEU. In: Faull J, Nikpay A (eds) The EU law of competition, 3rd edn. Oxford University Press

Dolmans M, Lin W (2017) Fairness and competition: a fairness paradox. Concurrences 4

Faull J et al (2014) Article 101 TFEU. In: Faull J, Nikpay A (eds) The EU law of competition, 3rd edn. Oxford University Press

Gal MS (2013) Abuse of dominance – exploitative abuses. In: Lianos I, Geradin D (eds) Handbook on European competition law: substantive aspects. Edward Elgar Publishing Ltd

Graafsma F, Cornelis J (2007) The EC's green paper on trade defence instruments: guillotine on anti-dumping or smokescreen for more basic predicaments? Global Trade Cust J 2(7/8):255

Heide-Jorgensen C (2013) The relationship between Article 101 (1) TFEU and Article 101 (3) TFEU. In: Heide-Jorgensen C and others (eds) Aims and values in competition law. DJØF Publications

Hoffmeister F (2015) Modernising the EU's trade defence instruments: mission impossible? In: Herrmann C, Streinz R, Simma B (eds) Trade policy between law, diplomacy and scholarship: liber Amicorum in Memoriam Horst G. Krenzler. Springer

Hoffmeister F (2018) Artikel 1 AD-GVO. In: Krenzler HG, Herrmann C, Niestedt M (eds) EU-Außenwirtschafts- und Zollrecht. C.H. Beck

Hoffmeister F (2020) The devil is in the detail: a first guide on the EU's new trade defence rules. In: Weiß W, Furculita C (eds) Global politics and EU trade policy: facing the challenges to a multilateral approach. Springer

Jones A, Sufrin B, Dunne N (2019) EU competition law, 7th edn. Oxford University Press

Jung C (2015) Artikel 102 AEUV. In: Grabitz E, Hilf M, Nettesheim M (eds) Das Recht der Europäischen Union. C.H. Beck

Kellerbauer M (2019) Article 102 TFEU. In: Kellerbauer M, Klamert M, Tomkin J (eds) The EU treaties and the charter of fundamental rights. Oxford University Press, Oxford

Khan D-E, Suh C-KP (2015) Article 101 TFEU. In: Geiger R, Erasmus-Khan D, Kotzur M (eds) European Union treaties: Treaty on European Union, Treaty on the Functioning of the European Union. Beck/Hart, London

Khan D-E, Suh C-KP (2015) Article 102 TFEU. In: Geiger R, Erasmus-Khan D, Kotzur M (eds) European Union treaties: Treaty on European Union, Treaty on the Functioning of the European Union. Beck/Hart, London

Krzeminska-Vamvaka J (2012) Artikel 2 AD-GVO. In: Krenzler HG, Herrmann C, Niestedt M (eds) EU-Außenwirtschafts- und Zollrecht. C.H. Beck

Kuplewatzky N, Rusche M (2018) Artikel 3 AD-GVO. In: Krenzler HG, Herrmann C, Niestedt M (eds) EU-Außenwirtschafts- und Zollrecht. C.H. Beck

Mueller W, Khan N, Scharf T (2009) EC and WTO anti-dumping Law: a handbook, 2nd edn. Oxford University Press

Müller W (2018) The EU's new trade defence laws: a two steps approach. In: Bungenberg M and others (eds) The future of trade defence instruments – global policy trends and legal challenges. Springer

Nazzini R (2011) The foundations of European competition law: the objectives and principles of Article 102. Oxford University Press

Peeperkorn L, Verouden V (2014) The economics of competition. In: Faull J, Nikpay A (eds) The EU law of competition, 3rd edn. Oxford University Press

Podszun R (2016) The arbitrariness of market definition and an evolutionary concept of markets. Anti Bull 61(1):121

Rados N (2018) Artikel 4 AD-GVO. In: Krenzler HG, Herrmann C, Niestedt M (eds) EU-Außenwirtschafts- und Zollrecht. C.H. Beck

Schroeder D, Schuhmacher F, Stockenhuber P (2018) Artikel 101 AEUV. In: Grabitz E, Hilf M, Nettesheim M (eds) Das Recht der Europäischen Union. C.H. Beck

Temple Lang J (2002) Case T-58/99, Mukand and Others v. Council, Court of First Instance, Judgment of 19 September 2001. Common Mark Law Rev 39(3):633

Thompson R, Brown C, Gibson N (2018) Article 102 TFEU. In: Bailey D, John LE (eds) European Union law of competition, 5th edn. Oxford University Press

van Bael I, Bellis J-F (2019) EU anti-dumping and other trade defence instruments, 6th edn. Kluwer Law International

Whish R, Bailey D (2018) Competition law, 9th edn. Oxford University Press

Zimmer D (2016) The emancipation of antitrust from market-share-based approaches. Anti Bull 61(1):133

Chapter 4
The Objectives of EU Competition Law and Trade Defence Law

4.1 Introduction

As can be derived from the previous chapters, trade defence and competition law have been at the heart of the European integration process. In this chapter, an analysis on the objectives pursued by the two areas of law is undertaken. Historically, the objectives pursued by trade defence law and competition law converge to a certain extent. Today, however, any remaining similarities are outweighed by significant differences in the objectives they seek to attain. In outlining these divergences, the chapter lays the groundwork for the following section on key concepts used in both areas of law: structural differences in their interpretation and application can only be explained after having studied the objectives each area of law pursues. The identification of their underlying *ratio* is also a prerequisite for the step after next of this research, namely a critical evaluation of the ways in which trade defence law and competition law interact.

4.2 The Objectives of EU Competition Law

Two preliminary remarks have to be made before embarking on the analysis of the objectives of EU competition law. The first one once more pertains to the status of competition within the framework of the European Treaties. Chapter 2 concluded that while being of paramount importance to the realisation of the European integration project, competition law was never an objective of the European Union in its own right. Any argument made in determining the objectives of competition law must therefore be consequentialist: competition is protected not for its own sake but as a means to achieve certain policy objectives.[1] In this context, it should further be noted that according to the settled case law of the CJEU, the antitrust provisions of the EU Treaties have to be applied in light of the wider objectives of the European Union.[2] The central task must thus be to identify the objectives specific to EU competition policy while also respecting the overarching framework of Treaty objectives. Both Article 101 TFEU and Article 102 TFEU share the same purpose, namely ensuring the maintenance of undistorted competition within the internal market.[3] This also applies with regard to the EU Merger Regulation.[4] Due to the unity of purpose of the EU competition provisions,[5] any finding concerning the purpose underlying the protection of competition[6] in the EU legal system applies to all EU competition law provisions mentioned above.

In the EU legal system, it is the task of the CJEU to provide the authoritative interpretation of the competition provisions[7] and said interpretations are binding upon the Commission.[8] Despite the attention devoted to guidelines and statements published by the Commission by some authors, the chapter will hence focus on the jurisprudence of the Court in the interpretation and application of the competition provisions.[9]

---

[1] Lianos (2013), p. 41; with further references van Rompuy (2012), p. 25.

[2] Cf. e.g. *Éduard Leclerc v Au blé vert* (10 January 1985) C-229/83 8 (European Court of Justice); *Metro SB-Großmärkte GmbH & Co. KG v Commission* (Chap. 2, n 22) 20; *Europemballage Corporation and Continental Can Company Inc. v Commission of the European Communities* (Chap. 2, n 14) 23; *Consten and Grundig v Commission* (Chap. 3, n 16) 340. The demand for accomodating between EU antitrust policy objectives and other policy objectives increased with the shift from the market integration imperative to a broader economic, social and political agenda with the Treaty of Maastricht, cf. van Rompuy (2012), p. 173.

[3] *Konkurrensverket v TeliaSonera Sverige AB* (Chap. 2, n 62) 20–22, where the Court defined the objective of the competition rules referred to in Article 3 (1) lit. b) TFEU; *Europemballage Corporation and Continental Can Company Inc. v Commission of the European Communities* (Chap. 2, n 14) 25.

[4] This can already be taken from the fact that before the entry into force of the first merger control regulation in 1989, the control of concentrations was conducted on the basis of Article 102 TFEU, cf. *Europemballage Corporation and Continental Can Company Inc. v Commission of the European Communities* (Chap. 2, n 14). Today's EUMR is based on Article 103 TFEU—also part of the competition provisions mentioned in Article 3 (1) lit. b) TFEU—as well as Article 352 TFEU.

[5] Petit (2013), p. 405.

[6] As just mentioned, competition is not an objective of EU law of its own. Its protection hence has to contribute to the fulfilment of an 'ulterior objective'.

[7] Article 19 (1) TEU.

[8] Cf. Opinion of Advocate General Kokott in *British Airways v Commission*, C-95/04 P 2007 28 (23 February 2006): '*the Commission [has] to act within the framework prescribed for it (...) as interpreted by the Court of Justice*'.

[9] This does not mean that the Commission cannot propose interpretations to the Court. Indeed, a significant portion of the case law on competition matters concerns appeals against Commission decisions, and the Commission may thus have been more or less successful in convincing the Court of the interpretation it adopted, cf. Wils (2014), pp. 405, 415–416.

Second, as rightly noted by *Massarotto* and *Whish/Bailey,* competition law is susceptible to change. Historically, there has not been one single, unifying, policy underpinning the competition law of the EU. Competition policy is an expression of the current values and aims of society and as affected by changes in these values as other policy fields.[10] It is outside the scope of this study to provide an overview over the historical development of the objectives of EU competition law.[11] Instead, it confines itself to presenting those objectives that have consistently been addressed in the jurisprudence of the EU Courts in Luxembourg and those that have played a prominent role in the decisional practice of the Commission over the course of the last decades.

4.2.1 Welfare Standard

Whether competition should aim to achieve or protect a certain welfare standard, and if so, which one, is one of the focal points of the debate on the so-called 'more economic approach'. There is an extensive body of scholarly literature on the question of the economisation of competition law,[12] debating the possible advantages and drawbacks of focussing on the effects of an undertaking's behaviour on welfare in assessing the compatibility of said behaviour with the rules on competition.[13] Some authors favour the adoption of a consumer welfare standard, while others are proponents of a total welfare standard. Social—or total—welfare can be defined as the sum of the surplus of producers and consumers in a given industry, whereas consumer welfare is the difference between the sum of the consumers' willingness to pay for a product and what they actually paid for it.[14] The central difference between the advocates of a social and a consumer welfare standard is thus whose welfare is to be served.

4.2.1.1 The Promotion of Consumers' Welfare

A considerable number of scholarly contributions has argued in favour of EU competition law adhering to a consumer welfare standard, drawing support from the Commission's stance on the matter: beginning in the early 2000s, the Commission started to promote the economisation of competition law and promoted the

---

[10] Whish and Bailey (2018), p. 19; Massarotto (2018), p. 395.

[11] For a comprehensive study on this subject cf. van Rompuy (2012), Chapter 4.

[12] Heide-Jorgensen (2013), p. 100.

[13] C.f. e.g. Witt (2016); Drexl et al. (2011); Chiriță (2010), p. 417; Ehlermann and Marquis (2008); Albæk (2013); Gerber (2008). For a more recent contribution on the U.S.-perspective cf. Melamed and Petit (2019), p. 741; Glick (2018), p. 455.

[14] van Rompuy (2012), pp. 28–29.

consumer welfare objective.[15] Such a consumer welfare standard entails the application of the competition rules to deliver lower prices, greater output and choice, higher quality and more innovation to the benefit of consumers.[16]

4.2.1.2   The Promotion of Societal Welfare

It is true that the interests of consumers are mentioned in Article 101 (3) TFEU and Article 102 lit. b) TFEU. However, this does not prove that competition law is exclusively concerned with the protection of consumers. Most notably, Article 3 (3) TEU, which names the establishment of the internal market as one of the EU's objectives, does not limit the benefits accruing from the internal market to consumers. Instead, in accordance with the other paragraphs of Article 3 TEU, the internal market is to enhance overall societal welfare as a whole, and not only operate to the advantage of consumers. Further, regardless of its origin and precise content, the concept of a social market economy as included in Article 3 (3) TEU likewise is intended to contribute to societal welfare, and is not meant to benefit exclusively consumers.[17] Consequently, the EU competition provisions—which are essential in guaranteeing the functioning of the internal market[18]—equally are to contribute to the promotion of societal welfare.

This is supported by the jurisprudence of the CJEU. In its *TeliaSonera* judgment, the Court acknowledged that the EU is to establish an internal market pursuant to Article 3 (3) TEU and Protocol No. 27. This market is to include a system ensuring that competition is not distorted.[19] Given this link between the internal market and the competition rules, the Court concluded that the function of the competition rules is to prevent competition from being distorted to the detriment of the public interest, individual undertakings and consumers, thereby ensuring the well-being of the EU. Consequently, a finding of a competition law infringement does not require a

---

[15] Cf. e.g. Mario Monti, *The Future for Competition Policy in the European Union (SPEECH/01/340)* (2001); European Commission, 'Guidelines on the application of Article 81(3) of the Treaty' (n 167) paras. 13, 33; European Commission, 'Communication from the Commission: Guidance on the Commission's enforcement priorities in applying Article 82 of the Treaty to abusive exclusionary conduct by dominant undertakings' (n 195) para. 19 as well as the speeches delivered by Monti's successors, Neelie Kroes, *European Competition Policy – Delivering Better Markets and Better Choices (SPEECH/05/512)* (2005) (calling consumer welfare the standard applied by the Commission in assessing infringements of the EU rules on competition) and Joaquín Almunia, *Competition – what's in it for consumers? (SPEECH/11/803)* (2011) (naming consumer welfare as the guiding principle of EU competition policy).

[16] Jones et al. (2019), p. 39.

[17] On the concept of the social market economy cf. above p. 25.

[18] *Accession of the European Union to the European Convention for the Protection of Human Rights and Fundamental Freedoms* (18 December 2014) Opinion 2/13 172 (European Court of Justice).

[19] Cf. Protocol No. 27 on the Internal Market and Competition (12008M/PRO/27).

finding of direct consumer harm.[20] Instead, according to the jurisprudence of the CJEU on the interpretation of Articles 101 and 102 TFEU, the competition rules protect consumers in an indirect manner by means of an effective competitive structure[21] and the integration of national markets.[22]

Similarly, with regard to restrictions of competition 'by object' under Article 101 (1) TFEU, the Court has adjudged that no detriment to consumers' needs to be proven in order for the Commission to arrive at a finding of a restriction 'by object'.[23] This likewise shows that competition law is not exclusively concerned with the protection of consumer welfare. The rationale behind the categorisation of agreements as 'by object' restrictions is that they are inherently detrimental to competition on the internal market.[24] If agreements are presumed to have such an anticompetitive effect regardless of their possible effect on consumers, this must signify that the protection of competition cannot be equated with the protection of consumers.

Thus, the interpretation of the Treaties as adopted by the CJEU does not allow the conclusion that consumer welfare is the sole aim of EU competition law either. The adoption of a consumer welfare standard would be contrary to the open-textured nature of competition law,[25] which pursues wider objectives than 'just' the protection of consumers. Instead, as held by the Court in the aforementioned *TeliaSonera* judgment, the function of the competition rules is to prevent competition from being distorted to the detriment of the public interest, individual undertakings and consumers, thereby ensuring the well-being of the EU.[26] One can therefore argue that, relying on the teleological interpretation of the competition rules adopted by the Court,[27] EU competition law aims to enhance societal welfare instead of consumer welfare.

This is not to say, however, that the Commission and the CJEU have to align their decisional practice on the interpretation and application of the EU competition rules with a view to the respective decision's impact on societal welfare. Instead, in accordance with the view already taken by former Director-General for Competition

---

[20] *Konkurrensverket v TeliaSonera Sverige AB* (Chap. 2, n 62) 20–24; cf. also *SA Roquette Frères v Commission* (22 October 2002) C-94/00 42 (European Court of Justice).

[21] *Slovenská sporiteľňa* (7 February 2013) C-68/12 18 (European Court of Justice); *British Airways v Commission* (Chap. 3, n 75) 106; *Europemballage Corporation and Continental Can Company Inc. v Commission of the European Communities* (Chap. 2, n 14) 26.

[22] *GlaxoSmithKline Services Unlimited v Commission* (6 October 2009) joined cases C-501/06 P, C-513/06 P, C-515/06 P and C-519/06 61–64 (European Court of Justice); *Sot. Lélos kai Sia EE and others v GlaxoSmithKline AEVE Farmakeftikon Proïonton* (16 September 2008) joined cases C-468/06 to C-478/06 66–68 (European Court of Justice).

[23] *Koninklijke Wegenbouw Stevin BV v Commission* (27 September 2012) T-357/06 111 (General Court); *GlaxoSmithKline Services Unlimited v Commission* (n 22) 121.

[24] Cf. above p. 39.

[25] Zimmer (2008), p. 104.

[26] *Konkurrensverket v TeliaSonera Sverige AB* (Chap. 2, n 62) 20–22.

[27] Schweitzer and Klaus Patel (2012), p. 222.

Alexander Schaub, while the promotion of the public interest is the ultimate objective underlying competition policy, the day-to-day enforcement of competition law should not be preoccupied with achieving these benefits directly.[28] Instead, the promotion of long-term societal welfare by means of competition law is rather to be understood as a core principle which may be replaced by other, narrower tests or enforcement standards in individual cases, as is displayed *inter alia* in Article 101 (3) TFEU—which references the benefits for consumers—and the Court's jurisprudence in *Post Danmark I,* where the Court held that the negative effects produced by the abusive conduct might be counterbalanced by advantages in terms of efficiency that also benefit consumers.[29] It thus seems prudent to argue that it is only on the 'first stage' of the analysis, namely when assessing whether a certain behaviour infringes EU competition law provisions, that EU competition law is not directly concerned with consumer benefits.[30] Coming back to the question posed at the beginning of this paragraph, despite its fundamental importance, societal welfare must therefore be considered an indirect objective of competition law rather than a direct one.[31]

4.2.1.3 The Role of Efficiency

Competitive markets are presumed to be efficient, thereby furthering welfare. Consequently, competition law aims to enhance societal welfare by ensuring efficient—and hence competitive—markets. Thus, efficiencies play a central role in the competitive assessment of a firm's behaviour and its impact on the competitive situation on a given market.[32] It has however to be defined when markets are deemed efficient and how trade-offs between different types of efficiencies[33] are to be handled. These questions are linked to the choice of a welfare standard. Indeed, economic efficiencies can only be assessed if it is defined how one measures market performance beforehand—i.e. with a view to its impact on consumer welfare or on societal welfare.[34] Efficiency is thus better viewed as an indicator of the extent to which

---

[28] Schaub (1998).

[29] *Post Danmark AS v Konkurrencerådet* (Chap. 3, n 69) 41, referencing *British Airways v Commission* (Chap. 3, n 75) 86 and *Konkurrensverket v TeliaSonera Sverige AB* (Chap. 2, n 62) 76.

[30] Zimmer (2008), pp. 103–104.

[31] Nazzini puts it this way: '*The objective of the law must inform the construction of open-textured principles and concepts but is not the same as the concept of the rules*', Nazzini (2011), p. 45.

[32] Cf. with further references Ezrachi (2018), p. 10.

[33] One usually differentiates between allocative efficiency, productive efficiency and dynamic efficiency. With further references cf. Whish and Bailey (2018), p. 6.

[34] Nazzini (2011), pp. 33–38; van Rompuy (2012), p. 43.

the objective of increasing welfare is achieved.[35] It is for this reason that efficiency itself is not a stand-alone concept, but relative to a given objective.[36]

4.2.2   Market Integration

The objective of market integration has remained at the heart of EU competition law, as provided for by Article 3 (3) TEU and Protocol No. 27.[37] Most importantly, the rules on competition form the necessary complement to the basic freedoms, by preventing private actors from erecting barriers to intra-EU trade.[38] At the same time, the free movement of goods and services as provided for by the basic freedoms heightens the degree of competition within the European Union. It is for this reason that market integration and competition rules have been described as a '*two-way street*'.[39] As elaborated upon earlier, the nexus between competition law and market integration is particularly visible in the wording of the TFEU competition provisions, as agreements or abuses of a dominant position are prohibited as '*incompatible with the internal market*'[40] as well as in the division of competences between the Union and its Member States.[41]

Since the beginning of the European integration process, the competition rules have routinely been interpreted and enforced with the explicit purpose of furthering integration between the Member States' economies.[42] In this context it should be

---

[35]This also appears to have been the Commission's stance on the matter in its first report on competition policy, where it highlighted the positive effects of competition on allocative, dynamic and productive efficiency. Here, efficiency is not an end in itself but a means of enhancing societal welfare within the European Union, European Commission, 'First Report on Competition Policy' (Brussels, Luxembourg 1972) 11.

[36]Nazzini (2011), p. 33. Akman identifies efficiency as the '*original objective*' of the EU competition rules based on the Spaak Report, Akman (2009), p. 267. However, this does not acknowledge that the use of *travaux préparatoires* is rejected concerning the interpretation of the EEC Treaty, cf. Opinion of Advocate General Mayras in *Reyners v Belgium*, C-2/74 (28 May 1974) and ignores that efficiency was not an end in itself in the Spaak Report either. Monti describes efficiency as one of the core values of EU competition law, but failes to provide arguments as to why this should be the case, cf. Monti (2007), pp. 46–47.

[37]According to Protocol No. 27 (n 19), the internal market as set out in Article 3 of the TEU includes a system ensuring that competition is not distorted.

[38]Parret (2012), p. 65; Immenga and Mestmäcker (2019) C para. 12.

[39]Ibáñez Colomo (2016), pp. 749, 750.

[40]The same applies to the EU Merger Regulation, which likewise assesses concentrations with a view to their compatibility with the now internal market, cf. Article 2 (1) of Council Regulation (EC) No 139/2004 of 20 January 2004 on the control of concentrations between undertakings (Chap. 3, n 78).

[41]Cf. above p. 16.

[42]Ibáñez Colomo (2016), p. 749; Whish and Bailey (2018), p. 23. On the interpretation of the Treaty's competition rules by the Commission and the Court with a view to upholding the single market ideal of the Treaty: Albors-Llorens (2002). Cf. also *Accession of the European Union to the*

noted that the market integration objective never existed in a vacuum itself but has to be understood within the framework of the EU Treaties. Article 3 (1) TEU prescribes that it is the aim of the European Union to promote the well-being of the European peoples, hence to enhance societal welfare. Accordingly, in addition to its economic dimension, the market integration objective also contains a social dimension.

4.2.3   Ensuring Effective Competition on the Internal Market

Since their early jurisprudence, the courts of the EU have consistently held that the European competition provisions prohibit practices detrimental to the competitive structure on a given market.[43]

This aspect is closely related to the protection of the competitive process. Examining the impact of a certain conduct on the preservation of a 'competitive market structure' requires at least a comparison between two states of affairs, one in which the conduct under review is likely to have a certain impact on the market and one in which such conduct is absent. This comparison can only be made by examining the 'competitive process', i.e. the dynamic interaction of firms over a specified period. Therefore, the term 'competitive market structure' is equivalent to the 'competitive process' and the terms can be used interchangeably.[44]

The protection of the competitive process needs to be distinguished from the question whether EU competition law aims to protect competitors. The Court has repeatedly stated that the latter is not the case. Firms are allowed, and even encouraged to improve their products, lower prices and expand choice, even if this pushes rivals out of the market that are less efficient or less attractive to consumers— as long as their behaviour conforms with the boundaries set by EU competition law.[45]

As the EU Treaties do not provide further information on what exactly is encompassed by the phrase of the 'protection of the competitive process' or the

---

European Convention for the Protection of Human Rights and Fundamental Freedoms (Chap. 4, n 18) 172, with the Court adjudicating that the pursuit of the EU's integration objective is entrusted to a number of *'fundamental provisions'*, which include those on competition policy, and *French Republic v Commission* (19 March 1991) C-202/88 41 (European Court of Justice).

[43] *InnoLux Corp. v Commission* (27 February 2014) T-91/11 84 (General Court); *British Airways v Commission* (Chap. 3, n 75) 103–108; *GlaxoSmithKline Services Unlimited v Commission* (Chap. 4, n 22) 63; *Europemballage Corporation and Continental Can Company Inc. v Commission of the European Communities* (Chap. 2, n 14) 26.

[44] Nazzini (2011), p. 15.

[45] *Intel Corporation Inc. v Commission* (6 September 2017) C-413/14 P 133–134 (European Court of Justice); *GlaxoSmithKline Services Unlimited v Commission* (n 22) 63; *Post Danmark AS v Konkurrencerådet* (Chap. 3, n 69) 22.

'protection of a competitive market structure',[46] it thus must be determined to what extent competition in the internal market is to be safeguarded by the application of the competition rules. In its jurisprudence concerning infringements of Article 101 TFEU and Article 102 TFEU, the CJEU appears to regard 'effective competition' as the degree of competition to be protected by the EU competition rules.[47] The term does not seem to be linked to any particular theory or model of competition,[48] opposite to terms such as 'workable' or 'perfect' competition.[49] Instead, 'effective competition' has been described by the Court as *the degree of competition necessary for the attainment of the objectives of the Treaty.*'[50]

Various authors have expressed doubts as to whether the protection of 'effective competition'—which seems to be the appropriate level of protection awarded to a 'competitive market structure'—is a self-standing objective of competition law.[51] Already the definition of 'effective competition' provided by the Court as the level of competition necessary to ensure the attainment of the Treaties' objectives shows an inherent connection to the Union's market integration objective. This corresponds to the analysis provided by *Nazzini,* who held that the protection of a competitive market structure cannot be an objective of competition law, as it always requires having recourse to an additional normative standard.[52] As elaborated upon above, the rationale behind the protection of competition and a competitive market structure is the presumption that competition will bring about favourable results for society.[53] The preservation of the competitive process can therefore only be an intermediate objective of EU competition law. The pursuit of this intermediate goal ultimately serves the attainment of the ulterior objectives of competition law, namely the

---

[46] Article 173 (1) TFEU declares that the actions of the Member States and the EU in the area of industrial policy shall be in accordance with a system of *'competitive markets'*. This is a reference to the Union's economic policy concept as laid out in Articles 119 (1) and 120 TFEU, the core of which is the *'principle of an open market economy with free competition'*, Lurger (2018) para. 11.

[47] *Europemballage Corporation and Continental Can Company Inc. v Commission of the European Communities* (Chap. 2, n 14) 25; *GlaxoSmithKline Services Unlimited v Commission* (27 September 2006) T-168/01 109 (Court of First Instance); *Metro SB-Großmärkte GmbH & Co. KG v Commission* (Chap. 2, n 22) 20; *Europemballage Corporation and Continental Can Company Inc. v Commission of the European Communities* (Chap. 2, n 14) 25.

[48] Whish and Bailey (2018), p. 17.

[49] On the different theories and models of competition cf. Bishop and Walker (2007).

[50] *GlaxoSmithKline Services Unlimited v Commission* (n 47) 109. The objectives referred to herein were the objectives of the EC Treaty. Also in its *Metro I* judgment, the Court of Justice held that the degree of competition necessary is the degree necessary to ensure the observance of the basic requirements and the attainment of the objectives of the EEC Treaty, cf. *Metro SB-Großmärkte GmbH & Co. KG v Commission* (Chap. 2, n 22) 20. However, here the Court of Justice used the phrase *'workable competition'*, cf. also above p. 17.

[51] Cf. Bishop and Walker (2007), pp. 20–21; Jones et al. (2019), p. 25; Nazzini (2011), p. 17; Ahlborn and Padilla (2008), p. 76, with *Bishop/Walker* and *Ahlborn/Padilla* linking the level of protection of the competitive process to the benefits it delivers to European consumers.

[52] Nazzini (2011), p. 17.

[53] Cf. above p. 71.

establishment of the internal market and consequently also the promotion of societal welfare.[54]

4.2.4 Promoting Fair Competition

Another concept that frequently features as a possible objective of EU competition law is the promotion of fairness.[55] The concept itself is of a multi-faceted nature. The subsequent section therefore aims to present the different elements of the concept and to assess their role within the framework of EU competition law.

4.2.4.1 Procedural Fairness

The concept of fairness can assume procedural as well as substantive forms. Regarding its procedural aspects, there is a wide consensus that just treatment in the course of an (antitrust-) investigation is fundamental, as it enhances the legitimacy of the substantive outcome.[56] While the importance of those procedural facets of 'fairness' is uncontested, they are not objectives of competition law. Rather, they are an expression of the fundamental rights as recognised by the Charter of Fundamental Rights of the EU, the European Convention on Human Rights and the constitutional traditions common to the Member States being at the heart of the EU's legal structure, as well as respect for those rights.[57]

4.2.4.2 Substantive Fairness

The question of whether EU competition law should concern itself with guaranteeing substantive fairness has triggered a vivid debate among EU law scholars.[58] Articles

---

[54] Zimmer (2012), p. 490.

[55] Cf. e.g. Gerber (2008). On the multiple dimensions of the concept of 'fairness' in competition law in general cf. Ducci and Trebilcock (2019), p. 79.

[56] Marco Colino (2019), p. 329. Cf. further Kokott and Dittert (2018).

[57] *Accession of the European Union to the European Convention for the Protection of Human Rights and Fundamental Freedoms* (n 18) 167–169; *Yassin Abdullah Kadi and others v Council* (3 September 2008) joined cases C-402/05 P and 415/05 281–283 (European Court of Justice). On the development of the 'individual rights' dimension within EU law cf. Mestmäcker (1994).

[58] Cf. e.g. the 13th annual conference of the Global Competition Law Centre, *Fairness in Competition Law and Policy: Significance and Implications*, 25–26 January 2018, Brussels; Criticising the incorporation of fairness concerns in EU competition law analysis Forrester (2004), p. 919; Ahlborn and Padilla (2008).

101 and 102 TFEU do reference the concept of fairness,[59] revealing a concern for fairness in the behaviour of undertakings *vis-à-vis* consumers[60] as well as producers.[61] Furthermore, the preamble of the TFEU calls for concerted action in order to guarantee fair competition.[62]

On a more abstract level, the competition provisions have been characterised as the 'rules on fair play' on the internal market. It is advanced that a rationale underlying these rules is the hypothesis that society as a whole, competitors and consumers would be off worse if singular players could distort competition in their favour.[63] However also under this line of reasoning, while competition rules are said to be intended to achieve fairness, the ultimate objective of competition law is once more assumed to be long-term societal welfare. Said objective is to be achieved *inter alia* through the application of competition rules. These provisions in turn have to be fair and equitable in order to promote the willingness of firms and individuals to engage in market operations, thereby furthering the aggregate well-being of individuals.[64] This does not make fairness an objective of EU competition law in the strict sense, but rather a test to be applied in the design and application of the relevant competition provisions.[65] However, the notion of fairness itself is too imprecise in order to provide competition authorities or courts with a workable concept or enforcement standard. It needs to be translated into operational rules and standards. Putting it with the former Director-General for Competition *Johannes Laitenberger*, '*fairness only rings true if it is understood as a call to rigour, coherence and consistency*'.[66]

Commissioner for Competition *Margrethe Vestager* has frequently emphasised that competition rules also serve to give the consumers *'the power to demand a fair deal'*, by shopping around to find a better price, or presenting them with a wider

---

[59] Article 101 (3) TFEU requires that a '*fair share*' of the efficiencies of an otherwise restrictive agreement must be passed on to consumers. Article 102 lit. a) TFEU lists the imposition of '*unfair purchase or selling prices or other unfair trading conditions*' as one possible abuse of a dominant position.

[60] In Article 101 (3) TFEU and Article 102 lit. a) TFEU.

[61] In Article 102 lit. a) TFEU.

[62] The preamble to the TFEU reads: '(. . .) *recognising that the removal of existing obstacles calls for concerted action in order to guarantee steady expansion, balanced trade and fair competition, (. . .)*'.

[63] Kokott and Dittert (2018), p. 410.

[64] Along these lines cf. also Zimmer (2008), p. 107.

[65] Cf. also Gerard (2018), p. 211. Zimmer recognises a 'fairness dimension' of competition law insofar as it protects the rights of producers as well as those of consumers, Zimmer (2008), pp. 105–106. While this is certainly correct, this rather is an expression of the character of the EU as a community based on the rule of law, which has to observe the rights it has accorded to all its citizens.

[66] Johannes Laitenberger, *EU competition law in innovation and digital markets: fairness and the consumer welfare perspective* (2017).

choice of products.[67] Indeed, concerns regarding vertical fairness—understood as fairness between consumers and producers—are visible in Article 102 lit. a) TFEU, which prohibits exploitative abuses of market power such as excessive pricing and is hence *prima facie* indicative of distributive concerns in EU competition law. The unfairness of this behaviour is inferred from its economic inefficiency and the loss of welfare incurred by the dominant undertaking's customers.[68]

Another aspect of the fairness debate revolves around the issue of horizontal fairness as fairness in the interactions of competitors.[69] Pursuant to the jurisprudence of the Court, a system of undistorted competition, as laid down in the Treaties, can only be guaranteed if equality of opportunity is secured as between the various economic operators.[70] Hence, the Court regards equality of opportunities as one central aspect of the fairness dimension of EU competition law. In *Deutsche Telekom,* the Court specified that equality of opportunities signifies that an undertaking and its equally efficient competitor are to be placed on equal footing.[71] From this perspective, equality of opportunities is not an objective of EU competition law, but a test to be applied to the behaviour of undertakings in assessing whether said behaviour conforms to the EU competition provisions.[72]

Such horizontal fairness concerns relating to equality of opportunities between undertakings feature most prominently in the application of Article 102 TFEU. According to the settled jurisprudence of the CJEU, an exclusionary abuse of a dominant position occurs where a dominant undertaking resorts to methods other than competition on the merits.[73] The Court has characterised such behaviour as hindering fair competition between economic operators.[74] While the content of the concept of 'competition on the merits' needs to be defined itself, it can be understood as referring to competition based on quality, price, innovation and functionality.[75] Limiting the methods of competition firms may resort to thus serves to ensure equality of opportunities between economic operators, safeguarding the fairness of the competitive process.

---

[67] Margrethe Vestager, *Global markets and a fair deal for consumers* (2019); Margrethe Vestager, *Fairness and competition* (2018).

[68] Dolmans and Lin (2017), p. 57.

[69] Ducci and Trebilcock (2019), p. 93.

[70] *Motosykletistiki Omospondia Ellados NPID (MOTOE)* (1 July 2008) C-49/07 230 (European Court of Justice); *Connect Austria Gesellschaft für Telekommunikation GmbH* (22 May 2003) C-462/99 83–84 (European Court of Justice); *BPB Industries and British Gypsum v Commission* (1 April 1993) T-65/89 94 (Court of First Instance).

[71] *Deutsche Telekom AG v Commission* (14 October 2010) C-280/08 P 233 (European Court of Justice).

[72] Nazzini (2011), p. 148. Cf. also Ducci and Trebilcock (2019), pp. 93–98, who define 'horizontal fairness' as equal access to markets for competitors.

[73] *Hoffmann-La Roche v Commission* (Chap. 3, n 26) 91.

[74] *BPB Industries and British Gypsum v Commission* (n 70) 94.

[75] Dolmans and Lin (2017), pp. 44–47, referring to *Post Danmark AS v Konkurrencerådet* (Chap. 3, n 69) 21; *Intel Corporation Inc. v Commission* (n 45) 133–134. Cf. also above p. 43 et seq.

The conclusion of this section must therefore be that EU competition law is concerned with fairness to a certain extent. These 'fairness concerns' are best conceived as relating to the social rationale of EU competition law, with said social rationale ultimately informing the discretion permissible under established legal standards.[76] The notion of 'fairness' itself is too imprecise to provide the competition authorities and courts with workable enforcement standards. For these reasons, EU competition law integrates fairness concerns in specific competition law concepts or standards. Regarding horizontal fairness as between economic operators, fairness is best understood as relating to equality of opportunities between the various economic operators. This equality of opportunities, however, only extends to as efficient firms: inefficient firms are not protected against competition by more efficient ones, even if this leads to their departure from the market.[77]

4.2.5   Conclusions

The set of objectives EU competition law seeks to achieve encompasses the promotion of societal welfare, the market integration objective, and the protection of a competitive market structure. Other principles informing the interpretation of the EU competition rules without being objectives *strictu sensu* themselves include fairness concerns, in particular horizontal fairness as equality of opportunities between economic operators.

The last issue thus is how conflicts between these at times contradicting concepts may be resolved. The solution to this question lies in the hierarchy of objectives as sketched out above: conflicts between the different objectives are to be resolved in favour of the objective of market integration, as it presents the only true immediate objective of competition law.[78] At the same time, it should be recalled that EU competition law will always have to contribute to the overarching objectives of the European Union,[79] such as industrial policy. However, while doing so, the objectives specific to competition law must not be neglected in favour of more general policy objectives of the European Union, such as wider regulatory concerns.[80] Its character as a policy first and foremost directed at both ensuring and preserving market integration must be safeguarded. Yet, it should be noted that the Treaties

---

[76]Gerard (2018), p. 212, referring to Vestager, *Fairness and competition* (n 67). Cf. also the foreword by then Director-General of the Directorate-General for Competition Johannes Laitenberger, European Commission, 'Annual Activity Report of DG Competition 2016' (7 December 2016) 2.

[77]Cf. also the Court's jurisprudence in *Intel Corporation Inc. v Commission* (n 45) 133–134; *Post Danmark AS v Konkurrencerådet* (Chap. 3, n 69) 21.

[78]Also arguing in favour of a resolution of conflicts between the objectives of the EU in favour of the market integration principle Lianos (2013), p. 42.

[79]van Rompuy (2012), p. 202.

[80]Lianos (2013), p. 42.

themselves provide for the market integration objective to be accorded lesser relevance than non-economic, societal values in some instances, as explicitly pre-scribed *inter alia* by Article 36 TFEU and the *Cassis-de-Dijon* jurisprudence of the CJEU.[81]

4.3 The Objectives of EU Trade Defence Law

The following section examines the objectives of EU trade defence law. The EU's trade defence instruments form part of the EU's common commercial policy.[82] The aims pursued by the trade defence rules thus have to conform to the objectives of the CCP. For this reason, the section will be structured as follows: first, the general objectives of the common commercial policy will be introduced. In a second step, the specific objectives of the EU's trade defence instruments will be presented. At this point, it is expedient to recall that the specific objectives of the EU's trade defence rules as well as the objectives of its CCP may not run counter to the remainder of the Union's policies, as provided for by Article 7 TFEU and Article 21 (3) subpara. 2 TEU.

4.3.1 The Objectives and Principles Governing the Common Commercial Policy

As already indicated in Chap. 2, it is only since the entry into force of the amend-ments introduced by the Treaty of Lisbon that the EU Treaties set out an explicit mandate for the European Union's external action as well as a set of objectives to which that action should be directed and principles by which it should be guided.[83] Another significant change brought about by the Treaty of Lisbon is the integration of the CCP into the wider plane of the EU's external and internal action, as apparent from Articles 3 (5), 21 TEU and Articles 205 and 207 (1) TFEU.

---

[81] *Rewe-Zentral AG v Bundesmonopolverwaltung für Branntwein* (20 February 1979) 120/78 8 (European Court of Justice).

[82] *Free Trade Agreement with Singapore* (Chap. 2, n 87) 42–43.

[83] Cremona (2017a), p. 7.

4.3.1.1   Integration of the Common Commercial Policy Into the Wider Plane of the EU's External Action by the Treaty of Lisbon

As indicated *supra*, the integration of the common commercial policy into the general framework of the external action of the European Union follows from the wording of Articles 3 (5), 21 TEU and Articles 205 and 207 (1) TFEU.

While Article 21 (1) TEU reiterates the EU's commitment to its founding principles in its external relations,[84] Article 21 (2) TEU gives a list of objectives the EU aims to achieve in its external action. The enumeration contains objectives such as fostering the sustainable economic, social and environmental development of developing countries with the primary aim of eradicating poverty (Article 21 (2) lit. d) TEU), or environmental protection (Article 21 (2) lit. f) TEU). It is hence apparent that the EU's common commercial policy is set not only to achieve classical, commercial objectives, such as the integration of all countries into the world economy through the progressive abolition of restrictions on international trade (Article 21 (2) lit. e) TEU), but also non-commercial objectives. At this point, it should be emphasised that the use of trade policy to achieve non-commercial policy objectives had been taking place already before the Treaty of Lisbon, a practice approved by the Court[85]: The EU's common commercial policy measures routinely integrated non-commercial policy concerns, such as environmental or labour issues.[86]

Further, Article 21 (3) subpara. 2 TEU mandates the European Union to ensure consistency between its internal and its external policies.[87]

4.3.1.2   Free and Fair Trade

In examining the Union's trade defence instruments as a part of the common commercial policy, the reference to 'free and fair trade' contained in Article 3 (5) TEU, to which the EU shall contribute, is of particular interest.

---

[84] The parallelism between the EU's internal and external action has already been noted in Chap. 2, cf. above p. 18. Cf. further Cremona (2011), p. 280.

[85] Cf. e.g. *Commission v Council (Energy Star Agreement)* (12 December 2002) C-281/01 39, 43 (European Court of Justice). On the historical developments underlying the integration of non-trade objectives cf. Jaremba (2020), pp. 163, 164–165.

[86] Cremona calls this '*a Treaty-based sanction to what has always been a characteristic of the CCP*', namely the use of trade policy to achieve broader political and non-trade objectives, Cremona (2017b), p. 498.

[87] Cf. above p. 30.

4.3.1.2.1   Free Trade

As mentioned, Articles 3 (5) and 21 TEU also include some classical trade objectives, in particular the EU's contribution to free trade (Article 3 (5) TEU) and the integration of all countries into the world economy, including through progressive abolition of restrictions on international trade (Article 21 (2) lit. e) TEU). These norms reference a trade policy participating in multilateral efforts towards trade liberalisation, a commitment dating back to the foundations of the EEC.[88] It is generally understood that the notion of free trade refers foremost to the EU's membership in the WTO and to the obligations flowing from said membership.[89] For the purposes if this work, in particular the obligations arising from the agreements annexed to the Marrakesh Agreement,[90] such as the GATT 1994,[91] the ADA[92] and the ASCM,[93] are of relevance.

4.3.1.2.2   Fair Trade

While the general scope and content of the objective of free trade is largely uncontested, there is debate as to what can be subsumed under the notion of 'fair' trade. One could assume that fair trade exclusively refers to compliance with the rules set out under the regime of the WTO, such as the ADA or the ASCM, which outline the WTO members' options for action against trading practices that are perceived as unfair.[94] Such a reading would run parallel to the prevailing understanding of free trade in the sense that it refers to the compliance of one's trade policy with the WTO-regime. Free trade would then be stressing the liberalisation aspect of the GATT 1994, whereas fair trade would be referring to specific trade practices prohibited under the regime of the GATT 1994. However, this would constitute a rather narrow interpretation, not taking account of the non-commercial objectives contained in Article 3 (5) and 21 (2) TEU.

The relevance of non-commercial objectives for the EU's CCP was highlighted in the Court's reasoning in *Opinion 2/15,* where it held that the objective of sustainable

---

[88] Ackermann et al. (2018), pp. 373, 374.

[89] Ibid, basing their reasoning on *International Fruit Company NV and others v Produktschap voor Groenten en Fruit* (12 December 1972) joined cases 21 to 24/72 10–13 (European Court of Justice).

[90] 'Marrakesh Agreement Establishing the World Trade Organization (Uruguay Round Agreement)' (1867 U.N.T.S. 154, 15 April 1994).

[91] 'General Agreement on Tariffs and Trade 1994: Agreement Establishing the World Trade Organization, Annex 1A' (1867 U.N.T.S. 190).

[92] 'Agreement on Implementation of Article VI of the General Agreement on Tariffs and Trade 1994: Agreement Establishing the World Trade Organization, Annex 1A' (Chap. 1, n 16).

[93] 'Agreement on Subsidies and Countervailing Measures: Agreement Establishing the World Trade Organization, Annex 1A' (Chap. 1, n 13).

[94] Cremona and Marín Durán (2013), p. 151, also using this interpretation as a starting point for their analysis.

development forms an integral part of the common commercial policy.[95] Consequently, the fair trade the EU is to contribute to must be understood as also including non-commercial aspects of trade. Only this interpretation is reflective of the equal status of non-commercial and commercial objectives in the EU's external relations as set out by Articles 3 (5), 21 TEU.

If it is concluded that the notion of fair trade is *per se* to be understood as including non-commercial aspects, the next question that needs to be addressed is which aspects exactly are covered by it. The objectives of the protection of human rights (Article 21 (2) lit. b) TEU), the promotion of the economic and social development of developing countries with the primary aim of eradicating poverty (Article 21 (2) lit. d) TEU) as well as solidarity and mutual respect among peoples (Article 3 (5) TEU) suggest that the rights of those producing the goods being exported to the EU have to be observed. Hence, one facet of fair trade is respect for human rights and especially workers' rights, in particular by promoting compliance with standards set by the International Labour Organisation (ILO).[96] Second, in addition to fostering the economic and social development of developing countries, the Union shall do the same with regard to their environmental development (Article 21 (2) lit. d) TEU). The set of objectives of Article 21 (2) TEU further includes the sustainable development of the earth (Article 21 (2) lit. f) TEU). In the above-mentioned *Opinion 2/15*, when elaborating upon the relevance of sustainable development objectives, the Court argued that the inclusion of a chapter on non-commercial objectives in the free trade agreement concluded between the EU and its Member States and Singapore ensures that '*trade between them takes place in compliance with the obligations that stem from the international agreements concerning social protection of workers and environmental protection*'.[97] The Court further held that account must be taken of Articles 9 and 11 TFEU, which respectively provide that the EU shall take into account the requirements linked to the guarantee of adequate social protection and that the EU is to integrate environmental protection requirements into the definition and implementation of its policies, and that '*Article 3(5) TEU obliges the European Union to contribute, in its relations with the wider world, to "free and fair" trade.*'[98]

Hereby, the Court not only linked the notion of fair trade to sustainable development objectives, but it effectively defined the notion of 'sustainable development' in terms of multilateral conventions on labour rights and environmental protection.[99]

The relevance the EU attaches to pursuing such non-commercial objectives within its common commercial policy is evidenced, *inter alia*, by the inclusion of chapters on matters of sustainable development in its trade agreements and, as

---

[95] *Free Trade Agreement with Singapore* (Chap. 2, n 87) 147. On the impact of the judgment cf. Cremona (2018), p. 231.

[96] Cf. also Vedder (2013), p. 121.

[97] *Free Trade Agreement with Singapore* (Chap. 2, n 87) 152.

[98] Ibid 146.

[99] Ackermann et al. (2018), p. 384.

regards unilateral trade policy measures, by making access to the internal market conditional upon ratification and implementation of a number of international conventions related to human rights, labour rights, environmental protection and good governance within its Generalised Scheme of Preferences (GSP).[100] In this regard, EU law shows a certain emancipation from WTO law, where the notion of unfair trade is still understood as only encompassing trade violating the rules on dumping and subsidies.[101]

This broader understanding of fair trade as 'ethical' or 'equitable' trade[102] is also visible in the Commission's trade strategy 'Trade for all', which stipulates that it is one of the aims of the EU to ensure that economic growth goes hand in hand with social justice, respect for human rights, high labour and environmental standards, and health and safety protection. This also encompasses its trade policy.[103] A similar stance is reflected in the 2018 activity report prepared by DG TRADE. While the Commission's main focus as regards 'fair' trade continues to lie on ensuring that trade complies with the requirements of WTO law, the Commission devotes attention to the fact that the reformed EU's trade defence instruments are now also taking account of the costs incurred by the EU industry in complying with multilateral environmental agreements and ILO conventions. The Commission then clarifies that this is not only important in economic terms but also because it reflects the need to respect social and environmental concerns in international trade.[104]

4.3.1.3   The Specific Objectives and Principles Governing the EU's Common Commercial Policy

The specific policy objectives of the CCP are to be determined on the basis of Articles 206 and 207 TFEU. Said objectives have to remain within the frame set by the overall objectives and principles of the EU's external relations.[105] A *lex specialis*

---

[100]The specifics of this approach will be examined in more detail in Chap. 8, cf. below p. 253 et seq.

[101]van den Bossche and Zdouc (2017), p. 41.

[102]Cremona and Marín Durán (2013), p. 152.

[103]European Commission, 'Trade for all – Towards a more responsible trade and investment policy (COM(2015) 497)' (14 October 2015) 22.

[104]European Commission, '2018 Annual Activity Report of the Directorate-General for Trade' (15 July 2019) 23-24. Cf. further European Commission, 'Commission Staff Working Document: Midterm Evaluation of the Generalised Scheme of Preferences accompanying the document "Report from the European Commission to the European Parliament and the Council on the application of Regulation (EU) 978/2012 applying a Scheme of Generalised Tariff Preferences and repealing Council Regulation (EC) No 732/2008" (SWD(2018) 430 final)' (Brussels 4 October 2018) 34, where the Commission held that the special incentives scheme under its generalised system of preferences (the so-called GSP+ scheme) '*is an innovative tool that offers incentives and support for human rights, sustainable development and good governance in countries committed to implementing core international conventions in those areas. This is seen as essential to encourage fairness in global trade.*'

[105]Larik (2011), p. 17.

rule does not apply. Rather, as evident from the wording of the relevant provisions in the TFEU and the TEU and the provisions' respective location in the Treaties,[106] the content of the specific policy objectives is informed by the general principles and objectives of the European Union's external relations. Consequently, the CCP objectives may only be pursued to the extent that they do not run counter to the overarching, general objectives of the EU's external action.[107]

4.3.1.3.1   Trade Liberalisation

4.3.1.3.1.1   Scope

As proclaimed in Article 206 TFEU, the main objectives of the CCP are to contribute, in the common interest, to the harmonious development of world trade, to the progressive abolition of restrictions on international trade and foreign direct investment, and to the lowering of customs tariffs and the removal of other types of barriers.[108] This commitment to liberalising international commercial relations has been in place since the beginning of European integration, with already Article 110 of the EEC Treaty mandating an orientation of the common commercial policy towards the objective of trade liberalisation.[109] Effectively, Article 206 TFEU mirrors the commitment towards trade liberalisation expressed in the notion of 'free trade' in Article 3 (5) and the progressive abolition of restrictions on international trade mandated by Article 21 (2) lit. e) TEU. As indicated above, one dimension of the liberalisation objective is the abolition of trade-restrictive measures which violate the requirements of WTO law.[110]

That being said, while Article 206 TFEU is considered to be legally binding, the provision still permits the EU to adopt WTO-compliant trade restrictive measures which cause the EU to fall behind the current level of trade liberalisation.[111] A different interpretation would fail to take account of the fact that both Article 21 (2) lit. e) TEU and Article 206 TFEU regard trade liberalisation as a gradual

---

[106] Article 3 (5) TEU is located in the common provisions of the TEU, Article 21 TEU in the chapter on the general provisions of the European Union's external action. Article 205 TFEU prescribes that the Union's action on the international scene shall be guided by the principles, pursue the objectives and be conducted in accordance with the general provisions laid down in Article 21 TEU.

[107] Weiß (2014) para. 26.

[108] de Waele (2017), p. 80.

[109] Cf. above Ackermann et al. (2018) and the wording of Article 110 EEC Treaty: '*By establishing a customs union between themselves the Member States intend to contribute, in conformity with the common interest, to the harmonious development of world trade, the progressive abolition of restrictions on international exchanges and the lowering of customs barriers.*'

[110] Cf. above Ackermann et al. (2018).

[111] Weiß (2014) para. 16. Cf. also *Anton Dürbeck v Hauptzollamt Frankfurt am Main-Flughafen* (5 May 1981) C-112/80 44 (European Court of Justice), where the Court held that the liberalisation objective of Article 110 EC Treaty does not prevent the Community from enacting trade-restrictive measures. But see Dimopoulos (2010), p. 167, 169.

process.[112] This process does not necessarily have to be linear. As long as the general orientation of the common commercial policy as geared towards liberalised trade is not being called into question, a reading of Article 206 TFEU as prohibiting any measure restricting trade would be unduly strict. Further, by speaking of the 'harmonious' development of world trade, Article 206 TFEU adds an element of reciprocity: the EU is not obliged to liberalise its trade policy absent similar commitments from its trading partners.[113] Lastly and most importantly, as evident from the wording of Article 206 TFEU, the liberalisation of international trade always has to serve the common interest of the European Union and its Member States. Consequently, Article 206 TFEU does not prevent the European Union from adopting measures restricting trade, if omitting to do so would be contrary to its own interests or the interests of the Member States.[114]

4.3.1.3.1.2   Content

The mention of the objective of free trade alongside that of fair trade in Article 3 (5) TEU, the integration of all countries into the world economy (Article 21 (2) lit. e) TEU) as well as the other non-commercial policy objectives of Article 21 (2) TEU are further reflections of the fact that trade liberalisation cannot be seen as a self-determining objective. Instead, it also encompasses a 'fair' trade angle by aiming to achieve a balanced liberalisation of trade, which contributes to sustainability and development objectives as well as environmental protection.[115]

4.3.1.3.2   Uniformity

Even though not an objective of the common commercial policy in the strict sense, the principle of uniformity has been decisive in shaping this policy area.[116] It is visible in the first sentence of Article 207 (1) TFEU, which prescribes that the CCP shall be based on uniform principles. Article 207 (1) TFEU itself does not contain any of the principles on which the CCP should be based.[117] Instead, the principles it refers to can be found in Articles 3 (5) and 21 TEU.

---

[112] For example, both Article 21 (2) lit. e) TEU and Article 206 TFEU speak of the *'progressive'* abolition of restrictions on international trade.

[113] Weiß (2014), para. 10.

[114] *United Kingdom and Northern Ireland v Council of the European Union* (19 November 1998) C-150/94 67 (European Court of Justice); *Anton Dürbeck v Hauptzollamt Frankfurt am Main-Flughafen* (n 111) 44. It also follows from the above that there is no obligation to mirror the level of internal liberalisation at the external level. This was recognised by the Court in *EMI Records Limited v CBS United Kingdom Limited* (15 June 1976) C-51/75 17 (European Court of Justice).

[115] Weiß (2015a) para. 12.

[116] Cf. above p. 18 et seq.

[117] Weiß (2015b) para. 20.

4.3.2 The Objectives of the EU's Trade Defence Instruments

As can already be inferred from the remarks preceding this section, central conceptual differences between the rules on competition and those on trade defence become visible. Whereas competition law is a major policy area of the European Union's internal market policies itself, trade defence merely forms a sub-section of the European Union's common commercial policy. Consequently, its objectives and design have to be determined in light of the objectives of the CCP and, since the entry into force of the Treaty of Lisbon, the overarching principles and objectives applying to all areas of the Union's external policy.

4.3.2.1 Trade Defence Instruments as a Part of the Common Commercial Policy

Trade defence measures are an exception to the general trade liberalisation objective of the EU's CCP as contained in Article 206 TFEU. However, as noted above, Article 206 TFEU does not mandate an unconditional liberalisation of trade. Moreover, as mentioned, also under a narrow understanding of the concept of fair trade, the EU's commitment to fair trade in Article 3 (5) TEU includes upholding the rules of the WTO, which permit the imposition of trade defence measures in the event of trading practices that are perceived as being unfair.

Nevertheless, the overarching trade policy objective of liberalisation mandates a restrictive use of trade defence instruments. In order to ensure an appropriate balance between free trade and other legitimate objectives being struck, trade-restrictive measures have to be proportionate in the sense that they have to find their justification in the Treaties and have to be necessary.[118] Despite this, due to the wide margin of appreciation enjoyed by the Union institutions in the area of trade defence,[119] a judicial control of measures restricting trade is limited to assessing whether relevant procedural rules have been complied with, the facts on which the contested choice is based have been accurately stated, and whether there has been a manifest error in the appraisal of those facts or a misuse of powers.[120]

As already touched upon, the EU is a member to the WTO. Consequently, its trade defence instruments have to conform to the requirements flowing from its

---

[118]Dimopoulos (2010), p. 167; also holding that Article 21 TEU may not be used to legitimise purely protectionist policies: Weiß (2014) para. 26. Cf. further Opinion of Advocate General Léger in *Commission v NTN Corporation and Koyo Seiko*, C-245/95 9 (16 September 1997); *Anton Dürbeck v Hauptzollamt Frankfurt am Main-Flughafen* (n 111) 44.

[119]*Ikea Wholesale Ltd. v Commissioners of Customs and Excise* (27 September 2007) C-351/04 40 (European Court of Justice); *EEC Seed Crushers' and Oil Processors' Federation (FEDIOL) v Commission* (22 June 1989) C-70/87 26 (European Court of Justice); *Nachi Fujikoshi Corporation v Council and others* (7 May 1987) C-255/84 21 (European Court of Justice).

[120]*Ikea Wholesale Ltd. v Commissioners of Customs and Excise* (n 119) 41; *United Kingdom and Northern Ireland v Council of the European Union* (Chap. 4, n 114) 54.

WTO membership.[121] While it was not formally party to the old GATT 1947, it became a member of the WTO in its own right in 1995.[122] For this reason, and in accordance with Article XVI:4 of the Marrakesh Agreement, it has to ensure the conformity of its laws, regulations and administrative procedures with WTO law. Within the EU legal order, this obligation flows from 216 (2) TFEU explicitly stipulating that the agreements concluded by the Union are binding upon the EU institutions. This is also recognised by the CJEU, which considers the international agreements to which the EU is party an 'integral part' of EU law.[123]

4.3.2.2   The Economic Rationale Behind Trade Defence Instruments

Anticompetitive behaviour leads to less competitive pressure, resulting in inefficiencies, higher prices, less choice for consumers and overall negative effects on welfare.[124] In order to avoid such undesirable effects, competition provisions are necessary. This economic rationale of competition law is uncontested. For anti-subsidy measures, their basic economic rationale can likewise be found in the market-distortive effects of subsidisation, resulting in inefficiencies and ultimately also negative effects on welfare in the importing State.[125]

For anti-dumping law, the picture is much more unclear. From an economic perspective, the entry of new producers in the market leads to increased competitive pressure. The presence of foreign products itself results in a resource and wealth transfer from the exporter's home country to the country of destination, where consumers benefit from lower prices. Hence, *prima facie*, an increased influx of goods from other countries, even if exported at dumping prices, may be considered positive or even desirable.[126] Conversely, proponents of anti-dumping legislation argue that protectionist politics of the exporter's home country frequently lead to an asymmetry in market access, which results in artificial competitive advantages for companies operating from sanctuary home markets and serious disadvantages for companies in open markets. In the worst case, this can lead to the elimination of competitors which are more efficient than the dumper, ultimately resulting in a loss of economic resources in the importing country.[127] Moreover, the beneficial effects of an increased number of economic operators being active on the market will only

---

[121] Weiß (2014) para. 9; Krajewski (2012), p. 295.

[122] Egelund Olsen (2012), p. 3. The EU Member States continue to be parties to the WTO, and are bound by the Marrakesh Agreement establishing the WTO and the multilateral agreements concluded under the auspices of the WTO themselves, Herrmann and Streinz (2014) para. 88.

[123] R. & V. Haegeman v Belgian State (30 April 1974) C-181/73 5 (European Court of Justice).

[124] Cf. Bailey (2018) para. 1.016 with further references on the economic theory of competition.

[125] Sykes (2003), p. 2, 7. It is disputed, however, whether this applies to all types of subsidisation and under which circumstances the imposition of anti-subsidy measures is sensible from an economic perspective. For an in-depth discussion cf. Coppens (2014).

[126] Müller-Ibold (2018a), p. 548.

[127] Mueller et al. (2009) paras. I.09–I.16.

materialise if the dumping exporter's pricing strategy does not constitute a case of predatory behaviour which leads to the exit of the dumping exporter's competitors from their home market. In cases of such predatory—or otherwise anticompetitive—behaviour, dumping may ultimately result in negative effects on competition and on welfare.[128] However, studies have shown that only in very few cases dumping actually reflects a predatory pricing strategy and there is scant economic evidence that dumping indeed leads to undesirable welfare effects.[129] Instead, economic analysis has demonstrated that the aggregate welfare results of anti-dumping measures themselves are systematically negative for the importing country.[130] Lacking a sound economic rationale, anti-dumping measures are in practice more accurately described as a form of contingent protection.[131]

4.3.2.3 The Legal Rationale Behind Trade Defence Instruments

Notwithstanding the controversies revolving around the economic foundations of anti-dumping measures, from a political and a legal perspective, anti-dumping legislation remains an integral part of States' trade defence toolkit: Article VI GATT 1994 and the Anti-Dumping Agreement authorise the practice, as long as one stays within the specified bandwidth.[132] In spite of the scarce economic evidence, the proponents of anti-dumping legislation continue to refer to the alleged benefits to competition and overall societal welfare brought about by the imposition of anti-dumping measures. Moreover, a number of non-economic reasons are advanced to justify the need for the imposition of anti-dumping measures, which will be presented below.

---

[128] Arguing that it would be reasonable to limit the scope of the anti-dumping rules to cases where products are sold at below cost: Wegener Jessen (2012), p. 265.

[129] Cf. e.g. Sandkamp (2018); Prawitz and Kasteng (2013), p. 12 et seq; Derk Bienen, Dan Ciuriak and Timothée Picarello, 'Trade and Development Discussion Paper: Does Antidumping Address "Unfair" Trade? – The European Union's Experience' (2013); Bourgeois and Messerlin (1998); Willig (1998). Defending the necessity of anti-dumping measures also outside the scope of predatory dumping Peter Holmes and Jeremy Kempton, 'Study on the Economic and Industrial Aspects of Anti-Dumping Policy' (1997).

[130] With further references cf. Tavares de Araujo Jr. (2002), p. 161.

[131] For detailed criticism cf. e.g. Cho (2009), p. 357, 370 et seq; Lloyd (2005), p. 72 et seq, arguing that anti-dumping measures are not effective in restoring competition even in instances of predatory pricing. Cf. also the study by Conrad showing that national anti-dumping proceedings do not bring about an optimal international resource allocation, Conrad (2002), p. 563.

[132] de Waele (2017), p. 94. On the political economy underlying the continued application of anti-dumping measures cf. Macrory (2005), p. 487 et seq; Tharakan (1995), p. 1550 et seq.

4.3.2.3.1 Compensating for the Differences Between National and International Trade

Under the regime of the GATT 1994, each member determines its own level of market liberalisation. However, there is no reciprocity in the WTO system and the WTO system itself only provides limited instruments against market foreclosures.[133] Members may thus in principle be willing to liberalise access to their markets even absent similar commitments from other members, however only under the premise of being able to resort to trade defence instruments in order to mitigate trade deflections resulting from the unequal liberalisation of trade between all members. Indeed, studies have shown that the use of anti-dumping policies may contribute to reducing the resistance of domestic protectionist forces towards major tariff reforms.[134] Trade defence instruments can therefore be regarded as having a 'balancing' function.[135] In a similar vein, trade defence instruments have also been described as a sort of insurance policy or 'safety valve' against unforeseen trade pressures, allowing countries to take on deeper commitments in trade negotiations than they would otherwise be willing to make.[136] Both aspects imply that overall gains from trade liberalisation must in some instances be sacrificed if certain sectors of the domestic industry are experiencing injury due to competing imports.[137]

In this regard, anti-dumping measures are used to compensate for the lack of comprehensive market integration between two trading economic areas, or an asymmetry in market access.[138] It may however prove difficult to identify the exact reasons for the market segregation, and even more challenging to combat their root cause, as the EU will rarely have the political power to change another State's economic policy.[139] Furthermore, the monetary advantages an undertaking enjoys from the market segregation may not be quantifiable. For this reason, anti-dumping measures only serve as a second-best solution by preventing the economically undesirable effects of trade arising from said lack of reciprocity in market

---

[133] Jakob et al. (2014) para. 104.

[134] Ketterer (2018), p. 1111.

[135] Hoffmeister, 'AD-GVO 2016 vor Art. 1 [Erwägungsgründe]' (Chap. 1, n 18) para. 22. Cf. also the study conducted by Derk Bienen, Dan Ciuriak and Timothée Picarello, 'Anti-Dumping as Insurance Policy: What the "Grey Area" Measures Tell Us' (2013).

[136] On this aspect of anti-dumping measures cf. Bienen et al. (2013a); Tavares de Araujo Jr. (2002), p. 162. From this perspective, anti-dumping measures may even be regarded as welfare-enhancing in the sense that they implicitly permit governments to commit to deeper levels of trade liberalisation, Bienen et al. (2013a), p. 6 and Mueller et al. (2009) para. I.16. Despite this, Bienen et al. also note that the design of anti-dumping policy and the emphasis on 'unfair' trade in its justification makes it ill-suited to pursue this objective in a systematic and well-administered way, Bienen et al. (2012), p. 17.

[137] Bown and McCulloch (2015), pp. 1–2.

[138] Jakob et al. (2014), para. 129.

[139] Müller-Ibold (2018a), p. 548; Bienen et al. (2012), p. 8; Hoekman and Mavroidis (1996), p. 27, 30.

access, without addressing the market segregation itself.[140] As opposed to anti-dumping duties, countervailing duties directly tackle the competitive distortion caused by the subsidisation: the recipients of a countervailable subsidy receive a quantifiable competitive advantage, which the countervailing duty is intended to offset.[141]

4.3.2.3.2   Contributing to the Protection of Competition on the Internal Market

So far, trade defence policy has proven to be mainly concerned with the lack of reciprocity in market access at an international level and economic integration in general, and the issues arising therefrom. The next point in question then is to what extent these concerns accommodate a competition policy rationale.

As regards countervailing duties, the answer is relatively straight-forward: as stated above, countervailing duties are intended to offset the competitive distortion caused by the subsidisation. Here, the competition policy rationale is visible as ensuring an equality of opportunities in competition in the sense that States may not distort competition between undertakings by financially favouring some.[142] Concerning anti-dumping legislation, the answer is less clear.

4.3.2.3.2.1   *Common Roots and Present Disparities*

Traditionally, trade defence instruments have been characterised as the international trade analogue of internal market competition policies.[143] This connection between the two policy fields was apparent in the early legislation on trade defence: One of the first anti-dumping laws, which was introduced in Canada in 1904, was motivated by concerns over predation. Similarly, the 1916 U.S. Antidumping Act mirrored the concerns of antitrust law by extending the prohibition of price discrimination contained in the United States' domestic antitrust law to cases of price discrimination between foreign markets and U.S. markets.[144] Despite these common roots, nowadays, the conceptual differences between competition and trade defence law are substantial. As noted by *Finger* concerning the U.S. anti-dumping legislation, '*any mention of antitrust criteria (. . .) is gone. Antitrust's injury-to-competition standard has been replaced by a diversion-of-business standard.*'[145]

---

[140] Müller-Ibold (2018a), p. 548; Müller-Ibold (2018b), pp. 194–195.

[141] Jakob et al. (2014) para. 133.

[142] In a parallel to the rationale behind the EU's rules on the prohibition of State aid, cf. Rusche (2019) para. 5; Peretz and Mackersie (2018) para. 17.001.

[143] Cf. e.g. Barbuto (1994), p. 2048.

[144] For a more detailed account cf. Sykes and Cooper (1998), p. 14 et seq and Viner (1923), p. 239 et seq.

[145] Finger (1992), p. 129; cf. also Mavroidis (2016), p. 73.

This statement holds true for various jurisdictions. In particular, studies concerning the United States, Canada and the EU respectively, have shown that only a small fraction of anti-dumping investigations would also have been likely to be pursued under the relevant jurisdiction's domestic competition law.[146] This is substantiated by the European Union's experience following its 2004 enlargement. Before the accession of the new Member States, the European Community had a number of trade defence measures in place which were directed at products originating from the accession candidates. Following the accession, the measures were terminated. While the relevant practices were considered to fulfil the preconditions for the imposition of anti-dumping duties prior to the accession, the same practices were not pursued under the Community's competition rules after the accession.[147]

4.3.2.3.2.2   Protecting Fair Competition on the Internal Market

According to an often-cited phrase, anti-dumping policy contains a competition law rationale as it, too, is concerned with combatting unfair competition.[148] Moreover, as mentioned, Article 3 (5) TEU mandates that the EU contributes to international fair trade, which is traditionally understood as trade in accordance with the rules of the WTO.[149] It is thus expedient to elaborate on the content and the relevance of the concept of fairness in anti-dumping law.

Anti-dumping law is concerned with achieving horizontal fairness in a relatively direct manner, intended to ensure that the division of means of production is based on genuine comparative advantage.[150] Even though none of the legal texts which address the issue of dumping explicitly characterises dumping as an unfair trading practice,[151] the rationale of anti-dumping law as ensuring fair competition on the internal market has been affirmed by the jurisprudence of the CJEU.[152] Likewise, the Commission considers that the purpose of anti-dumping measures is, in general, to stop distortions of competition arising from unfair commercial practices and thus to re-establish open and fair competition on the internal market.[153] Hence, in

---

[146] Bienen et al. (2013b); Bourgeois and Messerlin (1998); Shin (1998).

[147] Prawitz and Kasteng (2013).

[148] Cf. *inter alia* Korkea-Aho and Sankari (2017), p. 543, 546; Koutrakos (2015), p. 357.

[149] Cf. above p. 84.

[150] Bienen et al. (2012), p. 1.

[151] Neither Article VI GATT 1994, nor the Anti-Dumping Agreement or the Basic Anti-Dumping Regulation actually characterise dumping as being unfair, Reymond (2015), pp. 104–105.

[152] *Industrie des poudres sphériques v Commission and others* (3 October 2000) C-458/98 P 91, 96 (European Court of Justice); *Industrie des poudres sphériques v Council* (15 October 1998) T-2/95 265, 345 (Court of First Instance).

[153] Commission Regulation (EEC) No 2140/89 of 12 July 1989 imposing a provisional anti-dumping duty on imports of certain compact disc players originating in Japan and South Korea recital 121; Commission Regulation (EC) No 1748/95 of 17 July 1995 imposing a provisional anti-dumping duty on imports of peroxodisulphates (persulphates), originating in the People's Republic of China recital 39, referring to the re-establishment of '*effective*' competition. Cf. also

anti-dumping law, the term fairness is used to denote an equality of opportunities between the various market operators. The unfairness of the dumper's behaviour is inferred from the fact that he enjoys certain competitive advantages resulting from the asymmetrical market access between his home country and the EU.[154]

The Commission, however, usually does not investigate whether there actually is any market segregation or insufficient competition law enforcement in the exporter's home country.[155] Similarly, it is not considered whether the dumping is an expression of the existence of unfair competitive advantages or whether there are legitimate economic reasons for the exporter to resort to such a practice.[156] Rather, the existence of dumping creates the irrefutable assumption that such impediments to competition do exist on the exporter's home market, which are revealed by the dumping practice. Dumping is thus treated as constituting an unfair trading practice *per se*,[157] with the verdict of unfairness not necessarily being based on the actions of the dumping exporter, but on the measures by its home State awarding protection to its exporters.[158]

4.3.2.3.2.3   Restoring Effective Competition on the Internal Market

After having established the fairness-rationale underlying anti-dumping law, it is to be assessed whether the imposition of anti-dumping measures is also intended to ensure the effectiveness of competition within the internal market. This would constitute another parallel with EU competition law. One of the objectives of EU competition law as identified by the jurisprudence of the CJEU is the protection of the competitive process or the protection of a competitive market structure, with the Court considering the protection of 'effective competition' as the appropriate level of competition to be preserved on the internal market.[159] Indeed, Article 21 (1) BADR holds that, when deciding whether to impose anti-dumping measures or not, the need to restore effective competition shall be given special consideration.[160]

However, the structure of Article 21 (1) BADR, taken together with the central rationale of anti-dumping measures, shows that despite its wording, the EU's anti-dumping legislation is not intended to safeguard a certain degree of competition within the internal market.

Kuplewatzky (2018), pp. 448, 455, concluding that the European Commission's goal in the imposition of anti-dumping duties is to equalise competitive conditions between foreign manufacturers and the EU industry.

[154] Jakob et al. (2014) para. 105.

[155] The new Article 2 (6a) BADR, dealing with the existence of '*significant distortions*' in the exporting producer's home country, is an exception to this. In detail on Article 2 (6a) BADR cf. below p. 162 et seq.

[156] Marceau (1994), p. 12 et seq.

[157] Reymond (2015), p. 110.

[158] Mueller et al. (2009) para. I.18.

[159] Cf. above p. 76 et seq.

[160] Article 21 (1) BADR.

It first serves to recall that one central argument put forward in favour of anti-dumping legislation is the need to ensure fair competition between local and third country producers. Here, the underlying assumption is that competition on the internal market is distorted in favour of the third country producers, which enjoy unfair advantages conferred to them by an advantageous competitive situation on their home markets. Once a finding of injury to the EU industry is made, a separate analysis concerning the effects of dumping on the competitive structure within the internal market is not necessitated: it is the perceived unfairness of a certain behaviour that justifies the imposition of anti-dumping measures, and not the impact of the behaviour on the competitive structure within the EU.[161]

Further, the main purpose of the Union interest test under Article 21 BADR is to decide whether there are compelling reasons to refrain from imposing anti-dumping measures, despite a finding of injury. Hence, the competition assessment carried out by the Commission in the course of an anti-dumping investigation under Article 21 (1) subpara. 2 BADR merely serves as a corrective, which may lead to the non-imposition of anti-dumping measures only in exceptional circumstances. This corrective function of Article 21 BADR likewise speaks against the protection of a certain degree of competition within the internal market being an objective of EU anti-dumping law.

Therefore, despite the wording of the provision indicating otherwise, the main object of the competition assessment under Article 21 (1) subpara. 2 BADR is not the impact of the dumping on the competitive situation on the internal market, but the impact of the imposition of anti-dumping measures. This likewise applies, *mutatis mutandis*, to the Union interest test carried out under Article 31 BASR. The current practice of the CJEU and the Commission[162] and earlier versions of the Union interest test confirm this: under previous versions of the EU trade defence legislation, the Community interest test was expressly designed to ensure that the EU institutions considered the possible negative impact of anti-dumping measures on the economy as a whole and on the processing industry and consumers before imposing any such measures.[163]

4.3.2.3.3 Welfare Standard

As elaborated upon above, the long-term economic rationale behind the imposition of trade defence measures is to prevent exporters from third States from forcing their

---

[161] It serves to recall the statement made by Finger (cf. above p. 93) who held that the relevant benchmark in anti-dumping procedures is not an '*injury to competition*'-standard, but a '*diversion-of-business*'-standard.

[162] For an overview cf. van Bael and Bellis (2019) § 6.02 [F].

[163] Bourgeois and Messerlin (1998), p. 132, referring to Articles 15 (1), 17 (1) of Regulation (EEC) No 459/68 of the Council of 5 April 1968 on protection against dumping or the granting of bounties or subsidies by countries which are not members of the European Economic Community (Chap 1, n 33).

European competitors out of the market by selling at dumped or subsidised prices, taking advantage of benefits they enjoy on their home markets they would not have under normal competitive circumstances and without being more efficient than their EU counterparts. Such a replacement of EU producers by less efficient non-EU producers would lead to reductions in efficiency, countering the long-term economic interests of the EU. If one follows this line of reasoning,[164] the appropriate welfare standard adhered to by trade defence instruments is that of long-term total welfare.[165]

However, as already visible in the fairness-rationale of anti-dumping policy, trade defence legislation places a particular emphasis on protecting the interests of the EU industry. In accordance with this, the EU Courts have expressly affirmed that it is the objective of the anti-dumping rules to protect the European industry from injury resulting from dumping.[166]

Nevertheless, from the early days of trade defence it was agreed that these instruments should be used only if in the overall economic interest.[167] In particular, while the imposition of anti-dumping measures or anti-subsidy measures might disadvantage other economic operators such as the users of the products covered by the measures, the assumption is that, at least in the long term, the elimination of trade distorting effects of injurious dumping and ensuring fair competition on the internal market is also of genuine interest to users.[168] To conclude, using the terminology developed in the previous section on the objectives of EU competition law, trade defence law pursues a total welfare objective. This, however, is best described as a meta-objective, with the core immediate objective of the EU trade defence legislation being the protection of the EU industry against 'unfair' competition from third country producers.

4.3.3   Conclusions

The integration of the EU's common commercial policy into the general framework of the EU's external relations through Articles 3 (5), 21 TEU and Article 205 TFEU also affects the interpretation of concepts that are central in defining and implementing the EU's common commercial policy, most notably the understanding of 'free and fair trade' as set out in Article 3 (5) TEU. Traditionally, the concept of 'fair' trade has been interpreted as referring only to trading practices violating the

---

[164]The lack of economic evidence to support this line of argument has already been presented, cf. above p. 90 et seq.

[165]Juramy (2018), pp. 511, 512; Bienen et al. (2012), p. 31.

[166]*Industrie des poudres sphériques v Council* (n 152) 265; *Banque Indosuez* (16 October 1997) C-177/96 21 (European Court of Justice); Herrmann (2008), p. 1907.

[167]Juramy (2018), p. 512.

[168]Mueller et al. (2009) para. 21.25. Again, economic theory does not support this assumption.

WTO rules on trade, warranting the imposition of trade-restrictive measures. Today, it must be understood as also including aspects of 'ethical' or 'equitable' trade, taking into account matters of environmental protection as well as respect for human rights.

As can already be inferred from Article 3 (5) TEU and its reference to 'free' trade as well as Article 21 (1) lit. e) TEU and Article 206 TFEU, trade liberalisation remains a core objective of the EU's common commercial policy. The use of trade defence instruments is a permissible exception to this commitment to the liberalisation of international trade. Indeed, trade defence legislation is an expression of the conventional understanding of 'fair' trade: here, trading practices are perceived as unfair where the exporting producers benefit from subsidisation by their home States or where they resort to dumping. Consequently, the core policy rationale offered for the imposition of trade defence measures is that they ensure that third country exporters do not gain unjustified competitive advantages compared to their European counterparts due to the competitive situation on their home market, coupled with market segregation between the exporter's home country and the EU internal market. In this sense, trade defence instruments are combatting the negative effects of a lack of market integration, hereby ensuring a 'level playing field' between all competitors on the internal market. The measures are further intended to contribute to long-term societal welfare by preventing welfare losses caused by the forced exit of domestic, more efficient competitors from the market. While this is a frequently offered line of reasoning offered by the advocates of trade defence measures, it must be observed that economic theory does not support this claim. Conversely, trade defence instruments are not intended to ensure the effectiveness of competition on the internal market (despite Article 21 (1) subpara. 2 BADR and Article 31 (1) subpara. 2 BASR indicating otherwise). Ensuring the effectiveness of competition—in the sense of the degree of competition necessary to ensure the functioning of the internal market—is not something to which the trade defence instruments contribute directly.

4.4 Chapter Conclusions

The shared historical roots of the two fields of law find expression in the coincidence of concerns originally fuelling the use of trade defence instruments with those underlying the application of competition law, namely concerns regarding predation and international price discrimination. In spite of these common origins, today, competition and trade defence law pursue decidedly divergent objectives. At first glance, the objectives of trade defence and competition policy still appear to converge to a certain degree: they both aim at promoting the efficient allocation of resources by ensuring that markets are open and competitive. Both policies further share the meta-objective of promoting economic efficiency and welfare through transparent and rule-based regimes, and they also both focus on eliminating barriers to market entry and market distortions.[169] Yet, significant differences between the objectives pursued can be discerned. To some extent, these divergences can be explained by the different spheres competition law and trade defence law are operating in: competition policy is part of the EU's internal policies, trade defence policy forms part of the EU's external relations. For this reason, the objective of anti-dumping legislation to compensate for asymmetries in market access between different countries does not find any equivalent in competition law, as this is an issue specific to international trade. Conversely, while it has been described as competition law's *raison d'être* to contribute to the integration process between the Member States, this cannot be said for trade defence instruments.

It is correct that both competition and trade defence law aim at ensuring fair competition on the internal market. Nonetheless, the importance attached to fairness concerns and the way in which they are integrated in the respective area of law differs. In competition law, fairness concerns are an expression of the social rationale of competition law—namely its contribution to societal welfare. In this sense, fairness concerns find only limited expression in EU competition law. In the instances where this is the case, neither the enforcement authorities nor the EU Courts base their reasoning directly on those fairness considerations. Instead, the concept of fairness is being translated into specific legal standards and tests in order to ensure predictability and legal certainty in the application of EU competition law. Additionally, it is important to note that while fairness concerns are a part of EU competition law, competition law is not enforced with the objective of ensuring 'fair' outcomes. Instead, EU competition law remains focussed on the protection of the competitive process itself, with the ulterior objective of contributing to the market integration objective and to enhance overall societal welfare. It further serves to recall that the verdict of unfairness—as specified by the abovementioned enforcement standards or tests—is not sufficient on its own to constitute a violation of the EU competition norms. Rather, the behaviour in question always has to affect trade between the EU Member States. In conclusion, fairness considerations do certainly play a role in EU competition law, but to a limited extent only.

Opposed to competition law, horizontal fairness—as equality of opportunities between all economic operators—is the principal objective behind trade defence law. Pursuant to the settled jurisprudence of the CJEU, it is the objective of trade defence instruments to prevent the EU industry from suffering injury caused by unfair trading practices of third country exporters.[170] In a parallel to horizontal fairness concerns in EU competition law, trade defence instruments are thus intended to ensure equality of opportunities between economic operators. However, the protection awarded by competition law extends to equally efficient operators only. Anti-dumping law does not make such a distinction. Instead, it is merely assumed that, absent the lack of market integration between the dumping exporting producer's

---

[169] Kennedy (2001), pp. 2–5.

[170] *Industrie des poudres sphériques v Council* (n 152) 265; *Banque Indosuez* (n 166) 21.

home market and the EU, he would not be able to compete efficiently with his EU competitors. Dumping is thus treated as constituting an unfair trading practice *per se.*

Consequently, while competition law and trade defence law are both intended to protect competition, they do so from different angles and do award different levels of protection to competition. These differences again result from the different spheres competition and trade defence law operate in, and in particular from trade defence instruments not contributing to the integration of the Member States' national markets. First, as EU competition law is concerned with anti-competitive practices on the internal market, it can address those competition-distorting practices themselves. Trade defence law, being concerned with international trade, can only make the distortions of competition arising from certain trading practices its focus of action, but it cannot prevent a third country from subsidising its industries, and it can only tackle the preconditions allowing a third-country exporter to dump to a very limited extent. It is for this reason that anti-dumping legislation has been described as an instrument to '*soothe*' the symptoms by limiting certain harmful effects on the domestic industry that result from the market segregation.[171] Second, competition law is concerned with safeguarding a specific degree of competition, with the applicability of the EU competition rules being independent from the degree of injury suffered by the EU industry. Opposed to this, trade defence law is not awarding any specific level of protection to the competitive process itself. Instead, it only seeks to prevent material injury to the Union industry.

Lastly, it has been shown above that both competition and trade-defence law are intended to foster overall societal welfare.[172] Other than in EU competition law, however, and rooted in the object of protection of trade defence instruments being the EU industry, the interests of the latter receive particular attention during anti-dumping and countervailing investigations.

References[173]

Ackermann T et al (2018) Playing by the rules – free and fair trade: editorial. Common Mark Law Rev 55(2):373

Ahlborn C, Padilla AJ (2008) From fairness to welfare: implications for the assessment of unilateral conduct under EC competition law. In: Ehlermann C-D, Marquis M (eds) European competition law annual: a reformed approach to Article 82 EC. Hart

Akman P (2009) Searching for the long-lost Soul of Article 82 EC. Oxford J Legal Stud 29, 267(2)

Albæk S (2013) Consumer welfare in EU competition policy. In: Heide-Jorgensen C et al (eds) Aims and values in competition law. DJØF Publications

---

[171] Müller-Ibold (2018a), p. 550.

[172] That is, if one follows the contested theory according to which trade defence measures prevent the elimination of competitors that are more efficient than the third country exporter, ultimately resulting in a loss of economic resources in the importing country, cf. above p. 90.

[173] All online sources were last accessed on 8 September 2021.

Albors-Llorens A (2002) Competition policy and the shaping of the single market. In: Barnard C, Scott J (eds) The law of the single European market: unpacking the premises. Hart

Bailey D (2018) Competition law and policy in the EU. In: Bailey D, John LE (eds) European union law of competition, 5th edn. Oxford University Press

Barbuto CM (1994) Toward convergence of antitrust and trade law: an international trade analogue to Robinson-Patman. Fordham Law Rev 62(7):2048

Bienen D, Ciuriak D, Picarello T (2012) Motives for using trade defence instruments in the European Union. BKP Trade and Development Discussion Paper 01/2012. Available at <https://www.bkp-development.com/attachments/article/279/BKP_DP_2012-01-Bienen-Ciuriak-Picarello-TDI-Motives.pdf>

Bienen D, Ciuriak D, Picarello T (2013a) Anti-Dumping as Insurance Policy: What the "Grey Area" Measures Tell Us. BKP Trade and Development Discussion Paper 02/2013, Available at <https://www.bkp-development.com/attachments/article/317/BKP_DP_2013-02-Ciuriak-Bienen-Picarello%202013%20-%20Grey_Area_Measures_and_AD.pdf>

Bienen D, Ciuriak D, Picarello T (2013b) 'Trade and Development Discussion Paper: Does Antidumping Address "Unfair" Trade? – The European Union's Experience. BKP Trade and Development Discussion Paper 01/2013. Available at <https://www.bkp-development.com/attachments/article/306/BKP_DP_2013-01-Bienen-Ciuriak-Picarello-Predatory_Dumping-rev.pdf>

Bishop S, Walker M (2007) The economics of EC competition law: concepts, application and measurement, 3rd edn. Sweet & Maxwell

Bourgeois J, Messerlin PA (1998) The European community's experience. In: Lawrence R (ed) Brookings Trade forum. Brookings Institution Press, Washington, DC

Bown CP, McCulloch R (2015) 'Antidumping and market competition: implications for emerging economies', EUI Working Papers RCAS. Available at <https://cadmus.eui.eu/bitstream/handle/1814/37522/RSCAS_2015_76.pdf?sequence=1>

Chiriță AD (2010) Undistorted, (Un)fair competition, consumer welfare and the interpretation of Article 102 TFEU. World Compet Law Econ Rev 33(3):417

Cho S (2009) Anticompetitive trade remedies: how antidumping measures obstruct market competition. North Carolina Law Rev 87(2):357

Conrad C (2002) Dumping and anti-dumping measures from a competition and allocation perspective. J World Trade 36(3):563

Coppens D (2014) WTO disciplines on subsidies and countervailing measures: balancing policy space and legal constraints. Cambridge University Press

Cremona M (2011) Values in EU foreign policy. In: Evans MD, Koutrakos P (eds) Beyond the established legal orders: policy interconnections between the EU and the rest of the world. Hart

Cremona M (2017a) A quiet revolution: the changing nature of the EU's common commercial policy. In: Bungenberg M and others (eds) European yearbook of international economic law 2017. Springer

Cremona M (2017b) The internal market and external economic relations. In: Koutrakos P, Snell J (eds) Research handbook on the law of the EU's internal market. Edward Elgar Publishing Ltd

Cremona M (2018) Shaping EU trade policy post-Lisbon: Opinion 2/15 of 16 May 2017. Eur Const Law Rev 14(1):231

Cremona M, Marín Durán G (2013) Fair trade in the European Union: regulatory and institutional aspects. In: Granville B, Dine J (eds) The processes and practices of fair trade: trust, ethics, and governance. Routledge

de Waele H (2017) Legal dynamics of EU external relations: dissecting a layered global player, 2nd edn. Springer

Dimopoulos A (2010) The effects of the Lisbon treaty on the principles and objectives of the common commercial policy. Eur Foreign Aff Rev 15(2):153

Dolmans M, Lin W (2017) Fairness and competition: a fairness paradox. Concurrences 4

Drexl J, Kerber W, Podszun R (eds) (2011) Competition policy and the economic approach: foundations and limitations. Edward Elgar Publishing Ltd

Ducci F, Trebilcock M (2019) The revival of fairness discourse in competition policy. Anti Bull 64(1):79

Egelund Olsen B (2012) Introduction. In: Egelund Olsen B, Steinicke M, Sørensen KE (eds) WTO law: from a European perspective. Wolters Kluwer

Ehlermann C-D, Marquis M (eds) (2008) European competition law annual: a reformed approach to Article 82 EC. Hart

Ezrachi A (2018, June 6) The goals of EU competition law and the digital economy. Oxford Legal Studies Research Paper 17/2018, Available at <https://papers.ssrn.com/sol3/papers.cfm?abstract_id=3191766>

Finger JM (1992) Dumping and antidumping: the rhetoric and the reality of protection in industrial countries. World Bank Res Observer 7(2):121

Forrester IS (2004) Article 82: remedies in search of theories? Fordham Int Law J 28(4):919

Gerard D (2018) Fairness in EU competition policy: significance and implications. J Eur Compet Law Pract 9(4):211

Gerber DJ (2008) The objectives of competition policy: protecting consumers, protecting the competitive process, fostering efficiency?: efficiency versus fairness: how relevant remains ordoliberalism?. In: Ehlermann C-D, Marquis M (eds) European competition law annual: a reformed approach to Article 82 EC. Hart

Glick M (2018) The unsound theory behind the consumer (and total) welfare goal in antitrust. Anti Bull 63(4):455

Heide-Jorgensen C (2013) The relationship between Article 101 (1) TFEU and Article 101 (3) TFEU. In: Heide-Jorgensen C and others (eds) Aims and values in competition law. DJØF Publications

Herrmann C (2008) Welthandelsorganisation (WTO). In: Terhechte J (ed) Internationales Kartell- und Fusionskontrollverfahrensrecht. Gieseking Buchverlag

Herrmann C, Streinz R (2014) Die Europäische Union als Mitglied der WTO. In: von Arnauld A (ed) Europäische Außenbeziehungen. Nomos

Hoekman BM, Mavroidis PC (1996) Dumping, antidumping and antitrust. J World Trade 30(1):27

Ibáñez Colomo P (2016) Article 101 TFEU and market integration. J Compet Law Econ 12(4):749

Immenga U, Mestmäcker E-J (2019) Einleitung. In: Immenga U, Mestmäcker E-J (eds) Wettbewerbsrecht: Band 1: Europäisches Kartellrecht, 6th edn. C.H. Beck

Jakob T, Müller W, Schultheiß C (2014) Vorb. Art. 101-109 AEUV. In: Schröter H and others (eds) Europäisches Wettbewerbsrecht, 2nd edn. Nomos

Jaremba U (2020) Non-economic values and objectives in EU trade policy: different models of externalization and enforcement. In: Weiß W, Furculita C (eds) Global politics and EU trade policy: facing the challenges to a multilateral approach. Springer

Jones A, Sufrin B, Dunne N (2019) EU competition law, 7th edn. Oxford University Press

Juramy H (2018) Anti-dumping in Europe: what about us(ers)? Global Trade Cust J 13(11):511

Kennedy KC (2001) Competition law and the World Trade Organisation: the limits of multilateralism. Sweet & Maxwell

Ketterer TD (2018) Anti-dumping use and its effect on trade liberalisation. Evidence for the European Union. World Econ 41(4):1111

Kokott J, Dittert D (2018) Das Konzept der Fairness im europäischen Wettbewerbsrecht. In: Kokott J, Pohlmann P, Polley R (eds) Europäisches, Deutsches und Internationales Kartellrecht: Festschrift für Dirk Schroeder zum 65. Geburtstag. Dr. Otto Schmidt

Korkea-Aho E, Sankari S (2017) External participants v. internal interests: principles of EU administrative law in anti-dumping investigations. Eur Pap 2(2):543

Koutrakos P (2015) EU international relations law, 2nd edn. Hart Publishing

Krajewski M (2012) The reform of the common commercial policy. In: Biondi A, Eeckhout P, Ripley S (eds) EU law after Lisbon. Oxford University Press, Oxford

Kuplewatzky N (2018) Defining anti-dumping duties under European Union law. Trade Law Dev 10(2):448

Larik J (2011) Much more than trade: the common commercial policy in a global context. In: Evans MD, Koutrakos P (eds) Beyond the established legal orders: policy interconnections between the EU and the rest of the world. Hart

Lianos I (2013) Some Reflections on the Question of the Goals of EU Competition Law. CLES Working Paper Series. Available at <https://papers.ssrn.com/sol3/papers.cfm?abstract_id=223 5875>

Lloyd PJ (2005) Anti-dumping and competition law. In: Macrory P, Appleton A, Plummer M (eds) The World Trade organization: legal, economic and political analysis, vol II. Springer Science and Business Media

Lurger B (2018) Artikel 173 AEUV. In: Streinz R (ed) EUV/AEUV, 3rd edn. C.H. Beck

Macrory P, Appleton A, Plummer M (eds) (2005) The World Trade Organization: legal, economic and political analysis, vol I. Springer Science and Business Media

Marceau G (1994) Anti-dumping and anti-trust issues in free trade areas. Clarendon Press

Marco Colino S (2019) The Antitrust F Word: fairness considerations in competition law. J Bus Law 5:329

Massarotto G (2018) From standard oil to Google: how the role of antitrust law has changed. World Compet 41(3):395

Mavroidis PC (2016) The regulation of international trade: vol I. GATT MIT Press

Melamed D, Petit N (2019) The misguided assault on the consumer welfare standard in the age of platform markets. Rev Ind Organ 54(4):741

Mestmäcker E-J (1994) On the legitimacy of European law. Rabels Zeitschrift für ausländisches und internationales Privatrecht 58(4):615

Monti G (2007) EC competition law. Cambridge University Press

Mueller W, Khan N, Scharf T (2009) EC and WTO anti-dumping Law: a handbook, 2nd edn. Oxford University Press

Müller-Ibold T (2018a) Antidumping and competition law – common origin, a life of their own and peaceful coexistence?. In: Kokott J, Pohlmann P, Polley R (eds) Europäisches, Deutsches und Internationales Kartellrecht: Festschrift für Dirk Schroeder zum 65. Geburtstag. Dr. Otto Schmidt

Müller-Ibold T (2018b) EU trade defence instruments and free trade agreements. In: Bungenberg M and others (eds) The future of trade defence instruments – global policy trends and legal challenges. Springer

Nazzini R (2011) The foundations of European competition law: the objectives and principles of Article 102. Oxford University Press

Parret L (2012) The multiple personalities of EU competition law: time for a comprehensive debate on its objectives. In: Zimmer D (ed) The goals of competition law. Edward Elgar Publishing Ltd

Peretz G, Mackersie D (2018) State aids. In: Bailey D, John LE (eds) European Union law of competition, 5th edn. Oxford University Press

Petit N (2013) The future of the Court of Justice in EU competition law. In: Court of Justice of the European Union (ed) The Court of Justice and the Construction of Europe: analyses and perspectives on sixty years of case-law: La Cour de Justice et la Construction de l'Europe: Analyses et Perspectives de Soixante Ans de Jurisprudence. Asser Press

Prawitz C, Kasteng J (2013) Effects on Trade and Competition of Abolishing Anti-Dumping Measures: The European Union Experience. Available at <https://unctad.org/system/files/non-official-document/ditc_ted_03042014Kommerskollegium2.pdf>

Reymond D (2015) Action antidumping et droit de la concurrence dans l'Union européenne. Dissertation, Panthéon-Assas

Rusche M (2019) Article 107 TFEU. In: Kellerbauer M, Klamert M, Tomkin J (eds) The EU treaties and the charter of fundamental rights. Oxford University Press, Oxford

Sandkamp A-N (2018) The Trade Effects of Antidumping Duties: Evidence from the 2004 EU Enlargement. IFO Working Papers, available at <https://www.ifo.de/DocDL/wp-2018-261-sandkamp-antidumping-duties-eu.pdf>

Schaub A (1998) Competition policy objectives. In: Ehlermann C-D, Laudati L (eds) European competition law annual 1997: The objectives of competition policy. Hart

Schweitzer H, Patel KK (2012) EU competition law in historical context: continuity and change. In: Schweitzer H, Patel KK (eds) The historical foundations of EU competition law. Oxford University Press

Shin HJ (1998) Possible instances of predatory pricing in recent U.S. antidumping cases. In: Lawrence R (ed) Brookings Trade Forum. Brookings Institution Press

Sykes AO (2003) The Economics of WTO Rules on Subsidies and Countervailing Measures', Coase-Sandor Working Paper Series in Law and Economics, Available at <https://chicagounbound.uchicago.edu/cgi/viewcontent.cgi?article=1515&context=law_and_economics>

Sykes AO, Cooper RN (1998) Antidumping and antitrust: what problems does each address? In: Lawrence R (ed) Brookings Trade Forum. Brookings Institution Press

Tavares de Araujo Jr. J (2002) Legal and economic interfaces between antidumping and competition policy. World Compet 25(2):159

Tharakan PKM (1995) Political economy and contingent protection. Econ J 105(433):1550

van Bael I, Bellis J-F (2019) EU anti-dumping and other trade defence instruments, 6th edn. Kluwer Law International

van den Bossche P, Zdouc W (2017) The law and policy of the World Trade Organization: text, cases and materials, 4th edn. Cambridge University Press

van Rompuy B (2012) Economic efficiency: the sole concern of modern antitrust policy?: Non-efficiency considerations unter Article 101 TFEU. Kluwer Law International

Vedder C (2013) Linkage of the common commercial policy to the general objectives for the Union's external action. In: Bungenberg M, Herrmann C (eds) Common commercial policy after lisbon. Springer

Viner J (1923) Dumping: a problem in international trade (re-print 1996). Kelley

Wegener Jessen P (2012) Anti-Dumping. In: Egelund Olsen B, Steinicke M, Sørensen KE (eds) WTO law: from a European perspective. Wolters Kluwer

Weiß W (2014) Vertragliche Handelspolitik der EU. In: von Arnauld A (ed) Europäische Außenbeziehungen. Nomos

Weiß W (2015a) Artikel 206 AEUV. In: Grabitz E, Hilf M, Nettesheim M (eds) Das Recht der Europäischen Union. C.H. Beck

Weiß W (2015b) Artikel 207 AEUV. In: Grabitz E, Hilf M, Nettesheim M (eds) Das Recht der Europäischen Union. C.H. Beck

Whish R, Bailey D (2018) Competition law, 9th edn. Oxford University Press

Willig RD (1998) Economic effects of antidumping policy. In: Lawrence R (ed) Brookings Trade Forum. Brookings Institution Press

Wils WPJ (2014) The Judgment of the EU General Court in Intel and the so-called more economic approach to abuse of dominance. World Compet 37:405

Witt A (2016) The more economic approach to EU antitrust law. Hart

Zimmer D (2008) On fairness and welfare: the objectives of competition policy. In: Ehlermann C-D, Marquis M (eds) European competition law annual: A reformed approach to Article 82 EC. Hart

Zimmer D (2012) The basic goal of competition law: to protect the opposite side of the market. In: Zimmer D (ed) The goals of competition law. Edward Elgar Publishing Ltd

Chapter 5
Terminological Overlaps and Conceptual Differences in the Concepts Used in EU Competition and Trade Defence Law

5.1 Introduction

As can already be derived from the introduction to the legal framework on trade defence and competition in the EU, a number of concepts are used in anti-dumping and countervailing procedures as well as in proceedings assessing possible violations of the competition rules. In practice however, the content of these concepts differs significantly. While trade defence and competition law recognise the concept of 'markets', market definition is undertaken on the basis of different criteria and for different reasons. Likewise, whereas the concept of dumping is recognised in both areas of law, it is used to denote different behaviour in EU trade defence and competition law. This also applies to the circumstances under which geographical price discrimination is deemed impermissible. Furthermore, even though the addressees of legal action taken by the EU institutions in the two areas of law are undertakings, competition and trade defence vary concerning the preconditions under which an undertaking may fall within the scope of the competition or trade defence rules respectively. In particular, EU trade defence legislation usually will not require for an exporting producer—or a group of exporting producers—to possess a certain degree of market power or to collude. This section explores these criteria with a view to the disparities in the objectives pursued by the respective legal order. It concludes by presenting the standards used to identify pricing practices considered objectionable under EU competition and anti-dumping law. As this is an issue specific to anti-dumping law, the basic anti-subsidy regulation will not be addressed in this last part of the analysis.

5.2 Differences Concerning Market Definition

Even though anti-dumping, anti-subsidy and competition rules all mention the concept of 'markets', its precise meaning and content differs.

In competition law, market definition plays a central role. Here, the notion of 'market' is usually used within the context of defining the 'market concerned', i.e. the market on which the potentially anticompetitive conduct takes place. In contrast, while the basic regulations also reference the term 'market', the competition law concept of the 'market concerned' does not appear in anti-dumping or countervailing legislation. Nonetheless, the application of the trade defence rules does depend on defining the product concerned—the product under investigation—and the like products.[1] Defining the substantive side of the market, i.e. product definition, is also a central part of the competition assessment carried out under the EU competition rules. Likewise, in another parallel to competition law, the application of the anti-dumping and anti-subsidy rules involves an assessment concerning the geographic area in which the dumping or the subsidisation takes place respectively and produces its effects.

As a preliminary remark, it should be noted that the Commission—as the institution responsible for market definition in competition and trade defence law—enjoys a wide margin of appreciation in both areas of law, since market definition entails an analysis of a complex economic situation. Judicial review of its market definition is therefore limited to assessing whether it based its findings on materially incorrect facts, or the assessment is vitiated by an error of law, manifest error of appraisal or misuse of powers.[2]

5.2.1 The Relevant Product Market

While market definition is relevant in both areas of law, the competition and trade defence rules go about defining the product market in different manners. One prominent example of this is the *Extramet* affair, in which parallel anti-dumping and antitrust investigations were being carried out. In the anti-dumping investigation, the EU institutions concluded that the 'product concerned' was primary calcium metal.[3] By contrast, in the proceedings relating to a possible violation of Article 102 TFEU, the Commission held there to be two separate product markets,

---

[1] In addition, it has also to be determined whether the product exported and the product sold on the exporter's home market are 'like', cf. above pp. 55 et seq.

[2] For competition law cf. *Confédération européenne des associations d'horlogers-réparateurs (CEAHR) v Commission* (15 December 2010) T-427/08 65–66 (General Court); for anti-dumping law cf. *Industrie des poudres sphériques v Council* (n 152 in Chap. 4) 204–205.

[3] Council Regulation (EC) 2557/94 of 19 October 1994 imposing a definitive anti-dumping duty on imports of calcium metal originating in the People's Republic of China and Russia recital 6.

even though the product in question was also primary calcium metal.[4] The following section intends to illustrate the differences in the criteria used for the product definition which ultimately lead to divergent results such as those of the *Extramet* case.

In anti-dumping law, the 'product concerned' and consequently also the 'like' product are defined mainly by having regard to their basic physical, technical or chemical characteristics. As the basic regulations prescribe that products only have to share the same basic characteristics, smaller and/or insignificant differences in their characteristics do not prevent them from being considered to belong to the 'product concerned'. Likewise, differences in the quality of products are irrelevant as long as they share the same basic characteristics and as long as the differences in quality do not lead to the products being put to different uses. In contrast, whether the products are interchangeable from the consumers' point of view or whether they are put to the same use are only secondary criteria in determining whether a product falls within the category of the 'product concerned'.[5] The same applies with regard to product definition in anti-subsidy investigations. In competition law on the other hand, the Commission routinely defines the relevant product market with a view to the demand substitutability, i.e. whether certain products, with respect to their characteristics, are particularly suitable for satisfying the consumers' needs and are only to a limited extent interchangeable with other products.[6] Here, the physical characteristics and the uses of the product merely serve as a starting point in determining the interchangeability of the products in question.

Moreover, according to the settled case-law of the Court, the competitive conditions on the market and the supply and demand structure must likewise be taken into consideration in order to arrive at a viable assessment as to the substitutability of products, and hence also regarding the competitive constraints a firm faces.[7] The question of interchangeability between the products thus is not merely an additive, facultative element of defining the product market in competition cases, but of an obligatory character. As just shown, this demand-side orientated concept of market definition does not have any equivalent in trade defence law. Instead, due to the facultative nature of the questions of interchangeability and consumer perception in defining the product concerned under EU anti-dumping law, its product definitions are usually wider than the scope of the product market in competition law.[8]

---

[4]Namely the upstream market of primary calcium metal and the downstream market for broken calcium metal, cf. *Industrie des poudres sphériques v Commission* (30 November 2000) T-5/97 (Court of First Instance).

[5]Cf. above p. 54 et seq.

[6]*Hilti AG v Commission* (n 74 in Chap. 3) 8, 11–14; *NV Nederlandsche Banden Industrie Michelin v Commission (Michelin I)* (n 27 in Chap. 3) 37.

[7]Cf. the jurisprudence cited above, n 43 in Chap. 3.

[8]Cf. the *Extramet* affair mentioned above (n 3 and n 4) and Commission Decision of 22 December 1987 relating to a proceeding under Article 85 of EEC (IV/32.306—Olivetti/Canon) (88/88/EEC) recital 34. Vandenbussche and Wauthy argue that this might disadvantage European firms through reversals of quality ranking, Vandenbussche and Wauthy (2001), p. 101.

This disparity can be explained by the different functions of market definition in competition and trade defence law: in competition law, market definition is a tool to identify the competitive constraints an undertaking faces in its business operations, which in turn may prevent it from adopting conduct which is detrimental to competition on the internal market.[9] For this reason, competition law requires the needs of the other market participants to be taken into account when defining the product market. On the other hand, in trade defence law, market definition is not intended to assess any competitive constraints but rather only to delineate the scope of the possible investigation and consequently also the products covered by the anti-dumping measures.[10] For this reason, market definition in anti-dumping law is not concerned with the questions of demand-side or supply-side substitution.[11] The Commission's stance—or more precisely, DG TRADE—in *Tyres* is illustrative in this regard. Here, one interested party had advanced that a previous CJEU judgment[12] and a decision by DG COMP[13] in the field of merger control according to which the market for retreated tyres was a separate product market from the market for new tyres were also relevant for the product definition in the anti-dumping investigation. However, DG TRADE considered the judgment and the decision by DG COMP to be irrelevant as market definition in a merger case focuses on demand-side and supply-side substitution whereas in an anti-dumping investigation, the market is defined by the physical, technical and chemical characteristics of the product concerned.[14] Again, the same applies for product definition in the course of anti-subsidy proceedings.

On a more abstract level, the different purposes of market definition in competition law and trade defence law can be explained by the different objectives pursued by the respective area of law: competition law aims to promote the market integration objective by protecting a competitive market structure. To a certain extent, it is concerned with the protection of the competitive process as such. Opposed to this,

---

[9]Cf. above p. 43.

[10]*Brosmann Footwear (HK) Ltd. and others v Council* (n 108 in Chap. 3) 131.

[11]In *Cold Rolled Flat Products*, the Commission held that the market definition in a merger case is irrelevant in defining the 'product concerned' in an anti-dumping investigation as the criteria examined in merger cases to define the market go far beyond those examined for the product concerned definition. In particular, the market definition in an anti-dumping case is defined by the physical characteristics of the product concerned and not the demand-side and supply-side substitution, Commission Implementing Regulation (EU) 2015/1429 of 26 August 2015 imposing a definitive anti-dumping duty on imports of stainless steel cold-rolled flat products originating in the People's Republic of China and Taiwan recitals 16–18.

[12]*NV Nederlandsche Banden Industrie Michelin v Commission (Michelin I)* (n 27 in Chap. 3) 32 et seq.

[13]European Commission, 'Case No COMP/M.4564—Bridgestone/Bandag' (Brussels 29 May 2007).

[14]Commission Regulation (EU) 2018/683 of 4 May 2018 imposing a provisional anti-dumping duty on imports of certain pneumatic tyres, new or retreaded, of rubber, of a kind used for buses or lorries, with a load index exceeding 121 originating in the People's Republic of China, and amending Implementing Regulation (EU) 2018/163 recital 79.

neither anti-dumping nor anti-subsidy measures are aimed at ensuring the existence of a certain degree of competition on the internal market. Instead, they are intended to combat the negative effects of 'unfair' trading practices on the internal market, thereby preventing injury to the European industry.[15] For these reasons, transposing the criteria used in one area of law to the other would run counter to the attainment of the objectives they pursue. In particular, transferring the criteria used to define the market in competition law to the area of trade defence would entail the risk of overly narrow market definitions in the area of anti-dumping. On the one hand, such an overly narrow market definition would be disadvantageous to the exporters, as it would be comparatively easier to find injury for a small product segment although the domestic industry is overall in a healthy state. On the other hand, it would be disadvantageous to the Union industry, as it would make the anti-dumping measures prone to circumvention.[16] Other risks of an overly narrow market definition, depending on the facts of the case, include a bias towards a finding of dumping or inflated dumping margins.[17] Identical concerns can be put forward considering the transposition of competition law criteria for product definition to anti-subsidy proceedings. It is for these reasons that the methods employed in EU competition law to define the relevant product market differ from those used to define the 'product concerned' and the 'like product' in the course of anti-dumping and anti-subsidy proceedings.

5.2.2 The Relevant Geographic Market

In competition law, market definition also requires the delineation of the relevant geographical market in order to identify the area in which the potentially anticompetitive conduct takes place. Just as it is the case for the relevant product market, defining the geographic market helps to identify the firms which impose a competitive constraint on the firm(s) under investigation.[18] Again, the SSNIP test is a key element in defining the geographic aspect of the market based on the supply and demand-side substitutability. The size of the geographic market varies from a local[19] to a global[20] scale.

---

[15] On the differences in the objectives of the two areas of law cf. Chap. 4, pp. 69 et seq.

[16] Mueller et al. (2009), para. 1.32.

[17] Reymond (2015), p. 203. It must be noted that, depending on the circumstances of the case, the market definition applied under competition law could also be wider than it is under anti-dumping law, Mueller et al. (2009), para. I.32.

[18] Cf. the sources cited above, n 46 in Chap. 3; Hoekman and Mavroidis (1996), p. 49.

[19] Cf. e.g. *Société alsacienne et lorraine de télécommunications et d'électronique (Alsatel) v SA Novasam* (5 October 1988) C-247/86 16–18 (European Court of Justice).

[20] Cf. e.g. Commission Decision of 24 May 2004 relating to a proceeding under Article 82 of the EC Treaty (Case COMP/C-3/37.792 Microsoft (C(2004)900 final) recital 427.

While proceedings concerning the violation of EU competition law usually only entail identifying one geographical market, namely the area in which the potentially anti-competitive conduct takes place, trade defence cases concern two separate geographical markets in the sense of two separate geographic areas with different conditions of competition: the internal market of the European Union and the exporter's home market.[21] Contrary to competition law, a precise delineation of the geographic market is not undertaken, neither regarding the internal market nor the exporter's home market.[22] Instead, the boundaries between the markets are equated with the national borders of the exporter's home country and the EU internal market respectively.[23] This has led commentators to conclude that the geographic market in anti-dumping law is of a political nature, opposed to the economic criteria used in delineating the borders of the geographic market in competition law.[24]

This is again a consequence of the different reasons for which market definition is undertaken in trade defence and competition law. In particular, defining the geographic market in anti-dumping and anti-subsidy law is not intended to identify competitive restraints to an undertaking's business operations. Instead, it is a factual precondition for identifying the exports which are causing injury to the Union industry and hence also for setting out the scope of the anti-dumping measures. While the first requires a precise definition of the geographic market by examining whether the competitive conditions in a certain area are sufficiently homogeneous, the second one does not. At this point, it serves to recall anti-dumping's core policy *ratio* according to which anti-dumping legislation is necessary in order to compensate for the lack of market integration between two trading economies,[25] i.e. for the heterogeneity in competitive conditions, in particular concerning market access. This leads to what is in effect a legal presumption as to the heterogeneity of competitive conditions in the exporter's home market and the EU internal market,[26] making a precise delineation of the geographic scope of the market superfluous. This also applies with regard to anti-subsidy proceedings, where the heterogeneity in competitive conditions can be inferred from the fact that the foreign government is granting subsidies to select companies.

---

[21] Reymond (2015), p. 187.

[22] Instead, as a rule, the geographic scope of the market extends to the whole territory of the European Union, with the exception being regional cases pursuant to Article 4 (1) lit. b) BADR.

[23] The exception again being regional cases, Article 4 (1) lit. b) BADR.

[24] Reymond (2015), p. 206.

[25] Cf. above p. 92.

[26] Reymond (2015), p. 207.

5.3   Differences Concerning the Authors of Practices Falling Within the Scope of EU Competition and Trade Defence Law

5.3.1   No Coordination Between the Exporters Required

Opposed to Article 101 TFEU, anti-dumping law does not require an element of collusion among the exporters. Neither does it set out certain elements concerning a connection between them that have to be fulfilled in order for the exporters to fall within the scope of an anti-dumping investigation, such as it would be the case for a finding of collective dominance under Article 102 TFEU. Put simply: anti-dumping law generally does not care whether the dumping exporters are acting jointly or separately. The mere fact that they all export the dumped product is sufficient for all of their exports to be included in the anti-dumping investigation. The same can be said for exporting producers of subsidised products. Compared to this collective assessment of the imported products, EU competition law focusses on the undertakings, and analyses the existence of specific links or collusion between them. This divergence can likewise be explained by the different objectives of the respective area of law: where competition law requires a certain form of connection between the undertakings, it is because these linkages are deemed to be detrimental to the competitive structure within the EU: either because the collusion itself is potentially harmful to competition (as it is the case under Article 101 TFEU) or because, by acting jointly, undertakings are being put in a position which enables them to act in certain ways which are considered harmful to the competitive structure (as it is the case concerning collective dominance under Article 102 TFEU). Opposed to this, trade defence law is not concerned with safeguarding the competitive structure on the internal market, but primarily with preventing injury to the European industry. As long as the exporting producers are all resorting to dumping, or trading subsidised products, thereby adding to the injury of the EU industry, the question of whether exporters are acting jointly or not does not influence the verdict of unfairness. This corresponds to the jurisprudence of the CJEU according to which anti-dumping proceedings do not concern the products of specific undertakings but all imports of a certain category of products from a third country.[27] In addition, it can be argued that, to a certain extent, competition law also serves to protect the economic freedom of market actors,[28] which on the one hand calls for a prohibition of certain practices

---

[27] *Since Hardware (Guangzhou) Co. Ltd. v Council* (18 September 2012) T-156/11 65 (General Court). This also explains why in some instances, where imports of a product from more than country are simultaneously subject to anti-dumping investigations, their effects on the Union industry are being assessed cumulatively, Article 3 (4) BADR. Again, the rationale here is that if the circumstances laid out in Article 3 (4) BADR are fulfilled, the exports contribute to the EU injury in a comparable way, which justifies them being assessed together, without the exporters being required to act jointly.

[28] Ramírez Pérez and van de Scheur (2012); Gormsen (2007), p. 329.

unduly restricting said economic freedom. On the other hand, it requires an individual assessment of each potentially anticompetitive practice. It is therefore necessary to weigh the economic rights of the parties involved. Such a requirement does not exist under the rationale of the BADR or the BASR. Rather, it considers the interests of the EU industry as *per se* worthy of protection *vis-à-vis* the dumping exporters.

In some instances, the basic regulations do take account of connections between undertakings. Under the regime of the BADR, where parties appear to be associated or to have a compensatory arrangement with each other, the prices between them may not be used to establish normal value[29] or the export price.[30] Similarly, where EU producers are related to the exporters or importers, or are themselves importers of the allegedly dumped or subsidised product, they may be excluded from the definition of the Union industry both in anti-dumping and countervailing proceedings.[31] However, in these instances, the point in question is not whether a certain practice is apprehended by the basic regulations, but only to assure a certain precision in determining the dumping margin and the injury respectively in order to guarantee the attainment of the objective of the EU's trade defence instruments: alleviating the injury of the EU industry caused by the presence of dumped or subsidised imports on the internal market. Lastly, in parallel to the practice of not determining individual dumping margins for related exporters,[32] the EU trade defence legislation does not require individual duty rates to be set for related exporters. This is done in order to ensure the efficiency of measures, as the imposition of individual dumping margins—or duties—may enable related exporting producers to channel their exports to the EU through the company with the lowest individual duty margin, thus rendering the measures ineffective.[33] In a similar vein, imported products produced by any other company not specifically mentioned in the operative part of an implementing regulation, including entities related to those specifically mentioned, cannot benefit from individual duty rates and are subject to the—higher—duty rate applicable to 'all other companies'.[34]

---

[29] Article 2 (1) subpara. 3 BADR.

[30] Article 2 (9) subpara. 1 BADR.

[31] Article 4 (1) lit. a) BADR and Article 9 (1) lit. a) BASR.

[32] This is not prescribed by the BADR, but done on a regular basis, cf. e.g. Commission Regulation (EC) 2005/2006 of 22 December 2006 imposing provisional anti-dumping duties on imports of synthetic staple fibres of polyesters (PSF) originating in Malaysia and Taiwan recitals 33-34; Council Regulation (EC) 2962/95 of 18 December 1995 repealing Regulations (EEC) No 868/90 and (EEC) No 898/91 imposing definitive anti-dumping duties on imports of certain welded tubes, of iron or non-alloy steel, originating in Yugoslavia except Serbia and Montenegro and Romania, and in Turkey and Venezuela respectively recital 39. For the BASR cf. e.g. Council Regulation (EC) No 74/2004 of 13 January 2004 imposing a definitive countervailing duty on imports of cotton-type bedlinen originating in India recital 210.

[33] Explicitly on anti-dumping measures: Commission Regulation (EC) 2005/2006 of 22 December 2006 imposing provisional anti-dumping duties on imports of synthetic staple fibres of polyesters (PSF) originating in Malaysia and Taiwan (n 32) recital 33.

[34] Cf. e.g. Commission Implementing Regulation (EU) 2019/244 of 11 February 2019 imposing a definitive countervailing duty on imports of biodiesel originating in Argentina recital 510; for anti-

5.3.2 No Market Power of the Exporters Required

In competition law, the market power of the undertakings involved in a potentially anti-competitive practice frequently plays a decisive role. For example, under Article 101 TFEU, certain 'by effect'-restrictions to competition may not be considered to cause an appreciable effect on competition due to a lack of market power of the parties involved[35] and a firm[36] must hold a dominant position on the internal market in order for its practices to be scrutinised under Article 102 TFEU to begin with. Similarly, when assessing a merger under the EUMR, the positions of the merging parties are analysed with a view as to whether them merging would create or reinforce a dominant position on the market, enabling them to significantly impede effective competition.[37] With the exception of 'by object'-restrictions under Article 101 TFEU,[38] it is hence assumed that companies have to possess a certain degree of market power in order to be able to negatively impact the competitive structure on the internal market. The same applies with regard to an appreciable effect on trade between the Member States being required for a practice to be caught by Article 101 TFEU or Article 102 TFEU. Appreciability can be appraised in particular by reference to the position and the importance of the relevant undertakings on the market for the products concerned.[39] In all areas of competition law, the market shares of the undertakings are a frequently used indicator for assessing an undertaking's market power.[40] These requirements concerning the market power of firms are once more an outflow of the objectives of competition law: safeguarding the competitive structure and ensuring the success of the internal market by preventing the re-erection of barriers to trade by private undertakings. Both of these objectives are only endangered by actions of undertakings that can potentially hamper their attainment, i.e. undertakings that possess a certain degree of market power.

---

dumping duties cf. Commission Implementing Regulation (EU) 2019/915 of 4 June 2019 imposing a definitive anti-dumping duty on imports of certain aluminium foil in rolls originating in the People's Republic of China following an expiry review under Article 11(2) of Regulation (EU) 2016/1036 of the European Parliament and of the Council recital 250.

[35] European Commission, 'Notice on agreements of minor importance which do not appreciably restrict competition under Article 101(1) of the Treaty on the Functioning of the European Union' (n 19 in Chap. 3).

[36] Or a multitude of firms acting jointly, cf. above p. 46.

[37] European Commission, 'Guidelines on the assessment of horizontal mergers under the Council Regulation on the control of concentrations between undertakings (2004/C 31/03)' para. 2.

[38] Due to their nature, 'by object'-restrictions are presumed to have a negative effect on competition *per se*, cf. above p. 39.

[39] Cf. e.g. *Javico International v Yves Saint Laurent Parfums* (n 17 in Chap. 3) 17.

[40] However, market shares are not the only instrument for examining the existence of market power, in particular as their importance may vary depending on the structure and characteristics of the market, cf. above p. 46.

In contrast, the BADR does not require the exporting producers to have a certain degree of market power.[41] On the contrary, an anti-dumping proceeding may already be initiated against countries whose imports represent a market share of at least 1%, unless such countries collectively account for 3% or more of Union consumption, in the case of which proceedings may also be initiated if their market share is below 1%.[42] Instead of focussing on the market power held by the exporters, EU anti-dumping law concentrates on the question of whether their imports are causing or threatening to cause material injury to the Union industry. The determination of injury is based on an examination of the volume of the dumped imports and the effect of the dumped imports on prices in the Union for like products, and the consequent impact of those imports on the Union industry. If the imports do not reach the threshold set out above, the injury shall normally be regarded as negligible.[43] This can again be explained by the fact that the BADR is not concerned with single producers, but with imports of a certain category of products from a third country,[44] and the injury they may cause to the Union industry. Neither of these considerations requires for the third country producers to have a certain degree of market power. A similar picture presents itself in countervailing proceedings, where the volume of subsidised imports likewise has to surpass a market share of 1%, unless such countries collectively account for 3% or more of Union consumption.[45] Again, if the imports do not reach the threshold set out above, the injury shall normally be regarded as negligible.[46]

Comparisons have been made with the low degree of market power—or rather the absence thereof—required by the BADR and a situation as described by the CJEU in the competition law case *Henninger Bräu*.[47] Here, the Court held that agreements between undertakings might violate Article 101 TFEU even if the market shares of the companies involved are comparatively low as long as there is a certain degree of market concentration and the agreement forms part of a series of similar contracts leading to a risk of market foreclosure.[48] The comparison is fitting insofar as a

---

[41] Arguing for the introduction of a dominance-criterion in anti-dumping law: Hoekman and Mavroidis (1996), p. 48.

[42] Article 5 (7) BADR.

[43] Article 9 (3) BADR (on the termination without measures; imposition of definitive duties) reads '*injury shall normally be regarded as negligible where the imports concerned represent less than the volumes set out in Article 5 (7) BADR*'.

[44] Cf. the sources cited above, n 27.

[45] Article 10 (9) BASR.

[46] Article 14 (4) BASR. In another difference to the BADR, Article 14 (4) BASR sets a different threshold for developing countries: here, the volume of subsidised imports shall also be considered negligible if it represents less than 4% of the total imports of the like product in the Union, unless imports from developing countries whose individual shares of total imports represent less than 4% collectively account for more than 9% of the total imports of the like product in the Union.

[47] Reymond (2015), p. 231.

[48] *Stergios Delimitis v Henninger Bräu AG* (28 February 1991) C-234/89 17–29 (European Court of Justice); European Commission, 'Notice on agreements of minor importance which do not

situation described in *Henninger Bräu* also takes account of the cumulative effect of a number of undertakings behaving in a similar manner, without examining whether there is any degree of coordination between the parties to the contracts. However, in addition to the market operators behaving similarly, this jurisprudence additionally sets out requirements regarding the structure of the market on which such behaviour takes place in order for the undertakings to be able to influence the effectiveness of competition despite their low market shares. Such a concern with the market structure is extraneous to trade defence law, where the mere fact that the undertakings' trading practices are similar is sufficient for their effects to be assessed cumulatively. The reason for this lies again in the imports being able to injure the EU industry, thereby triggering the 'fairness' rationale of trade defence law, irrespective of the competitive structure on the market.

To conclude, the lack of a requirement regarding the existence of market power can be explained by recalling that the EU's trade defence instruments are also intended to safeguard competition. However, opposed to competition law itself, which is primarily concerned with ensuring the effectiveness of competition, anti-dumping and anti-subsidy law are concerned with ensuring the fairness of competition between the EU industry and the third country exporters. The unfairness of certain behaviours manifests itself in the existence of a material injury caused by the presence of the dumped or subsidised imports. In order to alleviate said injury and restore fair competition between the market participants, anti-dumping or anti-subsidy measures are applied. This fairness-rationale applies regardless of the market power held by the exporters, which is why the EU's trade defence legislation does not require the exporting producers to hold a significant market share.

5.4   Differences Concerning Pricing Practices

As mentioned in the previous chapter on the objectives of competition and trade defence law, trade defence instruments are at times perceived as constituting the international trade analogue of internal market competition policies. This characterisation mirrors the concerns underlying early trade defence legislation. As discussed, the first Canadian anti-dumping legislation was motivated by concerns over predation, and U.S. anti-dumping legislation extended the prohibition of price discrimination to differential pricing practices between the U.S. market and the exporters' home markets.[49] The following section examines to what extent this early convergence in the concerns underlying the respective area of law is still visible in today's concepts of predatory pricing and price discrimination in EU competition and anti-dumping law.

---

appreciably restrict competition under Article 101(1) of the Treaty on the Functioning of the European Union' (n 19 in Chap. 3) para. 10, where a market share of at least 5% is required.

[49] Cf. above p. 93.

5.4.1 Discriminatory Pricing

Competition and anti-dumping legislation are both concerned with forms of geographical price discrimination. The concept of price discrimination itself has been defined as charging different customers or different groups of customers different prices for goods or services whose costs are the same or, conversely, charging a single price to customers for whom supply costs differ.[50] According to economic theory, in order to be able to price discriminate, firms do need some degree of market power on their home market. Further, arbitrage should be impossible in order to defeat resale possibilities between customers that would undermine the differential pricing scheme.[51] Other than what might be expected, the circumstances under which a differential pricing practice by an undertaking is prohibited in EU competition and trade defence law do not necessarily fulfil these criteria set by economic theory.

5.4.1.1 The Prohibition of Geographical Price Discrimination in EU Competition Law

Price discrimination exists in various forms within the internal market. While not all of them are problematic from a competition law perspective, they may however raise concerns under EU anti-discrimination law or conflict with the fundamental freedoms.[52] In EU competition law, Article 102 lit. c) TFEU prohibits price discrimination by prescribing that a dominant undertaking may not apply dissimilar conditions to equivalent transactions with other trading parties that place the other trading parties at a competitive disadvantage. The wording of the provision is clear insofar as it does not seek to prevent 'primary line' injury, i.e. instances in which a dominant undertaking injures its direct competitors, but only 'secondary line' injury, i.e. injury which is inflicted by the dominant firm on one of its customers by applying different prices to its own customers.[53]

In order for Article 102 lit. c) TFEU to be applicable, the dominant undertaking has to have treated equivalent transactions dissimilarly. This requires for the transactions between the dominant undertaking and its customers to be equivalent.[54]

---

[50] *Post Danmark AS v Konkurrencerådet* (n 69 in Chap. 3) 30. More precisely, price discrimination is selling at a price or prices such that the ratio of price to marginal costs is different in different sales, Posner (2001), pp. 79–80. This definition can also be transposed to the anti-dumping context.

[51] Hojnik (2019), pp. 23, 28; Papandropoulos (2007), p. 34.

[52] On price discrimination within the EU legal order cf. the overview provided by Hojnik (2019).

[53] Geradin and Petit (2006), pp. 479, 487. This corresponds with the jurisprudence of the CJEU in *British Airways*, where the Court held that Article 102 lit. c) TFEU aims to prevent a dominant undertaking from distorting competition on an upstream or a downstream market by (dis-)favouring the co-contractors of the dominant undertaking in the area of competition which they practice amongst themselves, *British Airways v Commission* (n 75 in Chap. 3) 143.

[54] de La Mano et al. (2014), para. 4.908.

Once the equivalence of the transactions has been established, the conditions applied to them have to be dissimilar, i.e. discriminatory. However, the discriminatory practice itself is not itself suggestive of an exclusionary abuse as prohibited by Article 102 lit. c) TFEU.[55] Instead, the discrimination has to place the dominant undertaking's contracting partners at a competitive disadvantage.[56] This in turn presupposes that a competitive relationship exists between the trading partners of the dominant undertaking,[57] even though the EU institutions have handled this requirement rather loosely in past cases.[58] Where these elements of abusive behaviour pursuant to Article 102 lit. c) TFEU have been established, the dominant undertaking may produce evidence in order to prove that its conduct is objectively justified.[59]

The requirement of the existence of a 'competitive disadvantage' reflects back on the objectives of competition law and on the economic effects of price discrimination. It is established in economic theory that a practice of price discrimination may have pro-competitive effects by increasing efficiency.[60] Only if the discriminatory practice creates an actual or potential anti-competitive effect is it prohibited under EU competition law. This illustrates the fact that EU competition law is not directly concerned with fairness considerations or the protection of competitors, but with the protection of the competitive process.[61]

---

[55] *Post Danmark AS v Konkurrencerådet* (n 69 in Chap. 3) 30.

[56] *MEO – Serviços de Comunicações e Multimédia SA v Autoridade da Concorrência* (19 April 2018) C-525/16 26–27 (European Court of Justice); *British Airways v Commission* (n 75 in Chap. 3) 144. The standard that has to be met in order for a 'competitive disadvantage' being deemed to exist is still unclear. In para. 25 of its *MEO* judgment, the Court held that Article 102 lit. c) TFEU does not require the discrimination to distort competition or to be capable of doing so. Instead, it suffices that the behaviour tends to lead to a distortion of competition between the business partners of the dominant undertaking. On this issue cf. Ritter (2019), p. 259. The requirement of a 'competitive disadvantage' furthermore prevents Article 102 lit. c) TFEU from being interpreted as a general anti-discrimination rule, Horvath et al. (2020), pp. 35, 43.

[57] *MEO – Serviços de Comunicações e Multimédia SA v Autoridade da Concorrência* (n 56 in this Chapter) 26–27; *British Airways v Commission* (n 8 in Chap. 4) 104–105.

[58] Cf. e.g. *Corsica Ferries* (n 60 in Chap. 3) and Commission Decision of 25 July 2001 relating to a proceeding under Article 82 of the EC Treaty: COMP/C-1/36.915—Deutsche Post AG—Interception of cross-border mail (2001/892/EC) recitals 124 et seq. However, in *Deutsche Post* the Commission held that in any event, the list of abuses in Article 102 TFEU is only indicative, so that the behaviour of Deutsche Post AG could be objected to under the first sentence of Article 102 TFEU even if it did not fulfil the requirements set out in Article 102 lit. c) TFEU.

[59] de La Mano et al. (2014), para. 4.895.

[60] OECD, 'Directorate for Financial and Enterprise Affairs—Competition Committee: Price Discrimination: Background Note by the Secretariat (DAF/COMP(2016)15)' (13 October 2016) 9 et seq.

[61] Opinion of Advocate General Wahl in *MEO – Serviços de Comunicações e Multimédia SA v Autoridade da Concorrência*, C-525/16 62 (20 December 2017).

The Commission and the CJEU have applied Article 102 lit. c) TFEU to cases of geographical price discrimination.[62] This form of price discrimination describes instances in which a dominant undertaking charges different prices for the same products or services in different geographical territories.[63] Such a geographical price discrimination based on the borders of EU Member States is only actionable under Article 102 lit. c) TFEU if these Member States belong to the same geographic market.[64] The comparison between the two transactions thus has to take place on the same market.[65] This also flows from the requirement that the dominant undertaking's customers have to be in competition with each other. Hence, Article 102 lit. c) TFEU should only apply to differential pricing practices taking place within the same geographic market.[66]

Nonetheless, even where these requirements are met, a prohibition of geographic price discrimination under Article 102 lit. c) TFEU has been met with criticism from the scholarly literature, both from an economic and a legal perspective.

From an economic perspective, charging different prices can be justified by the different economic circumstances and local conditions of competition. This has also been recognised by the jurisprudence of the CJEU.[67] In addition, price differentiation can even have pro-competitive effects, as it incentivises parallel trade (from Members State with lower prices to Member States with higher prices) and increases efficiency.[68] Indeed, introducing an outright ban to geographical price discrimination might lead to undesirable distributive effects and even run contrary to the central objective of the internal market: The existence of price divergences among Member States is the main driver for parallel trade within the Union, which in turn ensures that prices across Member States converge towards the lower prices.[69] It follows that an outright ban of geographic price discrimination would not be justified under EU competition law; indeed, it would even risk hampering economic integration between the Member States.[70] Instead, EU competition law should only apply in

---

[62]Two of the most prominent examples are *Tetra Pak International SA v Commission* (6 October 1994) T-83/91 (Court of First Instance) and *United Brands Company v Commission* (n 29 in Chap. 3).

[63]Jones et al. (2019), p. 562.

[64]Deselaers (2015), para. 425.

[65]Schröter and Bartl (2014), para. 246.

[66]Geradin and Petit (2006), p. 528.

[67]*United Brands Company v Commission* (n 29 in Chap. 3) 227; *Tetra Pak International SA v Commission* (n 62) 160. However, the CFI's judgment in *Tetra Pak II* also shows that it will be difficult for the dominant undertaking to prove that specificities concerning the conditions on local markets exist if the geographical market has been found to encompass all Member States on which the discriminatory behaviour takes place, cf. *Tetra Pak International SA v Commission* (n 62) 170; cf. also Jones et al. (2019), p. 394.

[68]*MEO — Serviços de Comunicações e Multimédia SA v Autoridade da Concorrência* (n 61) 61–63.

[69]Geradin and Petit (2006), p. 525.

[70]Ibid 485.

situations where the undertaking practicing geographical price discrimination seeks to prevent outside competition from parallel trade by maintaining artificial obstacles to trade, in effect compartmentalising markets. However, in these instances, the real objection to the undertaking's business practices is not the price discrimination itself but the market partitioning, which endangers the market integration objective.[71] The pursuit of the internal market objective requires fending off attempts by private firms to erect barriers to trade between Member States which allow them to price discriminate across barriers.[72] Based on this reasoning, authors have argued that there is no need to prohibit geographical price discrimination as a distinct abuse, as the measures taken by the dominant undertaking to compartmentalise the market it operates in would be actionable under EU competition law themselves.[73]

5.4.1.2 Dumping as a Form of Transnational Price Discrimination

Dumping as defined by Article VI GATT 1994 and Article 1 BADR covers a broad range of pricing practices, which all constitute a form of international price discrimination.[74] In the context of WTO law, this price differentiation between two segregated markets is usually equalled with price differentiation taking place between two States, i.e. transnational price discrimination.[75] Anti-dumping legislation is only concerned with one type of price discrimination, namely the selling of goods below normal value on one's own territory compared to the price charged by the exporter on its home market. Reverse dumping, i.e. selling goods at a higher price compared to the price of the product on the domestic market,[76] is not covered by the EU rules on anti-dumping. For this reason, anti-dumping legislation has been described as being of a 'one-directional' character.[77]

This reflects the two main rationales underpinning EU anti-dumping legislation. First, only low-priced imports potentially cause injury to one's domestic injury (the alleviation of which is one of the central reasons underlying the imposition of anti-dumping measures)—higher-priced imports do not. Second, anti-dumping law is concerned with ensuring the re-establishment of fair competition on one's own

---

[71] Thompson et al. (2018), para. 10.096; de La Mano et al. (2014), para. 4.899.

[72] Papandropoulos (2007), p. 34.

[73] Geradin and Petit (2006), p. 524. Such practices might violate Article 102 lit. a) TFEU; in addition, market partitioning practices do not comply with Article 101 (1) TFEU.

[74] Cf. e.g. Hoffmeister (2018), para. 8; Wegener Jessen (2012), pp. 263 et seq.; Viner (1923), pp. 4 et seq.

[75] Cf. already Viner (1923), pp. 3–4. It however also covers price differentiation taking place between a State and a customs territory—such as the EU—or between two customs territories, cf. the explanatory notes to the Marrakesh Agreement (n 90 in Chap. 4): 'The terms "country" or "countries" as used in this Agreement and the Multilateral Trade Agreements are to be understood to include any separate customs territory Member of the WTO.'

[76] Viner (1923), pp. 4–5.

[77] Reymond (2015), p. 254.

market. Here, competition is distorted by the presence of products sold by exporters making use of competitive advantages which are not genuine comparative advantages[78] to the detriment of the industry located on the exporting market. As the EU anti-dumping legislation is only concerned with re-establishing the fairness of the dumping exporters' behaviour *vis-à-vis* the EU's own industry, it is not concerned with the question of whether the exporters' pricing practices could equally be considered unfair to the industry in their domestic market. Consequently, EU anti-dumping legislation does not cover situations of reverse dumping; its perspective is always that of the impact the dumping may cause on the internal market.[79]

As noted in the introduction to this section, successful price discrimination usually requires the existence of a certain degree of market power for the undertaking in question to be able to practice differential pricing. Additionally, arbitrage should not be possible in order to defeat resale possibilities.[80] When transposing these requirements to the context of anti-dumping, it becomes apparent that the requirement concerning the existence of a certain degree of market power on part of the undertaking practicing discriminatory pricing is not necessarily met in anti-dumping investigations: an anti-dumping investigation can already be initiated against exporters with market shares as low as 1%.[81] Neither is the exporter's market power on his home market investigated. The reason behind the requirement of a certain degree of market power lies in the assumption that, in order for an undertaking to be able to price discriminate, it has to be able to set prices itself, i.e. it has to be a 'price maker' instead of a 'price taker'. This ability depends on the market power of an undertaking and on the competitive pressure exerted by the other undertakings operating on the market. In a highly competitive market, a seller could not sell identical products at different prices, because other sellers would concentrate on the high-price sector until the price in that sector had been driven down to the price in other sectors.[82]

In the case of dumping, the dumping exporters do not necessarily have to possess a certain degree of market power in order to price discriminate. Their ability to set lower prices on the EU internal market than they are charging on their home market is not dependent on their degree of market power on the internal market or the competitive pressure exerted by their EU counterparts. Instead, their ability to charge higher and in some instances even supra-competitive prices on their home markets follows from the market segregation between the domestic and the exporting market and, in some instances, their domestic market being a high-price market, possibly

---

[78] Such as market segregation or an ineffective domestic competition law.

[79] In fact, these applies to all forms of modern anti-dumping legislation including Article VI GATT 1994. For the same reason, anti-dumping legislation is not concerned with instances where the exporter is charging different prices on different export markets. The only form of price discrimination anti-dumping legislation is concerned with is selling below normal value on the export market.

[80] Cf. the sources cited above, n 55.

[81] Cf. Article 5 (7) BADR.

[82] Hojnik (2019), p. 29.

because of distortions to competition. These factors enable exporters to practice price discrimination in the same way as firms possessing a certain degree of market power can in competitive, non-foreclosed markets. Concerning the requirement of arbitrage being impossible, it has been noted that transnational price discrimination is in principle an expression of unwanted market segregation. The second precondition for an undertaking being able to successfully price discriminate is thus met in the case of dumping.

Anti-dumping legislation does not provide for justifications once the existence of dumping has been established.[83] However, steps are taken to identify the cases in which an actual price discrimination is taking place. For one, this is done by identifying the product concerned and the 'like product' in order to ensure that the products sold are to a certain degree comparable to each other. Second, when comparing the normal value and the export value, factors affecting price comparability are taken into account in order to distinguish those types of price differentiation that cannot be explained by those factors affecting the comparability of the normal value and the export price. Article 2 (10) BADR explicitly calls for this differentiation by prescribing that a fair comparison shall be made between the normal value and the export price. This 'fair' comparison entails that certain factors affecting price comparability have to be taken into account, such as quantity rebates or discounts or price differences resulting from the differences in the physical characteristics of the product concerned.[84] It is only when the difference between the normal value and the export price is not justified by the factors affecting price comparability as set out under Article 2 (10) BADR that the price differentiation will be considered a case of dumping as prohibited under the BADR. Beyond the possibilities foreseen in Article 2 (10) BADR, exporters cannot justify their practices of differential pricing.[85]

5.4.1.3 Lack of Comparability

Economic theory requires the existence of parallel trade for the possible beneficial effects of geographical price discrimination to materialise. Yet, both in the case of anti-dumping and competition policy, parallel trade is prevented either by agreements between undertakings or unilateral practices of dominant undertakings or even by measures taken by the State. Despite these similar initial considerations, the conditions under which geographical price discrimination is prohibited differ considerably in anti-dumping and competition law.

---

[83] Reymond (2015), p. 258.

[84] Cf. Article 2 (10) lit. a) to lit. k) BADR.

[85] Cf. e.g. *Ajinomoto Co. Inc. and The NutraSweet Company v Council* (18 December 1997) joined cases T-159/94 and T-160/94 127 (Court of First Instance), where the Court held that a difference in price elasticity between the domestic market and the exporting market could not be taken into account when assessing the normal value and the export price.

A parallel between the prohibition of differential geographical pricing in competition and anti-dumping law exists in that they both require an element of discrimination in the form of different prices being applied to equivalent situations. This is explicitly prescribed by Article 102 lit. c) TFEU and it is also apparent in Article 2 (10) BADR, which serves to identify factors affecting the comparability of the normal value and the export price. However, apart from this parallelism concerning the existence of a basic discrimination rationale, the concept of price discrimination covers fundamentally different situations in each field of law.

By prohibiting price discrimination which disfavours the dumping exporters' EU competitors, anti-dumping law outlaws 'primary line price discrimination'. In contrast, the prohibition of price discrimination as set out in Article 102 lit. c) TFEU targets 'secondary line discrimination' in the form of practices of a dominant undertaking harming the competitive situation of its customers on an up- or downstream market. In line with the rationale underlying the respective area of law, anti-dumping legislation is concerned with preventing price discrimination to the competitive disadvantage of the exporters' direct competitors, which leads to it addressing 'primary line' injury. Conversely, Article 102 lit. c) TFEU seeks to avert a dominant undertaking negatively influencing the competitive structure of an up- or downstream market, thereby causing 'secondary line' injury.

Second, the requirement of the undertaking's competitors suffering a 'competitive disadvantage' in order for a case of geographical price discrimination to be prohibited under Article 102 lit. c) TFEU does not have an equivalent in EU anti-dumping law, which instead requires for the EU industry to have suffered material injury. This as well as the focus of anti-dumping legislation on primary line discrimination is reflective of this policy area being focused on the immediate attainment of fairness in the competitive relationship between the EU industry and third country exporters. Instead, competition policy is indirectly concerned with ensuring fairness in the competitive relationship between market actors at best. It instead concentrates on safeguarding the competitive process within the internal market as such, which goes beyond the immediate competitive relationship between certain market actors.[86]

Third, in the context of anti-dumping policy, the geographical price discrimination usually takes place on two separate geographic markets,[87] namely on the

---

[86]Cf. also the Opinion of Advocate General Wahl in *MEO – Serviços de Comunicações e Multimédia SA v Autoridade da Concorrência* (n 61) 62–63: '*[A] differential pricing practice may have the consequence of increasing economic efficiency and thus the well-being of consumers. These are goals which, to my mind, should not be overlooked in the application of the rules of competition law, and they are (. . .) quite distinct from considerations of fairness. As the Court has repeatedly held, the rules of competition law are designed to safeguard competition, not to protect competitors. It should only be possible to penalise price discrimination, either under the law applicable to cartels or under the law applicable to abuses of a dominant position, if it creates an actual or potential anticompetitive effect. The identification of such an effect must not be confused with the disadvantage that may immediately be experienced, or suffered, by operators that have been charged the highest prices for goods or services.*'

[87]Marceau even calls this a presupposition, Marceau (1994), p. 11.

exporter's domestic market and the internal market. In contrast, because Article 102 lit. c) TFEU requires for the dominant undertaking's customers to be in a competitive relationship with each other, Article 102 lit. c) TFEU is only applicable to cases of geographical price differentiation taking place on the same geographic market.

Lastly and most importantly, the instances where geographical price discrimination was prohibited under EU competition law all seem to be cases where the actual concern was not so much the geographical price discrimination itself, but the market partitioning practices by the dominant undertaking enabling it to price discriminate. The imposition of such limitations to parallel trade within the internal market runs counter to the internal market objective of the EU. Regardless of whether one agrees with the standpoint presented above according to which this implies that there is no need to prohibit geographical price discrimination as an abuse under Article 102 lit. c) TFEU, the fact remains that putting a halt to market partitioning practices is a central concern of EU competition law.[88] Such a concern with ending market compartmentalisation practices is absent in the prohibition of geographical price discrimination in the form of dumping under the BADR. At this point, it is expedient to recall a central difference between the conceptions of competition law and anti-dumping law in that the latter has been characterised as a 'second best' solution in tackling the negative consequences of an asymmetrical market integration in international trade,[89] without addressing the market partitioning practices themselves. This also applies to the prohibition of geographical price discrimination in the two areas of law: in competition law, the prohibition of geographical price discrimination in effect results in a prohibition of the measures enabling undertakings to partition a market to begin with. It thus targets the root causes behind the differential pricing practice. In anti-dumping law, the prohibition of price discrimination only serves to alleviate the injury caused by the geographical price discrimination without addressing the circumstances which make the transnational price discrimination possible themselves.

5.4.2   Predatory Pricing

5.4.2.1   Competition Law

In the application of Article 102 TFEU, the term 'predatory pricing' generally refers to a below cost pricing campaign undertaken by a dominant firm[90] which has no economic purpose other than to eliminate or weaken the dominant firm's

---

[88] Cf. above p. 75.

[89] Müller-Ibold (2018), p. 550.

[90] Ibáñez Colomo (2016), pp. 709, 716.

competitors.[91] It usually involves a temporary, substantial reduction in price by the dominant firm in response to competition, at unprofitable or barely profitable price levels and pricing aimed at eliminating or disciplining a specific competitor.[92] The subsequent foreclosure of the rival may then enable the dominant undertaking to increase its prices to supra-competitive levels.[93] Should the dominant firm operate on multiple markets, the relationship between prices in its home market and the export market is not relevant in deciding whether the prices charged by the firm can be objected to under Article 102 TFEU or not.[94]

5.4.2.1.1 The *AKZO*-Test

In practice, it may prove challenging to distinguish between legitimate price competition and predatory pricing. In EU competition law, this distinction is made by comparing the prices charged by the dominant undertaking with the costs it incurs.[95] The CJEU has clarified which pricing practices it considers abusive in a number of judgments. According to the seminal *AKZO*-judgment of the CJEU, pricing below average variable cost (AVC) will be presumed to be in conflict with Article 102 TFEU, as a dominant undertaking has no economic interest in applying such prices[96] except that of eliminating competitors.[97] Consequently, the existence of a predatory intent on part of the dominant undertaking does not have to be proven separately; instead, the predatory intent is inferred from the *prima facie* absence of any legitimate economic reason for pricing below AVC. Nonetheless, the dominant undertaking can rebut this presumption by showing that such legitimate economic reasons do in fact exist.[98] On the other hand, if a dominant undertaking prices above its AVC, but below its average total costs (ATC), this will only be regarded abusive if the practice forms part of a plan for eliminating a competitor, as such prices may also drive equally efficient competitors of the dominant undertaking from the

---

[91] Thompson et al. (2018), para. 10.078.

[92] Ibid.

[93] de La Mano et al. (2014), para. 4.298. Criticising the conditions under which predation is sanctioned in EU competition law as economically unsound: Funk and Jaag (2018), p. 292.

[94] Wagner-von Papp (2017), p. 309.

[95] On criticism regarding this reliance on price-cost tests cf. de La Mano et al. (2014), paras. 4.328–4.340.

[96] By setting a price which does not cover its variable costs, the undertaking fails to recover any of its production costs, Monti (2007), p. 179.

[97] *Tetra Pak International SA v Commission* (n 62) 147–148; *AKZO Chemie BV v Commission* (n 54 in Chap. 3) 71.

[98] Jones et al. (2019), pp. 388 et seq.; cf. also *France Télécom SA v Commission (Wanadoo)* (n 69 in Chap. 3) 109–111. On the possibilities for an undertaking to justify its pricing practice cf. below p. 126.

market.[99] Hence, opposed to the first alternative presented in the *AKZO*-judgment, the existence of predatory intent needs to be proven by the competition authority. In *Post Danmark I,* the Court further held that prices below ATC but above average incremental cost (AIC)[100] might still be considered abusive where anti-competitive effects of the pricing practice are found to exist.[101] In effect, the Court hereby laid down a further situation in which pricing below ATC but above AVC might be considered predatory even if no predatory intent on part of the dominant undertaking can be established. In these instances, the behaviour will be regarded as being abusive if there is proof of the likely exclusion of an equally efficient competitor, to the detriment of the consumer.[102]

The situations in which above-cost price cuts were deemed predatory appear to be tailored to the specifics of the relevant case.[103] In particular, in each of the cases in which above-cost price cuts were considered to conflict with Article 102 TFEU, the dominant undertakings had a position of 'super-dominance' or a quasi-monopoly and the exclusionary intent was clearly defined.[104]

Under EU law, the possibility of recoupment on part of the dominant undertaking does not have to be shown in order for its behaviour to be caught by Article 102 TFEU.[105] However, in *Wanadoo* the Court pointed out that the Commission is not precluded from finding that the possibility of recoupment is a relevant factor in assessing whether a pricing practice is abusive.[106]

While the Court includes objective and subjective elements in examining whether a pricing practice is considered to constitute predatory pricing, the objective elements—i.e. the price-cost analysis and, since *Post Danmark I,* the anti-competitive effects of the practice—seem to be of more relevance than the subjective 'predatory intent'-element. In a similar vein, the Commission's Guidance on the enforcement priorities in applying Article 82 of the EC Treaty to abusive exclusionary conduct by

---

[99] *Tetra Pak International SA v Commission* (n 62) 149; *AKZO Chemie BV v Commission* (n 54 in Chap. 3) 72. In these instances, the undertaking is at least recovering its marginal costs, which can be a rational short-term strategy. For this reason, predation cannot be inferred without evidence that the prices are set with the aim of ousting a competitor, Monti (2007), p. 179.

[100] Average incremental cost denotes the average change in the cost which results from a specified variation in output (i.e. the increment), averaged over the units of output supplied, Thompson et al. (2018), para. 10.080. Incremental costs are always comprised of variable costs, which fluctuate with the production volume, but they may also involve some allocation of common costs.

[101] *Post Danmark AS v Konkurrencerådet* (n 69 in Chap. 3) 40, 45.

[102] de La Mano et al. (2014), para. 4.342; Fritzsche and Marquier (2012), pp. 536, 538.

[103] de La Mano et al. (2014), para. 4.320 hold that above-cost price cuts were considered abusive in three sets of circumstances: (a) when the above-cost price cut is part of a wider exclusionary strategy; (b) when it is applied selectively by a quasi-monopolist to eliminate its only competitor; and (c) when it is aimed at preventing parallel trade. Ibáñez Colomo (2016), p. 717.

[104] *Irish Sugar plc v Commission* (n 57 in Chap. 3); *Alsthom Atlantique SA v Compagnie de Construction Mécanique Sulzer SA* (24 January 1991) C-339/89 (European Court of Justice).

[105] *France Télécom SA v Commission (Wanadoo)* (n 69 in Chap. 3) 110; *Tetra Pak International SA v Commission (Tetra Pak II)* (n 43 in Chap. 3) 44.

[106] *France Télécom SA v Commission (Wanadoo)* (n 69 in Chap. 3) 110–111.

dominant undertakings[107] also focusses on the cost-price-comparison as established by the case law of the CJEU.

5.4.2.1.2   The Commission's *Guidance*

In its just-mentioned Guidance, the Commission develops the *AKZO*-test further; modifying it to cost standards it considers to reflect economic reality better than the standards used by the Court. While equally focussing on a cost-price-analysis in order to determine whether a pricing practice can be deemed abusive, the cost benchmarks the Commission will usually use in establishing whether a certain pricing practice constitutes predatory pricing are average avoidable cost (AAC) and long-run average incremental cost (LRAIC). Long-run average incremental cost is the average of all the costs that a company incurs to produce a particular product.[108] To a certain extent, the Commission thus replaces the ATC-standard set by the *AKZO*-test with the LRAIC-standard.[109] In a second step, the Commission will examine whether a dominant undertaking's prices are below its AAC. In addition to AVC, AAC also cover those parts of the fixed costs which would have been avoided if the company had not produced a certain additional amount of output, in this case the amount allegedly the subject of abusive conduct. The Commission considers that failure to cover AAC indicates that the dominant undertaking is sacrificing profits in the short term and that an equally efficient competitor cannot compete without incurring a loss, leading to anti-competitive foreclosure.[110]

5.4.2.1.3   Justification

As EU law does not prohibit pricing below cost *per se*, even when an undertaking's pricing practices are found to be *prima facie* objectionable, the undertaking can provide justification for its behaviour by demonstrating that the behaviour is either objectively necessary or that the exclusionary effect the behaviour is causing is counterbalanced or outweighed by efficiencies also benefiting consumers.[111] An undertaking may also rebut the presumption of its behaviour being predatory by

---

[107] European Commission, 'Communication from the Commission: Guidance on the Commission's enforcement priorities in applying Article 82 of the Treaty to abusive exclusionary conduct by dominant undertakings' (n 51 in Chap. 3).

[108] Ibid paras. 26–27.

[109] Fuchs (2019), para. 240.

[110] European Commission, 'Communication from the Commission: Guidance on the Commission's enforcement priorities in applying Article 82 of the Treaty to abusive exclusionary conduct by dominant undertakings' (n 51 in Chap. 3) paras. 26–27.

[111] *Post Danmark AS v Konkurrencerådet* (n 69 in Chap. 3) 41.

showing that it is in fact pursuing legitimate economic interests.[112] To a limited extent, a dominant undertaking might also rely on the so-called 'meeting competition defence' and argue that a lowering of its prices was necessary in order to align its prices with those of its competitors. However, in *Wanadoo* the CJEU held that a dominant undertaking does not have an absolute right in this regard.[113] In general, the EU institutions have been reluctant in accepting any of the above reasons as a justification for a *prima facie* violation of Article 102 TFEU, which has led commentators to argue that in particular the efficiency defence possesses more of a '*rhetorical than an actual relevance*'.[114]

5.4.2.2   Anti-dumping Law

While predation concerns are still frequently cited as a rationale behind anti-dumping legislation, the conditions under which a pricing practice will be considered to justify the imposition of measures under the BADR differ significantly from those applied under Article 102 TFEU: The normal value of a product is usually the sales price, e.g. a price at which the producer can cover its ATC and at which he generates a profit. Consequently, even the price asked on the exporting market might still be sufficient to cover the exporter's total cost and thus be well above a level at which the pricing practice would be objectionable under EU competition law. However, anti-dumping law does not analyse the exporter's cost structure. Instead of comparing costs, as will be set out below, anti-dumping law compares price levels. This results in a significantly broader spectrum of pricing practices falling within the definition of 'dumping' than would be deemed to constitute predatory pricing under Article 102 TFEU.

5.4.2.2.1   Comparing Price Levels

A product is considered to be dumped if its export price is less than its 'normal value'.[115] Usually, the normal value is established by having regard to the sales of the product in the ordinary course of trade in the exporter's home market.[116] Hence, opposed to Article 102 TFEU, it is not the costs an undertaking incurs and the prices it charges that are being compared, but two prices. Consequently, as mentioned, if

---

[112] *France Télécom SA v Commission (Wanadoo)* (n 69 in Chap. 3) 111; cf. also *Sot. Lélos kai Sia EE and others v GlaxoSmithKline AEVE Farmakeftikon Proïonton* (n 22 in Chap. 4) 68. First accepted as a defence in *United Brands Company v Commission* (n 29 in Chap. 3) 189–190, where the Court also held that the behaviour in question cannot be countenanced if its actual purpose is to strengthen or abuse the dominant position.

[113] *France Télécom SA v Commission (Wanadoo)* (n 69 in Chap. 3) 47–48.

[114] Fuchs (2019), p. 163.

[115] Article 1 (2) BADR.

[116] Article 2 (1) BADR.

the exporter's domestic market for some reason is a high-price market, the exporting producer may still be selling well above total costs on the EU internal market. Yet, already the fact that his export prices are lower than his domestic prices will result in the applicability of the BADR.[117] It is irrelevant whether the prices charged on the internal market are profitable or not: below cost pricing on part of the exporters is not a direct concern of anti-dumping law; it is focussed on comparing price levels.

By comparing the costs incurred by a dominant undertaking and the prices it charges, Article 102 TFEU limits the prohibition of predatory pricing to pricing practices that are able to eliminate an equally efficient competitor from the market, as this would entail negative consequences on the market structure. Opposite to this, the protection the BADR awards to the EU industry is not restricted to as efficient EU competitors of the exporter. This was explicitly stated by the Court in *Canon Inc.* with regard to the injury assessment in anti-dumping investigations. The complainant *Canon* had argued that it would not be in the interests of the Community to protect inefficient producers. Therefore, the EU institutions would have to differentiate between efficient and inefficient EU producers in determining the injury caused by the presence of dumped imports.[118] However, this line of reasoning was rebutted by the Court, as it held that the fact that a Union producer is facing difficulties attributable in part to causes other than the dumping is not a reason for depriving that producer of all protection against the injury caused by the dumping.[119]

5.4.2.2.2 Pricing Below Cost and the 'Ordinary Course of Trade'-Requirement

The costs the exporter incurs are relevant insofar as domestic sales made at a loss will be regarded as not having taken place within the 'ordinary course of trade'. Sales are considered to have been made at a loss if they do not cover the undertaking's total production costs plus selling, general and administrative expenses (SG&A).[120] If the domestic prices are below this level, the normal value may not be determined on the basis of said prices, but on the basis of the cost of production in the country of origin plus a reasonable amount of selling, general and administrative costs and for profits or on the basis of representative export prices.[121] Commentators have noted that this entails that dumping is considered to be taking place even in situations where the export price is lower than the computed normal value, consisting of total costs plus a reasonable profit margin.[122] Clearly, in these instances, the constructed 'normal

---

[117] Schroeder (1991), pp. 540, 545.

[118] *Canon Inc. and others v Council* (5 October 1988) joined cases 277 and 300/85 61–62 (European Court of Justice).

[119] Ibid 63.

[120] Article 2 (4) BADR.

[121] Article 2 (3) BADR.

[122] Reymond (2015), pp. 249–350, 314.

value' is above the price levels that give rise to predation concerns under EU competition law.

The reason behind the 'ordinary course of trade'-requirement has been cited by the Court as ensuring that the normal value of the product corresponds as closely as possible to the normal price of the like product on the domestic market of the exporter. Consequently, any sale which is made under conditions that are not reflective of the normal commercial practice for sales of the like product does not constitute an appropriate basis on which to determine the normal value of the like product on that market.[123] For this reason, already sales made below total costs are deemed to constitute such an 'abnormal' business practice: under normal circumstances, a profit-oriented undertaking would not price in a way which does not enable it to cover the cost it incurs.[124] Consequently, no differentiation between 'sales below total costs' and 'sales below variable costs'—as it is the case in competition law—is undertaken: pricing below cost is always considered to be an extraordinary commercial decision, regardless of the effects it may have on the producer's domestic market.[125] Compared with Article 102 TFEU, which only prohibits pricing below cost in a very limited set of circumstances, the BADR thus regards below cost-pricing as constituting a commercial abnormality *per se*. In particular, under Article 102 TFEU, a dominant undertaking may provide a justification for its pricing practices. Such an opportunity is not foreseen in the BADR: an exporter cannot defend its pricing practices on the grounds of the underlying causes, such as a downturn in the business cycle, market penetration or meeting its competitors' prices.[126] This is at least problematic insofar as pricing below cost may actually be an economically rational decision in some instances, and may hence also reflect the normal commercial practice in the exporter's domestic market.[127]

---

[123] *Council v Alumina d.o.o.* (1 October 2014) C-393/13 P 28 (European Court of Justice).

[124] Marceau (1994), pp. 13–14.

[125] Anti-dumping legislation is not concerned with the effects a potentially predatory pricing practice may have on the competitive structure in the exporter's domestic market. Hence, also under this perspective, it is not necessary for it to distinguish between different price-cost-ratios.

[126] Wegener Jessen (2012), p. 270.

[127] To some extent, those concerns are taken up by Article 2 (4) subpara. 1 BADR, which requires that sales below cost may only be disregarded if it is determined that they are made at prices which do not provide for the recovery of all costs within a reasonable period of time. According to Article 2 (4) subpara. 2 BADR, prices will not allow for a recovery of costs if they are below costs at the time of sale and below the weighted average costs of the period of investigation. This excludes instances in which a price will be considered to be at a loss at the time of the sale, however in the course of the investigation, costs fall to a degree that has made the price profitable. These cases usually concern the introduction of new products, Mueller et al. (2009), para. 2.49.

5.4.2.2.3   No Predatory Intent Necessary

Lastly, the Commission does not need to prove predatory intent on part of the exporters.[128] In competition law, the criterion of predatory intent limits the cases where below-cost pricing practices are considered objectionable to instances where these are directed against equally efficient competitors, the exclusion of which from the market would produce a negative effect on the competitive structure of the internal market. Conversely, as anti-dumping legislation is not primarily concerned with protecting the competitive structure of the internal market but with shielding the EU industry from the negative effects resulting from commercial practices that are regarded as unfair, it does not require any predatory intentions on part of the exporters.[129]

It thus comes as no surprise that while it is frequently advanced that anti-dumping legislation is intended to fight off predatory behaviour on part of the exporters, the instances in which such predatory behaviour can actually be identified are scarce. *Bourgeois* and *Messerlin* already made this observation in 1998. In applying a set of criteria relating *inter alia* to the market share of the exporters, the outcome of the anti-dumping investigation, the number of countries and the number of firms involved in a given case, they found that only 12 of 461 investigations between 1980 and 1997—that is, only 2%—were possible candidates for a closer examination of predatory behaviour.[130] More recent studies have arrived at similar conclusions.[131]

5.5   Chapter Conclusions

The preceding chapter has sought to highlight some of the central differences in the content of concepts that apply both in competition law and in the law on trade defence instruments. These differences were then examined in the light of the objectives of the respective field of law, as presented in the previous chapter. It follows that it is not so much the aspect of relatively little weight being given to consumers' interests in the anti-dumping investigation (as well as in the countervailing investigation)[132] which leads to central standards and concepts being ascribed a completely different content in competition and trade defence

---

[128] Müller-Ibold (2018), p. 545.

[129] In fact, early U.S. anti-dumping legislation contained an intent-requirement. However, the existence of predatory intent was hard to prove, which rendered the legislation largely ineffective, leading to an amendment of the U.S. anti-dumping legislation, Sykes and Cooper (1998), p. 18.

[130] Bourgeois and Messerlin (1998).

[131] Bienen et al. (2013). The authors developed a '*likelihood-of-predatory-practice-index*', which they in turn apply to the EU's anti-dumping investigations initiated between 2000 and 2010.

[132] In particular as competition law does not adhere to a 'consumer welfare standard' either, as described above.

law. Rather, while trade defence law is concerned with protecting the market participants from harm caused by trading practices which are considered unfair, competition law is focussed on the protection of competition on the market itself: first, by safeguarding the success of the internal market project by preventing the re-erection of barriers to trade and second, by protecting a competitive market structure. Both concerns are extraneous to the EU's trade defence legislation. Anti-dumping's direct concern with horizontal fairness, coupled with the absence of any structural concerns regarding the competitive situation on the internal market lead to differences in the understanding of concepts such as 'market' or 'predation' as well as their use in the two areas of law. Another result of these discrepancies is the general lack of relevance attached to the market power of the exporting producers in EU trade defence law. Conversely, the debate on the correct welfare standard to be pursued by competition law and the absence of a similar discussion in trade defence law does not appear to play a significant role here.

While the differences in the objectives pursued by the two fields of law serve to explain the different meaning and relevance attributed to concepts used both in competition and trade defence law, the question remains whether the requirement flowing from the Treaties that trade defence instruments must not be used in a protectionist manner is being observed. Accordingly, the next section of the thesis will be devoted to assessing first, the anti-competitive concerns trade defence proceedings can raise, second, in how far competition concerns are taken into account in the practice of the Commission as the investigating authority and third, whether the ideal situation of a *'peaceful coexistence'*[133] of trade and competition policy was bettered or worsened by the reforms introduced by the Trade Defence Modernisation Package.

References[134]

Bienen D, Ciuriak D, Picarello T (2013) 'Trade and Development Discussion Paper: Does Anti-dumping Address "Unfair" Trade? – The European Union's Experience. BKP Trade and Development Discussion Paper 01/2013. Available at <https://www.bkp-development.com/attachments/article/306/BKP_DP_2013-01-Bienen-Ciuriak-Picarello-Predatory_Dumping-rev.pdf>

Bourgeois J, Messerlin PA (1998) The European community's experience. In: Lawrence R (ed) Brookings Trade Forum. Brookings Institution Press

de La Mano M, Nazzini R, Zenger H (2014) Article 102 TFEU. In: Faull J, Nikpay A (eds) The EU law of competition, 3rd edn. Oxford University Press

Deselaers W (2015) Artikel 102 AEUV. In: Grabitz E, Hilf M, Nettesheim M (eds) Das Recht der Europäischen Union. C.H. Beck

---

[133] Müller-Ibold (2018).

[134] All online sources were last accessed on 8 September 2021.

Fritzsche A, Marquier J (2012) Kampfpreisunterbietung ohne Verdrängungsabsicht – das Ende des formbasierten Ansatzes in der europäischen Missbrauchsaufsicht? Zeitschrift für europäisches Wirtschaftsrecht (EuZW) 536

Fuchs A (2019) Artikel 102 AEUV. In: Immenga U, Mestmäcker E-J (eds) Wettbewerbsrecht: Band 1: Europäisches Kartellrecht, 6th edn, C.H. Beck

Funk M, Jaag C (2018) The more economic approach to predatory pricing. J Compet Law Econ 14(2):292

Geradin D, Petit N (2006) Price discrimination under EC competition law: another antitrust doctrine in search of limiting principles? J Compet Law Econ 2(3):479

Gormsen LL (2007) The conflict between economic freedom and consumer welfare in the modernisation of Article 82 EC. Eur Compet J 3(2):329

Hoekman BM, Mavroidis PC (1996) Dumping, antidumping and antitrust. J World Trade 30(1):27

Hoffmeister F (2018) AD-GVO 2016 vor Art. 1 [Erwägungsgründe]. In: Krenzler HG, Herrmann C, Niestedt M (eds) EU-Außenwirtschafts- und Zollrecht. C.H. Beck

Hojnik J (2019) Tell me where you come from and I will tell you the price: ambiguous expansion of prohibited geographical price discrimination in the EU. Common Mark Law Rev 56(1):23

Horvath R, Peeperkorn L, Rousseva E (2020) The preliminary ruling in MEO: closing the circle of Article 102 TFEU. J Eur Compet Law Pract 11(1–2):35

Ibáñez Colomo P (2016) Beyond the "more economics-based approach": a legal perspective on Article 102 TFEU case law. Common Mark Law Rev 53(3):709

Jones A, Sufrin B, Dunne N (2019) EU competition law, 7th edn. Oxford University Press

Marceau G (1994) Anti-dumping and anti-trust issues in free trade areas. Clarendon Press

Monti G (2007) EC competition law. Cambridge University Press

Mueller W, Khan N, Scharf T (2009) EC and WTO anti-dumping Law: a handbook, 2nd edn. Oxford University Press

Müller-Ibold T (2018) Antidumping and competition law – common origin, a life of their own and peaceful coexistence?. In: Kokott J, Pohlmann P, Polley R (eds) Europäisches, Deutsches und Internationales Kartellrecht: Festschrift für Dirk Schroeder zum 65. Geburtstag. Dr. Otto Schmidt

Papandropoulos P (2007) How should price discrimination be dealt with by competition authorities? Concurrences 34

Posner RA (2001) Antitrust law, 2nd edn. Chicago University Press

Ramírez Pérez SM, van de Scheur S (2012) The evolution of the law on Articles 85 and 86 EEC [Articles 101 and 102 TFEU]: ordoliberalism and its Keynesian challenge. In: Schweitzer H, Patel KK (eds) The historical foundations of EU competition law. Oxford University Press

Reymond D (2015) Action antidumping et droit de la concurrence dans l'Union européenne. Dissertation, Panthéon-Assas

Ritter C (2019) Price discrimination as an abuse of a dominant position under Article 102 TFEU: MEO. Common Mark Law Rev 56(1):259

Schroeder D (1991) Anti-trust Law Implications of EEC Anti-dumping proceedings. Rabels Zeitschrift für ausländisches und internationales Privatrecht 55(3):540

Schröter H, Bartl U (2014) Artikel 102 AEUV. In: Schröter H and others (eds) Europäisches Wettbewerbsrecht, 2nd edn. Nomos

Sykes AO, Cooper RN (1998) Antidumping and antitrust: what problems does each address? In: Lawrence R (ed) Brookings Trade Forum. Brookings Institution Press

Thompson R, Brown C, Gibson N (2018) Article 102 TFEU. In: Bailey D, John LE (eds) European Union law of competition, 5th edn. Oxford University Press

Vandenbussche H, Wauthy X (2001) Inflicting injury through product quality: how European antidumping policy disadvantages European producers. Eur J Polit Econ 17(1):101

Viner J (1923) Dumping: a problem in international trade (re-print 1996). Kelley

Wagner-von Papp F (2017) Competition law in EU free trade and cooperation agreements (and What the UK can expect after brexit). In: Bungenberg M and others (eds) European yearbook of international economic law 2017. Springer

Wegener Jessen P (2012) Anti-Dumping. In: Egelund Olsen B, Steinicke M, Sørensen KE (eds) WTO law: from a European perspective. Wolters Kluwer

Chapter 6
The Impact of the Trade Defence Modernisation Package on the Relationship Between the EU's Trade Defence Instruments and Competition: Anti-competitive Effects of Trade Defence Proceedings

6.1 Introduction

While competition and trade defence policy pursue the same underlying objective, namely the attainment of economic efficiency in resource utilisation and the advancement of overall economic welfare,[1] the preceding chapters already indicate that despite the historical convergence in the concerns underlying competition and trade defence, soon the objectives they sought to attain diverged.

Nonetheless, the Treaties prescribe that competition and trade defence shall operate in harmony, with the use of the EU's trade defence instruments not interfering with a system of undistorted competition.[2] These calls for harmony have been recognised by the EU institutions, which have repeatedly held that the purpose of anti-dumping proceedings *'is not and cannot be to enforce or encourage restrictive business practices'*.[3] This is also reflected in the opinion of Advocate General *Jacobs* in the *Extramet* case, in which he stated that while the Treaties allow for measures against dumping to be taken as a *'necessary evil'*, this must not be done without having regard for the EU competition rules. In order to avoid restrictions to competition caused by anti-dumping measures, it is thus essential to take competition policy considerations into account when deciding on the imposition of

---

[1] Hope (1998), pp. 2–3. Cf. also above p. 93 et seq. It should however be borne in mind that it is contested whether the imposition of trade defence measures actually fosters economic efficiency, with studies pointing to the contrary, cf. above p. 84.

[2] Cf. above p. 13 et seq.

[3] Cf. e.g. Commission Regulation (EEC) No 1361/87 of 18 May 1987 imposing a provisional anti-dumping duty on imports of ferro-silico-calcium/calcium silicide originating in Brazil recital 12.

P. Trapp, *The European Union's Trade Defence Modernisation Package*, EYIEL Monographs - Studies in European and International Economic Law 23, https://doi.org/10.1007/978-3-030-91363-2_6

anti-dumping measures.[4] These considerations apply, *mutatis mutandis*, also to anti-subsidy proceedings and the measures adopted under the rules of the BASR.

However, as pointed out above, the previous chapters strongly suggest that theory and reality might not converge. Indeed, authors have noted that in particular anti-dumping proceedings carry a risk of producing anti-competitive effects and being used for what is described as 'non-price predation' by the domestic industry, i.e. the filing of anti-dumping complaints with the objective of excluding foreign rivals from the domestic market.[5] In his well-known study on the European Communities' chemical cases, *Messerlin* went so far as to suggest that in markets where foreign competition had created difficulties for the creation and organisation of a cartel, EC firms used the EC anti-dumping law as a means of obtaining a *de facto* exemption from EC competition law. Further, he held that '*the capture of EC anti-dumping procedures for this purpose has been easy – so easy that it might be more appropriate to speak of "surrender" rather than a "capture"*'.[6]

The Commission appears to devote little attention to the issue. In an impact assessment accompanying the proposal for the modernisation of the EU's trade defence instruments, it was held that the Commission is only aware of one single instance of an overlap of anti-competitive behaviour on part of the complainant EU industry and the imposition of trade defence measures.[7] One could therefore be inclined to conclude that, for all the criticism voiced by scholars and practitioners alike, the actual risk of trade defence instruments causing further distortions to competition is rather limited. However, a study by *Laprévote* analysing the EU's anti-dumping measures imposed between 1998 and 2015 and the cartel decisions adopted over the same period paints a different picture. The study reveals several overlaps in cartel activity and anti-dumping periods and, even more frequently, periods of cartel activity preceding an anti-dumping period.[8] He further points out that the number of cases where anti-competitive behaviour on part of the Union industry occurred might still be underestimated, as his analysis did not take cartel decisions by national competition authorities into account and, due to the secretive nature of cartels, not all cartel behaviour is detected.[9] The Commission also

---

[4] Opinion of Advocate General Jacobs in *Extramet Industrie v* Council, C-358/89 32–34 (21 March 1991); cf. also Opinion of Advocate General van Gerven in *Nölle v Hauptzollamt Bremen-Freihafen*, C-16/90 33 (22 October 1991).

[5] Cho (2009), pp. 360–361.

[6] Messerlin (1990), p. 465.

[7] European Commission, 'Commission Staff Working Document – Impact Assessment accompanying the document "proposal for a regulation of the European Parliament and of the Council on the modernisation of trade defence instruments" (COM(2013) 192 final) (SWD(2013) 106 final)' (Brussels 10 April 2013) 38.

[8] Laprévote (2015), pp. 12–14.

[9] Ibid 14. The anti-dumping proceedings concerning imports of ceramic tableware and kitchenware originating in China serve as an example in this regard. Here, the exporting producers claimed that a cartel investigation launched by the German authorities had not been duly taken into account when establishing a causal relationship between the presence of dumped imports on the EU market and

acknowledges the latter aspect in the impact assessment just mentioned.[10] Thus, the issue of possible frictions between competition policy and the EU's trade defence instruments is far from being a purely theoretical one. Whereas the criticism voiced by authors such as *Laprévote* and *Messerlin* pertains to the strategic use of trade defence proceedings by domestic industries for anti-competitive purposes, it should further be considered that the effect of trade defence proceedings as restrictive to competition also extends to incidental restrictions to competition as well as a 'protectionist bias' in the formulation of the legislation governing the EU's trade defence instruments and their application. Consequently, the following two chapters will carry out a more in-depth assessment of the interactions between competition and trade defence law. More specifically, this chapter is set out to examine the restrictions to competition an anti-dumping or anti-subsidy procedure may entail. Chapter 7 will then be dedicated to identifying the protectionist bias in the EU's modernised trade defence legislation. Through these analyses, it will be assessed whether the statement made by *Hoffmeister* already referenced above according to which the EU's reformed basic regulations maintain their character as a '*proportionate remedy against unfair trade practices*'[11] can be agreed with.

6.2   The Anti-competitive Effects of Trade Defence Proceedings

When analysing the anti-competitive potential of trade defence proceedings and the imposition of anti-dumping or anti-subsidy measures, it is expedient to differentiate between their general, structural implications on the competitive situation on the internal market and the specific effects a certain part of a trade defence proceeding may have on competition.

6.2.1   General Restrictions to Competition

As outlined above, one argument put forward against trade defence instruments is that their use frequently results in the exit of foreign manufacturers from the

---

the injury suffered by the EU industry. The Commission however rejected this claim, holding that the macro-economic indicators had only been affected to a very limited extent, if any, cf. Council Implementing Regulation (EU) 412/2013 of 13 May 2013 imposing a definitive anti-dumping duty and collecting definitively the provisional duty imposed on imports of ceramic tableware and kitchenware originating in the People's Republic of China recitals 168–169.

[10] European Commission, 'Commission Staff Working Document – Impact Assessment accompanying the document "proposal for a regulation of the European Parliament and of the Council on the modernisation of trade defence instruments"' (n 7) 17.

[11] Hoffmeister (2020), p. 214.

importing market, leading to a smaller number of players on said market and hence to a reduction of the elasticity of demand faced by each of them.[12] Further, the effect of anti-dumping or countervailing measures will be to raise the prices of the imported product in order to enable the EU producers to protect their position on the market by either maintaining their prices or even being able to raise them.[13] Consequently, anti-dumping measures typically lead to a higher price level on the internal market. This stands in contrast with the objectives pursued by competition policy, which is generally concerned with keeping prices low by spurring efficiency.[14] This also applies to countervailing measures, as they likewise result in the prices of the imported subsidised products—and thus the price level in the importing country in general—to go up.

The Commission decision in *Siemens/Fanuc*[15] is illustrative in this respect. The decision concerned proceedings regarding a possible violation of now Article 101 TFEU by means of a number of agreements concluded between the Japanese producer of computers *Fanuc* and *Siemens*. Through the agreements, *Siemens* was granted exclusive selling rights for *Fanuc* computers for the whole of Europe. *Fanuc* also undertook not to grant manufacturing licenses for its computers to any third party in that territory, but only to *Siemens*. In its investigation, the Commission found that the selling price of *Fanuc's* products was on average 34% higher in the common market than the prices charged in Japan. The Commission considered that such a restrictive agreement, which isolated the common market from a potentially cheaper source of a product that it considered essential to the development of a major Community industry, might be of such a nature as to distort competition within the common market and to negatively affect trade between the Member States.[16] In other words, an agreement between undertakings leading to higher prices for the EU industry by means of isolating the EU market from lower-priced third country markets would raise objections under the EU competition rules. Conversely, such an isolation of the EU industry from lower-priced imports is exactly what is foreseen and accepted by the EU's trade defence rules.

In conclusion, the imposition of trade defence measures may produce a general anti-competitive effect on the EU industry in two regards: first, the EU industry producing the European counterpart of the product under investigation benefits from a lower number of players being active on the market.[17] This results in a general lessening of the degree of competition on the internal market. Secondly, the imposition of trade defence measures potentially diminishes the effectiveness and global competitiveness of the EU downstream industry dependent on the imported products

---

[12] Cf. above p. 90 and Bown and McCulloch (2015), p. 8.

[13] *Extramet Industrie v Council* (n 4) 30.

[14] Vandoren (1986), p. 8.

[15] Commission Decision of 18 December 1985 relating to a proceeding pursuant to Article 85 of the EEC Treaty (IV/30.739 – Siemens/Fanuc) (85/618/EEC).

[16] Ibid recital 24.

[17] In anti-dumping law, this is referred to as the 'like' product, cf. above p. 54.

for which prices increase as a consequence of the imposition of anti-dumping or countervailing measures.[18] Additionally, the adverse impact of the higher prices of the product subjected to anti-dumping or anti-subsidy measures on the downstream industry may also extend to more efficient competitors being able to force less competitive domestic rivals off the downstream market, which likewise results in a reduction of market players.[19] The exclusion of less efficient manufacturers is not objectionable under the rationale of EU competition policy *per se*.[20] However, it must still be noted that this constitutes a discrepancy with the protection afforded to the EU producers of the product concerned, as the EU institutions have repeatedly held that the protection awarded by its trade defence instruments is not limited to efficient EU producers.[21] This results in less efficient EU producers being able to successfully claim protection under the EU's anti-dumping and anti-subsidy instruments, even if it is established that their non-EU competitors outperform them in terms of efficiency.

Commentators have also observed that, in the long run, even the mere threat of protective measures or increases in protection can provide an inducement for foreign market operators to either downsize their exports to the relevant country or,[22] on the opposite, to relocate their production via direct investment in the importing country,[23] with the latter leading to adverse effects on the competitive situation on their domestic markets. In a similar vein, it has been put forward that already the existence of trade defence legislation may be used by members of a domestic cartel as a pretext either to monitor the prices of their foreign competitors or to pressure them that unless they join the cartel, they will face consequences through the initiation of anti-dumping or countervailing proceedings.[24] An often-quoted example in this regard is the case of anti-dumping duties on imports of ferro-silicon originating in Brazil. The domestic members of the cartel, which took place in Europe and the United States in the eighties and nineties, used anti-dumping duties to eliminate their third country competitors.[25] The Brazilian exporters disclosed this behaviour to the investigating authorities in the course of the anti-dumping proceedings carried out on Community level. However, while the Commission held that a finding of an infringement of the

---

[18] It can also be argued that the reduction of the volume of imports—which is an accepted result of the imposition of anti-dumping measures, cf. e.g. Council Implementing Regulation (EU) No 792/2011 of 5 August 2011 imposing a definitive anti-dumping duty and collecting definitively the provisional duty imposed on imports of certain ring binder mechanisms originating in Thailand recital 50—can cause additional issues for the EU downstream industry, such as shortages of supply.

[19] Bown and McCulloch (2015), p. 8.

[20] Cf. above p. 76 et seq and the Court's judgment in *Intel Corporation Inc. v Commission* (Chap. 4, n 45) 133, 134.

[21] *Canon Inc. and others v Council* (Chap. 5, n 118) 63. Cf. also above p. 59.

[22] On the trade diverting effects of anti-dumping measures cf. Hoai et al. (2017), p. 1128.

[23] Bown and McCulloch (2015), p. 8.

[24] Laprévote (2015), p. 10.

[25] For more details on the background of the case cf. Pierce (2000), pp. 726–729.

Community competition rules would *per se* warrant a review of the measures,[26] the measures were not repealed. Indeed, the duties were later re-instated in the EU on the assumption that the cartelist behaviour occurred before the period investigated by the Commission to determine the existence of dumping.[27]

6.2.2   Specific Restrictions to Competition

6.2.2.1   Restrictions Related to the Initiation of Proceedings: Preparation of an Anti-dumping Complaint

6.2.2.1.1   Information Exchanges as an Infringement of Article 101 (1) TFEU

As a rule, under the BADR and the BASR, the Commission will initiate an investigation into dumping or the presence of subsidised products on the internal market upon complaint by any natural or legal person, or any association not having legal personality, acting on behalf of the Union industry.[28] This usually requires for the EU producers to act jointly in order for their complaint to be considered as having been lodged 'on behalf of the Union industry'. A complaint will be considered to have been made by, or on behalf of, the Union industry where it is supported by more than 50% of the EU producers producing the like product. No investigation shall be initiated where less than 25% of Union producers producing the like product support the complaint.[29] The joint preparation of the complaint entails the EU producers exchanging information among themselves. As the complaint has to include *prima facie* evidence of injury, this information exchange necessarily entails the disclosure of sensitive business information, such as prices and customers, *vis-à-vis* one's competitors, which runs the risk of conflicting with Article 101 (1) TFEU.[30] According to the Court's *Suiker Unie* judgment, each competitor in the market must determine independently the policy that he intends to adopt in the common market. This strictly precludes any direct or indirect contact between such competitors, the object or effect of which is to disclose to a competitor the course of conduct which one has decided to adopt on the market.[31] It has been suggested that the exchange of sensitive business information in the preparation of a complaint

---

[26] Commission Regulation (EEC) No 1361/87 of 18 May 1987 imposing a provisional anti-dumping duty on imports of ferro-silico-calcium/calcium silicide originating in Brazil (n 3) recital 12.

[27] Laprévote (2015), p. 10.

[28] On the risks associated with the *ex officio* initiation of investigations cf. below p. 172.

[29] Article 5 (4) BADR and Article 10 (6) BASR.

[30] Stegemann (1990), p. 289.

[31] *Suiker Unie and others v Commission* (Chap. 3, n 59) 174.

potentially conflicts with the criteria set out in *Suiker Unie*.[32] However, transposing the *Suiker Unie* judgment to the situation of EU producers preparing an anti-dumping or an anti-subsidy complaint seems unconvincing, as such a restrictive interpretation would lead to the EU industry becoming more reluctant in initiating investigations for fears of committing an infringement of Article 101 (1) TFEU itself. This would not only risk undermining the rights of the EU industry awarded to it under the BADR and the BASR, but ultimately also hamper the effectiveness of the EU's trade defence instruments themselves.[33] Indeed, in a proceeding relating to a possible infringement of Article 101 TFEU committed by EU undertakings concerned about possible State aid granted by a Member State to their rivals, the Commission held that it

> obviously recognises the right of undertakings not only to notify the competent authorities – including the Commission where appropriate – of breaches of national or [EU] provisions but also their right to act collectively for this purpose, which necessarily presupposes the possibility of holding preparatory discussions among themselves.[34]

It seems prudent to apply this reasoning also to the preparation of anti-dumping or anti-subsidy complaints by the EU industry.[35,36] Nonetheless, anything going beyond what is necessary to make such a complaint might still conflict with Article 101 (1) TFEU.[37] In particular, undertakings may not 'take the law into their own hands': According to the Commission, *'[e]ven the prevention of alleged dumping practices does not justify attempts to regulate prices and markets through private agreements'*.[38]

---

[32] Schroeder (1991), pp. 542–543.

[33] Cf. also Müller-Ibold (2018), pp. 553–555.

[34] Commission Decision of 30 November 1994 relating to a proceeding under Article 85 of the EC Treaty (Cases IV/33.126 and 33.322 – Cement) (94/815/EC) recital 36.10.

[35] Also arguing in favour of the compatibility of information exchanges occurring in the course of the preparation of an anti-dumping complaint Bourgeois (1989), p. 63; Vandoren (1986), p. 3.

[36] In this regard, a comparison is frequently made with the legal situation in the U.S. In the United States, when determining whether lodging an anti-dumping or anti-subsidy complaint with the competent authorities is abusive, the so-called 'Noerr-Pennington Doctrine' applies. The doctrine gives antitrust immunity to domestic producers who cooperate and exchange information among themselves when filing anti-dumping suits with the authorities. However, the doctrine does not apply to 'sham petitions' that have the sole purpose of harassing rivals. On this cf. Cho (2009), p. 408 et seq; Davidow (1999), p. 682 et seq.

[37] Vandoren (1986), p. 3. In that regard, Müller-Ibold differentiates between the agreement in principle between competitors to cooperate in submitting a complaint to the Commission and the ancillary measures and steps that have to be taken in order to actually cooperate, Müller-Ibold (2018), p. 556.

[38] Commission Decision of 6 August 1984 relating to a proceeding under Article 85 of the EEC Treaty (IV/30.350 – zinc producer group) (84/405/EEC) recital 73. Cf. also the Commission Decision in *IFTRA*, where it held that the mere labelling of an agreement between undertakings as rules against unfair competition (which in this case also included rules on dumping) does not suffice to remove the agreement from the ambit of Article 101 TFEU, Commission Decision of 15 July 1975 relating to a proceeding under Article 85 of the EEC Treaty (IV/27.000 – IFTRA rules

While the Commission's guide 'How to Make an Anti-Dumping Complaint' advises the complainant to redact or summarise data which contain business secrets in the non-confidential version of the complaint,[39] it does not contain any information on how to avoid violating Article 101 (1) TFEU when preparing the complaint.

6.2.2.1.2   Filing of a Complaint as an Infringement of Article 102 TFEU

Furthermore, it has to be analysed whether the filing of a complaint can amount to an abuse of a dominant position under Article 102 TFEU and, if so, under which circumstances.[40] In *Industrie des Poudres Sphériques*, the leading case on this question in the area of trade defence law, the Court dismissed the applicant's argument that recourse to the anti-dumping procedure by the complainant EU industry constituted an abuse of a dominant position. It held that recourse to a remedy in law and in particular participation by an undertaking in an investigation conducted by the EU institutions does not constitute a violation of Article 102 TFEU. In the view of the Court, the assertion that having recourse to such a procedure is, of itself, contrary to Article 102 TFEU would amount to denying undertakings the right to avail themselves of legal instruments established in the interest of the European Union.[41] The Court further argued that it had not been proven that the EU industry had actually had the intention to use the anti-dumping procedure to exclude the applicant from the market.[42] Thus, without any additional factors proving the intent on part of the EU industry to exclude its foreign competitors, the initiation of an anti-dumping or anti-subsidy procedure on part of the dominant EU industry will not conflict with Article 102 TFEU.

Still, *Laprévote* argues, referring to the CJEU's more recent jurisprudence on matters of intellectual property in *ITT Promedia* and *Protégé International*, that in spite of the Court's stance in *Industrie des Poudres Sphériques* it cannot be excluded for the initiation of the proceedings to infringe Article 102 TFEU if the proceedings

---

for producers of virgin aluminium) (75/497/EEC) recital 9. Another example is the *Aluminium Imports from Eastern Europe* case, where the Commission stressed that dumping by third country producers does not permit the EU producers to enter into restrictive agreements, Commission Decision of 19 December 1984 relating to a proceeding under Article 85 of the EEC Treaty (IV.26.870 – Aluminium imports from eastern Europe) (85/206/EEC) recital 12.2.

[39] European Commission, 'How to Make an Anti-Dumping Complaint: A Guide' para. 6.

[40] One recent instance where this line of argument was employed by the exporting producers, but rebuffed by the Commission is Commission Implementing Regulation (EU) 2020/1336 of 25 September 2020 imposing definitive anti-dumping duties on imports of certain polyvinyl alcohols originating in the People's Republic of China recitals 10 et seq.

[41] *Industrie des poudres sphériques v Commission* (Chap. 5, n 4) 213.

[42] Ibid 214.

are manifestly unfounded and prove to be part of a plan to eliminate competition.[43] Indeed, building on the above, it cannot be excluded that the Court would have arrived at a different conclusion in *Industrie des Poudres Sphériques* had the applicant succeeded in providing sufficient evidence regarding the EU industry's intent to exclude its competitors from the market. Nonetheless, it should be borne in mind that, in the respective judgments cited by *Laprévote*, the Court stressed that access to the courts is a fundamental right and a general principle ensuring the rule of law. For these reasons, it is only in wholly exceptional circumstances that the fact that legal proceedings are brought is capable of constituting an abuse of a dominant position within the meaning of Article 102 TFEU.[44] In another procedure in the field of intellectual property law relied upon by *Laprévote* to support his line of reasoning, the Commission held that the use of procedures and regulations, including administrative and judicial processes with the '*clear purpose*' of excluding competitors carries a particular risk of being in violation of Article 102 TFEU in areas where the authorities or bodies applying such procedures or regulations have 'little or no discretion'.[45]

This restrictive stance of the Commission can be attributed to the fact that an actual risk of a competitor's competitive position being affected by the initiation of proceedings predominantly exists in areas where the authorities have only a limited discretionary power in deciding whether or not to grant the complainant's request concerning the initiation of proceedings. However, the Commission enjoys a wide margin of appreciation in the application of the BADR and the BASR, also with regard to the rejection of complaints by the EU industry.[46] This relatively burdensome initiation of proceedings for the complainant industry differentiates differentiates the area of trade defence from the area of intellectual property law, which is where the judgments referred to by *Laprévote* and the Commission decision mentioned above took place. Consequently, it can be called into doubt whether the risk of the initiation of an investigation pursuant to Article 5 BADR or Article 10 BASR resulting in the actual imposition of measures is comparable to an applicant's request for an injunction being granted under EU intellectual property rules. Indeed, Commission statistics show that of the 15 anti-dumping and anti-subsidy investigations

---

[43] Laprévote (2015), p. 14, referring to *Protégé International Ltd. v Commission* (13 September 2012) T-119/09 49 (General Court) and *ITT Promedia v Commission* (17 July 1998) T-111/96 55–56 (Court of First Instance).

[44] *Protégé International Ltd. v Commission* (n 43) 48; *ITT Promedia v Commission* (n 43) 60.

[45] Commission Decision of 15 June 2005 relating to a proceeding under Article 82 of the EC Treaty and Article 54 of the EEA Agreement (Case COMP/A.37.507/F3 – AstraZeneca) (C(2005) 1757) recital 747.

[46] A judicial review on the Commission's decision to reject a complaint will be limited to assessing whether the relevant procedural rules have been complied with, the facts on which the contested choice is based have been accurately stated, and whether there has been a manifest error in the appraisal of those facts or a misuse of powers, Rados (2018) para. 16.

concluded in 2019, one third was concluded without the imposition of measures.[47] For 2018, out of twelve new anti-dumping and anti-subsidy investigations, as many as eight did not result in the imposition of measures.[48] The statistics covering the previous years paint a similar picture. Consequently, the imposition of measures is far from being a near-automatic result of the initiation of a trade defence investigation. It further serves to recall that it is the Commission's practice to give informal advice to industries before they officially lodge a complaint. This practice contributes to lowering the share of 'unsuccessful' applications.[49] While this can be criticised as making trade defence proceedings intransparent,[50] it reduces the risk of 'sham' trade defence investigations even reaching the stage of the formal initiation of an investigation. In light of the above and also in light of the fundamental rights dimension stressed by the Court as well as the restrictive stance taken by the Commission, in line with the Court's reasoning in *Industrie des Poudres Sphériques*, it is thus only in wholly exceptional circumstances that the initiation of a trade defence investigation will give rise to concerns under Article 102 TFEU.

6.2.2.1.3   The Changes Introduced by the Trade Defence Modernisation Package

Regulation (EU) 2018/825 introduced changes concerning those who are able to put forward an anti-dumping and an anti-subsidy complaint with the Commission. Such a diversification of the parties able to initiate an investigation is *per se* welcome from a competition perspective, as facilitated access to trade defence instruments ensures that they are not used solely by well-organized industries and their representative organizations, with the aforementioned risks to competition this entails.

To begin with, trade unions now may support complaints under the reformed trade defence instruments.[51] If the Union industry withdraws the complaint, however, the trade union cannot uphold the complaint absent the support of the Union industry. During the reform process, it was considered to grant trade unions the right

---

[47] European Commission, 'Commission Staff Working Document accompanying the 37th Annual Report from the Commission to the Council and the European Parliament on the EU's Anti-Dumping, Anti-Subsidy and Safeguard Activities and the Use of Trade Defence Instruments by Third Countries (COM(2019) 158 final)' (SWD(2019) 141 final), Brussels 27 March 2019) 7–8.

[48] European Commission, 'Commission Staff Working Document Accompanying the 38th Annual Report from the Commission to the Council and the European Parliament on the EU's Anti-Dumping, Anti-Subsidy and Safeguard activities and the Use of trade defence instruments by Third Countries targeting the EU in 2019 (COM(2020) final) (SWD(2020) 71 final)', Brussels 30 April 2020) 7–8.

[49] On this practice cf. further European Court of Auditors, 'Special Report: Trade defence instruments: system for protecting EU businesses from dumped and subsidised imports functions well' (Luxembourg 2020) 23 et seq.

[50] Ibid.

[51] Article 5 (1) BADR and Article 10 (1) BASR.

to submit complaints to the Commission independently. Among others, an evaluation study commissioned by the Commission suggested that in order to ensure access
to trade defence instruments in situations where the interests of EU producers and
their workforce diverge (e.g. because of fears of retaliation), labour representatives
should also have the right to submit complaints.[52] Still, as noted by *Hoffmeister*, the
actual impact of such a right would have been negligible, since—as also indicated in
the evaluation study—it would only be of use if the workers' representation wishes
to bring a case against the will of the company management.[53] In such a scenario, a
complaint would be unlikely to contain all the necessary information as set out in
Article 5 (2) BADR and Article 10 (2) BASR respectively.[54] Consequently, given
the near impossibility of trade unions being able to submit a complaint satisfying the
conditions of Article 5 (2) BADR and Article 10 (2) BASR on their own, it is
commendable that the EU institutions ultimately refrained from following the
suggestions included in the evaluation study, and instead opted for a supporting
role of the trade unions.

Second, pursuant to the reformed basic regulations, the Commission shall facilitate access to the trade defence instruments for diverse and fragmented industry
sectors, largely composed of small and medium-sized enterprises (SMEs). This is to
be achieved by a number of measures, among others by providing general information and explanations on procedures and how to submit a complaint.[55] As *Vermulst*
put it, '*in anti-dumping cases organization means power*'.[56] This also applies under
the reformed anti-dumping and anti-subsidy regulations: as reiterated on the Commission's website, the complaint must still be lodged on behalf of at least 25% of the
total EU production of the product that the complaint is about.[57] In diverse and
fragmented industry sectors, it will hence require a bigger number of companies
supporting the complaint in order for this threshold to be met. The higher number of
companies active on the market also presents a bigger organizational challenge to
obtaining all the information necessary in order for a complaint to fulfil the conditions set out under the BASR and the BADR. For example, the so-called 'macro
indicators' must be provided for the whole EU industry. These include production,

---

[52] European Commission, 'Commission Staff Working Document – Impact Assessment accompanying the document "proposal for a regulation of the European Parliament and of the Council on the
modernisation of trade defence instruments"' (n 7) 20.

[53] Hoffmeister (2015), p. 374.

[54] Hoffmeister (2020), p. 225. Hoffmeister appears to argue that trade unions are able to bring a
complaint on their own under the modernised basic regulations. However, the wording of Article
5 (1) subpara. 2 BADR does not support this conclusion, reading that '*[c]omplaints may also be
submitted jointly by the Union industry (. . .) and trade unions, or be supported by trade unions*'
(emphasis added).

[55] Cf. Article 5 (1a) BADR and Article 10 (1a) BASR.

[56] Vermulst (2005), p. 112.

[57] European Commission, 'Trade defence: Help for SMEs', available at <https://ec.europa.eu/trade/
policy/accessing-markets/trade-defence/actions-against-imports-into-the-eu/help-for-smes/>.

capacity, sales in volume, market share and employment.[58] This information is inevitably harder to obtain where the industry is fragmented and consists of SMEs rather than a limited number of large market participants who are accustomed to providing the information necessary for a complaint to be accepted by the Commission. Consequently, while the Commission's awareness-raising strategy may contribute to informing SMEs regarding their rights under the EU's trade defence legislation, in practice complaints are likely to continue to be lodged mainly in sectors where the EU industry—and its respective representative organization—has been a frequent user of the trade defence instruments in the past. Statistics reveal that the majority of investigations under the modernised rules continue to be initiated upon complaints by the chemicals industry and the iron and steel industry. Both industries already were the main users of trade defence instruments in the years before the trade defence modernisation.[59] In only one instance did the Commission initiate an investigation where the Commission industry consisted largely of SMEs,[60] which was later terminated following the withdrawal of the complaint.[61] This imbalance was also noted by the European Court of Auditors (ECA) in its report on the EU's anti-dumping and anti-subsidy action. The ECA found that

> [a]lthough DG TRADE facilitates procedures for participating parties, it does very little outreach to increase awareness and use of TDIs among EU industries. Sectors such as steel and chemicals are well acquainted with TDIs, but other sectors are much less familiar with them. This means that industries experiencing unfair trade may not apply for and benefit from protective measures.[62]

As regards the impact of these changes on the possible violations of Articles 101 and 102 TFEU related to the initiation of an anti-dumping or anti-subsidy investigation, it should first be noted that none of the amendments discussed above explicitly addresses any concerns in this regard. This comes as no surprise, as the Commission's impact assessment on the effectiveness of the EU's trade

---

[58] European Commission, 'How to Make an Anti-Dumping Complaint' (n 39) 105.

[59] Cf. the lists contained in the Annexes of European Commission, '37th Annual Report from the Commission to the Council and the European Parliament on the EU's Anti-Dumping, Anti-Subsidy and Safeguard activities and the Use of trade defence instruments by Third Countries targeting the EU in 2018 (COM(2019) 158 final)' (Brussels 27 March 2019) and European Commission, 'Commission Staff Working Document Accompanying the 38th Annual Report from the Commission to the Council and the European Parliament on the EU's Anti-Dumping, Anti-Subsidy and Safeguard activities and the Use of trade defence instruments by Third Countries targeting the EU in 2019 (COM(2020) final) (SWD(2020) 71 final)' (n 48). Out of the 154 investigations initiated between 2009 and 2018, 47 concerned the chemicals sector, 57 the iron and steel industry.

[60] European Commission, Notice of initiation of an anti-dumping proceeding concerning imports of pins and staples originating in the People's Republic of China (OJ 2019 C 425/8) (18 December 2019).

[61] Commission Implementing Decision (EU) 2020/1202 of 14 August 2020 terminating the anti-dumping proceeding concerning imports of pins and staples originating in the People's Republic of China and subjecting imports of pins and staples originating in the People's Republic of China to surveillance.

[62] European Court of Auditors (n 49) 21.

defence instruments preceding the reform mentioned their potential to facilitate anti-competitive behaviour by the domestic industry only in passing.[63] Hence, the changes introduced by the Trade Defence Modernisation Package do not directly affect the possibility of the initiation of a trade defence investigation resulting in violations of EU competition law. If anything, by not calling attention to the need to observe the EU competition rules in preparing a complaint in its SME guide or in its guidelines on how to draft a complaint, it could be argued that the Commission indirectly increases the risk of violations of Article 101 (1) TFEU on part of companies active in highly fragmented and diverse industry sectors. SMEs might not be aware of the existing jurisprudence and Commission practice on the matter and might thus be at a greater danger of inadvertently infringing Article 101 (1) TFEU when exchanging information in the preparation of an anti-dumping or anti-subsidy complaint.

6.2.2.1.4   Conclusions and Further Considerations

The Commission itself has stated on various occasions that the purpose of trade defence proceedings is not and cannot be to enforce or encourage restrictive business practices.[64] The risk of infringements of Articles 101 and 102 TFEU related to the initiation of trade defence investigations appears relatively low. However, in order to minimise any remaining risks, further measures should be undertaken ensuring that already the first steps of an investigation are compliant with EU competition rules. One possible option of doing so would be for the Commission to include the relevant jurisprudence of the Court and its own decisional practice in its official documents, in particular in light of the increased focus on the participation of SMEs in trade defence proceedings. This would contribute to raising awareness among the EU industry that a misuse of its right to initiate an investigation might conflict with Articles 101, 102 TFEU.

6.2.2.2   Restrictions Related to the Imposition of Measures

Duties and undertakings, the two types of measures permissible against dumped or subsidised products under the basic regulations, have been criticised as facilitating infringements of Article 101 (1) TFEU on part of the companies active in a particular market or as having an inherently anti-competitive effect.

---

[63] European Commission, 'Commission Staff Working Document – Impact Assessment accompanying the document "proposal for a regulation of the European Parliament and of the Council on the modernisation of trade defence instruments"' (n 7) 17.

[64] Cf. e.g. already Commission Regulation (EEC) No 1361/87 of 18 May 1987 imposing a provisional anti-dumping duty on imports of ferro-silico-calcium/calcium silicide originating in Brazil (n 3) recital 12.

6.2.2.2.1   Undertakings

6.2.2.2.1.1   *Potential Restrictions to Competition*

Where a provisional affirmative determination of dumping and injury has been made, the Commission may accept satisfactory voluntary undertaking offers submitted by any exporter to revise his prises, if the injurious effect of the dumping is thereby eliminated.[65] The same applies once a provisional affirmative determination of subsidisation and injury has been made.[66]

The compatibility of price undertakings with Article 101 (1) TFEU has frequently been called into question. While some authors consider price undertakings to be less restrictive to competition than the imposition of duties,[67] others have denounced them as constituting nothing less but '*government-sponsored cartels*'.[68] This negative assessment is based on the fact that price undertakings not only result in a general increase in the price levels within the Union—with the negative effects for users and consumers this entails—but also regulate price competition between the market participants to a greater extent. Yet, while these detrimental effects on price competition within the EU are considered necessary to restore the fairness in competition between the EU industry and their foreign counterparts, price undertakings must not be mis-used for price increases going beyond what is necessary to achieve this objective. Both the EU industry and the exporting producers must thus refrain from utilising price undertakings as a conduit for practices violating Article 101 (1) TFEU, such as a coordination of prices.

Compared to duties, price undertakings are advantageous for the exporters as the higher rents resulting from the higher export prices remain with them, whereas the revenue created by anti-dumping duties accrues to the EU.[69] Unlike duties, which usually remain in force for at least five years,[70] the exporters can withdraw from the undertaking at short notice in the event of significant changes in the marketplace.[71] However, it is partly these advantages that make them susceptible to possible conflicts with Article 101 (1) TFEU: in order to ensure advantageous terms of an undertaking, the exporters may collude as a means of improving the terms of the price undertaking before making an undertaking offer to the Commission.[72] Further, since exporters will usually be keen to avoid the undertaking being replaced with duties upon violation of the undertaking, the exporters that are party to an

---

[65] Article 8 BADR. Theoretically, the BASR and the BADR also provide for the possibility of quantitative undertakings. However, the Commission no longer accepts 'pure' quantitative undertakings, cf. above p. 56.

[66] Article 13 BASR.

[67] Reymond (2015), p. 463.

[68] Vermulst (1987), p. 220.

[69] Steinbach (2014), p. 173.

[70] Cf. Article 11 (2) BADR.

[71] van Bael and Bellis (2019) § 7.13.

[72] Stegemann (1990), p. 289.

undertaking will monitor each other for not undercutting the undertaking price.[73] Indeed, in *Argentinian Biodiesel* the Commission explicitly considered that in view of the active role of the Argentine Chamber of Biofuels (CARBIO), the Commission would be able to monitor the undertakings effectively.[74] While the content of undertakings is usually confidential, depending on the intensity of the monitoring occurring on part of a firm's competitors or the industry's representative body, this might well conflict with Article 101 (1) TFEU, amounting to price fixing agreements.[75] This is particular so in instances where an industry's representative body is involved in the monitoring of undertakings.[76]

This leads to the second competition-related issue of price undertakings: they generally increase market transparency and, much like the preparation of a complaint on part of the Union industry, may be used as a conduit for the exchange of competitively sensitive information or price fixing on part of the European producers as well as the third country exporters.[77] While the Commission does not communicate the minimum price, the EU industry as well as domestic competitors of the exporting producers that are party to an undertaking can easily deduce from the exporter's market behaviour what the minimum prices are, in particular in highly concentrated markets where a certain degree of market transparency already exists.[78] Further, in highly concentrated markets with oligopolistic market structures, a reduced degree of competition among the EU producers might in turn enable them to keep their prices below the threshold set out in the price undertaking, without the risk of being outbid by the foreign producers.[79] Even though this might not infringe Article 101 (1) TFEU as long as there is no collusion among the EU industry regarding the pricing policies, it is nonetheless detrimental to competition as it reduces price competition in the entire market, with the price undertaking serving as the unofficial reference price.

It can be inferred from the above that the risk of the price undertaking being misused for anti-competitive purposes and the content of the price undertaking

---

[73] Steinbach (2014), p. 180.

[74] Commission Implementing Decision (EU) 2019/245 of 11 February 2019 accepting undertaking offers following the imposition of definitive countervailing duties on imports of biodiesel originating in Argentina (Chap. 3, n 146) recital 9; cf. also Commission Decision of 22 May 1990 accepting undertakings given in connection with the anti-dumping proceeding concerning imports of photo albums originating in South Korea and Hong Kong, and terminating the investigation (90/241/EEC) recital 45.

[75] Montag (2015), p. 385; Stegemann (1990), p. 289, pointing out that the risk of cartelisation also covers the EU industry (and/or the exporters) extending the scope of the price undertaking to other markets or goods.

[76] It has even been suggested that the mere attempt by a trade association representing the complainant industry to discover the minimum price agreed to by exporters in the context of a price undertaking might infringe Article 101 TFEU, Temple Lang (1987), p. 606.

[77] Montag (2015), p. 381.

[78] Schroeder (1991), p. 547.

[79] Steinbach (2014), p. 184.

becoming known increases in highly transparent markets, i.e. markets where the market players can easily discern their competitors' prices. With regard to undertakings accepted in anti-dumping investigations, *Steinbach* further argues that in instances where the analogue country method is used, a comparable degree of market transparency exists. He contends that in those situations, the competitors of the exporters can deduce the content of the price undertaking offer by adding the producers' costs in the analogue country and the 'regular' profit margin of 5% used by the Commission in its injury calculations.[80] This would also apply to calculations of normal value under the new methodology of Article 2 (6a) BADR, where the normal value is to be constructed exclusively on the basis of costs of production and sale reflecting undistorted prices or benchmarks, and which shall include an undistorted and reasonable amount of SG&A and for profits.[81] *Steinbach's* argument however appears to presuppose that the content of a price undertaking is equal to the costs of production borne by the producers in a representative country, plus a reasonable profit margin (i.e. the constructed normal value). This, however, is not necessarily the case. The Commission will only accept an undertaking offer if it is convinced that the price increase will be sufficient to eliminate the injurious effect of the dumping.[82] As the rules concerning the lesser duty rule apply accordingly to price undertakings,[83] the increase in the exporting producers' price levels is not always such to equal the constructed normal value. Instead, the price increases mandated by a price undertaking may be set at a lower, injury-eliminating level as a consequence of the lesser duty rule. In these instances, not even the exporting producers will necessarily be aware of the non-injurious price.[84] This applies regardless of the methodology one uses in the calculation of the normal value. Consequently, even if the EU industry were able to infer its competitors' production costs with some accuracy, this would still not automatically be reflective of the content of the price undertaking.

That being said, even if the minimum import price were to coincide with the constructed normal value, *Steinbach's* theory could not be followed for a number of other reasons, at least with regard to the practice adopted by the Commission under the analogue country methodology contained in Article 2 (7) BADR. While the Commission frequently indicates the profit margin it considers appropriate for the calculation of the export value,[85] it is doubtful whether the EU industry will have

---

[80] Ibid 183–184.

[81] Article 2 (6a) lit. a) BADR.

[82] Article 8 (1) subpara. 1 BADR and Article 13 (1) BASR. Cf. e.g. Commission Implementing Decision (EU) 707/2013 of 4 December 2013 confirming the acceptance of an undertaking offered in connection with the anti-dumping and anti-subsidy proceedings concerning imports of crystalline silicon photovoltaic modules and key components (i.e. cells) originating in or consigned from the People's Republic of China for the period of application of definitive measures recital 8.

[83] Article 8 (1) subparas. 3, 4 BADR and Article 13 (1) subparas. 3, 4 BASR.

[84] Kuplewatzky and Rusche (2020) para. 3.

[85] Cf. e.g. Commission Implementing Regulation (EU) 2017/141 of 26 January 2017 imposing definitive anti-dumping duties on imports of certain stainless steel tube and pipe butt-welding

detailed knowledge about the production costs borne by the producers of the product concerned in the analogue country. Such sensitive information is not included in the legislative acts published by the Commission; it merely communicates the methodology it used in calculating normal value.[86] This is in line with Article 19 (1) BADR, which prescribes that any information which is by nature confidential (for example because its disclosure would be of significant competitive advantage to a competitor) shall be treated as such by the authorities if good cause is shown.[87] Production costs can be considered to constitute such confidential information.[88] Indeed, the Commission itself also assumes this, as it advises the producers in an analogue country on how to prepare non-confidential versions of the questionnaire without disclosing their production costs in its questionnaire for analogue country producers.[89] Consequently, absent any official information on part of the Commission and given the fact that the production costs usually will not be disclosed during the investigation, it appears questionable whether it would actually be possible for the EU industry to obtain accurate information on the production costs which it could then use for illegal price fixing. Therefore, it cannot be concluded that a degree of price transparency comparable to that in oligopolistic markets[90] exits in the event of normal value construction under the analogue country method of Article 2 (7) BADR.

So far, the Commission has not accepted undertakings in investigations where the new methodology of Article 2 (6a) BADR was applied. Still, it is expedient to analyse whether the concern presented by *Steinbach* regarding the possible abuse of price undertakings for price fixing is valid under the new methodology. This would be the case if the use of the new methodology were to result in a high degree of transparency regarding the producers' costs of production. Under the new methodology, the Commission will construct normal value on the basis of costs of

---

fittings, whether or not finished, originating in the People's Republic of China and Taiwan (Chap. 3, n 117) recital 86.

[86] Commission Regulation (EU) No 513/2013 of 4 June 2013 imposing a provisional anti-dumping duty on imports of crystalline silicon photovoltaic modules and key components (i.e. cells and wafers) originating in or consigned from the People's Republic of China and amending Regulation (EU) No 182/2013 making these imports originating in or consigned from the People's Republic of China subject to registration recitals 78–85.

[87] It should also be noted that the protection of business secrets is a general principle of EU law. In addition, the maintenance of fair competition is an important public interest, the safeguarding of which can justify a refusal to disclose information which reveals business secrets, *Jinan Meide Casting Co. Ltd. v Council* (30 June 2016) T-424/13 165 (General Court).

[88] *Ajinomoto Co. Inc. and The NutraSweet Company v Council* (Chap. 5, n 85) 106.

[89] European Commission, 'Anti-Dumping Questionnaire for Producers in the Analogue Country', available at <https://trade.ec.europa.eu/doclib/docs/2013/december/tradoc_151941.pdf>. Cf. also Commission Implementing Regulation (EU) 2017/141 of 26 January 2017 imposing definitive anti-dumping duties on imports of certain stainless steel tube and pipe butt-welding fittings, whether or not finished, originating in the People's Republic of China and Taiwan (Chap. 3, n 117) recitals 126–127, where the Commission held that it could not disclose the company's figures underlying the Commission's price adjustment for confidentiality reasons.

[90] Both on the Union market and the exporters' home market.

production and sale reflecting undistorted prices or benchmarks. The sources the Commission may use include *inter alia* corresponding costs of production and sale in an appropriate representative country or undistorted international prices, costs, or benchmarks.[91] Just as it was the case in the application of the analogue country method, the Commission will not publicise the actual costs of production incurred by the producers in the appropriate representative country for confidentiality reasons.

The investigation in *Ironing Boards* serves as an example of the approach taken by the Commission under the new methodology. In the investigation concerning the imports of ironing boards from China, the Commission used data provided by Turkey, which was chosen as the appropriate representative country, as well as by two Turkish companies for establishing the costs of production and sale in accordance with Article 2 (6a) BADR. While the Commission disclosed the average import prices it assigned to the factors of production for ironing boards, the data was not company-specific but was sourced from a database. The labour costs incurred by the specific companies in their production of ironing boards likewise were not disclosed in the regulation, but rather only the average labour costs in the specific labour sector as listed by the Turkish Statistical Institute.[92] In establishing the undistorted manufacturing costs, the Commission relied on the information provided by the applicants in the review request on the usage of each factor (materials and labour) for the production of ironing boards. The Commission then multiplied the usage factors by the undistorted costs per unit observed in the representative country. Only in including the manufacturing overheads, SG&A and profit, the Commission relied on the data provided by the two Turkish companies.[93] Since the Commission has been criticised for the lack of transparency regarding its methods in calculating normal value under the previous version of Article 2 (7) BADR, it is *per se* a welcome development for the Commission to disclose its calculation methods in more detail.[94] However, the risk of the exporting producers' EU competitors being able to accurately calculate the exporting producers' total production costs appears

---

[91] Article 2 (6a) lit. a) BADR.

[92] Commission Implementing Regulation (EU) 2019/1662 of 1 October 2019 imposing a definitive anti-dumping duty on imports of ironing boards originating in the People's Republic of China following an expiry review pursuant to Article 11(2) of Regulation (EU) 2016/1036 of the European Parliament and of the Council recital 121.

[93] Ibid recitals 129–130. Cf. also the similar approach taken in Commission Implementing Regulation (EU) 2019/1267 of 26 July 2019 imposing a definitive anti-dumping duty on imports of tungsten electrodes originating in the People's Republic of China following an expiry review under Article 11(2) of Regulation (EU) 2016/1036 recitals 115 et seq; Commission Implementing Regulation (EU) 2019/1259 of 24 July 2019 imposing a definitive anti-dumping duty on imports of threaded tube or pipe cast fittings, of malleable cast iron and spheroidal graphite cast iron, originating in the People's Republic of China and Thailand, following an expiry review pursuant to Article 11(2) of Regulation (EU) 2016/1036 of the European Parliament and of the Council recitals 136 et seq.

[94] For example, in the *Tungsten Electrodes* case, the Commission did not disclose any of the information on which it based its calculations when first imposing provisional duties, cf. Commission Regulation (EC) No 1350/2006 of 13 September 2006 imposing a provisional

to have increased under the new methodology, given the more detailed information on the calculation methodology and the factors used therein contained in the implementing regulations. Nonetheless, as the Commission does not publish any company-specific information used in calculating the cost of production, but only information that is publicly available, the risk of this increase in transparency regarding the calculation of the constructed normal value facilitating breaches of Article 101 (1) TFEU appears to remain limited.

Ultimately, it should be borne in mind that this is not an issue arising solely in the context of price undertakings. Even though the danger of the EU and non-EU producers' prices being fixed at the same level is particularly high in the context of price undertakings, the issue of an increase in market transparency with the possible consolidation of price levels this entails arises in the context of normal value calculations under the new methodology in general.

6.2.2.2.1.2 Commission Practice

The Commission has a wide margin of appreciation in deciding whether to accept or reject an undertaking offer.[95] However, the Commission must state the grounds on which the rejection is based and it must not exceed the margin of discretion conferred to it.[96]

In the past, the Commission frequently accepted undertakings, particularly in anti-dumping proceedings, with studies showing that between 1981 and 2001, around 40% of anti-dumping investigations were concluded by implementing price undertakings.[97] More recently, there has been a sharp decline in the number of undertakings.[98] Over the last decade, the Commission only accepted undertaking offers in four anti-dumping investigations (out of 132 new investigations initiated in

---

anti-dumping duty on imports of certain tungsten electrodes originating in the People's Republic of China recitals 32–33 and 45–46.

[95] Cf. the reasons for the rejection of an undertaking given in Article 8 (3) BADR and Article 13 (3) BASR.

[96] *Cartorobica SpA v Ministero delle Finanze dello Stato* (27 March 1990) C-189/88 25 (European Court of Justice).

[97] Zanardi (2006), p. 591; cf. also Zanardi (2004), p. 403.

[98] A more recent study analysing the cases initiated in the period between 1995 and 2008 concluded that price undertakings were only a part of anti-dumping measures in 23% of all cases, with 'pure' price undertakings having been accepted in 15% of the cases. As mentioned above, 'pure' quantitative undertakings are no longer accepted by the Commission. This is advantageous from a competition perspective, since quantity undertakings make the supply of the affected imports completely inelastic, Stegemann (1990), p. 283.

the period between 01.01.2009 and 31.12.2019)[99] and in one anti-subsidy investigation (compared to 38 investigations initiated in the reference period).[100]

Commentators have attributed this decline to a number of factors, among them the official trade policy of the EU to give preferential treatment to the Eastern European accession countries and to conclude anti-dumping proceedings by means of price undertakings.[101] Consequently, after their accession to the EU in 2004, the use of price undertakings in anti-dumping proceedings declined. Further, while China heads the list of countries whose exports to the EU are affected by trade defence measures,[102] price undertakings are used only infrequently *vis-à-vis* Chinese exports, mostly due to difficulties concerning the monitoring and enforcement of the undertakings.[103] While the past rejections took place under the old BADR, it can be assumed that the arguments regarding the difficulties in the monitoring of an undertaking and in ensuring its effectiveness do also apply under the new Article 2 (6a) BADR.[104] An exception to this general downward trend as well as the tendency not to accept undertakings in proceedings involving products originating

---

[99] Commission Implementing Decision (EU) 707/2013 of 4 December 2013 confirming the acceptance of an undertaking offered in connection with the anti-dumping and anti-subsidy proceedings concerning imports of crystalline silicon photovoltaic modules and key components (i.e. cells) originating in or consigned from the People's Republic of China for the period of application of definitive measures (n 82); Commission Decision (EU) 279/2011 of 13 May 2011 accepting an undertaking offered in connection with the anti-dumping proceeding concerning imports of zeolite A powder originating in Bosnia and Herzegovina; Commission Decision (EU) 177/2010 of 23 March 2010 amending Decision 2006/109/EC by accepting three offers to join the joint price undertaking accepted in connection with the anti-dumping proceeding concerning imports of certain castings originating in the People's Republic of China; Commission Decision of 5 October 2009 accepting an undertaking offered in connection with the anti-dumping proceeding concerning imports of certain aluminium foil originating, inter alia, in Brazil (2009/736/EC).

[100] Commission Implementing Decision (EU) 2019/245 of 11 February 2019 accepting undertaking offers following the imposition of definitive countervailing duties on imports of biodiesel originating in Argentina (Chap. 3, n 146).

[101] '*The Commission (. . .) will give (. . .) a clear preference to price undertakings rather than duties in order to conclude anti-dumping cases where injury is found*', European Council, 'Essen Declaration on a Strategy for Central and Eastern Europe (Bulletin of the European Communities No. 12/1994)' (9 December 1994) 21.

[102] Cf. the statistics provided in European Commission, 'Commission Staff Working Document Accompanying the 38th Annual Report from the Commission to the Council and the European Parliament on the EU's Anti-Dumping, Anti-Subsidy and Safeguard activities and the Use of trade defence instruments by Third Countries targeting the EU in 2019 (COM(2020) final) (SWD(2020) 71 final)' (n 48) 7: of 121 anti-dumping measures in force at the end of 2019, 86 concerned imports originating in China. Of the 16 anti-subsidy measures in place, 7 concerned Chinese imports. This trend continued in 2020, cf. the statistics provided in European Commission, 'Commission Staff Working Document Accompanying the 39th Annual Report from the Commission to the Council and the European Parliament on the EU's Anti-Dumping, Anti-Subsidy and Safeguard activities and the Use of trade defence instruments by Third Countries targeting the EU in 2020 (COM(2021) 496 final) (SWD(2021) 234 final)' 5.

[103] Steinbach (2014), pp. 174–175.

[104] Article 2 (6a) BADR; cf. also van Bael and Bellis (2019) § 7.11.

in China were the *Solar Panels* proceedings, which concerned anti-dumping and anti-subsidy proceedings on components of solar panels.[105]

As mentioned, the Commission may refuse the acceptance of undertakings on competition grounds.[106] It appears, though, that competition arguments are not decisive in the Commission's considerations on whether or not to accept an undertaking.[107] Most importantly, even where the Commission did reject an undertaking offer on the basis of competition concerns, they did not pose the only reason for this rejection. Indeed, the Commission also based its reasoning on other considerations that would justify the rejection of an undertaking, most notably the insufficient removal of injury by the proposed undertaking.[108] Despite the scarce Commission practice in this respect, it is nevertheless possible to identify a set of criteria the Commission usually applies when considering competition law aspects. These criteria are presented hereafter.

Generally speaking, as the risk of undertakings having the effect of fixing a minimum export price is particularly high in transparent markets, the Commission has avoided accepting a price undertaking in markets with only a small number of exporters.[109] Similarly, where the EU industry consisted only of a small number of players, the Commission has also refrained from the use of price undertakings.[110] Opposite, due to monitoring and circumvention issues, the Commission usually will not accept undertakings if there is a high number of exporters.[111]

However, in the *Solar Panels* proceedings, the Commission accepted undertakings offered by 121 Chinese exporters. This is remarkable for a number of reasons. First, as indicated above, it constitutes an exception to the Commission's general

---

[105]Commission Implementing Decision (EU) 707/2013 of 4 December 2013 confirming the acceptance of an undertaking offered in connection with the anti-dumping and anti-subsidy proceedings concerning imports of crystalline silicon photovoltaic modules and key components (i.e. cells) originating in or consigned from the People's Republic of China for the period of application of definitive measures (n 82).

[106]Cf. above p. 61 et seq.

[107]Cf. e.g. Commission Implementing Decision (EU) 2019/245 of 11 February 2019 accepting undertaking offers following the imposition of definitive countervailing duties on imports of biodiesel originating in Argentina (Chap. 3, n 146) recital 53, where the Commission rejected concerns by the EU industry that the undertaking would conflict with EU competition law.

[108]Council Regulation (EC) No 221/2008 of 10 March 2008 imposing a definitive anti-dumping duty and collecting definitively the provisional duty imposed on imports of certain manganese dioxides originating in South Africa (Chap. 3, n 152) recitals 68–70; Council Regulation (EC) No 1965/98 of 9 September 1998 imposing a definitive anti-dumping duty on imports of polysulphide polymers originating in the United States of America and collecting definitively the provisional duty imposed recital 56; Council Regulation (EEC) No 2322/85 of 12 August 1985 imposing a definitive anti-dumping duty on imports of glycine originating in Japan recital 22.

[109]Steinbach (2014), p. 184.

[110]van Bael and Bellis (2019) § 7.14; cf. e.g. the regulations cited above, n 108.

[111]Cf. also Article 8 (3) BADR: '*Undertakings offered need not be accepted if their acceptance is considered impractical, such as where the number of actual or potential exporters is too great (. . .).*'

reluctance concerning the acceptance of undertakings. One could have assumed that, in light of the previous Commission practice, it would not have accepted the undertaking already due to the large number of exporters.[112] Most interesting however is the fact that the undertaking was offered by a group of exporting producers in cooperation with the China Chamber of Commerce for Import and Export of Machinery and Electronic Products (CCCME).[113] For one, this challenges the view that undertaking offers do not fall within the scope of Article 101 (1) TFEU, since they are unilateral commitments offered by single exporters.[114] *Montag* holds that

> it seems difficult to reconcile the concept of a single/joint minimum import price offer with the fundamental principles of competition law. Reaching an agreement on a single minimum price inherently seems to imply the exchange of competitively sensitive information between competing exporters (. . .). One could even argue that the joint price undertaking results in a price cartel.[115]

Indeed, an EU producer sought the annulment of the Commission Implementing Regulation in question, in part because he considered the Commission's decision to accept the undertaking offer to infringe Article 101 (1) TFEU. However, as the Court adjudged the action for annulment to be inadmissible, it did not decide on the substance of the claim.[116] While the Commission itself is not a direct addressee of Articles 101, 102 TFEU, its acts, being secondary legislation, must nonetheless comply with primary law.[117] In consequence, it does not seem unfathomable for a Commission decision accepting an undertaking offer which is based on the exporting producers coordinating prices among themselves to violate Article 101 (1) TFEU.

In determining whether the companies party to an undertaking could still be held liable for infringing Article 101 (1) TFEU in such a situation, some authors have referred, by analogy, to the ruling in *Thyssen Krupp*.[118] Here, the General Court rejected arguments that the Commission itself had initiated or encouraged conduct it

---

[112] Indeed, Van Bael and Bellis argue that the suggestion of a price undertaking by the Commission itself was due to the Commission considering that this type of measure would allow it to obtain a positive vote in support of definitive anti-dumping measures in the Trade Defence Instruments Committee, van Bael and Bellis (2019) § 7.11.

[113] Commission Implementing Decision (EU) 707/2013 of 4 December 2013 confirming the acceptance of an undertaking offered in connection with the anti-dumping and anti-subsidy proceedings concerning imports of crystalline silicon photovoltaic modules and key components (i.e. cells) originating in or consigned from the People's Republic of China for the period of application of definitive measures (n 82) recital 2.

[114] Montag (2015), p. 383.

[115] Ibid 390.

[116] *SolarWorld AG and others v Council* (1 February 2016) T-141/14 (General Court); upheld in *SolarWorld and others v Commission* (9 November 2017) C-204/16 P 16 (European Court of Justice).

[117] *Tetra Pak Rausing SA v Commission* (10 July 1990) T-51/89 25 (Court of First Instance).

[118] Montag (2015), p. 391.

later held to be in violation of EU competition law, mainly because the Commission had not been aware of all the exchanges of information occurring between the EU producers which it subsequently considered to infringe Article 101 TFEU. Thus, the Court upheld the Commission's infringement decision.[119] It seems questionable, though, whether it can be argued that the Commission is not aware of the fact that a joint price undertaking offer, such as the one presented by the CCCME and the Chinese exporters, will always entail the exchange of sensitive information among competitors in order to arrive at 'common ground' regarding the offer. Therefore, in line with its current general restrictive approach towards the acceptance of undertakings, the Commission should refrain from accepting joint undertaking offers. This applies even more where the decision to accept an undertaking has not been made on the basis of factual considerations regarding the appropriateness of the undertaking in offsetting the injury caused by the presence of dumped imports, but was instead motivated by political concerns, as it was the case in the *Solar Panels* proceedings.[120]

6.2.2.2.1.3   *The Changes Introduced by the Trade Defence Modernisation Package*

As elaborated upon, undertakings carry a considerable risk of conflicting with Article 101 (1) TFEU. Accordingly, the possibilities for their acceptance should, in principle, be limited. Although spurred by effectiveness rather than competition concerns, during the reform process, the European Parliament intended to limit the Commission's options in accepting undertaking offers by ensuring that it may only do so where the Commission can ensure that the undertaking effectively eliminates the injurious effect of the subsidisation or dumping.[121] Recital 17 of Regulation (EU) 2018/825 reflects this, prescribing that the Commission should only accept an offer for an undertaking where it is satisfied, based on a prospective analysis, that it effectively eliminates the injurious effect of dumping.[122] Articles 8 (1) BADR and 13 (1) BASR were adapted accordingly, now holding that an undertaking may only be accepted where it eliminates the injury.[123] Authors have considered this

---

[119] *Thyssen Stahl AG v Commission* (11 March 1999) T-141/94 328 et seq (Court of First Instance).

[120] On the background of the *Solar Panels* proceedings cf. Goron (2018), p. 103.

[121] European Parliament, 'Amendments adopted by the European Parliament on 5 February 2014 on the proposal for a regulation of the European Parliament and of the Council amending Council Regulation (EC) No 1225/2009 on protection against dumped imports from countries not members of the European Community and Council Regulation (EC) No 597/2009 on protection against subsidised imports from countries not members of the European Community', OJ 2017 C 93/261 amendments 31 and 58.

[122] Recital 17 of Regulation (EU) 2018/825 (Chap. 1, n 10). Even though the text only refers to the context of anti-dumping proceedings, it can be assumed that these concerns regarding the effectiveness of undertakings in eliminating the injury also extend to countervailing proceedings.

[123] The previous versions of Article 8 (1) BADR and Article 13 (1) BASR read that an undertaking offer will be accepted where the Commission *'is satisfied that the injurious effect of the dumping [or subsidies, respectively] is thereby eliminated'*.

requirement regarding the conduct of an analysis to impose stricter conditions upon the Commission for accepting undertakings.[124] In reality, however, aspects calling the effectiveness of the undertaking in eliminating the injury into question were among the most frequent reasons for the Commission to reject an undertaking offer even before the modernisation of the EU's trade defence instruments.[125] Consequently, these changes will likely not bring about any significant changes in the future Commission practice, since this concern regarding the effectiveness of the undertaking in eliminating the injury is already reflected in its past decisional practice. In view of the Commission's reluctance in accepting undertaking offers over the last years,[126] it might nonetheless add to the general downward trend regarding the termination of investigations by undertakings and to their decreasing relevance in the EU's trade defence practice.

The reformed Article 8 (1) subpara. 3 BADR and its counterpart, Article 13 (1) subpara. 3 BASR, prescribe that price increases shall be less than the margin of dumping or subsidisation if such increase would be adequate to remove the injury to the Union industry.[127] In anti-dumping investigations, when examining whether price increases up to the injury margin would be sufficient, Article 7 (2a) to (2d) BADR and the limitations to the application of the lesser duty rule prescribed therein apply accordingly.[128] The reforms to the BASR reflect the *per se* non-application of the lesser duty rule in anti-subsidy proceedings.[129] These modifications ensure coherence by prescribing that the Commission also takes the

---

[124] Hoffmeister (2020), p. 224.

[125] Cf. e.g. Commission Implementing Regulation (EU) 2019/1688 of 8 October 2019 imposing a definitive anti-dumping duty and definitively collecting the provisional duty imposed on imports of mixtures of urea and ammonium nitrate originating in Russia, Trinidad and Tobago and the United States of America recital 291, where it held that the proposed minimum import price was inadequate to remove the injurious effects of dumping, or Commission Implementing Regulation (EU) 2016/1247 of 28 July 2016 imposing a definitive anti-dumping duty and collecting definitively the provisional duty imposed on imports of aspartame originating in the People's Republic of China recital 138, where the Commission considered price undertakings to not be effective remedies for products with volatile costs of production.

[126] With some notable exceptions (which appear to at least in part have been motivated by political considerations) such as the *Solar Panels* case (Commission Implementing Decision (EU) 707/2013 of 4 December 2013 confirming the acceptance of an undertaking offered in connection with the anti-dumping and anti-subsidy proceedings concerning imports of crystalline silicon photovoltaic modules and key components (i.e. cells) originating in or consigned from the People's Republic of China for the period of application of definitive measures (n 82)) or the *Argentine Biodiesel* case, (Commission Implementing Decision (EU) 2019/245 of 11 February 2019 accepting undertaking offers following the imposition of definitive countervailing duties on imports of biodiesel originating in Argentina (Chap. 3, n 146)).

[127] The previous version of Article 8 (1) subpara. 3 BADR only read that the price increases under the undertaking *'should'* be less than the dumping margin if such increase would be adequate to remove the injury.

[128] Article 8 (1) subpara. 3 BADR.

[129] Article 13 (1) subparas. 3, 4 BASR.

concerns leading to the non-application of the lesser duty rule into account when deciding upon the acceptance of a price undertaking.

The amendments to the scope of application of the lesser duty rule result in the possibility of higher price increases under price undertakings. Compared to duties, price undertakings may be advantageous for the exporters since the additional revenue created by the sales at a higher price accrues to them. Consequently, one could assume that the non-application of the lesser duty rule in relation to undertakings is not as disadvantageous for exporting producers as it is in the case of the imposition of duties. Nonetheless, it must still be borne in mind that the higher the minimum import price is, the lower the chances for third country producers are to compete on prices. Even though this might provide an incentive for them to strengthen the non-price competitiveness of their products (such as quality, customer care etc.), the higher the minimum import price the bigger the changes made to their products would have to be in order for them to remain competitive.[130] Depending on the characteristics of the product concerned, this might not be possible to the full extent, e.g. concerning products that are imported at great quantities, but are of a relatively low quality. Consequently, a higher minimum import price might produce a 'chilling effect' on the level of exports to the European Union comparable to that of the imposition of duties.

Further, the BADR and the BASR now explicitly prescribe that reasons of general policy—which fall among the reasons for which the Commission may reject the acceptance of an undertaking—include the principles and obligations set out in environmental agreements and protocols thereunder to which the Union is a party as well as certain ILO conventions.[131] In general, their inclusion in the reformed provisions on the acceptance of undertakings is reflective of the heightened visibility of social and environmental concerns throughout the reformed BADR and BASR. Yet, given the broad discretion of the Commission in deciding upon the acceptance of undertakings, the Commission most likely would be able to reject an undertaking offer for environmental or social concerns as aspects of general policy even without an explicit reference to these issues being contained in the reformed basic regulations.

As the main reasons for the rejection of undertaking offers by the Commission are concerns regarding their effectiveness and practicability,[132] it is improbable that reasons of general policy will gain prominence as grounds for rejection under the reformed trade defence instruments. It is however being suggested that undertakings offered by exporters with very low social and environmental standards should not be accepted in general.[133] Even though this is not explicitly prescribed by the reformed

---

[130] Vandenbussche and Wauthy point out that the increased quality-competition faced by foreign exporters in the event of undertakings may ultimately even be harmful for the European producers through quality reversals, Vandenbussche and Wauthy (2001), pp. 103–104.

[131] Article 8 (3) BADR and Article 13 (3) BASR.

[132] Cf. van Bael and Bellis (2019) § 7.11 with examples of the Commission practice.

[133] Hoffmeister (2020), p. 225.

basic regulations, Regulation (EU) 2018/825 leaves the door open to such an approach, with its recital 12 prescribing that where a country under measures withdraws from multilateral environmental agreements or from core ILO conventions, an interim review should be initiated. This review can result in the withdrawal of acceptance of the undertakings in force.[134] It could be argued that if undertakings can be withdrawn due to an insufficient level of social and environmental protection prevailing in the country of export, *a fortiori,* any undertaking offer from exporting producers located in such a country should not be accepted as a matter of principle. So far, this is not reflected in the Commission practice under the reformed rules, which is guided by the same considerations as under the old rules: the Commission continues to reject undertaking offers mainly out of concerns regarding the monitoring of the undertakings and their effectiveness in remedying the injury caused by the presence of the dumped or subsidised imports respectively.[135]

During the reform process, the European Parliament submitted amendments to the Commission proposal seeking to increase the transparency of undertakings. One amendment—which was included in the final text of Regulation (EU) 2018/825— required parties which offer an undertaking to provide a meaningful non-confidential version of such undertaking which would be made available to the interested parties to the investigation, the European Parliament and the Council.[136] Moreover, the amendments submitted by Parliament prescribed that before accepting any such offer, the Commission would have to consult the Union industry with regard to the main features of the undertaking.[137] This second aspect was not included in the Regulation. Although Parliament's proposal did not indicate that the Commission would have had to base its final decision on the impact received, the EU industry would have played a considerably more active role in the process leading up to the acceptance of undertaking offers. An amendment of the basic regulations to this

---

[134] Recital 12 of Regulation (EU) 2018/825 (Chap. 1, n 10).

[135] The Commission has rejected undertaking offers on a number of occasions since the Trade Defence Modernisation Package entered into force. However, in none of the instances, the reasons for the rejection of the offer lay in insufficient compliance with social and environmental standards. Cf. e.g. Commission Implementing Regulation (EU) 2020/353 of 3 March 2020 imposing a definitive anti-dumping duty and definitively collecting the provisional duty imposed on imports of steel road wheels originating in the People's Republic of China recital 90; Commission Implementing Regulation (EU) 2019/2092 of 28 November 2019 imposing a definitive countervailing duty on imports of biodiesel originating in Indonesia recitals 490–500; Commission Implementing Regulation (EU) 2019/1688 of 8 October 2019 imposing a definitive anti-dumping duty and definitively collecting the provisional duty imposed on imports of mixtures of urea and ammonium nitrate originating in Russia, Trinidad and Tobago and the United States of America (n 125) recitals 289–299.

[136] European Parliament, 'Amendments adopted by the European Parliament on 5 February 2014 on the proposal for a regulation of the European Parliament and of the Council amending Council Regulation (EC) No 1225/2009 on protection against dumped imports from countries not members of the European Community and Council Regulation (EC) No 597/2009 on protection against subsidised imports from countries not members of the European Community (COM(2013)0192)' (n 121) amendments 32 and 59.

[137] Ibid.

effect would have been problematic for several reasons. Firstly, it should be recalled that the central role of the EU industry throughout the entire investigation can be explained by the core rationale of the trade defence instruments, namely the protection of the EU industry against unfair competition.[138] As noted by *Eeckhout*, this translates into a central administrative role for the complainants representing the EU industry.[139] Nonetheless, a situation must be avoided where it so much as appears that it is not the Commission, as the competent investigating authority, but the EU industry who determines the course of an investigation. Such criticism regarding an undue influence of the EU industry is already expressed regarding other parts of an investigation, and it would inevitably have been raised again if a mandatory consultation of the EU industry on the main characteristics of the proposed undertakings had been introduced in the reformed basic regulations. Further, such an increase in the influence of the EU industry would have entailed the risk of the Commission's decisions on the acceptance of undertakings being perceived as no longer being driven by purely factual considerations, but also by protectionist reflexes on part of the EU industry expressed in its submissions to the Commission regarding the acceptance of undertakings. For such reasons, it is appropriate that the amendment was not included in the final text of Regulation (EU) 2018/825. Instead, under the modernised basic regulations, the EU industry must only be given the opportunity to comment on the main features of the undertaking.[140]

Lastly, undertaking offers must now be made five days prior to the end of the period during which representations may be made pursuant to Article 20 (5) BADR and Article 30 (5) BASR respectively. This modification is intended to counter the practice of exporting producers to submit undertaking offers 'last minute' before the adoption of measures.[141]

6.2.2.2.1.4   Conclusions and Further Considerations

As shown above, the acceptance of undertakings entails the risk of practices conflicting with Article 101 (1) TFEU by both the EU industry and the exporting producers. This is not addressed in the EU's modernised trade defence legislation or the Commission's practice. On the contrary, the Commission's decision to accept a joint undertaking offer in the *Solar Panels* proceedings could even be viewed as the Commission wilfully ignoring competition-related issues associated with the acceptance of undertakings. Overall, given the risks to competition connected to undertakings, the downward trend regarding the acceptance of undertaking offers is a positive development—even though the Commission's more restrictive stance on the manner is not so much motivated by competition concerns but by concerns relating to the efficiency of undertakings.

---

[138] Cf. above p. 94 et seq.

[139] Eeckhout (2011), p. 9.

[140] Article 8 (4) subpara. 2 BADR and Article 13 (4) subpara. 2 BASR.

[141] Hoffmeister (2020), p. 225.

The modifications regulating the acceptance of undertaking offers as introduced by the amending Regulation (EU) 2018/825 are likely to reinforce this downward trend. The integration of social and environmental concerns in the provisions regulating the acceptance of undertakings, in line with the general tone of the Trade Defence Modernisation Package, is unlikely to bring about significant changes to the Commission practice. It can be assumed that the main reasons for the (non-) acceptance or the withdrawal of undertakings will continue to be rooted in concerns relating to their effectiveness and their monitoring. Competition concerns do not figure among the amendments made to the provisions governing undertakings. However, particularly in light of the Commission's practice in *Solar Panels*, further legislative changes to the basic regulations are warranted. Possible avenues for amending the rules of the basic regulations to better address competition concerns raised by undertakings are thus explored in the following.

It has been criticised that, in the event of a violation of undertakings, the Commission only has one effective sanction, namely to impose an anti-dumping or a countervailing duty, with only very limited options regarding the retroactive levying of such duties.[142] According to *Stegemann*, intermediate sanctions would be needed that could be used to tackle 'minor' violations of undertakings before they become serious enough to warrant the withdrawal of the acceptance of an undertaking.[143] Even if one disregards difficulties of definition, such as determining which violations of undertakings would be considered 'minor', it should be recalled that the WTO framework prohibits specific action against dumping or subsidisation of exports from another member outside the measures provided for in the ADA and the ASCM respectively.[144] It is doubtful whether additional options, such as monetary sanctions imposed upon single exporters for violations of the undertaking would be in compliance with this. This is even more so as both WTO law and EU law acknowledge that the imposition of trade defence measures does not have any punitive character but is only intended to offset the negative effects of the presence

---

[142] The Commission may only levy duties retroactively within the framework provided by the BADR and the BASR. In the past, the Commission has sought to circumvent these limitations by declaring undertaking invoices issued by exporting producers void where it is determined that the producers violated the terms of their undertaking, resulting in the retroactive levying of the anti-dumping or countervailing duties the exporters would have had to pay. However, the General Court held this practice to be in violation of the system concerning the retroactive application of anti-dumping duties as set out in the basic regulation. *Jiangsu Seraphim Solar System Co. Ltd. v Commission* (8 July 2020) T-110/17 137–138, 151 (General Court), currently under appeal in C-439/20 P.

[143] Stegemann (1990), p. 280. At this point, it should be noted that in accordance with the principle of proportionality, inadvertent or minimal violations of undertakings will not result in its withdrawal, but in the exporting producer being given a warning, Kuplewatzky and Rusche (2020) para. 27.

[144] Article 18.1 ADA and Article 32.1 ASCM. Cf. also *United States – Continued Dumping and Subsidy Offset Act of 2000 (Byrd Amendment)* (16 September 2003) WT/DS217/R (Panel Report) and Adamantopoulos (2008) para. 22.

of dumped products on the importing country's market.[145] However, it appears that sanctions for violations of an undertaking would carry such a punitive character, effectively punishing the exporter for continuous dumping or the export of subsidised products instead of merely offsetting the negative effects caused by the respective trading practice. Consequently, the legal feasibility of *Stegemann*'s suggestion under WTO law must be called into question.

What should however be taken into consideration is to explicitly provide the Commission with the opportunity of withdrawing the acceptance of an undertaking where it is established that the undertaking gives rise to competition concerns. Several possible avenues for effectively addressing anti-competitive behaviour on part of the exporting producers arising in the context of undertakings present themselves. For one, it could be argued that—given that it is one of the objectives of the trade defence instruments to re-establish a 'level playing field'[146]—it is an inherent obligation of the parties to an undertaking to not misuse the undertaking in a way that is causing further distortions of competition. Under such an interpretation, the Commission would be able to hold that an exporter violated his obligations under the undertaking if he uses it in a manner that contradicts Articles 101, 102 TFEU. This would permit the Commission to immediately withdraw its acceptance of the undertaking pursuant to Article 8 (9) BADR or Article 13 (9) BASR respectively. The precise scope of the exporter's obligations is, however, set out in the decision by which the Commission accepts the undertaking, which in turn is based upon an offer made by the exporter. It thus seems questionable to argue that the exporters assumed any commitments going beyond the explicit obligations contained in the legislative act that would permit the Commission to withdraw the undertaking. This would be in conflict with the principle of legal certainty. Therefore, without any specific reference to the EU competition rules in an undertaking, the violation of competition law provisions within the context of an undertaking cannot be considered a violation of the terms of the undertaking, enabling the Commission to withdraw its acceptance of the undertaking.

One could further consider a violation of EU competition law to constitute a circumstance permitting the initiation of an interim review. Under the relevant provisions of the basic regulations, a review shall be initiated where the request contains sufficient evidence that the existing measure is not, or is no longer, sufficient to counteract the dumping or the countervailable subsidy which is causing injury.[147] It could be reasoned that a review is also warranted *a fortiori* where there is sufficient evidence that the measure is not only insufficiently alleviating the injury caused by the dumped or subsidised imports, but is instead causing injury itself due to its competition-distorting effects. Further, it is already the Commission's practice to withdraw its acceptance of undertakings where it considers the undertaking to no

---

[145] In detail on the character of anti-dumping duties cf. Kuplewatzky (2018).

[146] Cf. above p. 94 et seq.

[147] Article 11 (3) BADR and Article 19 (2) BASR.

longer be workable.[148] Anti-competitive behaviour occurring within the context of undertakings can be considered to limit the efficacy of the undertaking in alleviating the injury to the EU industry, warranting the conclusion that the undertaking likewise is unworkable under such circumstances.

Such an interpretation would however cause issues concerning the choice of the appropriate injury standard. Under EU trade defence law, injury to the EU industry is to be alleviated. Conversely, under EU competition law, practices causing injury to the competitive process itself are prohibited. In particular, in the event of practices violating Article 101 (1) TFEU 'by object', no economically adverse effect of a firm's behaviour on competition within the EU needs to be proven for the Commission to conclude that the conduct in question infringes Article 101 (1) TFEU.[149] Given the above, it appears that most anti-competitive practices occurring in the sphere of undertakings would be considered 'by object'-restrictions to competition, such as horizontal price fixing agreements.[150] Therefore, in this regard the issue would arise of whether the understanding adopted by the EU institutions according to which certain practices are inherently detrimental to competition would also suffice for an interim review to be initiated under the basic regulations or whether a separate 'injury to the EU industry'-analysis would have to be conducted by the Commission. Thus, simply maintaining that practices violating Articles 101, 102 TFEU cause injury to the EU industry within the meaning of the BADR and the BASR would risk conflating the different injury standards of EU competition and EU trade defence law.

Accordingly, in order to address violations of EU competition law arising within the context of undertakings in an adequate manner, further changes to the BASR and the BADR are required. These changes can occur either in the context of the norms addressing interim reviews or in the norms regulating the circumstances under which the Commission may withdraw undertakings. On balance, amending Article 8 (9) BADR and Article 13 (9) BASR as explicitly including violations of EU competition law among the reasons for which the Commission may withdraw its acceptance of an undertaking seems preferable. First, the gravity of breaches of EU competition law warrants the automatic withdrawal and imposition of duties.[151]

---

[148] Cf. e.g. Council Regulation (EC) No 1279/2007 of 30 October 2007 imposing a definitive anti-dumping duty on certain iron or steel ropes and cables originating in the Russian Federation, and repealing the anti-dumping measures on imports of certain iron or steel ropes and cables originating in Thailand and Turkey recitals 200–201.

[149] Cf. above p. 39.

[150] In EU competition law, price fixing agreements are generally characterised as a 'by object'--violation of Article 101 (1) TFEU, cf. with further references Barr (2018) para. 5.041.

[151] Pursuant to the Court's jurisprudence, the exercise of the discretion awarded to the Commission in determining whether, in accordance with the principle of proportionality, it is necessary to withdraw the acceptance of an undertaking if it has been infringed, is subject to review by the EU judicature, *Usha Martin Ltd. v Council and Commission* (22 November 2012) C-552/10 P 32 (European Court of Justice). Given the integral importance of EU competition law in ensuring the success of the internal market, no issues concerning the principle of proportionality regarding the

Moreover, the detrimental effects to competition caused by the anti-competitive conduct of the EU industry and/or the exporters do not necessarily materialise themselves on the market of the product concerned by the investigation. Instead, if the undertaking is used as a means of fixing a minimum price (in violation of Article 101 (1) TFEU), the distortions to competition may also materialise on the downstream market on which the cartel members' customers are present. This stands in contrast to the focus of interim reviews on the effects of the measure on the EU industry directly competing with the subsidised or dumped products. The issue of the divergent injury standards in competition and trade defence law has already been noted. Accordingly, the *telos* and the systematics of the provisions on the initiation of interim reviews exclude amendments addressing violations of competition law in the context of undertakings. When compared with the rules on interim review, the greater flexibility and speed with which a withdrawal of an undertaking can occur under Articles 8 (9) BADR and Article 13 (9) BASR is an additional advantage. Lastly, it should be noted that an exporter may bring an action for annulment as well as action for damages if he contests that the withdrawal of the undertaking is warranted under Article 8 (9) BADR or Article 13 (9) BASR, in particular if the alleged violations of the undertaking did not occur.[152] This can be transposed to the situation at hand if a Commission decision finding an infringement of the EU competition rules—on which the Commission bases its withdrawal of the undertaking—is later overturned by the CJEU.

6.2.2.2.2   Duties

6.2.2.2.2.1   *Potential Restrictions to Competition*

Duties are the second alternative means of offsetting the injury caused by the presence of dumped or subsidised products that is foreseen in the BADR and the BASR respectively. Compared with price undertakings, they present a much lower risk of violations of Article 101 (1) TFEU. This is because there are no legitimate reasons for firms to organize themselves or to cooperate on anything once the remedy is imposed. Further, import prices remain more variable if an *ad valorem* or specific anti-dumping duty is imposed than they would if fixed minimum import prices were set by undertakings.[153] However, again in comparison with undertakings, it is said that duties produce a greater 'chilling effect' on the level of imports to the European Union, as sales are more profitable for exporters if undertakings are accepted by the Commission.[154] While this prospect of additional revenue might

---

withdrawal of an undertaking following a breach of EU competition law on part of the exporters should arise.

[152] *Commission v Fresh Marine* (24 October 2000) T-178/98 46 (Court of First Instance).

[153] Stegemann (1990), p. 293.

[154] As explained above, this is due to the fact that the additional profit accrues to the exporters themselves, whereas where duties are imposed, their revenue accrues to the European Union.

also encourage exporters to strengthen the non-price aspects of competition, such as the quality of the products offered by them or their services and sales organisation,[155] a similar incentive is absent in the event of the imposition of duties. It is argued that this 'chilling effect' further extends to potential market entrants.[156]

6.2.2.2.2.2   Commission Practice

Complimentary to the less frequent acceptance of undertakings by the Commission, the vast majority of anti-dumping and anti-subsidy measures now are *ad valorem* duties. This is a positive development from a competition policy perspective, as duties in general provide for greater price flexibility and lesser opportunities for information exchanges among the exporters and/or the EU industry liable to conflict with Article 101 (1) TFEU. Conversely, the negative effect of duties on the level of imports can be avoided to some extent by making use of the lesser duty rule.

6.2.2.2.2.3   The Changes Introduced by the Trade Defence Modernisation Package

The application of the lesser duty rule is a central tool in limiting the 'chilling effect' brought about by the imposition of duties since it—as indicated by its name—results in a lower duty level. This in turn leads to a smaller decline in the level of exports to the EU and has a lesser deterrent effect on current or future exporters. The smaller degree of the lessening of competitive pressure is favourable from a competition perspective.[157] Under the reformed BADR, the lesser duty rule will not apply in certain instances,[158] and it will be generally inapplicable under the reformed BASR.[159] While the validity of these changes to the scope of application of the lesser duty rule will be discussed in detail below,[160] it can be stated that its non-application will result in higher anti-dumping and countervailing duties being imposed,[161] thereby reducing the incentives of exporters to export to the European Union.

---

[155] Stegemann (1990), p. 294; cf. also above p. 148.

[156] Ibid 289.

[157] Rovegno and Vandenbussche (2012), p. 445. Pauwels, Vandenbussche and Weverbergh point out that lesser duty rules, if open to manipulation by domestic firms, may have undesirable effects on welfare. In particular, under a lesser duty rule a domestic firm has the incentive to contract its production quantities in order to increase the injury margin. This might, under certain circumstances, lead to a lower overall welfare than a pure dumping margin system. Pauwels et al. (2001), p. 75.

[158] Article 7 (2a) BADR prescribes that the Commission may decide not to apply the lesser duty rule in the event of raw material distortions.

[159] Article 12 (1) subparas. 3, 4 BASR and Article 15 (1) subparas. 3, 4 BASR.

[160] Cf. below p. 192 et seq.

[161] This is illustrated by a comparative analysis of average anti-dumping duty levels in the EU, Canada and the U.S. between 1989 and 2009, which reveals the overall average duty level in the EU for the entire period to be 30%, against 70% for the USA and 47% for Canada. Moreover, the

6.2.2.2.2.4 *Conclusions and Further Recommendations*

The imposition of duties presents a much smaller risk of violations of Article 101 (1) TFEU. They may, however, produce a greater 'chilling effect' on the level of imports into the EU. This effect can be minimised to some extent by making use of the lesser duty rule. As noted, the limitations to the scope of application of the lesser duty rule likely will result in higher duty levels, reducing the level of imports into the EU to a greater extent. This, correspondingly, will have an adverse impact on the degree of competition on the internal market. Accordingly, the limitations to the scope of application of the lesser duty rule must be criticised at this point of the analysis.

6.3 Chapter Conclusions

This chapter has revealed that trade defence investigations may be used as a conduit for anti-competitive practices by both the EU industry and the exporting producers. Whereas the risk of a submission of a complaint by the EU industry to the Commission with the objective of an investigation being initiated conflicting with Articles 101, 102 TFU appears modest, it must be taken into consideration that, given their lower degree of familiarity with the EU's trade defence instruments, in particular SMEs run in danger of violating EU competition law when preparing a complaint to the Commission. Accordingly, it would be advisable for the Commission to adapt its guidelines and documents to include the relevant jurisprudence of the Court and its own decisional practice, strengthening awareness among the entire EU industry that a misuse of its right to initiate an investigation might conflict with EU competition law. This would be advisable since it is a declared objective of the reformed basic regulations to facilitate access to trade defence instruments for SMEs.[162]

Similarly, whereas the imposition of duties produces a greater chilling effect on the level of imports into the EU, the risk of violations of EU competition law associated with the imposition of anti-dumping or countervailing duties appears rather low. A different picture presents itself with regard to price undertakings, which may be used as a vehicle for pricing practices conflicting with Article 101 (1) TFEU in a number of scenarios. However, competition concerns rarely play a role in the Commission's considerations when deciding upon the acceptance or rejection of undertaking offers. It is recommended that the Commission changes its practice in that regard. In particular, the Commission should refrain from accepting joint undertaking offers and offers presented in oligopolistic markets, as the risk of the minimum import price being used for price coordination practices is

---

maximum duty level registered in the EU during the reference period was 96.8%. For the U.S., the maximum was 386%, for Canada 226%, Rovegno and Vandenbussche (2012), p. 445.

[162] Cf. Article 5 (1a) BADR and Article 10 (1a) BASR.

particularly high in these two situations. Moreover, amendments to the basic regulations are necessary to allow the Commission to react more efficiently in situations where it is revealed that the undertaking is used for anti-competitive purposes. Regarding price coordination among the exporting producers, this is best achieved by explicitly including violations of EU competition law provisions among the reasons listed in Article 8 (9) BADR and Article 13 (9) BASR for which an undertaking can be withdrawn.

References[163]

Adamantopoulos K (2008) Article VI GATT. In: Wolfrum R, Stoll P-T, Koebele M (eds) WTO – trade remedies. Martinus Nijhoff Publishers

Barr F (2018) Cartels. In: Bailey D, John LE (eds) European Union law of competition, 5th edn. Oxford University Press

Bourgeois J (1989) Antitrust and trade policy: a peaceful coexistence? European community perspective I. Int Bus Lawyer 17(2):58

Bown CP, McCulloch R (2015) 'Antidumping and market competition: implications for emerging economies', EUI Working Papers RCAS. Available at <https://cadmus.eui.eu/bitstream/handle/1814/37522/RSCAS_2015_76.pdf?sequence=1>

Cho S (2009) Anticompetitive trade remedies: how antidumping measures obstruct market competition. North Carolina Law Rev 87(2):357

Davidow J (1999) Antitrust issues arising out of actual or potential enforcement of trade laws. J Int Econ Law 2(4):681

Eeckhout P (2011) Administrative Procedures in EU External Trade Law. Note Prepared for the Directorate-General of Internal Policies of the European Parliament. Available at <https://www.europarl.europa.eu/RegData/etudes/note/join/2011/432758/IPOL-JURI_NT(2011)432758_EN.pdf>

Goron C (2018) Fighting against climate change and for fair trade: finding the EU's interest in the solar panels dispute with China. China-EU Law J 103

Hoai NT, Toan NT, Van PH (2017) Trade diversion as firm adjustment to trade policy: evidence from EU anti-dumping duties on Vietnamese footwear. World Econ 40(6):1128

Hoffmeister F (2015) Modernising the EU's trade defence instruments: mission impossible? In: Herrmann C, Streinz R, Simma B (eds) Trade policy between law, diplomacy and scholarship: liber Amicorum in Memoriam Horst G. Krenzler. Springer

Hoffmeister F (2020) The devil is in the detail: a first guide on the EU's new trade defence rules. In: Weiß W, Furculita C (eds) Global politics and EU trade policy: facing the challenges to a multilateral approach. Springer

Hope E (1998) Introduction. In: Hope E, Mæleng P (eds) Competition and trade policies: Coherence or conflict? Routledge

Kuplewatzky N (2018) Defining anti-dumping duties under European Union law. Trade Law Dev 10(2):448

Kuplewatzky N, Rusche M (2020) Artikel 8 AD-GVO. In: Krenzler HG, Herrmann C, Niestedt M (eds) EU-Außenwirtschafts- und Zollrecht. C.H. Beck

Laprévote FC (2015) Antitrust in wonderland: trade defense through the competition looking-glass. Concurrences 1

---

[163] All online sources were last accessed on 8 September 2021.

Messerlin PA (1990) Anti-dumping regulations or pro-cartel law? The EC chemical cases. World Econ 13(4):465

Montag F (2015) Price undertakings in anti-dumping law: recent trends and considerations from a competition law perspective. In: Herrmann C, Streinz R, Simma B (eds) Trade policy between law, diplomacy and scholarship: liber Amicorum in Memoriam Horst G. Krenzler. Springer

Müller-Ibold T (2018) Antidumping and competition law – common origin, a life of their own and peaceful coexistence?. In: Kokott J, Pohlmann P, Polley R (eds) Europäisches, Deutsches und Internationales Kartellrecht: Festschrift für Dirk Schroeder zum 65. Geburtstag. Dr. Otto Schmidt

Pauwels W, Vandenbussche H, Weverbergh M (2001) Strategic behaviour under European anti-dumping duties. Int J Econ Bus 8(1):75

Pierce RJ (2000) Antidumping law as means of facilitating cartelization. Anti Law J 67(3):725

Rados N (2018) Artikel 5 AD-GVO. In: Krenzler HG, Herrmann C, Niestedt M (eds) EU-Außenwirtschafts- und Zollrecht. C.H. Beck

Reymond D (2015) Action antidumping et droit de la concurrence dans l'Union européenne. Dissertation, Panthéon-Assas

Rovegno L, Vandenbussche H (2012) Anti-dumping practices in the EU. In: Gaines SE, Olsen BE, Sørensen KE (eds) Liberalising trade in the EU and the WTO: a legal comparison. Cambridge University Press

Schroeder D (1991) Anti-trust Law Implications of EEC Anti-dumping proceedings. Rabels Zeitschrift für ausländisches und internationales Privatrecht 55(3):540

Stegemann K (1990) EC anti-dumping policy: are price undertakings a legal substitute for illegal price fixing? Weltwirtschaftliches Archiv 126(2):268

Steinbach A (2014) Price undertakings in EU anti-dumping proceedings – an instrument of the past? J Econ Integr 29(1):165

Temple Lang J (1987) European Community antidumping and competition laws, their actual and potential application to EFTA countries. Tidsskrift for Rettsvitenskap 100(3):590

van Bael I, Bellis J-F (2019) EU anti-dumping and other trade defence instruments, 6th edn. Kluwer Law International

Vandenbussche H, Wauthy X (2001) Inflicting injury through product quality: how European antidumping policy disadvantages European producers. Eur J Polit Econ 17(1):101

Vandoren P (1986) The interface between antidumping and competition law and policy in the European community. Legal Issues Econ Integr 13(2):1

Vermulst E (2005) The 10 major problems with the anti-dumping instrument in the European community. J World Trade 39(1):105

Vermulst EA (1987) Antidumping law and practice in the United States and the European Communities: a comparative analysis. North Holland

Zanardi M (2004) Anti-dumping: what are the numbers to discuss at Doha? World Econ 27(3):403

Zanardi M (2006) Antidumping: a problem in international trade. Eur J Polit Econ 22(3):591

Chapter 7

The Impact of the Trade Defence Modernisation Package on the Relationship Between the EU's Trade Defence Instruments and Competition: Identifying the Protectionist Bias

7.1 Introduction

In addition to identifying potential conflicts with EU competition law provisions that may arise out of trade defence proceedings, it must be analysed to what extent EU trade defence legislation incorporates general competition policy concerns. It must further be ensured that the basic regulations are not designed or applied in a way that is unduly favouring the interests of the EU industry, i.e. in a protectionist manner. This would ultimately distort competition in the internal market and run counter to the objective of EU trade defence legislation to re-establish fair competition as equality between economic operators.[1] In fact, it is an often-voiced criticism that the protection awarded to EU producers under the trade defence instruments goes beyond what is necessary to achieve this objective. This criticism extends to a number of aspects of trade defence proceedings, and it has been voiced continuously by scholars and practitioners alike over the last decades.[2] With regard to the modernised basic regulations, this criticism can be raised in particular with regard to the new methodology of Article 2 (6a) BADR, the limitations to the scope of application of the lesser duty rule and the new rules on injury margin calculation. Finally, the regulations' focus on the *ex officio* initiation of investigations and the more recent practice of the Commission to include non-economic interests in its Union interest analysis under Article 21 BADR and Article 31 BASR deserve further attention with regard to the balance between protecting competition and protectionism struck under the amended basic regulations. As can be derived from the above, for the most part, the chapter is limited to an analysis of the changes made to the substantive law of EU trade defence legislation. The only exceptions to this are the new provisions concerning the *ex officio*-initiation of anti-dumping investigations by

---

[1] Cf. above p. 94 et seq.

[2] Cf. e.g. Pachmann (2005); Baetge (1998), p. 653; Bierwagen (1990); Kulms (1990), pp. 301–302.

© The Author(s), under exclusive license to Springer Nature Switzerland AG 2022
P. Trapp, *The European Union's Trade Defence Modernisation Package*, EYIEL Monographs - Studies in European and International Economic Law 23, https://doi.org/10.1007/978-3-030-91363-2_7

the Commission, given the risk for a politicisation of the use of the EU's trade defence instruments this poses.

7.2   Identifying the Protectionist Bias

7.2.1   Ex officio *Initiations of Investigations*

In November 2012, China initiated anti-dumping and anti-subsidy investigations on imports of polysilicon from the EU into China. The decision was taken only two months after the EU had announced the initiation of anti-dumping and anti-subsidy proceedings concerning imports of crystalline silicon photovoltaic modules and key components originating in China.[3] This parallelism continued during the proceedings that followed, with the Chinese Ministry of Commerce accepting a price undertaking by the main target of the Chinese duties, the German polysilicon producer *Wacker Chemie AG*, shortly after the European Commission and Chinese solar panel producers had reached a similar agreement. After the EU decided not to extend its measures in August 2018, the Chinese Ministry of Commerce likewise dropped its duties on EU polysilicon with effect from 1st November 2018. According to the Commission, in retaliating for the imposition of trade defence measures by the European Union, the Chinese authorities '*carefully mirrored every single move by the EU in the Solar Panels case*'.[4]

This high-profile case undoubtedly added to the feeling that the EU's trade defence instruments lacked effectiveness in the fight against retaliation by third countries, a concern also expressed by stakeholders in the course of the reform process.[5] Particularly the firms lodging a complaint with the Commission might be the target of subsequent retaliatory action taken by the governments in their export markets. In order to avoid such repercussions, the Commission will treat the identity of the complainants as confidential where it considers that such a risk of retaliation exists.[6] Another avenue of avoiding specific companies to become the target of

---

[3] European Commission, Notice of initiation of an anti-dumping proceeding concerning imports of crystalline silicon photovoltaic modules and key components (i.e. cells and wafers) originating in the People's Republic of China (OJ 2012 C 269/5) (6 September 2012).

[4] European Commission, 'Commission Staff Working Document accompanying the 37th Annual Report from the Commission to the Council and the European Parliament on the EU's Anti-Dumping, Anti-Subsidy and Safeguard Activities and the Use of Trade Defence Instruments by Third Countries (COM(2019) 158 final)' (Chap. 6, n 47) 57.

[5] Cf. the statements made in European Commission, 'Commission Staff Working Document – Impact Assessment accompanying the document "proposal for a regulation of the European Parliament and of the Council on the modernisation of trade defence instruments"' (Chap. 6, n 7) 93 et seq.

[6] Cf. e.g. Commission Implementing Regulation (EU) 2018/1012 of 17 July 2018 imposing a provisional anti-dumping duty on imports of electric bicycles originating in the People's Republic of China and amending Implementing Regulation (EU) 2018/671 recital 11; Commission

retaliatory action is to initiate investigations *ex officio*. While the Commission may initiate investigations *ex officio* in special circumstances,[7] in the past, the Commission has only made use of this option in two instances.[8] Addressing the concerns voiced by stakeholders regarding the insufficient protection against retaliatory actions, recital 6 of Regulation (EU) 2018/825 now explicitly prescribes that these special circumstances under which the Commission may initiate proceedings should include the threat of retaliation by third countries. Consequently, under the modernised basic regulations, if the Commission considers a threat of retaliation to exist, this will automatically qualify as a special circumstance[9] enabling the Commission to initiate an investigation. Furthermore, the Union producers are now requested to cooperate with the Commission in investigations that were initiated *ex officio*.[10] Even though the Trade Defence Modernisation Package did not formally extend the list of scenarios under which investigations may be initiated *ex officio*, the focus on the fight against retaliation might nevertheless be a gateway for further politicisation of the EU trade defence rules. In essence, the Commission can decide on its own when it deems a threat of retaliatory action to exist and when it would consider it suitable to initiate an investigation. Even though the Commission generally enjoys a wide margin of discretion in EU trade defence law,[11] the complete absence of guidelines and previous practice as to which circumstances would warrant the conclusion that a threat of retaliation does exist is worrisome.[12] In addition to the risk of over-protection being awarded to the EU producers and the trade defence instruments becoming increasingly politicised, authors have noted that since many of the EU's trading partners emulate its practices, they might well replicate the EU's practices, including any trend of an increasing number of investigations being imitated *ex officio*.[13] This could result in the EU producers

---

Regulation (EU) No 1205/2013 of 26 November 2013 imposing a provisional anti-dumping duty on imports of solar glass from the People's Republic of China recital 11; Commission Regulation (EU) No 513/2013 of 4 June 2013 imposing a provisional anti-dumping duty on imports of crystalline silicon photovoltaic modules and key components (i.e. cells and wafers) originating in or consigned from the People's Republic of China and amending Regulation (EU) No 182/2013 making these imports originating in or consigned from the People's Republic of China subject to registration (Chap. 6, n 86) recital 9.

[7] Article 5 (6) BADR and Article 10 (8) BASR.

[8] European Commission, *Statement by EU Trade Commissioner Karel De Gucht on mobile telecommunications networks from China* (2013). The case was later settled in the Joint Committee. The other case concerned synthetic fibre ropes from India, Commission Regulation (EC) No 18/98 of 7 January 1998 imposing a provisional anti-dumping duty on imports of synthetic fibre ropes originating in India.

[9] Vermulst (2014), p. 20.

[10] Article 6 (9) BADR and Article 11 (11) BASR.

[11] Cf. the sources cited above, Chap. 4, n 119.

[12] Cf. also Vermulst and Sud (2013), p. 205. In its report, the ECA likewise recommends the Commission to clarify which circumstances should trigger an *ex officio* investigation, European Court of Auditors (Chap. 6, n 49) 31–32.

[13] Vermulst (2014), p. 20.

themselves becoming the target of trade defence measures in third States more frequently, thereby offsetting any benefits obtained by a higher level of protection resulting from a higher number of investigations being initiated *ex officio* by the Commission.

Moreover, it can be called into question whether *ex officio* initiations of investigations alone are sufficient to shield the EU industry from retaliatory action. Third States might not necessarily follow the route taken by China in the *Solar Panels* case and target the EU counterpart of the industry affected by the imposition of trade defence measures, but instead opt to make other EU industries active in their markets the subject of measures.[14] Moreover, the efficiency of *ex officio* investigations must be called into question. Lacking the EU industry's cooperation, it will be much more difficult for the Commission to obtain the data necessary for its investigation to proceed. Where an EU producer decides to cooperate—absent any actual obligation to do so—he might still make himself a target of retaliatory action.[15] On the contrary, an EU producer's decision not to cooperate might be an expression of him prioritising other commercial interests, such as protecting his sales opportunities on the export market, over his need for protection by means of trade defence measures.[16] As the anti-dumping and anti-subsidy regulations' primary objective is to offset injury suffered by the EU industry, it must be considered whether pursuing an investigation without any cooperation on part of the EU industry would not contravene the interests of the EU industry, in effect disadvantaging it more than it would have been absent the imposition of measures. Even though the Commission has not initiated any new investigations *ex officio* under the reformed basic regulations so far, it must still be concluded that the changes made by the Trade Defence Modernisation Package are unwelcome insofar as they might lead to a more active use of Article 5 (6) BADR and Article 10 (8) BASR. In addition to the risks of the provisions being used for protectionist purposes and a possibly increased politicisation of trade defence measures, for the reasons set out above, it must further be called into question whether an increased number of *ex officio* initiations of investigations would actually have the desired effect of protecting the EU industry against retaliatory action.

7.2.2   The New Non-standard Methodology for Constructing Normal Value in Anti-dumping Investigations

The new methodology has attracted a great deal of attention among legal scholars and practitioners alike. The reactions oscillate between praising the reform as

---

[14]Ibid 21.

[15]Hoffmeister holds that the '*soft obligation*' laid out in Article 5 (6) BADR might still to some extent act as a '*shield*' against retaliatory acts, Hoffmeister (2020), pp. 220–221.

[16]Vermulst and Sud (2013), p. 205.

showing that the EU is capable of adapting its trade defence instruments to changing economic circumstances[17] and fierce criticism. A significant part of the negative assessment of the changes introduced by the Trade Defence Modernisation Package is directed at the questionable WTO law-compatibility of the new methodology.[18] Closely related to this is the assessment of the new methodology in essence being the old non-market economy methodology of Article 2 (7) BADR *in disguise*,[19] a critique fuelled by the structural similarities between the two approaches[20] and the Commission's references to findings from previous investigations conducted under the old methodology in investigations concerning products originating in China carried out under Article 2 (6a) BADR.[21]

Moreover, the new methodology can be disapproved of for a number of other reasons. One central point of criticism is that it disadvantages the exporting producers located in countries to which the new methodology applies: the benchmarks used in constructing normal value under the new methodology inflate the dumping margin,[22] thereby leading to higher duty levels. This likewise applies with regard to the sources used in calculating normal value.[23] Taken together, these factors will lead to the application of the new methodology resulting in higher dumping margins and hence higher duty levels[24] which will significantly impede market access for dumped products originating in countries to which the new methodology is applied. This, in turn, is advantageous to the EU industry. These market foreclosure effects

---

[17] Müller (2018), p. 61.

[18] On this cf. below Chap. 9, p. 275 et seq.

[19] Vermulst and Sud (2018), p. 253. The critics of the new methodology further point at a Commission impact assessment concerning the possible change in the calculation methodology of dumping regarding the People's Republic of China revealing that the application of the new methodology would result in comparable duty levels, with the average duty level only being 3.86% lower than under the old analogue country method, European Commission, 'Commission Staff Working Document Impact Assessment: Possible change in the calculation methodology of dumping regarding the People's Republic of China (and other non-market economies) (SWD (2016) 370 final)' (Brussels 9 November 2016) 40.

[20] On this cf. Shadikhodjaev (2018), p. 895; Vermulst and Sud (2018), p. 254.

[21] Cf. e.g. Commission Implementing Regulation (EU) 2019/1662 of 1 October 2019 imposing a definitive anti-dumping duty on imports of ironing boards originating in the People's Republic of China following an expiry review pursuant to Article 11(2) of Regulation (EU) 2016/1036 of the European Parliament and of the Council (Chap. 6, n 92) recital 60; Commission Implementing Regulation (EU) 2019/915 of 4 June 2019 imposing a definitive anti-dumping duty on imports of certain aluminium foil in rolls originating in the People's Republic of China following an expiry review under Article 11(2) of Regulation (EU) 2016/1036 of the European Parliament and of the Council (Chap. 5, n 34) recital 50. Cf. also the references to previous investigations in European Commission, 'Commission Staff Working Document on Significant Distortions in the Economy of the People's Republic of China for the Purposes of Trade Defence Investigations (SWD(2017) 483 final/2)' (Brussels 20 December 2017) 428 et seq, and 460 et seq.

[22] Vermulst and Sud (2018), p. 251; Vermulst and Dion Sud (2018), p. 77.

[23] Cf. e.g. Shadikhodjaev (2018), p. 898.

[24] Particularly when viewed together with the changes to the scope of application of the lesser duty rule, cf. below p. 192 et seq.

are further reinforced by the limitations to the scope of application of the lesser duty rule, which will be discussed in detail in the subsequent section of this study.

7.2.2.1   The Criteria Used in Establishing the Existence of Significant Distortions

The new methodology of Article 2 (6a) BADR is intended to address the issue of correctly determining the normal value for products originating in a country where the costs incurred by exporting producers are significantly distorted.[25] As can be derived from the factors used to establish the existence of significant distortions listed in Article 2 (6a) lit. b) BADR, these distortions arise from interventions of the exporting producer's home State in the economy, leading to costs and prices not being the result of free market forces.[26] A comparable, albeit more general line of reasoning put forward is that the use of domestic prices and costs is not appropriate if the government of the exporting country interferes in the economy in a way which goes significantly beyond the regulatory function of the State.[27] The elements relevant in determining whether such distortions exist include *inter alia* the presence of the State in firms allowing the State to interfere with respect to prices or costs, public policies or measures discriminating in favour of domestic suppliers or otherwise influencing free market forces, an inadequate enforcement of bankruptcy, corporate or property laws, and wage costs being distorted.[28]

Various authors have noted the new methodology to be couched in very imprecise terms. In particular the above-mentioned criteria used to arrive at a finding of the existence of significant distortions are considered to lack a proper definition, therefore being open to expansive interpretation by the Commission.[29] This increase in flexibility was an outcome intended by the Commission. In a hearing before the Committee on International Trade of the European Parliament on the subject of the reform, *Joost Korte,* then Deputy Director-General in DG TRADE, explicitly stated that the Commission would prefer not to be *'pinned down on very specific criteria', but instead retain the 'freedom to (...) decide as the markets develop'*.[30] This wish for room for manoeuvre on part of the Commission as the investigating authority

---

[25] Hoffmeister (2020), p. 214.

[26] Article 2 (6a) lit. b) BADR. Cf. also recital 3 of Regulation (EU) 2017/2321 (Chap. 1, n 9): '*In light of experience gained in past proceedings, it is appropriate to clarify the circumstances in which significant distortions affecting to a considerable extent free market forces may be deemed to exist.*'

[27] Müller (2018), p. 57.

[28] Article 2 (6a) lit. b) BADR.

[29] Vermulst and Sud (2018), p. 251.

[30] Committee on International Trade (INTA) of the European Parliament, 'Joost Koorte at the Public Hearing on EU Trade Defence Instruments' (28 February 2017) at 18:27, available at <http://www.europarl.europa.eu/news/en/news-room/20170223IPR63789/committee-on-international-trade-28022017-(pm)>.

might be understandable. Even so, the result of the list contained in Article 2 (6a) lit. b) BADR being non-exhaustive and the elements included in it lacking a precise definition is that the Commission's discretion in deciding on the existence of significant distortions is significant, with the legal uncertainty this ensues.[31]

It must further be questioned whether the inclusion of some of the factors in the list in Article 2 (6a) lit. b) BADR is justified under the reasons given for introducing the new methodology, according to which it is intended to deal with situations where a producer's costs and prices are not the result of supply and demand. This applies especially with regard to the element of distorted wage costs. In its report on the existence of significant distortions in the Chinese economy (the 'China Report'), the elements assessed by the Commission with regard to Chinese wages include the non-ratification of core ILO conventions, among those conventions relating to the right to organize and collective bargaining. Concerning the non-ratification of ILO conventions relating to the right to organize and collective bargaining and freedom of association, the Commission argues that, absent the recognition of equal rights of employers and employees, the wages will not be market based wages. Market based wages are understood as wages that have been freely bargained between workers and management in an undistorted economic environment.[32]

This assumption stands on rather shaky feet. If one follows the Commission's market-liberal approach of the costs of production having to be the result of the free play of market forces, the lack of regulation—*inter alia* by means of international conventions—is in no way detrimental to the wage level being based purely on supply and demand.[33] On the contrary, the Commission's focus on the ratification and implementation of certain ILO conventions[34] seems to acknowledge that, absent any regulation protecting workers' rights, workers run in danger of being disadvantaged when negotiating with their employers. Such regulation, however, restricts the free play of market forces by awarding the workers specific rights. Hence, the Commission's statements that the lack of ratification of ILO conventions entails that wage levels are not reflective of the free play of market forces is contradictory. Likewise, the line of argument pursuant to which the new methodology is intended to address interferences with the economy that go significantly beyond the regulatory function of the State does not hold regarding the non-ratification of international

---

[31] Also noted by Vermulst and Dion Sud (2018), p. 75.

[32] European Commission, 'Commission Staff Working Document on Significant Distortions in the Economy of the People's Republic of China for the Purposes of Trade Defence Investigations (SWD(2017) 483 final/2)' (n 21) 328, 332.

[33] Also noted by Huyghebaert (2019), p. 420.

[34] In this regard cf. also European Commission, 'Commission Staff Working Document on Significant Distortions in the Economy of the Russian Federation for the Purposes of Trade Defence Investigations (SWD(2020) 242 final)' (Brussels 22 October 2020) 353, where problems with observance of two ILO conventions are noted.

conventions in general or an insufficient enforcement of the State's domestic laws.[35]

In addition to the criterion of wage costs being distorted in Article 2 (6a) lit. b) BADR, recital 4 of Regulation (EU) 2017/2321 provides a further basis for the inclusion of social and environmental standards in the calculation of normal value under the new methodology. The recital states that when assessing the existence of significant distortions, relevant international standards should be taken into account by the Commission, where appropriate. This includes core ILO conventions and relevant multilateral environmental conventions. As can be derived from the wording of the recital as well as the non-binding character of the recitals themselves, the Commission is not obligated to have regard to such concerns when assessing the existence of significant distortions. Nonetheless, the Commission's China Report and its report on the existence of significant distortions in the Russian economy (the 'Russia Report') are testimony to the relevance the Commission attaches to these standards. The reference to the lack of ratification of core ILO conventions in the China Report has already been mentioned.[36] Moreover, the Russia Report elaborates upon deficiencies regarding the implementation of select ILO conventions by Russia[37] and further dedicates a section to the implementation of environmental standards.[38]

It should be noted that the basic regulations do not contain any information as to which level of social and environmental protection would be considered adequate when deciding upon the existence of significant distortions based on an insufficient level of social and environmental protection. In the 2019 expiry review concerning *Organic Coated Steel*, the Commission noted that the request for the initiation of an expiry review had identified a number of alleged additional distortions in the form of *inter alia* low environmental standards. Relying on an OECD report on environmental enforcement and compliance in China from 2006, the Commission accepted the argument made by the applicant that the Chinese government offered indirect support to steel manufacturers by failing to enforce basic environmental standards when contrasted with Union producers, which have to adhere to stricter environmental standards.[39] At this point, it is worth emphasising that the assessment

---

[35] Article 2 (6a) lit. b) BADR names the '*lack, discriminatory application or inadequate enforcement of bankruptcy, corporate or property laws*' one of the factors to be taken into account when establishing the existence of significant distortions.

[36] European Commission, 'Commission Staff Working Document on Significant Distortions in the Economy of the People's Republic of China for the Purposes of Trade Defence Investigations (SWD(2017) 483 final/2)' (n 21) 328, 332.

[37] European Commission, 'Commission Staff Working Document on Significant Distortions in the Economy of the Russian Federation for the Purposes of Trade Defence Investigations (SWD(2020) 242 final)' (n 34) 352–353.

[38] Ibid 185–188.

[39] Commission Implementing Regulation (EU) 2019/687 of 2 May 2019 imposing a definitive anti-dumping duty on imports of certain organic coated steel products originating in the People's Republic of China following an expiry review pursuant to Article 11 (2) of Regulation (EU) 2016/1036 of the European Parliament and of the Council recitals 51–52.

conducted by the Commission appears to go beyond the question of whether the relevant international standards, as can be derived from multilateral environmental agreements, are being complied with. Instead, the Commission compares the level of environmental protection in China with the one prevailing in the EU, effectively making the EU environmental standards the benchmark for the environmental policies of other States. Given the high standard of environmental protection in the EU, such a comparison will almost inevitably result in the conclusion that the degree of environmental protection in the other country is insufficient.

Even if one were to accept this unilateral benchmarking, the question remains why a lower level of environmental protection would warrant the conclusion that significant distortions exist, leading to the domestic costs and prices being disregarded when calculating the normal value. If one recalls the rationale provided for the introduction of the new methodology, namely the significant interference of the State in the economy or such interferences resulting in the domestic data not being reflective of the free play of market forces, none of these reasons apply with regard to a country having a—at least from an EU-perspective—deficient system of environmental protection or an inadequate protection of workers' rights. Rather, the criteria used to establish the existence of significant distortions, among those social and environmental considerations, address policy decisions that provide the exporting country's domestic industry with an advantage over foreign competitors in general.[40]

In conclusion, the new methodology goes beyond its declared objective of focussing on those State interventions in the economy which result in the prices or costs in the exporting country no longer reflecting the free play of market sources. Instead, it targets all forms of government action which potentially confer a competitive advantage on the non-EU industry as the competitors of the EU industry, irrespective of whether this affects the reliability of domestic prices and costs in the exporting country in establishing normal value. As such, the new methodology constitutes an attempt at addressing situations where EU companies suffer a competitive disadvantage when competing internationally. As elaborated upon in Chap. 4, the assumption underlying the imposition of anti-dumping measures is that the third country exporting producers are enjoying competitive advantages that are not the result of genuine comparative advantages, such as superior efficiency. Instead, the ability to sell goods below normal value on the internal market is seen as an expression of the exporting producer enjoying unfair competitive advantages through government measures foreclosing the exporting producer's home market to foreign competitors, or an inadequate competition law enforcement.[41] Under the line of argument advanced to justify the use of anti-dumping measures, they are not directed against actual comparative advantages enjoyed by exporting producers,

---

[40] On the question whether this warrants not basing the calculation of normal value on the exporting producers' domestic prices pursuant to Article 2.2 ADA cf. Huyghebaert (2019), p. 425 and below Chap. 9, p. 276 et seq.

[41] Cf. above p. 94 et seq.

such as those resulting from lower wage or environmental costs. Even though the objective of the EU's trade defence instruments of contributing to fair trade may also include social and environmental aspects,[42] the approach adopted by the new methodology of comprehensively approximating competitive conditions is thus not covered by the *ratio* underlying the use of anti-dumping legislation.

Taken together with the discretion awarded to the Commission in the application of Article 2 (6a) BADR, the inclusion of aspects of social or environmental dumping in the new methodology has the potential of overly benefitting the EU industry, going beyond the remediation of any actual detrimental effects caused by the exporting producers selling at prices below normal value.

Furthermore, as the new methodology is also concerned with distortions arising from the subsidisation of raw materials, attention must be paid in the event of parallel anti-subsidy and anti-dumping investigations to ensure that the same subsidisation is not addressed in both investigations (so-called 'double counting' or 'double remedies'). Offsetting the same subsidisation twice is not only impermissible under Article 14 (1) subpara. 2 BADR and the corresponding provisions of WTO law.[43] Moreover, it must be objected to under the overarching fairness-rationale pursued by EU trade defence law. Since the market distorting effects of subsidies are already addressed in the anti-subsidy investigation, taking them into account again when determining the existence of significant distortions unfairly disadvantages the exporting producers instead of levelling the playing field between them and their EU counterparts. The *Glass Fibre Fabrics* case constituted the first instance of parallel antidumping and countervailing investigations since the legislative changes introduced by Regulation (EU) 2017/2321 and Regulation (EU) 2018/825 entered into force. Here, the Commission opted for the deduction of the full subsidy amount from the dumping duty rate as it applied the new methodology in order to avoid the same subsidisation being taken into account in both investigations.[44]

7.2.2.2   The Evidence Used in Establishing the Existence of Significant Distortions

Compared to the previous version of the non-market economy methodology contained in Article 2 (7) BADR, the amending Regulation (EU) 2017/2321 shifted the burden of proof regarding the application of the new non-standard

---

[42] Cf. the section of the objectives of the EU's trade defense instruments above, p. 82 et seq. In detail on the amendments relating to social and environmental standards cf. below Chap. 8, p. 253 et seq.

[43] On the WTO compatibility of the reformed basic regulations cf. below Chap. 9, p. 275 et seq.

[44] Commission Implementing Regulation (EU) 2020/776 of 12 June 2020 imposing definitive countervailing duties on imports of certain woven and/or stitched glass fibre fabrics originating in the People's Republic of China and Egypt and amending Commission Implementing Regulation (EU) 2020/492 imposing definitive anti-dumping duties on imports of certain woven and/or stitched glass fibre fabrics originating in the People's Republic of China and Egypt recitals 1117–1118, 1122, 1136 and Article 2.

methodology.[45] Under the old Article 2 (7) BADR, individual exporters located in a country that was classified as a non-market economy could apply for market economy treatment but had to provide sufficient evidence that market economy provisions prevailed for them in respect of the manufacture and sale of the product concerned.[46] Now, it is the applicants in an investigation who have to provide sufficient evidence justifying the application of the new non-standard methodology of Article 2 (6a) BADR.[47] However, the Commission ensured that this would not result in an additional burden being imposed on the complainants. Pursuant to Article 2 (6a) lit. c) BADR, it is for the Commission to prepare country- or sector-wide reports on the existence of significant distortions where it has well-founded indications of the possible existence of such distortions as referred to in Article 2 (6a) lit. b) BADR.[48] Such reports and the evidence on which they are based are placed on the file of any investigation relating to that country or sector. When filing a complaint or a request for a review, the Union industry may rely on the evidence referred to in the report in order to meet the standard of evidence as required by Article 5 (9) BADR.[49]

Therefore, the Commission report in effect creates a rebuttable presumption of the existence of significant distortions in the economy of the country that is the subject of the Commission report.[50] It follows that the introduction of the new methodology, while formally shifting the burden of proof, did not lead to a significant change in the situation compared to the non-market economy methodology used under the previous version of the basic anti-dumping regulation. The Commission practice under the new methodology will be addressed in more detail in the following section.[51] It should already be mentioned at this point, however, that the practice under the

---

[45] Shadikhodjaev (2018), p. 897.

[46] Article 2 (7) lit. b), c) BADR.

[47] Article 2 (6a) lit. e) and Article 5 (9) BADR.

[48] The report itself does not have to be issued in a legally binding form; it being issued in the form of a Commission Staff Working Document is sufficient, cf. Commission Implementing Regulation (EU) 2021/546 of 29 March 2021 imposing a definitive anti-dumping duty and definitively collecting the provisional duty imposed on imports of aluminium extrusions originating in the People's Republic of China, recitals 109–110.

[49] Article 2 (6a) lit. d) BADR. Cf. also European Commission, *The EU is changing its anti-dumping and anti-subsidy legislation to address state induced market distortions* (2017): '[I]t is the Commission who will have the additional work to establish that significant distortions exist in a particular country. When lodging a request for the initiation of an anti-dumping investigation EU industry will be able to rely on the Commission's detailed country and sector level reports as evidence that distortions exist' and Commission Implementing Regulation (EU) 2021/546 of 29 March 2021 imposing a definitive anti-dumping duty and definitively collecting the provisional duty imposed on imports of aluminium extrusions originating in the People's Republic of China (n 48) recital 113, where it is held that, *pro forma*, the existence of a report is not a precondition for applying the new methodology of Article 2 (6a) BADR. What counts are the findings that the significant distortions are relevant in the case at hand.

[50] Shadikhodjaev (2018), p. 898.

[51] Cf. below p. 186 et seq.

reformed BADR shows that, for the purposes of triggering the use of the non-standard methodology of Article 2 (6a) BADR, it is sufficient for the complainant to refer to the Commission report on the existence of significant distortions. The Commission relies heavily on its own findings concerning the existence of significant distortions in justifying the application of Article 2 (6a) BADR, with additional evidence provided by the complainant industry only being of minor importance.[52] Conversely, as long as there is no such Commission report, no anti-dumping complaints by the EU industry calling for the application of Article 2 (6a) BADR will be put forward. Hence, while it is correct that the report itself does not contain a conclusion on the existence of significant distortions for the purposes of an investigation as such,[53] one has to agree with *Vermulst/Sud*, who consider a finding of distortions a '*self-fulfilling prophecy*' once the Commission has issued a report on the country under investigation.[54] Lastly, while the reformed basic regulation provides for the possibility to rebut the significant distortions claim,[55] the chances of an individual exporter being able to provide sufficient information in order to successfully rebut the significant distortions claim for the sector he is active in or his home country's economy as a whole are slim.[56] This likewise applies to Article 2 (6a) lit. a) BADR, which provides the possibility of using an exporting producer's costs if he can provide sufficient evidence that his own costs are undistorted, as it will prove difficult for an individual exporter to produce enough evidence supporting his claim if he is located in a country where the Commission has found significant distortions to exist.[57]

---

[52] Cf. e.g. Commission Implementing Regulation (EU) 2019/1198 of 12 July 2019 imposing a definitive anti-dumping duty on imports of ceramic tableware and kitchenware originating in the People's Republic of China following an expiry review pursuant to Article 11(2) of Regulation (EU) No 2016/1036 recitals 63–127; Commission Implementing Regulation (EU) 2019/915 of 4 June 2019 imposing a definitive anti-dumping duty on imports of certain aluminium foil in rolls originating in the People's Republic of China following an expiry review under Article 11(2) of Regulation (EU) 2016/1036 of the European Parliament and of the Council (Chap. 5, n 34) recitals 55–106.

[53] Müller (2018), p. 59.

[54] Vermulst and Sud (2018), p. 254. But cf. Commission Implementing Regulation (EU) 2021/546 of 29 March 2021 imposing a definitive anti-dumping duty and definitively collecting the provisional duty imposed on imports of aluminium extrusions originating in the People's Republic of China (n 48), recital 115, where the Commission emphasises that the issuing of a report does not replace the actual investigation.

[55] Article 2 (6a) lit. c) BADR.

[56] Vermulst and Sud (2018), p. 255, cf. e.g. Commission Implementing Regulation (EU) 2020/1534 of 21 October 2020 imposing a definitive anti-dumping duty on imports of certain prepared or preserved citrus fruits (namely mandarins, etc.) originating in the People's Republic of China following an expiry review pursuant to Article 11(2) of Regulation (EU) 2016/1036 of the European Parliament and of the Council, recitals 87–88, 91–93, 105, where the Chinese producers unsuccessfully tried arguing that the Chinese sector for canned citrus fruits was not affected by significant distortions.

[57] Ibid; cf. also Commission Implementing Regulation (EU) 2020/1428 of 12 October 2020 imposing a provisional anti-dumping duty on imports of aluminium extrusions originating in the

7.2.2.3 The Benchmarks Used in Constructing Normal Value

Pursuant to Article 2 (6a) lit. a) BADR, the sources the Commission may use in constructing normal value include corresponding costs in an appropriate representative country, undistorted international prices, costs or benchmarks, or domestic costs. Article 2 (6a) lit. a) BADR does not contain a hierarchy. This has led authors to assume that, drawing on Article 2 (5) BADR, undistorted domestic costs should be used as a priority option.[58] When having regard to recital 5 of Regulation (EU) 2107/2321, however, it appears as though undistorted domestic costs actually are not the primary benchmark on which to base the construction of normal value. The recital reads that domestic costs may also be used in constructing normal value, but only to the extent that they are positively established not to be distorted, on the basis of accurate and appropriate evidence.[59] Further, the practice of the Commission under the new methodology shows that Article 2 (6a) BADR is a stand-alone provision, not to be applied in conjunction with Article 2 (3), (5) BADR.[60] Therefore, no conclusions can be inferred from the hierarchy contained in Article 2 (5) BADR. The corresponding costs in an appropriate representative country or undistorted international prices are the preferred avenues in constructing normal value instead.[61]

Of these other two alternative benchmarks, the corresponding costs from an appropriate representative country with a similar level of economic development are being used more frequently. However, the Commission has at times had recourse to different sources when establishing normal value, replacing the costs of single factors of production with international benchmarks where it considered it inappropriate to use the prices in the representative country.[62]

People's Republic of China recitals 76 et seq, where the exporters failed at providing sufficient evidence that their own domestic costs were undistorted.

[58] Shadikhodjaev (2018), p. 898.

[59] Recital 5 of Regulation (EU) 2017/2321 (Chap. 1, n 9).

[60] Cf. the calculation of the normal value in Commission Implementing Regulation (EU) 2019/1693 of 9 October 2019 imposing a provisional anti-dumping duty on imports of steel road wheels originating in the People's Republic of China; Commission Implementing Regulation (EU) 2019/915 of 4 June 2019 imposing a definitive anti-dumping duty on imports of certain aluminium foil in rolls originating in the People's Republic of China following an expiry review under Article 11(2) of Regulation (EU) 2016/1036 of the European Parliament and of the Council (Chap. 5, n 34); Commission Implementing Regulation (EU) 2019/687 of 2 May 2019 imposing a definitive anti-dumping duty on imports of certain organic coated steel products originating in the People's Republic of China following an expiry review pursuant to Article 11 (2) of Regulation (EU) 2016/1036 of the European Parliament and of the Council (n 39).

[61] Hoffmeister (2020), p. 217.

[62] Commission Implementing Regulation (EU) 2020/776 of 12 June 2020 imposing definitive countervailing duties on imports of certain woven and/or stitched glass fibre fabrics originating in the People's Republic of China and Egypt and amending Commission Implementing Regulation (EU) 2020/492 imposing definitive anti-dumping duties on imports of certain woven and/or stitched glass fibre fabrics originating in the People's Republic of China and Egypt (n 44) recitals 192, 229;

In order for a country to be considered the appropriate representative country, it not only has to have a similar level of economic development as the exporting country, but the relevant data further has to be readily available. What is more, where there is more than one such country, preference shall be given, where appropriate, to countries with an adequate level of social and environmental protection.[63] This is a deviation from the criteria used in selecting the appropriate 'analogue country' under the old non-market economy methodology of Article 2 (7) BADR, where the Commission determined the then 'analogue country' by having regard to the conditions of production and competition in the country under investigation, for example relating to the access to raw materials. Aspects of social and environmental protection were irrelevant.[64] Under the new methodology, the Commission has to examine whether the potential representative countries comply with core ILO conventions as well as relevant multilateral environmental conventions.[65]

So far, social and environmental aspects have only played a decisive role in the *Organic Coated Steel* case, where the Commission was presented with the choice between Malaysia and Mexico as possible representative countries. The Commission ultimately considered Mexico to be the appropriate representative country, since it—as opposed to Malaysia—had ratified '*all core ILO conventions except for the convention on the right to organize and to bargain collectively*'.[66] As remarked by the ECA, this is a rather formalistic approach, since the mere ratification of a convention does not necessarily reflect the actual level of social or environmental protection in the country under investigation.[67] It should further be recalled that the lack of ratification of the same convention was considered a key factor in establishing the existence of significant distortions in the Chinese economy with regard to wage costs.[68] Apparently, the Commission did not harbour similar concerns regarding a distortion of wage costs in Mexico caused by its non-ratification of

---

Commission Implementing Regulation (EU) 2019/1693 of 9 October 2019 imposing a provisional anti-dumping duty on imports of steel road wheels originating in the People's Republic of China (n 60) recitals 137–140, 158.

[63] Article 2 (6a) lit. a) BADR. Similarly, under the reformed Article 2 (7) BADR, where there is more than one possible appropriate representative country, preference shall be given, where appropriate, to countries with an adequate level of social and environmental protection. Thus, the objections voiced in the following parts of the thesis regarding the inclusion of such considerations at this stage of the investigation likewise apply to the calculation of a product's normal value under Article 2 (7) BADR.

[64] Loets (2018), p. 313.

[65] Recital 6 of Regulation (EU) 2017/2321 (Chap. 1, n 9).

[66] Commission Implementing Regulation (EU) 2019/687 of 2 May 2019 imposing a definitive anti-dumping duty on imports of certain organic coated steel products originating in the People's Republic of China following an expiry review pursuant to Article 11 (2) of Regulation (EU) 2016/1036 of the European Parliament and of the Council (n 39) recitals 110–112.

[67] European Court of Auditors (Chap. 6, n 49) 40.

[68] European Commission, 'Commission Staff Working Document on Significant Distortions in the Economy of the People's Republic of China for the Purposes of Trade Defence Investigations (SWD(2017) 483 final/2)' (n 21) 328, 332.

said ILO convention. For reasons of coherence, however, the factors that caused the Commission to reject the prices and costs in the exporting country as distorted should likewise result in the rejection of the prices and costs in a possible representative country if the same factors are present there. Similarly, the inclusion of social and environmental standards in the selection of the representative country must not result in the exporting country being required to meet higher social and environmental standards when determining the existence of significant distortions than the (potential) representative country.

In the already mentioned guide 'How to Make an Anti-Dumping Complaint', the Commission specifies that an indicative list of the conventions that are considered relevant in selecting the appropriate representative country can be found in Annex VIII of Regulation (EU) No 978/2012 (GSP Regulation).[69] As regards the list of relevant multilateral environmental conventions, the GSP Regulation does not list agreements concluded later than 2001—and thus does not include the Paris Agreement of 2015,[70] widely considered a milestone in the fight against climate change. It should further be mentioned that Annex VIII of the GSP Regulation contains 15 ILO conventions, whereas the list of ILO conventions given in Annex Ia to the basic regulations is significantly shorter, encompassing only half the number of conventions.[71] While the reference to the GSP Regulation in the Commission guide does not possess any legal value, a harmonisation of the conventions that are regarded as relevant when considering social and environmental standards at different points of the anti-dumping investigation is warranted already for reasons of legal clarity. No argument can be made to justify the application of dissimilar levels of social and environmental standards depending on the stage of the investigation.

Accordingly, the basic anti-dumping regulation should be amended to extend the scope of application of Annex Ia to the BADR explicitly also to the assessment of the existence of significant distortions and the choice of the appropriate representative country. This would avoid legal uncertainty and limit the discretion of the Commission in deciding what it considers an appropriate level of social and environmental protection in an investigation. As of now, this is not the case: as the amendments introduced by Regulation (EU) 2018/825 did not concern the calculation of the dumping margin, the relevant provisions of the BADR were not amended to

---

[69] Regulation (EU) No 978/2012 of the European Parliament and of the Council of 25 October 2012 applying a scheme of generalised tariff preferences, cf. European Commission, 'How to Make an Anti-Dumping Complaint' (Chap. 6, n 39) 17.

[70] Paris Agreement (FCCC/CP/2015/L.9/Rev.1) (12 December 2015). It could be argued that since the Paris Agreement was adopted within the framework of the U.N. Framework Convention of Climate Change, it is of relevance in determining the relevant multilateral agreements under the GSP Regulation and consequently also under the BADR. However, the explicit mention of the Kyoto Protocol—likewise included within the UNFCCC—and the lack thereof regarding the Paris Agreement seem to exclude such an interpretation. It should further be noted that the GSP Regulation is currently undergoing re-evaluation. Hence, the list of conventions given in the Annex might be updated to include, *inter alia*, the Paris Agreement.

[71] Annex Ia to the BADR. On the abolition of the lesser duty rule in the event of raw material distortions in anti-dumping investigations cf. the next section, p. 192 et seq.

harmonise the level of social and environmental protection the EU requires in its trading partners at different stages of an investigation.

Lastly, it should be noted that the inclusion of social and environmental standards in the selection of the representative country is *per se* detrimental to the objective of using alternative benchmarks to calculate the prices and costs of producers in the exporting country, absent the distortions caused by State intervention, as accurately as possible.[72] Since the higher social and environmental standards in the representative country usually result in higher domestic costs and prices, the constructed normal value does not reflect the undistorted costs in the exporting producers' home country to the best extent possible. Moreover, this increased level of domestic costs and prices will lead to duty levels being inflated even further, as mentioned above.[73]

7.2.2.4 Commission Practice

While the number of investigations where the new methodology has been applied is still relatively low, it is nonetheless possible to make some observations pertaining to the Commission's practice under Article 2 (6a) BADR. Whereas some specific aspects of investigations conducted under the new methodology have already been mentioned in the preceding sections, the following passage will present a more general overview of the approach adopted by the Commission in applying the new methodology.

To begin with, even though the list of factors in Article 2 (6a) lit. b) BADR is non-exhaustive, the Commission will usually not have regard to other criteria on the basis of which to establish the existence of significant distortions. An exception to this approach was the investigation concerning *Organic Coated Steel*, where, as set out above, the Commission accepted the applicant's arguments regarding a lower level of environmental protection in the Chinese steel sector when determining the existence of significant distortions.[74] In a similar vein, arguments submitted by the complainant citing the lack of controls regarding the adherence to environmental standards as a factor having an impact on exporting producers' prices in China were included in the Commission's assessment regarding the existence of significant

---

[72] Akritidis and Sneji argue that the element of a country having to be of a '*similar level of economic development*' in order for it to be considered an '*appropriate representative country*' is also reflective of the Panel's findings in *EU – Biodiesel (Argentina)*, where it held that the purpose of the methodology of constructed normal value is to identify an appropriate proxy for the price '*of the like product in the ordinary course of trade in the domestic market of the exporting country*' when that price cannot be used (cf. *European Union – Anti-Dumping Measures on Biodiesel from Argentina* (29 March 2016) WT/DS473/R para. 7.233 (Panel Report)), Akritidis and Sneij (2018), p. 139.

[73] Cf. above p. 165 et seq.

[74] Commission Implementing Regulation (EU) 2019/687 of 2 May 2019 imposing a definitive anti-dumping duty on imports of certain organic coated steel products originating in the People's Republic of China following an expiry review pursuant to Article 11 (2) of Regulation (EU) 2016/1036 of the European Parliament and of the Council (n 39) recital 52.

distortions in *Polyvinyl Alcohols.*[75] The inclusion of social and environmental concerns in establishing whether significant distortions exist is foreseen in recital 4 of Regulation (EU) 2017/2321. Apart from that, the Commission has so far limited its investigations to the criteria explicitly mentioned in Article 2 (6a) lit. b) BADR in analysing the existence of significant distortions. Given the Commission's heavy reliance on its own reports in establishing the existence of significant distortions, this is not surprising, as the reports themselves are limited to an assessment of these factors. This leads to the second observation, namely that submissions made by the complainants concerning the existence of such distortions are near to irrelevant. For one, this can be explained by the fact that the complainants in investigations frequently do not present substantial new evidence pointing to the existence of significant distortions, but instead simply refer to the relevant Commission report in order to substantiate their claims regarding the applicability of Article 2 (6a) BADR.[76] In the instances where the complainants present such evidence, the Commission might use it to corroborate its sector-specific findings when assessing the existence of significant distortions in the sector under investigation.[77] For the most part, however, the Commission bases its findings on its own report, and rarely relies on the evidence provided by the complainants.

In its investigations under the new methodology, the Commission will address every aspect mentioned in the six indents of Article 2 (6a) lit. b) BADR. While its findings concerning the presence of State-owned enterprises on the market in question (first indent) or the degree of State presence in firms (second indent)[78] as well as concerning the existence of public policies or measures discriminating in favour of domestic suppliers or otherwise influencing free market forces (third indent)[79] usually are sector-specific and contain detailed information on the policy

---

[75] Commission Implementing Regulation (EU) 2020/1336 of 25 September 2020 imposing definitive anti-dumping duties on imports of certain polyvinyl alcohols originating in the People's Republic of China (Chap. 6, n 40) recital 92.

[76] Cf. e.g. Commission Implementing Regulation (EU) 2020/508 of 7 April 2020 imposing a provisional anti-dumping duty on imports of certain hot rolled stainless steel sheets and coils originating in Indonesia, the People's Republic of China and Taiwan recital 107; Commission Implementing Regulation (EU) 2019/1267 of 26 July 2019 imposing a definitive anti-dumping duty on imports of tungsten electrodes originating in the People's Republic of China following an expiry review under Article 11(2) of Regulation (EU) 2016/1036 (Chap. 6, n 93) recital 46.

[77] Cf. e.g. Commission Implementing Regulation (EU) 2019/1693 of 9 October 2019 imposing a provisional anti-dumping duty on imports of steel road wheels originating in the People's Republic of China (n 60) recitals 56–58.

[78] Cf. e.g. Commission Implementing Regulation (EU) 2019/1379 of 28 August 2019 imposing a definitive anti-dumping duty on imports of bicycles originating in the People's Republic of China as extended to imports of bicycles consigned from Indonesia, Malaysia, Sri Lanka, Tunisia, Cambodia, Pakistan and the Philippines, whether declared as originating in these countries or not, following an expiry review pursuant to Article 11(2) of Regulation (EU) No 2016/1036, recitals 65 et seq. and 71 et seq.

[79] Cf. e.g. Commission Implementing Regulation (EU) 2020/776 of 12 June 2020 imposing definitive countervailing duties on imports of certain woven and/or stitched glass fibre fabrics originating in the People's Republic of China and Egypt and amending Commission Implementing

measures in force, such sector-specific information will not be included for all factors listed in Article 2 (6a) lit. b) BADR. Instead, for some of the other criteria included in Article 2 (6a) lit. b) BADR, the Commission regularly bases its line of argument on the findings concerning the existence of significant distortions in the economy at large that are contained in the report, concluding that absent evidence to the opposite being presented, these distortions also exist in the sector under investigation. One example of this approach are the Commission's findings regarding wage costs being distorted (fifth indent). Here, the Commission has used the exact same paragraphs for every single investigation concluded so far,[80] with only one Commission implementing regulation referencing additional evidence of wage costs being distorted.[81] *Reinhold/Van Vaerenbergh* attribute this to the different nature of the criteria contained in Article 2 (6a) lit. lit. b) BADR: while the first half is more sector-specific itself, the second half relates to distortions in the economy of the exporting producer's home country at large.[82]

The China Report further contains four chapters addressing distortions in specific sectors.[83] In the instances where the Commission makes sector-specific findings with regard to the existence of significant distortions, it will rely on the information contained in those chapters. Since the China Report frequently refers to findings made under the old methodology of Article 2 (7) BADR, this entails the re-use of

---

Regulation (EU) 2020/492 imposing definitive anti-dumping duties on imports of certain woven and/or stitched glass fibre fabrics originating in the People's Republic of China and Egypt (n 44) recitals 123–138; Commission Implementing Regulation (EU) 2019/915 of 4 June 2019 imposing a definitive anti-dumping duty on imports of certain aluminium foil in rolls originating in the People's Republic of China following an expiry review under Article 11(2) of Regulation (EU) 2016/1036 of the European Parliament and of the Council (Chap. 5, n 34) recitals 71–89.

[80] Compare e.g. Commission Implementing Regulation (EU) 2020/776 of 12 June 2020 imposing definitive countervailing duties on imports of certain woven and/or stitched glass fibre fabrics originating in the People's Republic of China and Egypt and amending Commission Implementing Regulation (EU) 2020/492 imposing definitive anti-dumping duties on imports of certain woven and/or stitched glass fibre fabrics originating in the People's Republic of China and Egypt (n 44) recitals 143–145; Commission Implementing Regulation (EU) 2020/39 of 16 January 2020 imposing a definitive anti-dumping duty on imports of peroxosulphates (persulphates) originating in the People's Republic of China following an expiry review pursuant to Article 11(2) of Regulation (EU) 2016/1036 of the European Parliament and of the Council recitals 55–57 and Commission Implementing Regulation (EU) 2019/1259 of 24 July 2019 imposing a definitive anti-dumping duty on imports of threaded tube or pipe cast fittings, of malleable cast iron and spheroidal graphite cast iron, originating in the People's Republic of China and Thailand, following an expiry review pursuant to Article 11(2) of Regulation (EU) 2016/1036 of the European Parliament and of the Council (Chap. 6, n 93) recitals 89–91.

[81] Commission Implementing Regulation (EU) 2020/909 of 30 June 2020 imposing a definitive anti-dumping duty on imports of ferro-silicon originating in Russia and the People's Republic of China, following an expiry review pursuant to Article 11(2) of Regulation (EU) 2016/1036 recital 89.

[82] Reinhold and Van Vaerenberg (2021), p. 196.

[83] European Commission, 'Commission Staff Working Document on Significant Distortions in the Economy of the People's Republic of China for the Purposes of Trade Defence Investigations (SWD(2017) 483 final/2)' (n 21) chapters 14–17.

information gathered for the purposes of another methodology, which adds to the criticism of the new methodology simply being a re-packaged non-market economy methodology.[84] Besides, given that some of the anti-dumping investigations referenced in the China Report were concluded more than a decade ago,[85] it is questionable whether the information used by the Commission is still valid today, and accurate enough to justify the conclusion that distortions exist in the sector under investigation at the time of the current investigation. The *Ceramics* investigation of 2019 is illustrative in that regard. Here, when establishing whether there was an inadequate enforcement of bankruptcy, corporate and property laws (fourth indent) in the Chinese ceramics sector, the Commission referred to its China Report in order to establish that the ceramics industry had benefitted from State intervention with regard to purchases of land use rights.[86] While the China Report itself was published in 2017, its source is an anti-dumping investigation concerning the Chinese ceramics sector from 2012, resulting in the Commission effectively basing its findings regarding the existence of significant distortions in part on an investigation which was concluded seven years ago. The use of such potentially outdated information risks undermining the validity of the Commission's findings in anti-dumping investigations using the new methodology.

Once the Commission is satisfied that significant distortions do exist, it will go on to construct normal value. While the potential sources used in establishing normal value include the domestic costs, provided that they are found to be undistorted, and undistorted international prices, costs, or benchmarks, the Commission uses the corresponding costs of production and sale in an appropriate representative country wherever possible.[87] This once more highlights the similarities between the old non-market economy methodology of Article 2 (7) BADR and the new methodology contained in Article 2 (6a) BADR.

It is yet unclear how the Commission will proceed in anti-dumping investigations concerning Russia following the publication of the Russia Report. Compared to the China Report, the information used is more recent. This can in part be attributed to the absence of a similar reservoir of EU legislative acts under the old basic regulations addressing the existence of State interventions in the economy, as there is for China. In another difference to the China Report, the Russia Report places a significant emphasis on the Russian energy sector, with the corresponding chapter

---

[84]Cf. the sources cited above, n 19.

[85]European Commission, 'Commission Staff Working Document on Significant Distortions in the Economy of the People's Republic of China for the Purposes of Trade Defence Investigations (SWD(2017) 483 final/2)' (n 21) 429, where the Commission references an anti-dumping investigation from 2005 in footnote 1533.

[86]Commission Implementing Regulation (EU) 2019/1198 of 12 July 2019 imposing a definitive anti-dumping duty on imports of ceramic tableware and kitchenware originating in the People's Republic of China following an expiry review pursuant to Article 11(2) of Regulation (EU) No 2016/1036 (n 52) recital 98.

[87]On the few exceptions where this was not the case cf. the sources cited above, n 62.

accounting for a fifth of the entire report.[88] Conversely, the Report's findings in other chapters, such as those addressing the development of a land market and potential distortions in land prices[89] or distortions of the Russian labour market[90] remain superficial. Given that the findings on some chapters of the Russia Report are much less compelling than those in the China Report as regards establishing a high degree of State intervention in parts of the economy, it remains to be seen whether the Commission will maintain its previous practice of addressing each of the criteria mentioned in Article 2 (6a) lit. b) BADR when applying the new methodology to exports originating in Russia.

7.2.2.5   Conclusions

Coming back to the question posed at the beginning of this section, namely whether the new methodology introduced by Article 2 (6a) BADR unduly protects the EU industry against imports originating in countries for which significant distortions are deemed to exist, the answer is that this is indeed the case. The criteria used in establishing the existence of significant distortions lack a precise definition and are open to expansive interpretation by the Commission. While the new methodology is ostensibly aimed at addressing the excessive intervention of the State in the economy, particularly the relevance attached to social and environmental standards in establishing the existence of significant distortions does not fit this rationale. Instead, the criteria address an array of situations where the EU industry suffers a genuine comparative disadvantage when competing internationally. This includes the use of the non-standard methodology—with the higher dumping margins this entails—in the event of what is at times referred to as 'social and environmental dumping'.[91] Even if one were to agree with the policy rationale offered for the new methodology *per se*, the EU might find itself confronted with accusations of operating double standards, considering another State's policy measures to constitute an excessive intervention in the economy in the course of an anti-dumping investigation, while operating comparable policy measures itself: in *Aluminium Extrusions,* citing a

---

[88] European Commission, 'Commission Staff Working Document on Significant Distortions in the Economy of the Russian Federation for the Purposes of Trade Defence Investigations (SWD(2020) 242 final)' (n 34) 204–293.

[89] Cf. e.g. the chapter summary: '*The Government does not set or apply norms which would result in affecting the cost of land, neither in law nor in practice. Nonetheless, prices do not fully reflect market indicators due to a number of factors. Moreover, at the level of laws, environmental impacts of various types of industrial activities are not reflected in the prices of land which diminishes the incentives of economic operators to improve their environmental track record*', ibid 188.

[90] Cf. the chapter summary on the chapter of the Russian labour market, ibid 185–186.

[91] In the hearing before the INTA Committee, Joost Korte, when asked whether the significant distortions could also cover questions of social dumping and taxation issues, acknowledged this, as he replied '*[T]oday, this is impossible. (. . .) In the future, and since the criteria are a lot more flexible, I think there is a certain openness there*', Committee on International Trade (INTA) of the European Parliament (n 30) at 18:28.

number of EU laws, the exporting producers pointed out that the aids they received were comparable to the ones granted in the EU to high-tech enterprises in order to achieve aims of public interest. This argument was, however, not taken up by the Commission.[92]

Moreover, any double counting must be objected to under the overarching fairness-rationale put forward to justify the use of trade defence instruments.

The evidence used in establishing the existence of significant distortions likewise is subject to criticism. While formally only one among various sources upon which the Commission's findings regarding the existence of significant distortions can be based, the Commission practice has revealed that the Commission will rely predominantly on the report it itself has drafted, making the finding of the existence of significant distortions once a Commission report exists a near-automatic one. This confers a significant advantage to the complainants, while the chances of rebutting the findings contained in the respective report are low. In particular with regard to the China Report, the practice of basing the conclusion that significant distortions exist on findings made in previous trade defence investigations risks the China Report itself and consequently also the reasoning of the Commission in its anti-dumping investigations under the new methodology being based on potentially outdated information. Moreover, the at times generic reasoning of the Commission in concluding that significant distortions exist must be criticised.

Finally, basing the selection of the appropriate representative country on an adequate level of social and environmental protection must be regarded as a further element of the new methodology driving duty levels up. This also impacts negatively on the accuracy of the constructed normal value in the best possible representation of the cost and price levels in the exporting country. Further, the significant discretion awarded to the Commission in determining which level of social and environmental protection exactly it deems sufficient when applying the new methodology must be objected to. The same applies to the corresponding lack of clarification in this regard provided for in the basic regulations, particularly in light of the reference to the GSP Regulation contained in the Commission's guide 'How to Make an Anti-Dumping Complaint'.

If viewed benevolently, the inclusion of social and environmental concerns in the new methodology could be considered an attempt at a re-orientation of the EU's trade defence instruments in line with the Treaties' understanding of 'fair' trade as also encompassing aspects of 'ethical' or 'equitable' trade.[93] However, the way in which these standards were incorporated does not square with the objectives given for the new methodology. Instead, they run the risk of being instrumentalised in a way that contributes to artificially inflating the constructed normal value, resulting in higher dumping margins and the EU industry being awarded over-protection.

---

[92] Commission Implementing Regulation (EU) 2020/1428 of 12 October 2020 imposing a provisional anti-dumping duty on imports of aluminium extrusions originating in the People's Republic of China (n 57) recital 76.

[93] Cf. above p. 84 et seq.

7.2.3   Protectionism in the Level of Measures Imposed: The Changed Scope of Application of the Lesser Duty Rule and the Reformed Injury Margin Calculation

7.2.3.1   The Lesser Duty Rule

7.2.3.1.1   The Lesser Duty Rule as a Central Feature of the Basic Regulations

Before the amending Regulation (EU) 2018/825 entered into force, the lesser duty rule was a central feature of EU anti-dumping and anti-subsidy law and practice. The rule prescribes that the amount of the duty should not be based on the margin of dumping or subsidisation, but that it should be set at a lower level if such lesser duty would be adequate to remove the injury to the Union industry.[94] A corresponding provision exists for price increases under undertakings, the amount of which likewise is to be lower than the margin of dumping or subsidisation if such increase is adequate to remove the injury to the Union industry.[95] This obligates the EU institutions to calculate the so-called 'injury margin', i.e. the level of duty that would be adequate to remove the injury.[96] Consequently, the level of an anti-dumping or countervailing duty equals the margin of dumping or subsidisation respectively or the amount necessary to remove the injury sustained by the EU industry, whichever is the lower of the two margins.[97] By applying the lesser duty rule, the European Union goes beyond its obligations under WTO law, which leaves the decision to apply a lesser duty rule at the discretion of the importing Members.[98] When contrasting the average duty level within the EU with that of other major users of trade defence legislation, it becomes apparent that the application of the lesser duty rule has had a significant impact on duty levels, with the duties imposed by the EU being considerably lower than those of e.g. Canada or the United States.[99] In limiting the duty level to the injury margin, the EU trade defence legislation commits itself towards the remediation of the harm caused to the EU industry by the dumped

---

[94] Articles 7 (2) and 9 (4) subpara. 2 BADR and Articles 12 (1) subpara. 3 and 15 (1) subpara. 4 BASR.

[95] Article 8 (1) subpara. 3 BADR and Article 13 (1) subpara. 4 BASR.

[96] Luo (2010), p. 131.

[97] Mueller et al. (2009) para. 14.03.

[98] *European Union – Anti-Dumping Measures on Certain Footwear from China* (28 October 2011) WT/DS405/R para. 7.924 (Panel Report); *United States – Anti-Dumping and Countervailing Measures on Steel Plate from India* (28 June 2002) WT/DS206/R para. 7.116 (Panel Report).

[99] For a comparison of average anti-dumping duty levels in the EU, U.S. and Canada between 1989 and 2009 cf. Rovegno and Vandenbussche (2012), pp. 445–446; European Commission, '37th Annual Report from the Commission to the Council and the European Parliament on the EU's Anti-Dumping, Anti-Subsidy and Safeguard activities and the Use of trade defence instruments by Third Countries targeting the EU in 2018 (COM(2019) 158 final)' (Chap. 6, n 59) 3.

or subsidised imports, without foreclosing the market to foreign imports.[100] In particular, the lesser duty rule prevents the measure from factoring in the Union industry's inefficiencies, and thus precludes prices from increasing above the non-injurious level because of such inefficiency.[101] Thus, the lesser duty rule limits the possible detrimental effects to competition of anti-dumping and anti-subsidy proceedings.[102] The above reasoning has led authors to conclude that the measures are not intended to have a punitive or a deterring effect.[103] Instead, it is commonly understood that trade defence measures aim at restoring the level playing field between domestic and foreign suppliers, essentially being of a corrective nature.[104]

The central importance of the lesser duty rule in equalising competitive conditions on the internal market was also emphasised in the jurisprudence of the CJEU. In *Distillerie Bonollo*, Advocate General *Tanchev* held that the lesser duty rule is an expression of the effective competition objective of anti-dumping duties,[105] relying *inter alia* on the General Court's jurisprudence in *Canadian Solar Emea*. There, the General Court found that the lesser duty rule in anti-dumping proceedings serves to balance the interests of the exporting producers, importers, industry and consumers of the EU and expresses, in respect of EU trade defence measures, the general principle of proportionality.[106] Advocate General *Trstenjak* employed the same reasoning in *Moser Baer India* with regard to anti-subsidy proceedings, arguing that the lesser duty rule is intended to reduce the conflict between the concept of trade protection for the EU industry from subsidised imports and the principle of having an EU industry that is as competitive as possible, with the lowest possible prices for customers of the product concerned within the Union. She further stressed that the imposition of countervailing duties must not afford the Community industry

---

[100] On the lesser duty rule in anti-dumping proceedings cf. Commission Regulation (EEC) No 920/93 of 15 April 1993 imposing a provisional anti-dumping duty on imports of certain magnetic disks (3, 5 microdisks) originating in Japan, Taiwan and the People's Republic of China recital 78.

[101] Laprévote (2015), p. 8, deriving this limiting effect also from the Court of First Instance's judgment in *EFMA*, where it held that in calculating the injury margin, the target profit must be limited to what the Union industry could reasonably count on under normal conditions of competition, *European Fertilizer Manufacturers' Association (EFMA) v Council* (28 October 1999) T-210/95 60 (Court of First Instance). In detail on the *EFMA* judgment and profit margin calculation cf. below p. 203 et seq.

[102] Laprévote (2015), p. 8.

[103] On anti-dumping duties Kuplewatzky (2018), p. 455. Cf. also *Industrie des poudres sphériques v Commission and others* (Chap. 4, n 152) 91, where the Court held that the adoption of anti-dumping duties is a protective and preventive measure against unfair competition resulting from dumping practices, not a penalty or a measure aimed at giving a competitive advantage to the Union industry.

[104] On anti-dumping duties Vermulst and Sud (2013), p. 205 and Opinion of Advocate General Sharpston in *Council v Gul Ahmed Textile Mills Ltd.*, C-638/11 P 60 (25 March 2013).

[105] Opinion by Advocate General Tanchev in *Distillerie Bonollo v Commission*, C-461/18 P 93 (23 April 2020).

[106] *Canadian Solar Emea GmbH and others v Council* (28 February 2017) T-162/14 190 (General Court), upheld on appeal in *Canadian Solar Emea GmbH and others v Council* (27 March 2019) C-236/17 P 168 (European Court of Justice); cf. also Vermulst and Dion Sud (2018), p. 84.

a greater competitive advantage over subsidised imports.[107] Consequently, while serving to limit the detrimental effects to competition caused by the imposition of anti-dumping or anti-subsidy measures, the lesser duty rule simultaneously ensures that the character of anti-dumping and anti-subsidy duties remains a corrective rather than a punitive or deterrent one.[108]

7.2.3.1.2   The Changes Introduced by the Trade Defence Modernisation Package

The limitations to the scope of application of the lesser duty rule by Regulation (EU) 2018/825 appear to run counter to the attainment of these objectives. Since the regulation entered into force, the lesser duty rule applies in anti-subsidy proceedings only where the Commission can clearly conclude that it is not in the Union's interest to impose the duty at the amount of the subsidy margin.[109] In anti-dumping proceedings, the lesser duty rule will not be put to use if raw material distortions are found to exist and the Commission can clearly conclude that it would be in the Union's interest to base the amount of duty not on the injury but the dumping margin.[110] The rules governing undertakings were adapted accordingly.[111]

The modifications to the lesser duty rule were deemed necessary by the EU institutions in order to not give a further advantage to exporters who already benefit from major distortions of the level playing field.[112] It was argued that the active involvement of third country governments, helping their own companies to outcompete their EU counterparts by means of subsidies or distorting the raw material price, warranted a more principled reaction, i.e. the imposition of duties based on the full subsidy or dumping margin.[113] Additionally, in the event of raw material distortions, limiting the duty level to the injury level might neutralise the injury suffered by the Union industry only in part, in particular where the exporting country's government can further lower its exporters' costs of production by reducing the prices to be paid for raw materials even more.[114] These concerns are also reflected in the recitals of Regulation (EU) 2018/825, which state *inter alia* that raw material distortions create additional distortions of trade. Because of such interference, the costs of raw materials do not reflect the operation of normal market forces of supply and demand for a given raw material. As a result, Union producers are not

---

[107] Opinion by Advocate General Trstenjak in *Moser Baer India Ltd. v* Council, C-535/06 P 170 (2 October 2008).

[108] Cf. also Hoffmeister (2013), p. 15.

[109] Article 12 (1) subpara. 4 and 15 (1) subpara. 4 BASR.

[110] Article 7 (2a), (2b) BADR and 9 (4) subpara. 2 BADR.

[111] Article 8 (1) subpara. 4 BADR and Article 13 (1) subparas. 3, 4 BASR.

[112] Müller (2017), p. 215.

[113] Hoffmeister (2015), p. 370; Prost (2014), p. 38.

[114] Scharf and Kuplewatzky (2019) para. 12.

only harmed by dumping, but suffer from additional distortions of trade compared to third-country downstream producers which benefit from artificially low-priced raw materials.[115] With regard to anti-subsidy investigations, the recitals express the intention to address the ever more pressing issue of distortions of trade caused by subsidies granted by third country governments in a more effective manner, in particular when contrasted with the steady reduction of the amount of State aid authorised by the Commission within the European Union over time.[116] Overall, the changes to the lesser duty rule are thus aimed at enhancing the effectiveness of the legal instruments.[117]

In line with the above, the Commission has expressed the view that the abolition of the lesser duty rule complies with the proportionality principle because of the additional need to protect trade in cases of subsidisation or where raw material distortions have been found to exist.[118] This line of argumentation however appears overly simplistic. In the event of raw material distortions and subsidisation, the exporting producers' home State actively supports the exporting activities of its industry. Such State measures might indeed pose a particular danger to undistorted, fair competition on the importing country's market. This, however, does not affect the question of whether the level of measures is proportionate in that it provides for a balancing of the interests of exporters and the domestic industry by only offsetting the injury suffered by said industry as a result of unfair trading practices. This applies regardless of whether these trading practices were made possible by State measures such as subsidisation of raw materials or not. Consequently, while there may be a political impetus to address State-induced distortions to competition also through the level of measures, there is no compelling reason why this would be appropriate under the legal considerations underlying the application of the lesser duty rule.

Lastly, the partial removal of the lesser duty rule is also intended to have a deterrent effect upon third country governments by dissuading them from allowing

---

[115]Recital 8 of Regulation (EU) 2018/825 (Chap. 1, n 10).

[116]Recital 10 of Regulation (EU) 2018/825 (Chap. 1, n 10).

[117]European Commission, 'Proposal for a Regulation of the European Parliament and of the Council amending Council Regulation (EC) No 1225/2009 on protection against dumped imports from countries not members of the European Community and Council Regulation (EC) No 597/2009 on protection against subsidised imports from countries not members of the European Community (COM(2013) 192 final)' (Chap. 3, n 163) 3. It should be noted that these arguments could also have been advanced to justify the non-application of the lesser duty rule in instances where the normal value is calculated by having recourse to Article 2 (6a) BADR, since the list of criteria given to establish the existence of significant distortions addresses the active involvement of third countries in their economies which is used to rationalise the non-application of the lesser duty rule under the reformed basic regulations. However, it cannot be inferred from the legislative materials that the EU legislators ever considered such a further reduction of the scope of application of the lesser duty rule.

[118]European Commission, 'Commission Staff Working Document – Impact Assessment accompanying the document "proposal for a regulation of the European Parliament and of the Council on the modernisation of trade defence instruments"' (Chap. 6, n 7) 3.

or engaging in such trade distortive conduct.[119] In this respect, Regulation (EU) 2018/825 challenges the prevailing understanding of anti-dumping and anti-subsidy duties as being corrective in nature. Rather, the EU legislative organs now explicitly intend them to sanction those practices that are considered particularly trade distorting, and to discourage the EU's trade partners from resorting to such practices in the future.

Those opposing these limitations to the scope of application of the lesser duty rule have criticised the changes as going beyond the declared objective of ensuring the effectiveness of the EU's trade defence arsenal, instead resulting in excessive protection of the EU industry. Additionally, it was feared that in particular the non-application of the lesser duty rule in cases of raw material distortions would lead to a further politicisation of the EU trade defence instruments.[120]

Moreover, and standing in contrast to the objective of increased transparency and predictability in EU trade defence investigations,[121] the decision on whether to apply the lesser duty rule or not is yet another element in anti-dumping investigations where the Commission is being granted significant discretion.[122] Further, the Commission can base its findings regarding the existence of raw material distortions on multiple sources. The types of possible raw material distortions listed in Article 7 (2a) BADR are similar to the classification used in the *inventory on export restrictions on industrial raw materials* published by the Organization for Economic Co-operation and Development (OECD). However, this does not signify that in order for the Commission to have recourse to Article 7 (2a) BADR, a raw material distortion has to be listed in the relevant OECD catalogue.[123] This can already be taken from the wording of Article 7 (2a) BADR, which is only linked to the OECD catalogue in that it makes use of the typology the inventory uses.[124] In any case, as the OECD catalogue does not contain up-to-date information on raw material distortions currently operated by governments—the present database only includes information up until 2019—the Commission could not base its findings concerning raw material distortions for the post-2019 period on the OECD catalogue. Other possible resources in establishing the existence of raw material distortions include *inter alia* the database of the International Monetary Fund (IMF) or the Trade Policy Review published by the WTO. Consequently, while Article 7 (2a) BADR defines which types of practices can be considered to constitute raw material distortions, the

---

[119] Hoffmeister (2015), p. 370.

[120] Vermulst and Sud (2013), p. 205.

[121] Cf. recital 3 of Regulation (EU) 2018/825: '(. . .) [C]ertain provisions of the Regulations should be amended in order to improve transparency and predictability (. . .).'

[122] Cornelis (2018), p. 541. On the additional Union interest analysis to be carried out by the Commission cf. below p. 243.

[123] To that effect Hoffmeister (2020), p. 221.

[124] This can also be taken from the Commission's communication on the reformed trade defense instruments, European Commission, 'Factsheet: Europe's Trade Defence Instruments: Now Stronger and More Effective' (7 June 2018) 3, available at <http://trade.ec.europa.eu/doclib/docs/2018/june/tradoc_156921.pdf>.

reference to the OECD database does not serve as a truly limiting element, leaving the list of possible raw material distortions essentially open-ended.[125]

The 17%-threshold, intended to ensure that only raw material distortions that strongly influence the competitiveness of economic operators can trigger the application of the new rules,[126] is also the subject of discussion. The threshold itself is applied countrywide, with the Commission examining whether a raw material distortion accounts on average for more than 17% of the costs of production in the country under investigation.[127] The threshold is calculated by reference to prices on 'representative international markets' and not by reference to the producer's actual cost. This signifies that even if the raw material accounts for less than 17% of the cost of production of an exporting producer in the country under investigation, the threshold can be crossed if the raw material's undistorted value on international markets is used as a reference.[128]

While some authors have suggested that an individual exporter should be exempted from the application of the higher duty if he can prove that the distorted raw material accounts for less than 17% in his cost of production,[129] so far, there is no Commission practice in that regard. However, given that the threshold was introduced in order to ensure that only distortions affecting the competitiveness of economic operators trigger the application of the new rules,[130] their application would not be warranted in situations where a producer does not see his competitiveness increase as a result of raw material distortions because the share of the distorted raw material does not surpass the limit of 17% in his individual production cost.

A similar problem presents itself in situations where an individual exporting producer can show he does not benefit from the raw material distortions, e.g. because he is using a substitute material.[131] Again, it can be argued that in

---

[125] Cornelis (2018), p. 541.

[126] Müller (2018), p. 49.

[127] Cf. e.g. Commission Implementing Regulation (EU) 2019/576 of 10 April 2019 imposing a provisional anti-dumping duty on imports of mixtures of urea and ammonium nitrate originating in Russia, Trinidad and Tobago and the United States of America recital 210, where the Commission held that the raw material in question accounted for more than 50% of the total cost of production as reported by the two cooperating Russian exporting producers. Before, authors had assumed that the existence of raw material distortions would be examined for each cooperating producer separately, van Bael and Bellis (2019) § 6.01.

[128] Cornelis (2018), p. 541, as exemplified in Commission Implementing Regulation (EU) 2020/508 of 7 April 2020 imposing a provisional anti-dumping duty on imports of certain hot rolled stainless steel sheets and coils originating in Indonesia, the People's Republic of China and Taiwan (n 76) recital 210. He further notes that it is unclear whether the 17%-threshold also applies to processing of raw materials that is done in-house, as this too has an important impact in determining whether the threshold is met.

[129] Cornelis (2018), p. 541.

[130] Müller (2018), p. 49.

[131] Hoffmeister (2020), pp. 221–222. In the *Urea and Ammonium Nitrate* case it is indicated that this can indeed be of relevance in the application of Article 7 (2a) BADR, as the Commission explicitly held that the Russian producers of the product concerned took advantage of the distortions

those situations the competitiveness of the exporting producer is not affected, which should result in Article 7 (2a) BADR not being applied. Indeed, the Commission's practice under the reformed basic regulations points towards Article 7 (2a) BADR not being applicable in such circumstances: in *Urea and Ammonium Nitrate*, the Commission rebutted exporting producers' claims that the countrywide determination with regard to the existence of the raw material distortion and the subsequent decision to set measures at the level of the dumping margin could not be applied to the individual companies without assessment of their individual situation. The Commission noted that

> due to the nature of some of the distortions found on the Russian gas market, the individual behaviour of the exporting producers was irrelevant, as they benefited from the distorted natural gas price resulting from export restrictions and export tax regardless of their individual source of supply of natural gas.[132]

Given this caveat in the Commission's line of argumentation, it can be assumed that Article 7 (2a) BADR would not have been applied if the Russian producers had been able to demonstrate that, despite the structural nature of the raw material distortions put in place by the Russian government, they did not profit from said distortions.

Where the Commission can establish the existence of raw material distortions, it will move on to conduct a special Union interest test as set out in Article 7 (2b) BADR. The Commission needs to positively establish that it would be in the Union's interest to determine the amount of the duties in accordance with Article 7 (2a) BADR, i.e. to set the duty level at the dumping margin instead of the injury margin.[133]

As noted by Advocate General *Sharpston*,

> an anti-dumping duty is not a sanction designed to punish a dumping exporter for his behaviour. It is rather (clumsy though it may be) a mechanism designed to redress, as nearly as possible, an imbalance considered unfair to the domestic industry.[134]

The same applies, *mutatis mutandis*, with regard to countervailing duties. In particular in light of the rhetoric adopted by the co-legislators during the reform process, it appears as though this characterisation of anti-dumping and countervailing duties as primarily corrective mechanisms does no longer fully apply to duties levied under the modernised basic regulations. Likewise, by going beyond what is necessary to offset the injury incurred by the EU industry, the

---

identified, Commission Implementing Regulation (EU) 2019/576 of 10 April 2019 imposing a provisional anti-dumping duty on imports of mixtures of urea and ammonium nitrate originating in Russia, Trinidad and Tobago and the United States of America (n 127) recital 219.

[132] Commission Implementing Regulation (EU) 2019/1688 of 8 October 2019 imposing a definitive anti-dumping duty and definitively collecting the provisional duty imposed on imports of mixtures of urea and ammonium nitrate originating in Russia, Trinidad and Tobago and the United States of America (Chap. 6, n 125) recitals 214–215.

[133] On the Union interest analysis cf. in detail below p. 243.

[134] *Council v Gul Ahmed Textile Mills Ltd.* (n 104) 60.

non-application of the lesser duty rule upsets the balance between the interests of the exporting producers, importers, industry and consumers of the EU[135] in favour of the interests of the EU industry. The potential of the EU industry being awarded excessive protection is further increased by the lack of predictability in the application of the lesser duty rule, in particular regarding the unclarities surrounding the provisions on raw material distortions, coupled with the Commission's discretion in carrying out the Union interest test when deciding on the application of the lesser duty rule. Given that the EU's practice of incorporating the lesser duty rule was lauded internationally as reducing conflicts between competition law and trade defence law,[136] the limitations to its scope of application are all the more regrettable.

7.2.3.1.3 Commission Practice

The following section examines the Commission practice under the reformed basic regulations in light of the findings made above. Given that, so far, the Commission has always set the level of measures at the margin of subsidisation when applying the reformed provisions of the BASR,[137] the section's focus will be on the Commission practice under the BADR.

7.2.3.1.3.1 *Urea and Ammonium Nitrate*

At present, the Commission has identified the existence of raw material distortions in three investigations. However, in *Aluminium Extrusions*, no detailed examination of Article 2 (7a) BADR was undertaken, as the dumping margin was higher than the injury margin.[138] The first instance where this was the case concerned *Urea and*

---

[135] On the lesser duty rule serving to maintain said balance cf. *Canadian Solar Emea GmbH and others v Council* (n 106) 190.

[136] Matsushita et al. (2015), pp. 406–407.

[137] Commission Implementing Regulation (EU) 2020/870 of 24 June 2020 imposing a definitive countervailing duty and definitively collecting the provisional countervailing duty imposed on imports of continuous filament glass fibre products originating in Egypt, and levying the definitive countervailing duty on the registered imports of continuous filament glass fibre products originating in Egypt recitals 412–414; Commission Implementing Regulation (EU) 2020/776 of 12 June 2020 imposing definitive countervailing duties on imports of certain woven and/or stitched glass fibre fabrics originating in the People's Republic of China and Egypt and amending Commission Implementing Regulation (EU) 2020/492 imposing definitive anti-dumping duties on imports of certain woven and/or stitched glass fibre fabrics originating in the People's Republic of China and Egypt (n 44) recitals 1113–1115; Commission Implementing Regulation (EU) 2020/379 of 5 March 2020 imposing a provisional countervailing duty on imports of continuous filament glass fibre products originating in Egypt recital 215; Commission Implementing Regulation (EU) 2019/1344 of 12 August 2019 imposing a provisional countervailing duty on imports of biodiesel originating in Indonesia recital 206.

[138] Commission Implementing Regulation (EU) 2020/1428 of 12 October 2020 imposing a provisional anti-dumping duty on imports of aluminium extrusions originating in the People's Republic of China (n 57) recitals 347–348.

Ammonium Nitrate originating in Russia. When deciding upon the level of the measures to be imposed, the Commission found that raw material distortions existed with regard to natural gas, which was the main raw material of the product under investigation. These included the existence of an export tax of 30%, the operation of a dual pricing system for domestic and export sales, and reserving the exclusive right for the export of gas in a gaseous state to the State-owned gas supplier *Gazprom*.[139]

When carrying out the Union interest test under Article 7 (2b) BADR, the Commission is to examine all pertinent information, such as spare capacities in the exporting country, competition for raw materials and the effect on supply chains for Union companies. In *Urea and Ammonium Nitrate,* the Commission ultimately concluded that it would be in the Union's interest to base the duty level on Article 7 (2a) BADR, i.e. not to apply the lesser duty rule. It based this decision on the spare capacities in Russia, which could be used to increase exports to the EU.[140]

In the past, the investigating authorities frequently noted that anti-dumping measures are not intended to foreclose competition, but only to restore a level playing field.[141] However, the line of reasoning adopted by the Commission in analysing the spare capacities, in particular the express intention to avoid an increase in Russian exports to the EU, demonstrates that the Commission intended to augment the degree of market foreclosure by imposing duties up to the full dumping margin.

Another element of the Union interest test under Article 7 (2b) BADR is the analysis of the competitive situation concerning raw materials. Here, the Commission found that Russian producers have an unfair advantage *vis-à-vis* Union producers with regard to natural gas due to the regulation in the Russian market. In particular, Russian producers have access to artificially low gas prices in the domestic market.[142] At the same time, the Commission found that the Union producers are negatively affected by the price discrimination caused by the regulations in question, which makes them pay considerably higher prices than those paid by Russian producers.[143] The assessment of the competitive situation concerning raw

---

[139]Commission Implementing Regulation (EU) 2019/576 of 10 April 2019 imposing a provisional anti-dumping duty on imports of mixtures of urea and ammonium nitrate originating in Russia, Trinidad and Tobago and the United States of America (n 127) recitals 210–215.

[140]Ibid recitals 222–226.

[141]Cf. e.g. Council Regulation (EC) No 393/2009 of 11 May 2009 imposing a definitive anti-dumping duty and collecting definitively the provisional duty imposed on imports of certain candles, tapers and the like originating in the People's Republic of China recital 131; Council Regulation (EC) No 1942/2004 of 2 November 2004 imposing a definitive anti-dumping duty and collecting definitively the provisional duty imposed on imports of okoumé plywood originating in the People's Republic of China recital 52; Council Regulation (EC) No 437/2004 of 8 March 2004 imposing definitive anti-dumping duty and collecting definitively the provisional duty imposed on imports of large rainbow trout originating in Norway and the Faeroe Islands recitals 75–77.

[142]Commission Implementing Regulation (EU) 2019/576 of 10 April 2019 imposing a provisional anti-dumping duty on imports of mixtures of urea and ammonium nitrate originating in Russia, Trinidad and Tobago and the United States of America (n 127) recitals 227–230.

[143]Ibid recital 229.

materials as carried out by the Commission in *Urea and Ammonium Nitrate* thus does not provide substantial new information. This comes as no surprise, as certain types of raw material distortions—such as export taxes or dual pricing schemes—will *per se* be liable to distort competition in favour of domestic producers.

Lastly, the Commission considered the impact of the imposition of measures on the supply chain and on the downstream industry to be marginal, with the costs incurred by farmers as the ultimate users of the product concerned increasing only to a limited extent.[144]

7.2.3.1.3.2 Hot Rolled Stainless Steel

The second instance where the Commission had to decide on the non-application of the lesser duty rule pursuant to Article 7 (2a), (2b) BADR was the *Hot Rolled Stainless Steel* case.[145] The investigation concerned imports of steel originating *inter alia* in Indonesia and China.

With regard to Indonesia, the Commission established the existence of raw material distortions concerning nickel ore, which represented more than 17% of the total costs of production of the product under investigation. This led to the Indonesian price for nickel ore being significantly lower than the price in the representative international market, which the Commission regarded to be the Philippines.[146] Concerning China, the investigation confirmed the existence of raw material distortions on a number of raw materials. The investigation further established that, for each of the sampled companies, at least one of the raw materials represented more than 17% of their total cost of production of the product under investigation.[147] In determining the price for the raw materials in the representative international market, the same sources were used as for the construction of the normal value in accordance with Article 2 (6a) lit. a) BADR.[148] As Brazil had been selected as the appropriate representative country, the Commission relied mostly on import prices in Brazil to establish normal value for the raw materials.[149]

---

[144] Ibid recitals 231–234.

[145] Commission Implementing Regulation (EU) 2020/1408 of 6 October 2020 imposing a definitive anti-dumping duty and definitively collecting the provisional duty on imports of certain hot rolled stainless steel sheets and coils originating in Indonesia, the People's Republic of China and Taiwan; Commission Implementing Regulation (EU) 2020/508 of 7 April 2020 imposing a provisional anti-dumping duty on imports of certain hot rolled stainless steel sheets and coils originating in Indonesia, the People's Republic of China and Taiwan.

[146] Commission Implementing Regulation (EU) 2020/508 of 7 April 2020 imposing a provisional anti-dumping duty on imports of certain hot rolled stainless steel sheets and coils originating in Indonesia, the People's Republic of China and Taiwan (n 76) recitals 342–346.

[147] Ibid recitals 347–348.

[148] Ibid recital 349.

[149] Ibid recital 190. For some raw materials for which there was no benchmark or the available benchmark was considered non-representative on the basis of the imports statistics into Brazil, the Commission used benchmarks based on undistorted prices or other reasonable data, Commission Implementing Regulation (EU) 2020/508 of 7 April 2020 imposing a provisional anti-dumping

When conducting the Union interest test under Article 7 (2b) BADR, the Commission again assessed the spare capacities and the competition for raw materials in the exporting countries. While these factors did not call the Union interest in setting the duty level at the dumping margin into question, the interests of users ultimately led the Commission to conclude that it would not be in the Union interest to make use of Article 7 (2a) BADR. The Commission found that if duties were to be imposed pursuant to Article 7 (2a) BADR, the potential impact of measures would be disproportionate in view of the possible strong negative effects on supply chains for certain Union companies and on users. Under such a scenario, the user industry—particular those users which purchase significant volumes from exporting producers located in China or Indonesia—might be unduly affected and could become loss making as a result.[150]

7.2.3.1.4   Conclusions and Further Recommendations

Analysing the investigations conducted by the Commission under the reformed basic regulations, a number of observations can be made. First, where the Commission has replaced the exporting producer's raw material costs in calculating normal value with other sources due to interventions of his home government, it will later have recourse to the same sources used when establishing normal value when determining the price in the representative international market under Article 7 (2a) BADR. Second, the Union interest test-criterion of the existence of spare capacities will be used as a means of justifying the imposition of higher duties, leading to a higher degree of market foreclosure against imports from the country under investigation. This market foreclosing effect is intended to protect the Union industry from a high(er) level of imports originating in the country under investigation. Third, the examination of the competitive situation regarding raw materials so far has failed to develop any real relevance. Instead, it merely confirms the findings made by the Commission on the existence of raw material distortions, which almost inevitably result in a competitive disadvantage suffered by the Union industry. Fourth, concerning the possible negative impact of higher duty levels on the market participants in the EU, the profitability of users of the product concerned is of central importance. Fifth, while the Commission ultimately refrained from making use of Article 7 (2a) BADR in *Hot Rolled Stainless Steel*, the investigation nonetheless illustrates that the parallel application of the new methodology and Article 7 (2a) BADR has the potential of significantly inflating the level of duties imposed.

---

duty on imports of certain hot rolled stainless steel sheets and coils originating in Indonesia, the People's Republic of China and Taiwan (n 76) recital 192.

[150] Commission Implementing Regulation (EU) 2020/508 of 7 April 2020 imposing a provisional anti-dumping duty on imports of certain hot rolled stainless steel sheets and coils originating in Indonesia, the People's Republic of China and Taiwan (n 76) recitals 368–377.

In the present investigation, the dumping margin for some of the Chinese exporting producers was as high as 108.4%, with the injury margin only being 17%.[151]

When viewed in conjunction with the above findings regarding the limitations to the scope of application of the lesser duty rule, the Commission practice shows that anti-dumping and anti-subsidy measures are no longer intended to correct competitive imbalances, but to act as a deterrent and foreclose the Union market to foreign imports to a greater extent. This upsets the balance between the competing interests as established by the lesser duty rule in favour of the interests of the EU industry. The Union interest test is not able to remedy this. While it might ensure that an appropriate balance between the interests of the complainant industry and the up- and downstream users of the product concerned is struck, it does not address the issue of higher duty levels having an overall negative impact on the competitive situation on the internal market by factoring in the EU's inefficiencies, resulting in price increases above the non-injurious level because of such inefficiencies. These competition concerns do not find expression in the Union interest test under Article 7 (2b) BADR. Concerning the application of the lesser duty rule under the reformed BASR, given the fact that in none of the investigations concluded up to now the Commission received any information that might have led it to conclude that the lesser duty rule should apply, the lesser duty rule is *de facto* abolished in anti-subsidy investigations.

7.2.3.2 Injury Margin Calculation: Systematic Inaccuracies and Protectionist Tendencies

The calculation of the injury margin is closely connected to the application of the lesser duty rule, as the amount of the duties shall be based on the injury margin and not on the margin of dumping or subsidisation, if such lesser duty is sufficient to remove the injury to the Union industry. The changes to the application of the lesser duty rule introduced by the Trade Defence Modernisation Package have just been presented.[152]

7.2.3.2.1 The 'Undercutting' and the 'Underselling' Methodology

In the instances where the lesser duty rule is still applicable, however, the calculation of the injury margin is of central importance. Although neither the WTO treaties nor the basic regulations contain any precise methodology on how to calculate the injury margin, in practice, the Commission will typically have recourse to either the 'price

---

[151] Ibid recital 381.
[152] Cf. above p. 192 et seq.

undercutting' or the 'price underselling' method.[153] When determining the injury margin by using the price undercutting method, the Commission will compare the import prices with the prices of 'like' goods of the Union industry.[154] The Commission has stressed that its margin of discretion in assessing this injury factor is limited only by the need to base conclusions on positive evidence and to make an objective examination.[155] The 'price undercutting methodology' in essence consists of a comparison between the prices charged by the exporting producers and the EU industry producing 'like' products. Adjustments for factors affecting price comparability, such as differences in physical characteristics and the stage of transactions, are made.[156] However, in the majority of cases, the Commission will find that it is not possible to compare the prices of the exporting producers and the EU industry, as the prices of the latter have been depressed as a result of the dumped or subsidised imports, making them no longer profitable. Consequently, the Commission will base its determination of the injury margin on the so-called 'price underselling method'. Here, the Commission will compare the prices charged by cooperating exporting producers with a 'target price'. The difference between the exporting producers' prices and the target price is then expressed as a percentage of the export price of the exporting producers.[157] The target price represents the price which the Union industry would be able to achieve absent the 'unfair' competition of dumped and subsidised products on the internal market. In order to obtain the target price, the Commission may use the actual sales prices of the Union producers, adjusted to a break-even point, and adding a profit margin which may have been reasonably achieved in the absence of injurious dumping or subsidisation. Another means of determining the target price is to set it at the level of prices that would be required to cover the costs of production incurred by the EU industry and to obtain a profit before tax on sales of the like product that could have been achieved under normal competitive circumstances.[158]

Authors have noted in particular the 'underselling' methodology to be a highly theoretical exercise, given the uncertainties surrounding the determination of the

---

[153] On criticism regarding injury margin calculation in general cf. Vermulst and Graafsma (2007), p. 27; Tharakan et al. (2006), p. 653; Vandenbussche and Wauthy (2001).

[154] *Transnational Company 'Kazchrome' AO and ENRC Marketing AG v Council* (30 November 2011) T-107/08 55 (General Court).

[155] Commission Implementing Regulation (EU) 2019/1688 of 8 October 2019 imposing a definitive anti-dumping duty and definitively collecting the provisional duty imposed on imports of mixtures of urea and ammonium nitrate originating in Russia, Trinidad and Tobago and the United States of America (Chap. 6, n 125) recital 127; Commission Regulation (EU) 2018/683 of 4 May 2018 imposing a provisional anti-dumping duty on imports of certain pneumatic tyres, new or retreaded, of rubber, of a kind used for buses or lorries, with a load index exceeding 121 originating in the People's Republic of China, and amending Implementing Regulation (EU) 2018/163 (Chap. 5, n 14) recital 167.

[156] In detail cf. van Bael and Bellis (2019) § 4.11 [A] [2].

[157] Ibid § 7.04 [A] [2].

[158] Ibid.

price level of the EU industry in the absence of dumped imports.[159] This is further exacerbated by a number of issues relating to the data used in computing the injury suffered by the Union industry, both for the price undercutting and the price underselling methodology. The first issue relates to the confidentiality of the underlying data. The pricing information of the EU producers as well as the export prices of the foreign producers are considered confidential information and are thus not available to the opposing parties.[160] As only the EU institutions have full access to the relevant information in calculating the injury margin, it proves challenging for the parties to the proceedings to follow the Commission's calculation methods or to preview to what extent injury margins will operate as an adequate limit on the level of duties.[161] The second issue likewise concerns the sources of the data to be used for calculating the injury margin. Factors such as production, production capacity and prices of individual Union producers may vary widely, leading to different outcomes in determining the injury margin.[162] In the past, the investigating authorities have used the data of the most efficient Union producer[163] or have based their assessment on the situation of a representative Union producer,[164] both of which may present a distorted picture of the microeconomic situation of the Union industry. However, the most frequent method adopted in the current Commission practice appears to base the determination of the duty level necessary to eliminate the injury on the data of the sampled EU producers. The data is then used to determine e.g. average sales prices (in the event of the price undercutting methodology)[165] or the average non-injurious price of the like product sold by the sampled EU producers (price underselling

---

[159] Luo (2010), p. 132.

[160] Horlick and Vermulst (2007), p. 4; Vermulst (2005), p. 111; Vermulst and Waer (1991), p. 7.

[161] Vermulst and Waer (1991), p. 7.

[162] Ibid 18.

[163] Commission Regulation (EEC) No 3019/86 of 30 September 1986 imposing a provisional antidumping duty on imports of standardized multi-phase electric motors having an output of more than 0,75 kW but not more than 75 kW, originating in Bulgaria, Czechoslovakia, the German Democratic Republic, Hungary, Poland, Romania and the USSR recital 21.

[164] Council Regulation (EEC) No 3339/87 of 4 November 1987 imposing a definitive anti-dumping duty on imports of urea originating in Libya and Saudi Arabia and accepting undertakings given in connection with imports of urea originating in Czechoslovakia, the German Democratic Republic, Kuwait, the USSR, Trinidad and Tobago and Yugoslavia and terminating these investigations recital 45.

[165] Cf. e.g. Commission Implementing Regulation (EU) 2019/1693 of 9 October 2019 imposing a provisional anti-dumping duty on imports of steel road wheels originating in the People's Republic of China (n 60) recital 203; Commission Regulation (EU) No 513/2013 of 4 June 2013 imposing a provisional anti-dumping duty on imports of crystalline silicon photovoltaic modules and key components (i.e. cells and wafers) originating in or consigned from the People's Republic of China and amending Regulation (EU) No 182/2013 making these imports originating in or consigned from the People's Republic of China subject to registration (Chap. 6, n 86) recital 265.

methodology).[166] In *Canon v Council,* Advocate General *Slynn* held that since '*the costs of production of the [EU] producers differ from one to another, it is not possible to give each of them the same degree of protection against dumping*', however it would be entirely consistent with the BADR to apply an average degree of protection.[167] These considerations also apply, *mutatis mutandis,* to injury margin calculations under the BASR.

It follows from the above that, when the Commission uses the underselling methodology, the determination of the target profit margin is of utmost relevance in calculating the target price. As first held by the Court in its *EFMA* judgment, the profit margin must be limited to the profit margin which the Union industry could reasonably count on under normal conditions of competition, in the absence of dumped or subsidised imports. It would not be consistent with the basic regulations to allow the Union industry a profit margin that it could not have expected even if there were no dumped or subsidised products with which it competes.[168] Consequently, the profit margin can not be set at a level sufficient to restore prices at an undistorted, normal level but only at a level that could be achieved in the absence of dumped or subsidised imports on the EU market.[169] Furthermore, the Commission must provide sufficient reasons for the determination of the profit margin.[170] The methodology used by the Commission in calculating the profit margin is not made public; however, the parties to the proceedings may request additional information on that matter from the Commission.[171] The discretion enjoyed by the Commission in this regard is substantial, in particular since there are no fixed guidelines concerning the choice of the normative cost of production or rate of profit.[172] The Commission frequently calculates the profit margin by going back to a past representative time span before the investigation period where the level of imports of the product concerned into the EU is lower.[173] In other investigations, the target profit

---

[166]Commission Implementing Regulation (EU) 2019/576 of 10 April 2019 imposing a provisional anti-dumping duty on imports of mixtures of urea and ammonium nitrate originating in Russia, Trinidad and Tobago and the United States of America (n 127) recital 204.

[167]Opinion of Advocate General Slynn in *Canon Inc. and others v Council*, joined cases 277 and 300/85 19888 05731-5791 (8 March 1988).

[168]*European Fertilizer Manufacturers' Association (EFMA) v Council* (n 101) 60; confirmed *inter alia* in *Gold East Paper (Jiangsu) Co. Ltd. and others v Council* (11 September 2014) T-443/11 245 (General Court). The General Court also extended this reasoning to anti-subsidy investigations, cf. *Gold East Paper (Jiangsu) Co. Ltd. and others v Council* (11 September 2014) T-444/11 287 (General Court).

[169]This was one of the pleas brought forward by the applicants in *Gold East Paper (Jiangsu) Co. Ltd. and others v Council* (n 168) 248 et seq.

[170]*Yuanping Changyuan Chemicals Co. Ltd. v Council* (20 May 2015) T-310/12 199–203 (General Court).

[171]Cf. *Gold East Paper (Jiangsu) Co. Ltd. and others v Council* (n 168).

[172]Tharakan et al. (2006), p. 656. Said discretion has led the authors to conclude that '*the actual determination of injury margins remains something of a black box*'.

[173]Cf. e.g. Commission Regulation (EU) 2018/683 of 4 May 2018 imposing a provisional anti-dumping duty on imports of certain pneumatic tyres, new or retreaded, of rubber, of a kind used for

set by the Commission reflected the high up-front investment needs and risks involved in a particularly capital intensive industry.[174] In another investigation, the Commission arrived at the target profit margin by simulating

> how the recovery of the Union industry from the recession caused by the economic and financial crisis in 2009 might have developed if it had not been interrupted by the high volumes of price depressing imports.[175]

These varying approaches have led authors to conclude that

> in practice, the profit margin is set by the Commission on the basis of considerations which vary from case to case and are based on product and market considerations, the relevance of which depends on the level of the injury margin that the Commission wishes to reach.[176]

7.2.3.2.2 The Modifications Introduced by the Trade Defence Modernisation Package

7.2.3.2.2.1 The Introduction of a de minimis Target Profit

The modifications introduced to the calculation of the injury margin were considered necessary to better reflect the underlying economic reality, as the old rules were no longer sufficient to adequately remove the injury caused to the Union industry by the presence of dumped or subsidised imports on the internal market.[177] While the old basic regulations were silent on exactly how to calculate the target price or the target profit margin, the amending Regulation (EU) 2018/825 is considerably more explicit in this regard. When establishing the target profit, the level of profitability to be expected under normal conditions of competition, as well as further aspects such as the level of profitability before the increase of imports from the country under investigation, the level of profitability needed to cover full costs and investments, research and development and innovation are to be taken into account.[178]

---

buses or lorries, with a load index exceeding 121 originating in the People's Republic of China, and amending Implementing Regulation (EU) 2018/163 (Chap. 5, n 14) recital 254: '[T]his was considered the year in the [injury assessment] period considered that resembled most normal conditions of competition because the volume of Chinese imports was the lowest and the average import price was the highest.'

[174] Council Implementing Regulation (EU) No 451/2011 of 6 May 2011 imposing a definitive anti-dumping duty and collecting definitively the provisional duty imposed on imports of coated fine paper originating in the People's Republic of China recitals 156 et seq.

[175] Commission Implementing Regulation (EU) 2016/1778 of 6 October 2016 imposing a provisional anti-dumping duty on imports of certain hot-rolled flat products of iron, non-alloy or other alloy steel originating in the People's Republic of China recital 223.

[176] van Bael and Bellis (2019) § 7.04 [A] [2].

[177] Müller (2018), p. 48.

[178] Article 7 (2d) BADR and Article 12 (1b) BASR. It should be noted however that to some extent, this was already the case under the old regulations, where profit margins were established also by having regard to the research and development costs, the 'specialisation' of the product under investigation etc. Here, goods with short economic or technical life cycles tended to be assigned

Furthermore, the target price is to reflect the costs incurred by the Union industry resulting from multilateral environmental agreements and ILO Conventions. This includes future costs the Union industry will incur during the period of the application of the measure.[179] Both amendments will enable the EU industry to claim higher target profits than it would have been able to under the old basic regulations.[180] Further, the profit margin shall not be lower than 6%,[181] ruling out the possibility of the profit margin being set at a lower level, as it sometimes had been in the past.[182] This in turn will lead to higher injury margins, ultimately resulting in higher duties in investigations where the lesser duty rule still applies.

What is more, it must be called into question whether such a fixed minimum target price complies with the *EFMA* standard, which states that the target profit must be limited to the level of profitability to be expected under normal conditions of competition. If the Commission now sets the target profit at the minimum level of 6% even if the profitability of the EU industry did not reach that level in the past, this clearly sets the target profit well above the level of profitability the EU industry could have hoped to achieve even in the absence of dumped or subsidised products.

At the point of writing, the Commission has had recourse to the minimum target profit as set out in the basic regulations in four investigations.[183] Due to the still

---

relatively high profit margins on the grounds that investments were assumed to be amortised over a short period, Tharakan et al. (2006), p. 656.

[179] Article 7 (2d) BADR and Article 12 (1b) BASR. The provisions read *'[w]hen establishing the target price, the actual cost of production of the Union industry, which results from multilateral environmental agreements, and protocols thereunder, to which the Union is a party, of from International Labour Organisation (ILO) Conventions listed in Annex Ia to this Regulation, shall be duly reflected.'* For better readability, references to the protocols concluded thereunder will be omitted hereinafter.

[180] Hoffmeister (2020), p. 223.

[181] Article 7 (2c) second sentence BADR and Article 12 (1a) second sentence BASR.

[182] Cf. e.g. Commission Implementing Regulation (EU) 2018/1012 of 17 July 2018 imposing a provisional anti-dumping duty on imports of electric bicycles originating in the People's Republic of China and amending Implementing Regulation (EU) 2018/671 (n 6) recital 260; Commission Implementing Regulation (EU) 2016/388 of 17 March 2016 imposing a definitive anti-dumping duty on imports of tubes and pipes of ductile cast iron (also known as spheroidal graphite cast iron) originating in India recital 118; Council Regulation (EC) No 1420/2007 of 4 December 2007 imposing a definitive anti-dumping duty on imports of silico-manganese originating in the People's Republic of China and Kazakhstan and terminating the proceeding on imports of silico-manganese originating in Ukraine recital 166; Commission Regulation (EC) 2005/2006 of 22 December 2006 imposing provisional anti-dumping duties on imports of synthetic staple fibres of polyesters (PSF) originating in Malaysia and Taiwan (Chap. 5, n 32) recital 172.

[183] Commission Implementing Regulation (EU) 2021/983 of 17 June 2021 imposing a provisional anti-dumping duty on imports of aluminium converter foil originating in the People's Republic of China recital 371; Commission Implementing Regulation (EU) 2020/1336 of 25 September 2020 imposing definitive anti-dumping duties on imports of certain polyvinyl alcohols originating in the People's Republic of China (Chap. 6, n 40) recital 652; Commission Implementing Regulation (EU) 2020/492 of 1 April 2020 imposing definitive anti-dumping duties on imports of certain woven and/or stitched glass fibre fabrics originating in the People's Republic of China and Egypt (n 44) recitals 524–525; Commission Implementing Regulation (EU) 2019/1693 of 9 October 2019

limited number of investigations conducted under the new basic regulations, it is too early to draw any definite conclusions whether this is a general trend or reflective of the specific characteristics in the industries concerned in the respective investigations. However, so far, the reformed basic regulations have led to the outcome predicted above, namely an increase in the duty levels.

In addition to the compatibility of the *de minimis* profit margin with the *EFMA* standard being questionable *per se*,[184] the methodology for calculating the profit margins can be criticised for a number of other reasons.

7.2.3.2.2.2 A General 'Increase of Imports from the Country Under Investigation'

The Commission's initial proposal on the reform of the EU's trade defence instruments of 2013 encompassed the publication of guidelines concerning four core aspects of trade defence investigations, including on the subject of the calculation of the target profit margin. While the EU legislators ultimately refrained from including such guidelines in the Trade Defence Modernisation Package, the Commission's drafts on the guidelines are still available.[185] Concerning the calculation of the target profit margin, the draft guidelines provided that the profit margin obtained by the EU industry in a period in which the dumped and/or subsidised imports did not have any negative effects on the situation of the Union industry should serve as a basis for determining the target profit.[186] This would have been in line with the above-mentioned judgment of the General Court in *EFMA*, which stated that the target profit margin must be limited to what the Union industry could reasonably count on under normal conditions of competition, in the absence of the dumped imports.[187] These 'normal conditions of competition' referred to in the *EFMA* judgment also include competition from non-dumped/subsidised products from

---

imposing a provisional anti-dumping duty on imports of steel road wheels originating in the People's Republic of China (n 60) recitals 264–265.

[184] None of the official documents available provides guidance as to why 6% was chosen as the appropriate minimum target profit. The legislative documents only indicate that the Council's original negotiating position considered 5% adequate. During the inter-institutional negotiations between Council, Commission and Parliament, the minimum target profit of 6% was agreed upon, leading to this benchmark being included in the Council position on the Commission's legislative proposal and ultimately in the modernised basic regulations themselves, cf. Council of the European Union, 'Note from the Presidency to the Permanent Representatives Committee on the subject of the proposal for a Regulation of the European Parliament and of the Council amending Regulation (EU) No 2016/1036 on protection against dumped imports from countries not members of the European Union and Regulation (EU) No 2016/1037 on protection against subsidised imports from countries not members of the European Union (15530/17): Analysis of the final compromise text with a view to agreement' (Interinstitutional file 2013/0103 (COD), Brussels 15 December 2017) 4.

[185] European Commission, 'DG Trade Working Document: Draft Guidelines on the Determination of the Profit Margin Used in Establishing the Injury Margin' (Brussels 2013), available at <https://trade.ec.europa.eu/doclib/docs/2013/april/tradoc_150840.pdf>.

[186] Ibid para. 6.

[187] *European Fertilizer Manufacturers' Association (EFMA) v Council* (n 101) 60.

third countries competing with the products of the EU industry, with the possible negative effects on the profitability of the operations of the EU industry this might entail. Given the above, it is noteworthy that the reformed basic regulations do not limit themselves to the period before the presence of dumped or subsidised imports on the Union market in calculating the target profit margin of the EU industry. Instead, they refer to the time before the increase of imports from the country under investigation in general as a relevant factor in calculating the target profit margin.[188] This potentially permits the Commission to calculate the target profit based on the profitability levels of the EU industry before it faced any relevant competitive pressure from imports originating in the country under investigation, regardless of whether they were subsidised, dumped or none of the two.

This must be criticised for three reasons, which will be set out in more detail in the following section: first, the wording of the reformed basic regulations stands in conflict with the rules on injury assessment. Second, it contradicts the basic principles set out in the *EFMA* judgment and third, it risks blurring the lines between the anti-dumping and anti-subsidy instruments of the EU and its general safeguards instruments.

First, concerning the conflict with the rules on injury assessment contained in the basic regulations, it must be recalled that the provisions explicitly state that the injury assessment shall be based *inter alia* on an objective examination of the volume of the dumped or subsidised imports in the European Union.[189] Thus, imports for which no or only a *de minimis* dumping or subsidy margin has been established have to be excluded from the analysis. Consequently, during the injury assessment, the finding of dumping or subsidisation has to be made at the level of each individual exporter instead of at a country wide level in order for imports to be included in the examination on the level of dumped or subsidised goods being imported into the EU.[190] Opposed to this individual approach adopted under the injury assessment, by focussing on a general increase of the level of imports from the country under investigation, the modernised rules on the calculation of the target profit margin appear to follow a countrywide approach without regard for the dumping or subsidisation levels of individual exporters. This risks the injury assessment and the injury margin calculations to be guided by different standards, and the injury margin to be conflated.

Second, such a focus on a general increase in imports in calculating the target profit margin might be in conflict with the principles set out in the *EFMA* judgment. As mentioned, the basic regulations are not intended to give protection against any competitive pressure exerted by any imports but only against unfair import

---

[188] Article 7 (2c) BADR and Article 12 (1a) BASR.

[189] Article 3 (2) BADR and Article 8 (1) BASR.

[190] Mueller et al. (2009) para. 3.23. This is also prescribed by WTO law, cf. *European Communities – Countervailing Measures on Dynamic Random Access Memory Chips from Korea* (17 June 2005) WT/DS299/R para. 7.302 (Panel Report) on the interpretation of Article 15.2 ASCM.

competition resulting from an increase in dumped or subsidised imports. For this reason, it seems questionable to base the target profit calculations simply on the profit margin achieved by the EU industry at a time where the import level was at its lowest, without further information on whether a later increase in imports is actually attributable to dumping or subsidisation.[191] The Commission has been following this approach in the investigations it conducts under the reformed basic regulations, choosing the level of profitability before imports from the country under investigation increased.[192] This does not represent a change to its practice under the old basic regulations.[193] Under both regimes, the Commission argues that a certain year or period within the injury assessment period resembles normal conditions of competition the most, because here the volume of imports from the country under investigation was at its lowest, or conversely, that this is not the case because of the increase of imports from the country or countries now under investigation.[194] In a way, the approach taken by the EU institutions—in particular the Commission as the investigating authority—can be explained by the fact that it would be nearly impossible to retroactively assess whether the imports were already being dumped or subsidised before the investigation period. It is far less complicated for the investigating authorities to simply assume that any increase in imports witnessed over the period chosen for the assessment of the injury indicators is due to dumping or subsidisation. It can be argued that this logic echoes the 'original sin' of anti-dumping policy, namely the assumption that dumping itself is always an expression of some sort of unfair competitive advantage, such as market segregation or an inefficient competition law on the exporting producer's home market.[195] By extension, basing the target profit determination on the EU industry's level of profitability

---

[191] At this point, it has to be borne in mind that the periods for the examination of the trends relating to the injury assessment and the period for which the existence of dumping and injury are determined are not identical, cf. e.g. Commission Implementing Regulation (EU) 2020/492 of 1 April 2020 imposing definitive anti-dumping duties on imports of certain woven and/or stitched glass fibre fabrics originating in the People's Republic of China and Egypt (n 44) recital 46.

[192] Commission Implementing Regulation (EU) 2020/705 of 26 May 2020 imposing a provisional anti-dumping duty on imports of certain heavyweight thermal paper originating in the Republic of Korea recitals 143–144, 146; Commission Implementing Regulation (EU) 2020/508 of 7 April 2020 imposing a provisional anti-dumping duty on imports of certain hot rolled stainless steel sheets and coils originating in Indonesia, the People's Republic of China and Taiwan (n 76) recital 331; Commission Implementing Regulation (EU) 2020/492 of 1 April 2020 imposing definitive anti-dumping duties on imports of certain woven and/or stitched glass fibre fabrics originating in the People's Republic of China and Egypt (n 44) recitals 524–525; Commission Implementing Regulation (EU) 2019/1693 of 9 October 2019 imposing a provisional anti-dumping duty on imports of steel road wheels originating in the People's Republic of China (n 60) recitals 264–265.

[193] Cf. the examples given above, n 173.

[194] Commission Regulation (EU) 2018/683 of 4 May 2018 imposing a provisional anti-dumping duty on imports of certain pneumatic tyres, new or retreaded, of rubber, of a kind used for buses or lorries, with a load index exceeding 121 originating in the People's Republic of China, and amending Implementing Regulation (EU) 2018/163 (Chap. 5, n 14) recital 254 and the examples given above, n 971.

[195] Cf. e.g. Mueller et al. (2009) paras. I.06 et seq.

at the time where the share of imports from the country under investigation is at its lowest implicitly assumes that any increase in imports is rooted in these unfair competitive advantages already existing before the investigation period for which the existence of dumping is established. Yet, the compatibility of the Commission's practice to base its target profit calculations on the profit margin achieved by the EU producers at a time where the import level was at its lowest with the standard set out in *EFMA* must be called into doubt.

Third, the reformed basic regulations' focus on a general increase of imports from the country under investigation concerning the injury margin assessment risks blurring the line between the EU's safeguards instruments, which are the appropriate means for addressing concerns regarding a general increase in the volume of imports into the EU, and the EU's anti-dumping and anti-subsidy legislation.[196] Hence, the present formulation further adds to the criticism that anti-dumping or countervailing measures are frequently used as a means of avoiding the specifics of a safeguards investigation.[197]

In the light of the arguments presented above, it would thus have been appropriate to align the provisions on the calculation of the injury margin with the wording used in the provisions on injury assessment by limiting the target profit to the level of profitability achieved before the presence of dumped or subsidised imports above a negligible level was first established. Moreover, it should be called upon the Commission to adapt its practice accordingly, instead of equalling any increase in imports of the products under investigation with an increase in the imports of dumped or subsidised products, without the dumping or the existence of subsidisation actually having been established for this point in time.

7.2.3.2.2.3   The Level of Profitability Needed to Cover Full Costs and Investments, Research and Development and Innovation

As mentioned, the reformed basic regulations also rely on the level of profitability needed to cover full costs and investments, research and development (R&D) and innovation in calculating the target profit.[198] The practice of the Commission under the reformed legal instruments suggests that, in order for the Commission to take past research and innovation costs into account, the EU producers will have to make

---

[196]Cf. Article 15 (1) of Regulation (EU) 2015/478 of the European Parliament and of the Council of 11 March 2015 on common rules for imports (Chap. 3, n 85): *'Where a product is imported into the Union in such greatly increased quantities and/or on such terms or conditions as to cause, or threaten to cause, serious injury to Union producers, the Commission, in order to safeguard the interests of the Union, may, (. . .) alter the import rules for the product in question (. . .).'*

[197]It should further be noted that the reformed injury margin calculation is the only place where the basic regulations speak of the *'country under investigation'*. Usually, and in line with the general spirit of the basic regulations as focussing on certain products, they refer to the *'product under investigation'* or the *'product concerned'*. On the relationship between safeguards, anti-dumping and anti-subsidy investigations cf. van Bael and Bellis (2019) § 1.09.

[198]Article 7 (2c) BADR and Article 12 (1a) BASR.

a substantiated claim in this regard.[199] If the Commission accepts such a claim, it will adapt the non-injurious price for the individual exporter accordingly.[200] At this point, it once more serves to recall the counterfactual-standard set in *EFMA* as well as the stance originally taken by the Commission in its draft guidelines on the calculation of the target profit: the target profit must only reflect what the EU industry could reasonably have expected in the absence of dumped or subsidised products. This does not signify that it will be set at a level that would be desirable for the EU industry as ensuring the survival of the Union industry and/or an adequate return on capital.[201] Indeed, as established in *EFMA*, such an approach would contradict the basic regulations' rules on injury and the lesser duty rule,[202] and in essence amount to protectionism. However, the reformed basic regulations seem to set the target profit precisely at such an optimal level, namely at the level of profitability needed to cover full costs and investments, without having regard as to whether the EU industry could reasonably have expected to achieve such a profit margin over the the period during which the trade defence measures are in force.[203]

Moreover, the wording of the reformed rules leaves open whether the target profit margin should be calculated only on the basis of the costs for R&D and innovation that concern the product under investigation or whether costs resulting from the development of e.g. new products could be included. If the Commission's reasoning in *Acesulfame Potassium*, an investigation carried out under the old BADR, is regarded as indicative, it seems more probable that only those costs relating to the product under investigation will be considered when determining the target profit level. In the above-mentioned investigation, in establishing the profitability of the Union industry, the Commission deducted from the reported costs all R&D costs and marketing that it considered to be of an exceptional nature in the sense that they

---

[199] Commission Implementing Regulation (EU) 2020/492 of 1 April 2020 imposing definitive anti-dumping duties on imports of certain woven and/or stitched glass fibre fabrics originating in the People's Republic of China and Egypt (n 44) recitals 524–525; Commission Implementing Regulation (EU) 2019/1693 of 9 October 2019 imposing a provisional anti-dumping duty on imports of steel road wheels originating in the People's Republic of China (n 60) recitals 264–265. In fact, the questionnaires for EU producers in trade defence investigations specifically ask for any such investments foregone or R&D costs incurred.

[200] Commission Implementing Regulation (EU) 2020/508 of 7 April 2020 imposing a provisional anti-dumping duty on imports of certain hot rolled stainless steel sheets and coils originating in Indonesia, the People's Republic of China and Taiwan (n 76) recital 332.

[201] European Commission, 'DG Trade Working Document: Draft Guidelines on the Determination of the Profit Margin Used in Establishing the Injury Margin' (n 185) para. 4.

[202] *European Fertilizer Manufacturers' Association (EFMA) v Council* (n 101) 60.

[203] In the past, the Commission has at times called the economic soundness of investments made by the EU industry into question, such as when the industry decided to invest into new production facilities, even though it had suffered losses on the like product for many years, Council Regulation (EC) No 1331/2007 of 13 November 2007 imposing a definitive anti-dumping duty on imports of dicyandiamide originating in the People's Republic of China recitals 94–97.

related to a new product, albeit a product falling within the product scope of the ongoing investigation.[204]

To conclude, while the amending Regulation (EU) 2018/825 explicitly incorporated the counterfactual established in *EFMA* into the rules on profit margin calculation, other parts of the reformed provisions on the calculation of the target profit seem to contradict said counterfactual. One explanation for this apparent contradiction could be that the inclusion of the *EFMA* standard is intended to ensure that, even though the wording of the reformed basic regulations appears to be in conflict with the *EFMA* standard, the assessments carried out under the reformed basic regulations still have to comply with said standard. Of course, such an interpretation would strip the other factors included in the target profit calculation of any relevance, and the contradiction between the General Court's judgment in *EFMA* and the minimum target profit of 6% set out in Article 7 (2c) BADR and Article 12 (1a) BASR remains unsolved.

7.2.3.2.2.4   Social and Environmental Standards

With the EU institutions repeatedly emphasising that trade is not only about exporting goods, but also about exporting values,[205] the inclusion of social and environmental standards in various parts of the reformed basic regulations does not come as a particular surprise. This extends to the injury margin calculations, and more precisely the target price calculations, albeit the main reason for their inclusion lies in a more accurate reflection of the costs incurred by the EU industry in complying with social and environmental standards. As touched upon above, under the reformed rules on the calculation of the target price, the investigating authorities may not only take into account the EU industry's past costs which result from multilateral environmental agreements to which the EU is party, or from ILO Conventions listed in Annex Ia to the basic regulations, but its future costs in that regard as well.[206]

The issue of whether and how to account for investments made by the EU industry in order to meet the requirements of EU environmental legislation is not a new one. It already arose during the injury assessment carried out under the rules of

---

[204] Commission Implementing Regulation (EU) 2015/787 of 19 May 2015 imposing a provisional anti-dumping duty on imports of acesulfame potassium originating in the People's Republic of China as well as acesulfame potassium originating in the People's Republic of China contained in certain preparations and/or mixtures recitals 66–67.

[205] European Commission, 'Trade for all – Towards a more responsible trade and investment policy (COM(2015) 497)' (Chap. 4, n 103) 22.

[206] Article 7 (2d) BADR and Article 12 (1b) BASR. Conversely, future additional costs incurred by the exporting producers in complying with social and environmental legislation in their home country are irrelevant in the investigation and will not be added to the exporting producers' export prices, Commission Implementing Regulation (EU) 2020/1524 of 19 October 2020 imposing a definitive anti-dumping duty and definitively collecting the provisional duty imposed on imports of certain heavyweight thermal paper originating in the Republic of Korea recitals 78 et seq.

the previous versions of the basic regulations. When analysing whether the economic situation of the EU industry had worsened over the injury assessment period, the microeconomic indicators analysed by the investigating authorities included—and still include—the investments made by the EU industry. Usually, a downward trend in investments will be regarded as being indicative of the situation of the EU industry worsening, whereas a healthy or even increasing level of investments may point against the EU industry suffering injury. Under the previous versions of the basic regulations, if the investments made over the period considered were the result of legal requirements, a stable or even improving level of investments would not be regarded as indicating that the EU industry's economic situation was developing well.[207] Likewise, the Commission rebutted arguments by importers that costs stemming from environmental requirements break the causal link between the presence of dumped or subsidised imports and the deteriorating economic situation of the EU industry.[208] While the investigating authorities acknowledged that some of the costs borne by the EU industry were incurred in order to meet legal requirements and were not the result of free spending decisions by the EU industry, they stopped short of considering these costs as an additional cost factor when calculating the target price as part of the injury margin assessment. Put differently, money that was not spent voluntarily on part of the EU industry would not be regarded as reflecting

---

[207] Commission Regulation (EC) No 1071/2007 of 18 September 2007 imposing a provisional anti-dumping duty on imports of coke of coal in pieces with a diameter of more than 80 mm (Coke 80+) originating in the People's Republic of China recital 54; Commission Regulation (EC) No 994/2007 of 28 August 2007 imposing a provisional anti-dumping duty on imports of ferro-silicon originating in the People's Republic of China, Egypt, Kazakhstan, the former Yugoslav Republic of Macedonia and Russia recitals 99–100; Commission Regulation Regulation (EC) No 1259/2005 of 27 July 2005 imposing a provisional anti-dumping duty on imports of tartaric acid originating in the People's Republic of China recital 72. More recent examples include Commission Implementing Regulation (EU) 2020/1534 of 21 October 2020 imposing a definitive anti-dumping duty on imports of certain prepared or preserved citrus fruits (namely mandarins, etc.) originating in the People's Republic of China following an expiry review pursuant to Article 11(2) of Regulation (EU) 2016/1036 of the European Parliament and of the Council (n 56) recital 194; Commission Implementing Regulation (EU) 2019/1259 of 24 July 2019 imposing a definitive anti-dumping duty on imports of threaded tube or pipe cast fittings, of malleable cast iron and spheroidal graphite cast iron, originating in the People's Republic of China and Thailand, following an expiry review pursuant to Article 11(2) of Regulation (EU) 2016/1036 of the European Parliament and of the Council (Chap. 6, n 93) recital 237 and Commission Implementing Regulation (EU) 2019/687 of 2 May 2019 imposing a definitive anti-dumping duty on imports of certain organic coated steel products originating in the People's Republic of China following an expiry review pursuant to Article 11 (2) of Regulation (EU) 2016/1036 of the European Parliament and of the Council (n 39) recital 212. Instead, the Commission will have regard to the return on investments in assessing the development of the economic situation of the EU industry over the period considered.

[208] Commission Implementing Regulation (EU) 2020/508 of 7 April 2020 imposing a provisional anti-dumping duty on imports of certain hot rolled stainless steel sheets and coils originating in Indonesia, the People's Republic of China and Taiwan (n 76) recital 324; Commission Decision (EU) 81/2013 of 13 February 2013 terminating the anti-dumping proceeding concerning imports of white phosphorus, also called elemental or yellow phosphorus, originating in the Republic of Kazakhstan recitals 137–138.

positively on the economic situation of the EU industry in the assessment of the injury incurred by the EU industry. At the same time, the Commission would not consider it to affect the causal link between the presence of dumped or subsidised imports and the deteriorating situation of the EU industry. The reformed basic regulations develop the approach adopted in the previous versions of the basic regulations further, and extend its logic to the injury margin assessment. Since the costs of complying with legally required social and environmental standards are not borne voluntarily by the companies, not only do these costs have to be disregarded during the injury assessment, but they instead must be taken into account as additional costs when calculating the target price. This applies correspondingly with regard to those social and environmental costs which have not yet been incurred by the companies, but which can be reasonably expected to be incurred during the period of application of the measures.

As observed by authors shortly after the completion of the reform process, these changes to the target price calculation will be of particular relevance with regard to the costs incurred under the EU's emissions trading scheme,[209] and indeed, these were the environmental costs the Commission focussed on in *Urea and Ammonium Nitrate*. Here, the Commission argued that the costs the EU industry would have to bear also comprised the additional future costs to ensure compliance with the EU Emissions Trading Scheme (ETS), which is a cornerstone of the EU's policy in complying with multilateral environmental agreements. The additional costs were calculated on the basis of the average estimated additional EU Allowances[210] which will have to be purchased by the EU industry during the life of the measures.[211] The Commission added an additional cost of 3.7% incurred by the EU industry to the non-injurious price. The implementing regulation itself does not contain any information on how the Commission established this additional cost, but a note to the file on the matter is available for inspection by interested parties.[212] In the regulation imposing the definitive measures, the Commission revised its calculation of the costs for complying with the EU ETS. As the prices for EU Allowances were projected to be higher than what had been assumed under the provisional regulation, the additional cost for compliance with the ETS too was considered to be higher than what had been established.[213] After final disclosure, the representative body of the

---

[209] Müller (2018), p. 49.

[210] Under the EU Emissions Trading Scheme, the term 'allowances' denotes the right to emit one tonne of carbon dioxide equivalent during a specified period, Article 3 lit. a) Directive 2003/87/EC of the European Parliament and of the Council of 13 October 2003 establishing a scheme for greenhouse gas emission allowance trading within the Community and amending Council Directive 96/61/EC.

[211] Commission Implementing Regulation (EU) 2019/576 of 10 April 2019 imposing a provisional anti-dumping duty on imports of mixtures of urea and ammonium nitrate originating in Russia, Trinidad and Tobago and the United States of America (n 127) recital 202.

[212] Ibid recital 201.

[213] Commission Implementing Regulation (EU) 2019/1688 of 8 October 2019 imposing a definitive anti-dumping duty and definitively collecting the provisional duty imposed on imports of mixtures

complainant EU industry tried to argue that the average price for EU Allowances had increased even further, basing its line of argument on data from a source different from the one that the Commission had used at the provisional and definitive stage. However, as the Commission considered it to be of '*utmost importance*' that there is clarity about the source and the timing of the benchmark, the Commission did not re-evaluate its past calculations.[214] Likewise, the Commission examined the costs resulting from complying with the EU ETS in *Aluminium Extrusions*,[215] *Aluminium Flat Products*[216] and *MEG*.[217] Similar to the approach adopted by the Commission in *Urea and Ammonium Nitrate*, the Commission disclosed its calculation methodology and the data used in these investigations.

The Commission further considered environmental costs in *Hot Rolled Stainless Steel, Hot Rolled Flat Steel, Heavyweight Thermal Paper* and *Stainless Steel*. Compared to the reasoning contained in the investigations mentioned in the previous paragraph, the reasoning given in these implementing regulations is significantly briefer. Here, the respective legislative act only states that

> in accordance with Article 7(2d) of the basic regulation, the Commission assessed the future costs resulting from Multilateral Environmental Agreements, and protocols thereunder, to which the Union is a party, that the Union industry will incur during the period of application of the measure pursuant to Article 11(2). Based on the evidence available, the Commission established an additional cost between EUR (. . .) per tonne, which was added to the non-injurious price.[218]

---

of urea and ammonium nitrate originating in Russia, Trinidad and Tobago and the United States of America (Chap. 6, n 125) recital 195.

[214] Ibid recital 197.

[215] Commission Implementing Regulation (EU) 2020/1428 of 12 October 2020 imposing a provisional anti-dumping duty on imports of aluminium extrusions originating in the People's Republic of China (n 57) recitals 341 et seq.

[216] Commission Implementing Regulation (EU) 2021/582 of of 9 April 2021 imposing a provisional anti-dumping duty on imports of aluminium flat-rolled products originating in the People's Republic of China, recitals 468 et seq.

[217] Commission Implementing Regulation (EU) 2021/939 of 10 June 2021 imposing a provisional anti-dumping duty on imports of mono ethylene glycol originating in the United States of America and the Kingdom of Saudi Arabia, recitals 263 et seq.

[218] Commission Implementing Regulation (EU) 2021/854 of 27 May 2021 imposing a provisional anti-dumping duty on imports of stainless steel cold-rolled flat products originating in India and Indonesia, recital 169; Commission Implementing Regulation (EU) 2021/9 of 6 January 2021 imposing a provisional anti-dumping duty on imports of certain hot-rolled flat products of iron, non-alloy or other alloy steel originating in Turkey recital 168; Commission Implementing Regulation (EU) 2020/705 of 26 May 2020 imposing a provisional anti-dumping duty on imports of certain heavyweight thermal paper originating in the Republic of Korea (n 192) recital 147; Commission Implementing Regulation (EU) 2020/508 of 7 April 2020 imposing a provisional anti-dumping duty on imports of certain hot rolled stainless steel sheets and coils originating in Indonesia, the People's Republic of China and Taiwan (n 76) recital 333. Cf. further Commission Implementing Regulation (EU) 2021/940 of 10 June 2021 imposing a provisional anti-dumping duty on imports of birch plywood originating in Russia recital 174, where the Commission also mentions costs resulting from ILO Conventions that the Union industry will occur in its injury margin calculation.

No information regarding the origins of that additional cost or the methodology used in calculating said cost is given and the implementing regulations do not contain any information as to whether a note to the file on the matter is available for inspection by interested parties.

While the logic of including social and environmental costs in the injury margin assessment is sound itself, a number of issues related to their inclusion arises nonetheless. These will be presented below, as well as proposals relating to their solution.

Defining the ratione materiae

The first issue is to define the *ratione materiae* of Article 7 (2d) BADR and Article 12 (1b) BASR. The broader their scope of application, the more possibilities there are for costs to be included in the calculation of the target price, which in turn leads to higher injury margins and ultimately to higher duties. As mentioned before, the initial investigations under the new rules suggest that it is the costs resulting from the EU ETS that will be of particular importance under Article 7 (2d) BADR and Article 12 (1b) BASR when considering environmental costs. It remains to be seen whether this is also the case in future investigations and which other environmental costs the Commission includes when establishing the target price.

There is next to no guidance on the Commission's approach towards social costs. While it in some instances has noted that investments were prompted by the desire to increase safety of production,[219] there is no explicit mention of costs related to social standards in the Commission's past practice, and until now, there has not been any under the reformed basic regulations either. In any event, given the wide margin of discretion enjoyed by the Commission in the injury margin assessment,[220] in addition to the precise calculation of additional social and environmental costs being likely to prove factually challenging for the Commission, the outcomes of such calculations will be difficult to challenge before the CJEU. This adds potential for more legal uncertainty for the parties involved in trade defence investigations.

It further has to be clarified which costs exactly can be regarded as 'resulting' from the EU's obligations under international social and environmental legislation. First, it should be noted that the wording of the basic regulations would permit their application both to costs that are the direct result of the EU's obligations under multilateral environmental agreements and ILO conventions and to those costs for

---

[219] Commission Implementing Regulation (EU) 2019/687 of 2 May 2019 imposing a definitive anti-dumping duty on imports of certain organic coated steel products originating in the People's Republic of China following an expiry review pursuant to Article 11 (2) of Regulation (EU) 2016/1036 of the European Parliament and of the Council (n 39) recital 212.

[220] Commission Implementing Regulation (EU) 2019/73 of 17 January 2019 imposing a definitive anti-dumping duty and definitively collecting the provisional duty imposed on imports of electric bicycles originating in the People's Republic of China recital 206.

which this is the case only indirectly.[221] One possible avenue of delineating the provisions' scope of application is to distinguish between costs resulting from compulsory legislation and those arising from general efforts of the EU industry to contribute to the industry's eco-efficiency or an improvement in workplace conditions, without this being explicitly mandated by EU social or environmental legislation. When applying this standard, the costs arising from the purchase of emission allowances fall within the first category, as the EU industry is legally obligated to acquire said EU Allowances in order to conduct its business activities. This too appears to have been the case for the examples given above on environmental standards in the injury assessment under the old basic regulations, where it was stated that the companies had to make certain investments in order to comply with EU environmental legislation. Consequently, the Commission practice both under the old and the new rules points at Article 7 (2d) BADR and Article 12 (1b) BASR only being applied in instances where a certain cost factor is directly attributable to the EU industry having to comply with EU environmental or social legislation.[222]

While this narrows the scope of application of Article 7 (2d) BADR and Article 12 (1b) BASR, such an interpretation of the provisions creates legal certainty for the parties involved in trade defence proceedings by restricting the Commission's discretion as to which costs it may subsume under Article 7 (2d) BADR and Article 12 (1b) BASR. At the same time, such a restrictive interpretation is warranted in order to prevent the new rules from being abused for protectionist purposes. The provisions must not be used in a manner which permits the EU industry to benefit from unreasonably high target prices by claiming on a large scale that costs it is going to incur during the lifetime of the measures are the result of social and environmental legislation. In addition, a narrow interpretation of which costs can be considered as 'resulting' from the EU's commitments under multilateral environmental agreements and the relevant ILO conventions has the advantage of being enforcer-friendly as it provides the Commission with relatively clear guidelines on which costs fall within the scope of application of the relevant provisions.

---

[221] It merely states that the costs must '*result*' from the commitments assumed by the EU industry under multilateral environmental agreements and ILO conventions and their respective protocols.

[222] Interestingly, in the questionnaires sent out to the EU producers in the above-mentioned *Heavyweight Thermal Paper* investigation, the Commission not only asked for the costs that can be attributed directly to the respondent having to comply with EU environmental and labour standards, but also for any other investment aimed at reducing emissions, as well as other 'indirect costs' which result from multilateral environmental agreements and from ILO conventions. This does not call the statement made above into question, as the application of Articles 7 (2d) BADR and Article 12 (1b) BASR also depends on the companies being able to provide sufficient proof that the costs are incurred as a consequence of legal requirements flowing from obligations assumed by the EU under multilateral environmental agreements and ILO conventions, European Commission, 'Questionnaire for the Union producers in case AD659 – Thermal Paper (Certain Heavyweight)', available at <http://trade.ec.europa.eu/tdi/case_details.cfm?id=2419>.

Overlaps with EU State Aid Law

The reformed provisions on the calculation of the target price further present a number of issues related to the issue of over-compensating the EU industry, creating possible frictions between EU State aid law and the EU's trade defence legislation. More specifically, EU companies may receive compensation from their home States for the costs that arise in complying with EU social and environmental legislation that are included in the calculation of the target price. Article 7 (2d) BADR and Article 12 (1b) BASR are silent on how to address this matter. The ETS serves as an example of this overlap. As a consequence of the implementation of the emissions trading scheme, installations that purchase and use electricity from their suppliers will see a rise in their so-called 'indirect emission costs', i.e. the costs passed on by their power providers of using allowances to cover the emissions from power generation to their customers.[223] In order to avoid those energy-intensive industries from relocating their production or making new investments outside the EU (frequently referred to as 'leakage'), the ETS Directive allows the Member States to compensate sectors and subsectors if they face such indirect costs to a significant extent, provided that such financial measures are in accordance with EU State aid rules.[224] Hence, the existing ETS legislation already provides the option of granting companies compensation for certain costs they incur as a result of EU environmental legislation. Consequently, allowing these additional costs to be taken into account again when calculating the target price under the reformed basic regulations would amount to granting the EU industry double compensation. This, however, would be in conflict with the rationale of the EU's trade defence legislation as being intended to restore a 'level playing field'[225] and instead provide unfair competitive advantages to the EU industry, which would in essence see their competitive situation being unduly strengthened. The Commission has not yet adopted a unified approach in addressing this issue. In some investigations, it will ask EU producers in their questionnaires in ongoing anti-dumping investigations to indicate any compensation they received for the indirect emission costs borne by them.[226] Likewise, in *Aliuminium Flat-Rolled Products* and *Aluminium Converter Foil*, the respective implementing regulations indicated that account was taken of any compensation received by the Member States when having regard to the ETS in calculating the target profit.[227] However, so far, this is not the case for all of the implementing

---

[223] European Commission, 'EU ETS Handbook' (2015) 60–65.

[224] Article 10a (6) of Directive 2003/87/EC of the European Parliament and of the Council of 13 October 2003 establishing a scheme for greenhouse gas emission allowance trading within the Community and amending Council Directive 96/61/EC (n 210).

[225] Cf. above p. 31 et seq.

[226] European Commission, 'Questionnaire for the Union producers in case AD659 – Thermal Paper (Certain Heavyweight)' (n 222).

[227] Cf. Commission Implementing Reglation (EU) 2021/983 of 17 June 2021 imposing a provisional anti-dumping duty on imports of aluminium converter foil originating in the People's Republic of China recitals 372 et seq; Commission Implementing Regulation (EU) 2021/582 of

regulations where the Union industry's ETS costs were taken into consideration in establishing the target price. Indeed, in the investigation concerning *MEG*, the implementing regulation—which was published only one week before the implementing regulation imposing a provisional anti-dumping duty on aluminium converter foil was—did not elaborate on the issue.[228]

It should however be remarked that this only concerns the specific issue of compensation provided by the Member States for the costs that have arisen as a result of the implementation of the ETS. Apart from this, the questionnaires do not ask the EU producers to declare whether they have received compensation for the costs incurred by them as the result of having to comply with social and environmental standards in general. It should further be borne in mind that, even if such a section were to be introduced in the questionnaires, the EU producers will have to provide the Commission with accurate information on compensatory schemes on Member State level in order for the Commission to be able to take such schemes into account. Further, the situation may well arise that a producer correctly declares that he has received or will be receiving compensation under a State aid scheme operated by his home State. If the scheme however is found to be incompatible with EU State aid law after the trade defence measures are imposed, the EU producer will have to pay back said compensation. Following the logic presented above of avoiding undue double compensation, the EU producer's costs will then not have been taken into consideration during the anti-dumping or countervailing investigation in establishing the target price. The outcome of such a constellation is that the EU producer will not receive any compensation for the costs he incurs in adhering to EU social and environmental standards.

Lastly, and related to the issues presented above, the question remains of how the Commission will react in situations where DG TRADE is conducting an investigation under the basic regulations, and a compensatory scheme relevant to the correct determination of the target price is simultaneously under investigation by DG COMP for its compliance with EU State aid rules. In light of the fixed time limits in which an investigation has to be concluded under the basic regulations and the absence of such a fixed time frame for formal investigations in EU State aid law,[229] it might not be possible for DG TRADE to refrain from concluding its investigation until DG COMP has concluded its investigation under the EU State aid rules. This further

---

of 9 April 2021 imposing a provisional anti-dumping duty on imports of aluminium flat-rolled products originating in the People's Republic of China (n 216), recitals 468 et seq.

[228] Commission Implementing Regulation (EU) 2021/939 of 10 June 2021 imposing a provisional anti-dumping duty on imports of mono ethylene glycol originating in the United States of America and the Kingdom of Saudi Arabia (n 217), recitals 263 et seq.

[229] Article 9 (6) of Council Regulation (EU) 2015/1589 of 13 July 2015 laying down detailed rules for the application of Article 108 of the Treaty on the Functioning of the European Union reads that the '*Commission shall as far as possible endeavour to adopt a decision within a period of 18 months from the opening of the procedure.*' The preliminary examination has to be concluded within two months, Article 4 (5).

amplifies the risk that the EU industry will receive either double compensation for the social and environmental costs accrued or no compensation at all.

Such a major issue on the interactions between two areas of law and on how to resolve these interactions cannot be left entirely at the Commission's discretion. Consequently, further amendments to the basic regulations are necessary. As a first step, these should prescribe that any other compensation received in the past or during the prospective duration of the measures must be taken into account when establishing the target price pursuant to Article 7 (2d) BADR or Article 12 (1b) BASR in order to avoid situations of double compensation. While a harmonisation of the deadlines within which the Commission has to conclude its investigations under the basic regulations and the regulation laying down the rules for the application of Article 108 TFEU would be a straightforward solution, such a harmonisation seems both improbable and impractical given the different objectives and interests involved in the respective investigations. Consequently, rules addressing the issue of *ex post* divergences between EU trade defence and EU State aid law appear to be the best solution. *In concreto*, it could for example be required that an interim review has to be opened *ex officio* by DG TRADE whenever DG COMP issues a decision in the area of State aid affecting the calculation of the target price under Article 7 (2d) BADR and Article 12 (1b) BASR. Under such a rule, if a State aid investigation concluded after the imposition of measures under the basic regulations were to find that a State aid scheme is incompatible with EU law, an interim review re-calculating the target price of the EU industry, now including the EU industry's social and environmental costs, would have to be initiated. This would be in line with recital 12 of Regulation (EU) 2018/825, which states that interim reviews should be initiated, where appropriate, in cases where the Union industry faces increased costs from higher social and environmental standards. The situation at hand would differ from the one described in recital 12 insofar as the environmental and social standards would not necessarily have increased. Nevertheless, the situations are comparable in that both constellations lead to a change in the costs incurred by the EU producers in complying with these standards after the measures have been imposed, warranting the initiation of an interim review.

Double Compensation as a Result of Subsidies Granted by Third States

An identical issue of over-compensating the complainant industry arises also with regard to subsidies granted by third States. As the notion of the 'EU industry' within the meaning of the basic regulations comprises companies from third countries which produce the like product in the EU,[230] it cannot be excluded that a company located in the EU is receiving compensation from a non-EU State for the additional

---

[230]Rados (2018) para. 5. For example, in *CFL-i*, all four cooperating Union producers were part of multinational corporations, Council Regulation (EC) No 1205/2007 of 15 October 2007 imposing anti-dumping duties on imports of integrated electronic compact fluorescent lamps (CFL-i) originating in the People's Republic of China following an expiry review pursuant to Article 11(2) of Council Regulation (EC) No 384/96 and extending to imports of the same product consigned from

environmental and social costs it has to bear when operating on the EU internal market. Again, taking these costs into account when calculating the target price would lead to the company being compensated under two different regimes. While such a risk can be avoided with regard to State aid granted by EU Member States by adapting the basic regulations accordingly, the same is significantly more difficult regarding subsidies granted by third States. This is so because it will prove more challenging for the Commission to gain knowledge of subsidy schemes operated by third States and to assess them with regard to the extra costs borne by the companies as a result of EU social and environmental legislation. At this point, it serves to recall that the Commission is currently in the process of proposing new legislation on how to address foreign subsidies and their market-distortive effect within the EU.[231] Depending on the precise content of the new instruments to be adopted, further overlaps between the novel rules on foreign subsidies and the rules on social and environmental costs contained in Article 7 (2d) BADR and Article 12 (1b) BASR cannot be excluded. Adopting a similar approach to the one just presented with regard to subsidies granted by EU Member States, rules allowing for the *ex officio* initiation of an interim review whenever the EU adopts a legislative act on the market-distorting effects of foreign subsidies under the new instruments could be integrated in the basic regulations.

Lack of Transparency

Article 296 TFEU requires the Commission to state reasons when imposing anti-dumping or countervailing measures. According to the case law of the EU Courts, the statement of reasons as required by Article 296 TFEU must show clearly and unequivocally the reasoning of the EU authority which adopted the contested measure, so as to inform the persons concerned of the justification for the measure adopted and thus to enable them to defend their rights and the EU Courts to exercise their powers of review.[232] Due to the factual and legal complexity of the subject matters of anti-dumping and countervailing regulations, the Commission is not required to specify every matter dealt with in the regulation or to address all the arguments relied on by the parties concerned.[233] The Commission must nonetheless set out clear and unequivocally the facts and the legal considerations which are of

---

the Socialist Republic of Vietnam, the Islamic Republic of Pakistan and the Republic of the Philippines, recitals 47 et seq.

[231] European Commission, 'White Paper on levelling the playing field as regards foreign subsidies (COM(2020) 253 final)' (Chap. 1, n 4).

[232] *Zhejiang Jiuli Hi-Tech Metals Co. Ltd. v Commission* (2020) T-307/18 179 (General Court); *Caviro Distillerie and others v Commission* (15 March 2018) T-211/16 102 (General Court); *Yuanping Changyuan Chemicals Co. Ltd. v Council* (n 170) 170; *NTN Toyo Bearing Co. Ltd. and others v Council* (1987) C-240/84 31 (European Court of Justice).

[233] van Bael and Bellis (2019) § 8.60 [B].

decisive importance in the context of the contested regulation.[234] Against the backdrop of this jurisprudence, it seems questionable whether reasoning as brief as the one contained in *Hot Rolled Stainless Steel* and *Heavyweight Thermal Paper* complies with the standard set out in the jurisprudence of the CJEU. In any event, given that one explicit objective of the reform of the basic regulations was to improve transparency and predictability,[235] it appears that the approach adopted by the Commission in taking social and environmental costs into account when calculating the target price is not conducive to this objective.

7.2.3.2.3   Conclusions and Further Recommendations

The legal issues arising in the context of the reform of the injury margin calculations when determining the target price are substantial. While the increase in transparency regarding the factors to be included in the target price calculation is an improvement, the factors themselves appear to conflict with the jurisprudence of the CJEU and the systematics of the basic regulations. The inclusion of a minimum target profit is not compatible with the *EFMA* standard.[236] In a similar vein, the calculation of the target profit based on the level of profitability needed to cover full costs and investments contradicts the *EFMA* judgment. Basing the target profit *inter alia* on the level of profitability before an increase of imports from the country under investigation in general must likewise be objected to for the reasons set out above.

   Another novelty in the target price calculations under the reformed basic regulations is the inclusion of costs incurred by the Union producers in complying with requirements arising from the EU's obligations assumed under international environmental agreements or ILO conventions. In order to limit the possibility of the new provisions being used in an overly extensive manner, the *ratione materiae* of the provisions should be limited to instances where a certain cost factor is directly attributable to the EU industry having to comply with environmental or social standards set by EU legislation. Here, the possible overlaps with EU State aid law or subsidies granted by third States present a potentially major issue that must be addressed through further amendments to the basic regulations.

7.2.4   The Union Interest in the Basic Regulations

The EU legislature did not change the substantive content of the Union interest test contained in Article 21 BADR and Article 31 BASR when reforming the EU's trade

---

[234] *Yuanping Changyuan Chemicals Co. Ltd. v Council* (n 170) 172; *Whirlpool Europe Srl v Council* (Chap. 3, n 107) 114.

[235] Recital 3 of Regulation (EU) 2018/825.

[236] *European Fertilizer Manufacturers' Association (EFMA) v Council* (n 101) 60.

defence instruments. However, due to its explicit mentioning of competition concerns, the test has been at the core of contributions addressing the relationship
between the EU's trade defence instruments and competition law.[237] Furthermore,
as touched upon in the section on the amendments to the lesser duty rule, the reform
did introduce a 'new' Union interest test which comes into play when determining
the level of duties to be imposed.[238] For these two reasons, the following section will
first provide an overview on the Union interest test. Subsequently, the new Union
interest test introduced by Regulation (EU) 2018/825 and the current practice of the
Commission in applying the Union interest tests will be presented. It will then be
established how the changes in the legislation and the approaches followed by the
Commission in applying these Union interest tests serve to better integrate
competition-related concerns in trade defence proceedings—or whether they alienate trade and competition even further.

7.2.4.1   Legislative History and Structure of the Union Interest Test

The Union interest test is a 'WTO plus'-obligation, meaning that it goes beyond the
obligations assumed by the EU under its membership in the WTO.[239] Both the ADA
and the ASCM provide for the opportunity of members introducing additional
criteria necessary for the imposition of anti-dumping or anti-subsidy measures,
without making this mandatory.[240] While the EU is not the only user of trade defence
instruments to include a public interest clause in its legislation—other countries such
as Canada, Brazil or Mexico do, too—the Union interest test is arguably the most
comprehensive one.[241] It comes into play when the Commission decides upon the
imposition of provisional[242] or definitive[243] measures as well as the suspension[244]
and the termination of measures following the withdrawal of the complaint.[245] It is
intended to ensure that the Union institutions do not intervene exclusively for the

---

[237] Cf. e.g. Müller-Ibold (2018), p. 566 et seq; Laprévote (2015), p. 4 et seq.

[238] Cf. above p. 198.

[239] Luo (2010), p. 137.

[240] Article 9.1 first sentence ADA reads: '*The decision whether or not to impose an anti-dumping duty in cases where all requirements for the imposition have been fulfilled (. . .) are decisions to be made by the authorities of the importing Member.*' The corresponding provision for the ASCM is contained in Article 19.2 first sentence ASCM. Cf. also *United States – Anti-Dumping Act of 1916 (European Communities)* (26 September 2000) WT/DS136/AB/R; WT/DS162/AB/R paras. 113, 116 (Appellate Body Report).

[241] Mueller et al. (2009) para. 21.02. On possible avenues for reform Sinnaeve (2007), p. 157.

[242] Article 7 (1) lit. d) BADR and Article 12 (1) lit. d) BASR.

[243] Article 9 (4) BADR and Article 15 (1) BASR.

[244] Article 14 (4) BADR and Article 24 (4) BASR.

[245] Article 9 (1) BADR and Article 14 (1) BASR.

benefit of private operators, without regard for the interests of other economic operators such as users or the downstream industry.[246] The test set out in Article 21 BADR and Article 31 BASR respectively requires a prospective analysis of the consequences of both applying and not applying the measures proposed in particular for the interests of the parties referred to in Article 21 (1) BADR and Article 31 (1) BASR.[247] At this point, it should be noted that the Union interest test is not a simple cost/benefit analysis, and the imposition of measures does not *per se* run against the Union interest if such measures have negative consequences for the importers, traders, users or consumers of the product under consideration.[248]

The Union interest test has a long tradition in EU trade defence law, with already the first regulation on protection against dumped or subsidised imports prescribing that duties are only to be imposed where *'the interests of the [Union] call for immediate intervention'*.[249] However, the regulation was silent on which factors were relevant in assessing the Union interest. In another deviation from today's version of the basic regulations, the Union interest test contained in the first trade defence regulation was a positive one, meaning that measures could only be imposed where the Union institutions concluded that this would be in the Union interest.

A successor of the regulation, Regulation (EC) 384/96, introduced what is essentially still today's version of the Union interest test. It lined out which interests exactly are to be considered when determining the Union interest and provided for an administrative procedure to be followed by the Commission in taking account of all views and information presented before it in the decision on whether or not the imposition of measures is in the Union interest.[250] In another change to the first trade defence legislation, the Union interest test became a negative instead of a positive one, meaning that measures will be imposed unless it can be shown that the negative impacts of the imposition of measures manifestly outweigh the positive effects:[251] *in dubio pro interventione*.[252]

---

[246] Wenig (1996), p. 215.

[247] *Committee of Polyethylene Terephthalate (PET) Manufacturers in Europe (CPME) v Council* (5 April 2017) T-422/13 144 (General Court); *Euroalliages and others v Commission* (8 July 2003) T-132/01 47 (Court of First Instance). Given the parallels between the two provisions, the reasoning employed by the CJEU in interpreting Article 21 BADR can be applied, *mutatis mutandis*, to Article 31 BASR.

[248] European Commission, 'DG Trade Working Document: Draft Guidelines on Union Interest' (Brussels 2013) paras. 7, 15.

[249] Article 15 (1) of Regulation (EEC) No 459/68 of the Council of 5 April 1968 on protection against dumping or the granting of bounties or subsidies by countries which are not members of the European Economic Community (Chap. 1, n 33).

[250] Article 21 of Council Regulation (EC) No 384/96 of 22 December 1995 on protection against dumped imports from countries not members of the European Community.

[251] Cf. Article 21 (1) third sentence Council Regulation (EC) No 3283/94 of 22 December 1994 on protection against dumped imports from countries not members of the European Community.

[252] Giannakopoulos (2011), p. 408.

This negative formulation is still in place in the current basic regulations,[253] effectively establishing a rebuttable presumption that the imposition of anti-dumping or anti-subsidy measures is in the Union interest once injurious dumping or subsidisation has been found to exist.[254] Consequently, the Union interest test only leads to the non-imposition of measures where the Commission can conclude that the interests against such action clearly outweigh the interest in eliminating the negative effects caused by the presence of dumped or subsidised imports.[255] This weighing of interests involves the appraisal of complex economic situations; judicial review of the assessment carried out by the Commission is limited.[256] Due to the presumption established in Article 21 (1) BADR and Article 31 (1) BASR that the imposition of measures is in the interest of the Union and the wide margin of discretion awarded to the Commission in applying the Union interest test, only a small number of proceedings has been terminated on Union interest grounds.[257]

More frequently, however, the Union interest test has impacted the form or duration of measures to be imposed. For instance, in the *Solar Panels* proceedings, the Commission limited the length of measures to 18 months on Union interest grounds, *inter alia* due to uncertainties regarding the measures' future impact on demand given changes in the EU State aid legislation.[258] In contrast, the Union interest test will not affect the level of duties levied on the dumped or subsidised goods.[259]

---

[253] Article 21 (1) third sentence BADR and Article 31 (1) third sentence BASR.

[254] European Commission, 'DG Trade Working Document: Draft Guidelines on Union Interest' (n 248) para. 13.

[255] *Hangzhou Duralamp Electronics Co. Ltd. v Council* (11 July 2013) T-459/07 182 (General Court).

[256] Ibid 181; *Euroalliages and others v Commission* (n 247) 47–48; Mavroidis (2016), p. 112.

[257] Mueller et al. (2009) para. 21.62. Instances where this was the case include Commission Decision (EU) 81/2013 of 13 February 2013 terminating the anti-dumping proceeding concerning imports of white phosphorus, also called elemental or yellow phosphorus, originating in the Republic of Kazakhstan (n 208) recitals 148, 190, 195; Commission Decision of 19 June 2007 terminating the anti-dumping proceeding concerning imports of synthetic staple fibres of polyesters (PSF) originating in Malaysia and Taiwan releasing the amounts secured by way of the provisional duties imposed (2007/430/EC) recitals 39–41; Council Regulation (EC) No 930/2003 of 26 May 2003 terminating the anti-dumping and anti-subsidy proceedings concerning imports of farmed Atlantic salmon originating in Norway and the anti-dumping proceeding concerning imports of farmed Atlantic salmon originating in Chile and the Faeroe Islands recitals 238–245.

[258] Commission Implementing Regulation (EU) 2017/366 of 1 March 2017 imposing definitive countervailing duties on imports of crystalline silicon photovoltaic modules and key components (i.e. cells) originating in or consigned from the People's Republic of China following an expiry review pursuant to Article 18(2) of Regulation (EU) 2016/1037 of the European Parliament and of the Council and terminating the partial interim review investigation pursuant to Article 19(3) of Regulation (EU) 2016/1037 recital 745.

[259] European Commission, 'DG Trade Working Document: Draft Guidelines on Union Interest' (n 248) para. 16. It should be mentioned that there have been isolated instances where the then Community interest test did impact the duty level, cf. Council Regulation (EEC) No 2322/85 of 12 August 1985 imposing a definitive anti-dumping duty on imports of glycine originating in Japan

7.2.4.2   The Interests Taken into Consideration

Pursuant to the basic regulations, a determination as to whether the Union's interest calls for intervention shall be based on an appreciation of all the various interests taken as a whole, including the interests of the domestic industry, users and consumers.[260] In such an examination, the need to eliminate the trade distorting effects of injurious dumping—or subsidisation—and to restore effective competition shall be given special consideration.[261] In carrying out the Union interest assessment, the Commission has to take account of all views and information presented before it. Accordingly, Article 21 (2) BADR and Article 31 (2) BASR provide a list of the economic operators eligible to present information before the Commission. Since the amendments introduced by Regulation (EU) 2018/825 entered into force, these include the entire Union industry—before the reform, this right was limited to the complainants—and trade unions. Apart from these modifications, importers and their representative associations, representative users and representative consumer organizations continue to be among those who can provide the Commission with information for its Union interest analysis.

As held by the General Court in *Euroalliages*, '*[i]t is for the Commission to determine in as objective a manner as possible whether a protective measure is in the [Union] interest*'.[262] Nonetheless, this does not preclude the Commission from placing an emphasis on the interests of the EU industry, who will usually be in support of the imposition of measures. This '*built-in bias*'[263] in favour of the EU industry's interests and hence the imposition of measures is already expressed in the negative formulation of the Union interest test. Indeed, the bias is a consequence of the EU's trade defence instruments' central immediate objective being the protection of the EU industry from unfair competition.[264] While the interests of other economic operators—such as users or consumers—are also to be taken into consideration, they are usually not sufficient for the Commission to conclude that the negative effects borne by them manifestly outweigh the benefits the imposition of measures would bring to the Union industry. Correspondingly, the Commission regularly rebuts arguments concerning the short-term disadvantages suffered by other economic operators by pointing out that the imposition of measures in fact serves their long-term interests. For example, when confronted with the argument that the imposition of measures will cause a shortage of supply for the users of the product concerned, the Commission will counter that the measures will not drive the foreign producers out the market, but merely restore a level playing field allowing the Union industry

---

(Chap. 6, n 108) recitals 17–18; Commission Regulation (EEC) No 997/85 of 18 April 1985 imposing a provisional anti-dumping duty on imports of glycine originating in Japan recital 31.

[260] Article 21 (1) first sentence BADR and Article 31 (1) first sentence BASR.

[261] Article 21 (1) third sentence BADR and Article 31 (1) third sentence BASR.

[262] *Euroalliages and others v Commission* (n 247) 54.

[263] Mueller et al. (2009) para. 21.59.

[264] Cf. above p. 94.

to compete on equal terms.[265] In doing so, the imposition of measures will protect the Union industry from distorted competition and ensure the producers' survival on the Union market, thereby ensuring long-term security of supply to the benefit of the users of the product concerned.[266] A similar line of argument is employed to dismiss claims that the imposition of measures restricts consumer choice or leads to higher prices.[267] This is a key difference to the assessment carried out by the Commission under the EU's competition law rules, where the impact of the market behaviour on part of the undertakings on consumers' interests is of critical relevance.[268] Such a balanced approach towards the interests of the different economic operators is lacking in EU trade defence law.

Furthermore, opposed to investigations carried out by the Commission concerning possible violations of EU competition law, trade defence investigations are substantially driven by the submissions of the interested parties.[269] This also applies to the Union interest assessment.[270] Therefore, a low level of cooperation or a lack of information put forward by representative users or consumer organizations will be taken as evidence by the Commission that the imposition of measures does not run counter to their interests.[271] Lastly, it should be taken into consideration that *Vermulst's* above-mentioned *dictum 'in anti-dumping [and anti-subsidy] cases*

---

[265] Council Regulation (EC) No 1331/2007 of 13 November 2007 imposing a definitive anti-dumping duty on imports of dicyandiamide originating in the People's Republic of China (n 203) recital 107.

[266] Commission Implementing Regulation (EU) 2021/939 of 10 June 2021 imposing a provisional anti-dumping duty on imports of mono ethylene glycol originating in the United States of America and the Kingdom of Saudi Arabia (n 217) recital 296; Commission Implementing Regulation (EU) 2015/763 of 12 May 2015 imposing a provisional anti-dumping duty on imports of certain grain-oriented flat-rolled products of silicon-electrical steel originating in the People's Republic of China, Japan, the Republic of Korea, the Russian Federation and the United States of America recital 230; Commission Regulation (EC) No 994/2007 of 28 August 2007 imposing a provisional anti-dumping duty on imports of ferro-silicon originating in the People's Republic of China, Egypt, Kazakhstan, the former Yugoslav Republic of Macedonia and Russia (n 207) recital 167.

[267] Commission Regulation (EU) No 513/2013 of 4 June 2013 imposing a provisional anti-dumping duty on imports of crystalline silicon photovoltaic modules and key components (i.e. cells and wafers) originating in or consigned from the People's Republic of China and amending Regulation (EU) No 182/2013 making these imports originating in or consigned from the People's Republic of China subject to registration (Chap. 6, n 86) recital 253.

[268] Cf. above p. 43 et seq.

[269] This is not to say that the Commission is limited to the information submitted by the parties in carrying out the Union interest test. Indeed, the Commission can take into consideration any information that might be relevant for its assessment, irrespective of its source, provided it is representative and reliable, cf. *Euroalliages and others v Commission* (n 247) 54.

[270] Cf. Article 21 (2) first sentence, (7) BADR and Article 31 (2) first sentence, (7) BASR.

[271] Commission Implementing Regulation (EU) 2019/1267 of 26 July 2019 imposing a definitive anti-dumping duty on imports of tungsten electrodes originating in the People's Republic of China following an expiry review under Article 11(2) of Regulation (EU) 2016/1036 (Chap. 6, n 93) recital 220.

organization means power[272] applies during the entire investigation. Opposed to well-organized business associations representing the Union industry, consumer organizations or users might find it significantly more difficult to meet the short procedural deadlines for a submission to the Commission,[273] and hence present their interests in an effective manner before the Commission.

7.2.4.2.1   Competition Concerns During the Union Interest Analysis

The explicit mention of the need to restore effective competition in Article 21 (1) BADR and Article 31 (1) BASR is taken as evidence that the Union institutions attempt to reconcile trade and competition policy when conducting investigations under the basic regulations, and to weigh the at times competing objectives of the two policies against each other.[274] Despite the wording of the provisions indicating otherwise at first sight, the competition assessment carried out under the Union interest test is primarily concerned with the potential negative impact on competition caused by the imposition of measures, and not with the effects on competition brought about by the presence of dumped or subsidised products on the internal market.[275] Advocate General *Jacobs* explicitly acknowledged the relevance of competition policy concerns when adopting measures in *Extramet*:

> [c]ases may arise (. . .) where failure to take account of competition policy considerations might lead to the adoption of anti-dumping measures which produce effects that are inconsistent with [competition] policy. It is therefore essential in my view that proper account be taken of competition policy considerations when the imposition of anti-dumping duties is being considered.[276]

The Commission also recognises the relevance of other Union policies, such as competition policy, when it conducts the Union interest analysis. However, the Commission has repeatedly stated that the protection of the Union industry against

---

[272] Vermulst (2005), p. 112.

[273] Cf. Article 21 (2), (3) BADR and Article 31 (2), (3) BASR. Cf. for example European Commission, Notice of initiation of an anti-dumping proceeding concerning imports of steel road wheels originating in the People's Republic of China (OJ 2019 C 60/7) (15 February 2019) 5.5, where the deadline was set at 37 days following the publication of the notice.

[274] Wenig (1996), p. 217.

[275] On this cf. already above p. 90. Cf. also European Commission, 'DG Trade Working Document: Draft Guidelines on Union Interest' (n 248) para. 8: *'[T]he Commission seeks information on the following questions in order to conduct the Union interest analysis: inter alia "Would measures reduce effective competition on the Union market? Would they create or strengthen an oligopolistic/monopolistic market structure or a dominant position on the market?"'*.

[276] *Extramet Industrie v Council* (Chap. 6, n 4) 33.

injurious dumping must be given priority over the interests of users to avoid potential negative effects on competition on the internal market.[277]

Laprévote refers to claims that the imposition of anti-dumping or anti-subsidy measures will have a detrimental impact on competition on the internal market as a '*competition defence*'.[278] Variations of this line of reasoning are allegations that the imposition of measures will lead to either the creation or the reinforcement of a dominant position,[279] or that the Union industry has been involved in cartelist activities in the past.[280] In such cases, the imposition of measures might not be in the Union interest in that it would strengthen the position of the Union industry, potentially reinforcing the market-distorting effects of previous anticompetitive behaviour by the Union industry. This would ultimately run counter to the declared objective of re-establishing fair competition within the internal market. The CJEU has adopted a restrictive stance as regards this type of defence. In *Industrie des Poudrés Spheriques,* the Court held that the fact alone that an EU undertaking possesses a dominant position on the internal market is not sufficient in itself to lead to the conclusion that the imposition of anti-dumping measures would run counter to the Union interest.[281]

In examining competition-related arguments during the Union interest analysis, DG TRADE will also be careful to stress that an analysis of the competition concerns in anti-dumping or anti-subsidy proceedings does not encompass a competition assessment in the strict legal sense, which can only be carried out by a competent competition authority.[282] Where investigations by DG COMP into anticompetitive

---

[277] Cf. e.g. Commission Implementing Regulation (EU) 2016/388 of 17 March 2016 imposing a definitive anti-dumping duty on imports of tubes and pipes of ductile cast iron (also known as spheroidal graphite cast iron) originating in India (n 182) recital 149; Commission Regulation (EEC) No 550/93 of 5 March 1993 imposing a provisional anti-dumping duty on imports of bicycles originating in the People's Republic of China recital 64.

[278] Laprévote (2015), p. 4.

[279] Commission Implementing Regulation (EU) 2021/546 of 29 March 2021 imposing a definitive anti-dumping duty and definitively collecting the provisional duty imposed on imports of aluminium extrusions originating in the People's Republic of China (n 48), recital 323; Commission Implementing Regulation (EU) 2021/9 of 6 January 2021 imposing a provisional anti-dumping duty on imports of certain hot-rolled flat products of iron, non-alloy or other alloy steel originating in Turkey (n 218) recitals 199 et seq; Commission Implementing Regulation (EU) 2020/1428 of 12 October 2020 imposing a provisional anti-dumping duty on imports of aluminium extrusions originating in the People's Republic of China (n 57) recital 316; Council Regulation (EC) No 1193/2008 of 1 December 2008 imposing a definitive anti-dumping duty and collecting definitively the provisional duties imposed on imports of citric acid originating in the People's Republic of China recital 74; Commission Regulation (EC) No 781/2003 of 7 May 2003 imposing a provisional anti-dumping duty on imports of furfuryl alcohol originating in the People's Republic of China recital 127.

[280] Commission Regulation (EC) No 1009/2004 of 19 May 2004 imposing a provisional anti-dumping duty on imports of certain graphite electrode systems originating in India recital 104.

[281] *Industrie des poudres sphériques v Council* (Chap. 4, n 152) 291 et seq.

[282] Commission Implementing Regulation (EU) 2016/388 of 17 March 2016 imposing a definitive anti-dumping duty on imports of tubes and pipes of ductile cast iron (also known as spheroidal graphite cast iron) originating in India (n 182) recitals 145, 149.

behaviour on part of the complainant industry are ongoing, they will usually not impact the Union interest analysis carried out by DG TRADE.[283] This restraint of the Commission—or more precisely, DG TRADE—in examining concerns regarding possible adverse effects on competition caused by the imposition of measures in detail leads to a certain reluctance in accepting competition defences. In the eyes of DG TRADE, also the fact that the Union industry was engaged in anti-competitive practices in the past does not deprive it of its right to obtain protection under the Union's trade defence legislation.[284] Arguments regarding the creation or reinforcement of a dominant position are likewise unlikely to prevail.[285] Here, the Commission's past practice includes instances of questionable uses of competition law concepts. One example of this is the *Sodium Cyclamate* case, where the Commission dismissed concerns expressed by an exporting producer that the imposition of measures would reinforce the dominant position of the Union industry.[286] The Commission further argued that '*the [Union] industry does not hold a dominant position since its market share was less than 50% during the [investigation period].*'[287] As set out before, however, market shares are not the only criteria DG COMP uses in determining whether an undertaking occupies a dominant position on a certain market in investigations concerning possible infringements of Article 102 TFEU. Moreover, there is no formal 'safe harbour' with regard to the market share held by an undertaking below which a firm is never found to be dominant. Instead, undertakings with a market share below 50% have been found dominant in investigations relating to violations of Article 102 TFEU.[288] Thus, brushing aside claims concerning the existence or reinforcement of a dominant position simply based on the market share of the Union industry is inconsistent with the practice of DG COMP and the CJEU in applying EU competition law.

---

[283] Council Regulation (EC) No 383/2009 of 5 May 2009 imposing a definitive anti-dumping duty and collecting definitively the provisional duty imposed on imports of certain pre- and post-stressing wires and wire strands of non-alloy steel (PSC wires and strands) originating in the People's Republic of China recital 69.

[284] Commission Regulation (EC) No 1009/2004 of 19 May 2004 imposing a provisional anti-dumping duty on imports of certain graphite electrode systems originating in India (n 280) recital 105.

[285] Cf. e.g. Commission Implementing Regulation (EU) 2021/1100 of 5 July 2021 imposing a definitive anti-dumping duty and definitively collecting the provisional duty imposed on imports of certain hot-rolled flat products or iron, non-alloy or other allow steel originating in Turkey recitals 268–272; Commission Implementing Regulation (EU) 2015/763 of 12 May 2015 imposing a provisional anti-dumping duty on imports of certain grain-oriented flat-rolled products of silicon-electrical steel originating in the People's Republic of China, Japan, the Republic of Korea, the Russian Federation and the United States of America (n 266) recital 226.

[286] Council Regulation (EC) No 435/2004 of 8 March 2004 imposing a definitive anti-dumping duty and collecting definitively the provisional duty imposed on imports of sodium cyclamate originating in the People's Republic of China and Indonesia recitals 83–84.

[287] Ibid recital 84.

[288] Cf. above p. 46 et seq.

Furthermore, in an expiry review in the *Citric Acid* proceedings, the Commission rejected arguments pertaining to a lack of competition on the Union market due to the fact that the entire Union industry was comprised of only two producers. It insisted that *'the fact that only two producers remained in the Union is (...) the result of the dumping practices of Chinese exporting producers'.*[289] It is evident that this circular line of reasoning does not address the concerns regarding a further lessening of competition on the citric acid market.[290] Addressing such concerns in more detail would have been appropriate in particular in light of the Union industry's strong market position: while the Commission did not disclose the market share held by the Union industry during the review investigation period, it did disclose that its market shares went up by 7% during the period considered.[291] Given that the Union industry's market share already was at 49% during the original investigation period,[292] before the imposition of anti-dumping measures, it can be assumed that the Union industry's market share on the market for citric acid now surpassed 50%. It was thus at a level at which undertakings have been considered as occupying a dominant position within the meaning of Article 102 TFEU.[293]

At the same time, DG TRADE's only superficial interest in competition concerns does not prevent it from having recourse to competition concepts to the detriment of exporting producers when carrying out the Union interest test, e.g. by referring to the *'monopoly of Chinese imports'.*[294]

The preceding section has identified a number of issues pertaining to the examination of competition concerns during the Union interest assessment, in particular relating to a superficial assessment of competition concerns and the imprecise use of competition law concepts. In line with this, the Commission's practice in addressing competition concerns during the Union interest analysis has been criticised by the ECA for rejecting parties' arguments to that effect without detailed justification. Another point of criticism put forward by the ECA is the retrospective focus of the competition analysis; with the prospective part of the assessment not including a detailed analysis of the measures' impact on targeted imports and the potential

---

[289] Commission Implementing Regulation (EU) 2015/82 of 21 January 2015 imposing a definitive anti-dumping duty on imports of citric acid originating in the People's Republic of China following an expiry review pursuant to Article 11(2) of Council Regulation (EC) No 1225/2009 and of partial interim reviews pursuant to Article 11(3) of Regulation (EC) No 1225/2009 recitals 154–155.

[290] Laprévote (2015), p. 7.

[291] Commission Implementing Regulation (EU) 2015/82 of 21 January 2015 imposing a definitive anti-dumping duty on imports of citric acid originating in the People's Republic of China following an expiry review pursuant to Article 11(2) of Council Regulation (EC) No 1225/2009 and of partial interim reviews pursuant to Article 11(3) of Regulation (EC) No 1225/2009 (n 289) recital 112.

[292] Council Regulation (EC) No 1193/2008 of 1 December 2008 imposing a definitive anti-dumping duty and collecting definitively the provisional duties imposed on imports of citric acid originating in the People's Republic of China (n 279) recital 45.

[293] Cf. the sources cited above, Chap. 3, n 54.

[294] Council Regulation (EC) No 1331/2007 of 13 November 2007 imposing a definitive anti-dumping duty on imports of dicyandiamide originating in the People's Republic of China (n 203) recital 108.

impact on the supply chains such as the availability of imports from other countries.[295]

7.2.4.2.2   Competition Concerns During the Injury Analysis

The Union interest test is not the only stage of an investigation where competition concerns are taken into account. The *'competition defence'*[296] will also be employed to challenge the existence of a causal link between the presence of dumped or subsidised imports and the injury sustained by the EU industry.[297] Given that the competition-related arguments put forward both by the Commission and the parties involved in trade defence proceedings during the injury assessment are identical to those presented during the Union interest assessment, the following paragraph will be dedicated to the injury assessment. This is done in order to present an accurate picture of how competition concerns are addressed over the course of a trade defence investigation.

As it is the case during the Union interest assessment, the Commission has adopted a restrictive approach towards accepting competition-related arguments during the injury assessment. Parallel to its approach during the Union interest assessment, ongoing investigations by DG COMP regarding possible anti-competitive behaviour on part of the EU industry will not result in DG TRADE negating the existence of a causal link between the dumping or the subsidisation and the injury suffered by the EU industry.[298] In the past, it has held that it is only where there is concrete evidence of anti-competitive behaviour that it is required to investigate such claims further.[299] Moreover, DG TRADE is of the opinion that as long as the anti-competitive behaviour did not take place during the injury assessment period, it does not affect the causality assessment.[300] This is also reflected in

---

[295] European Court of Auditors (Chap. 6, n 49) 25.

[296] Laprévote (2015), p. 4.

[297] Cf. e.g. Commission Implementing Regulation (EU) 2016/2005 of 16 November 2016 imposing a provisional anti-dumping duty on imports of certain lightweight thermal paper originating in the Republic of Korea recitals 114–115; Council Implementing Regulation (EU) 412/2013 of 13 May 2013 imposing a definitive anti-dumping duty and collecting definitively the provisional duty imposed on imports of ceramic tableware and kitchenware originating in the People's Republic of China (Chap. 6, n 9) recitals 168–171.

[298] Commission Regulation (EEC) No 1361/87 of 18 May 1987 imposing a provisional anti-dumping duty on imports of ferro-silico-calcium/calcium silicide originating in Brazil (Chap. 6, n 3) recital 12.

[299] Commission Implementing Regulation (EU) 2017/336 of 27 February 2017 imposing a definitive anti-dumping duty and collecting definitively the provisional duty imposed on imports of certain heavy plate of non-alloy or other alloy steel originating in the People's Republic of China recital 163.

[300] Commission Regulation (EC) No 1009/2004 of 19 May 2004 imposing a provisional anti-dumping duty on imports of certain graphite electrode systems originating in India (n 280) recital 92.

the Commission's pledge of 2013 to systematically open interim reviews in investigations where it has found that Union producers have engaged in anti-competitive practices, examining if and to what extent the measures are affected by the anti-competitive behaviour. The Commission restricted the pledge to cases where there was an overlap of the product concerned and the time periods of the anti-competitive behaviour and the injury assessment.[301] So far, the Commission's annual reports on the EU's trade defence instruments do not indicate that any review has been initiated on the grounds of anti-competitive behaviour of the Union industry. However, the Commission is currently carrying out two competition investigations possibly warranting the initiation of an interim review following a finding of violation of the EU competition rules on part of the EU industry.[302]

A closer examination of the Commission's line of reasoning reveals that requiring an overlap between the periods of anti-competitive behaviour and the injury assessment fails to take into account the possible long-term impact anti-competitive behaviour can have on the market structure. The *Wire Rods* anti-dumping investigation is illustrative in that regard. Here, the period chosen for the trends relevant for the assessment of injury covered the period from the beginning of 2004 to the end of March 2008.[303]

When imposing provisional measures, the Commission considered that

the investigation did not point to any particular problem concerning the competition between [Union] producers, or to any trade distorting effect which may explain the material injury found for the [Union] industry.[304]

Already before the imposition of definitive anti-dumping duties in July 2009, DG COMP had started an investigation concerning anti-competitive conduct of Union producers of prestressing steel, with prestressing steel being defined as '*metal wires (. . .) made of wire rod*'.[305] This investigation resulted in DG COMP fining 17 Union producers a total of EUR 269 million for operating a cartel that lasted almost 20 years, from the beginning of 1984 until September 2002.[306] In light of the period during which the anti-competitive behaviour was practiced lasting over two decades, the cartel had a significant and lasting impact on the market structure. Thus, it is reasonable to assume that the Union market for wire rods underwent changes

---

[301] European Commission, 'Communication by the European Commission to the Council and the European Parliament on Modernisation of Trade Defence Instruments (COM(2013) 191 final)' (10 April 2013) 2.5.3.

[302] European Commission, 'Case AT.40606: Farmed Atlantic Salmon' and European Commission, 'Case AT.40054: Ethanol benchmarks'.

[303] Commission Regulation (EC) No 112/2009 of 6 February 2009 imposing a provisional anti-dumping duty on imports of wire rod originating in the People's Republic of China and the Republic of Moldova recital 13.

[304] Ibid recital 154.

[305] Commission Decision of 30 June 2010 relating to a proceeding under Article 101 TFEU and Article 53 EEA Agreement (COMP/38.344 – Prestressing Steel) (C(2010) 4387 final) para. 2.

[306] Ibid para. 1.

following the break-up of the cartel. Given the temporal proximity between the cartelisation period and the period chosen for the assessment of injury trends, it cannot be excluded that these changes in the market structure extended to the latter, potentially distorting the injury indicators. These considerations, however, are not reflected in the anti-dumping proceeding. Neither was an interim review initiated, nor was the issue addressed in the expiry reviews carried out in the years that followed.

The line of reasoning adopted by the Commission further is too strict in that it confines the possibility for *ex officio* reviews to instances where the Commission itself has found that EU producers have engaged in anti-competitive behaviour, without regard for decisions by national competition authorities. When not limiting oneself to the EU level, however, additional decisions by national competition authorities that would merit the initiation of an interim review of measures currently in force can be found. An example of this is a decision taken by the German national competition authority, the *Bundeskartellamt*, in December 2019. The *Bundeskartellamt* imposed fines totalling around EUR 646 million on steel manufacturers for exchanging information and fixing the price for quarto plates in Germany. Quarto plates are hot-rolled flat steel products, used *inter alia* in in steel construction, bridge building, building construction, shipbuilding, boilers and pressure vessels, general mechanical engineering, wind tower and pipeline construction and in the offshore industry.[307] The anti-competitive conduct took place between 2002 and 2016.

In 2016, the EU, acting upon a complaint of the European Steel Association, introduced provisional anti-dumping duties on hot-rolled flat steel products originating in China, with the examination of trends relevant for the assessment of injury covering the period from 1 January 2012 to 31 December 2015. The uses of the product covered by the EU's anti-dumping duties coincide with the uses for the type of hot-rolled flat steel product produced by the industry fined by the German competition authority,[308] so that an overlap in the products concerned by the anti-dumping investigation and those that were the subject of the *Bundeskartellamt's* decision can be assumed to exist. Given the size of the German steel industry—it is the largest steel manufacturer within the EU, holding a market share of approximately 25%[309]—it is likely that any distortions of competition on the German steel market had an effect on the indicators used to assess whether the EU industry

---

[307] Bundeskartellamt, *Fallbericht: Rund 646 Mio. Euro Bußgeld gegen Stahlhersteller wegen Preisabsprachen bei Quartoblechen* (2019) B12-25/16.

[308] Commission Implementing Regulation (EU) 2016/1778 of 6 October 2016 imposing a provisional anti-dumping duty on imports of certain hot-rolled flat products of iron, non-alloy or other alloy steel originating in the People's Republic of China (n 175) recital 26: *'[T]hey are used (...) in construction (production of steel tubes), shipbuilding, gas containers, cars, pressure vessels and energy pipelines.'*

[309] The European Steel Association (EUROFER), 'European Steel in Figures: Covering 2011-2020' (2020) 16, available at <https://www.eurofer.eu/assets/Uploads/European-Steel-in-Figures-2020.pdf>.

suffered injury due to the presence of dumped imports. These include sales prices on the free market in the Union or the profitability of the EU industry. In the light of the above findings, it can be concluded that the initiation of an interim review of the measures in force concerning hot-rolled flat steel products, re-assessing the injury suffered by the EU industry and possibly also the Union interest, would be appropriate.

Another overlap between decisions taken by national competition authorities and products covered by anti-dumping measures can be found in the *Ceramics* proceedings. Here, the Commission refused to take into account ongoing investigations into competition law violations by members of the complainant Union industry during the initial anti-dumping investigation, which was carried out in 2012 and 2013.[310] The examination of the trends relevant for the assessment of injury began on 1 January 2008. In 2013, the German competition authority fined several producers of household porcelain for engaging in anti-competitive conduct between 1995 and the beginning of 2008.[311] The anti-competitive behaviour thus covered a period used for the injury assessment, with the possible effects on the accuracy of the injury assessment this entails set out above. None of the reviews carried out over the course of the following years addresses the decision taken by the German competition authority. Currently, the measures are set to remain in force until 2024.

7.2.4.2.3 Environmental Policy Concerns

As can be inferred from the above, the considerations that have been taken into account in the Commission's previous practice were usually limited to arguments relating to the interested parties' economic interests. Attempts at including general policy concerns—such as environmental policy—were rebuffed by the Commission on a regular basis.[312] According to *Hartmann*, this limitation can already be inferred from the parties listed in Article 21 (2) BADR, whose interests should be examined and who enjoy procedural rights under the Union interest test. Since these include only economic operators, only economic interests should be of relevance when carrying out the Union interest test.[313] Another argument put forward against the inclusion of non-economic interests in the Union interest analysis is that doing so would be paramount to opening '*Pandora's box*',[314] causing legal uncertainty and

[310] Council Implementing Regulation (EU) 412/2013 of 13 May 2013 imposing a definitive anti-dumping duty and collecting definitively the provisional duty imposed on imports of ceramic tableware and kitchenware originating in the People's Republic of China (Chap. 6, n 9) recital 169.

[311] Bundeskartellamt, *Bußgelder gegen Hersteller von Haushaltsgeschirr* (2013) B 12-14/10.

[312] Cf. e.g. Council Regulation (EC) No 1472/2006 of 5 October 2006 imposing a definitive anti-dumping duty and collecting definitively the provisional duty imposed on imports of certain footwear with uppers of leather originating in the People's Republic of China and Vietnam (Chap. 3, n 119) recital 281.

[313] Hartmann (2018) para. 33.

[314] Wenig (1996), p. 219.

opening the door to a possibly politicised and non-transparent application of the Union interest test. This reasoning can also be applied to investigations carried out under the BASR. As mentioned, this approach is reflected in the Commission's previous practice. In an investigation carried out in 2009, it held that

> Article 21 of the basic Regulation requires that special consideration shall be given to the need to eliminate trade distorting effects of injurious dumping and to restore effective competition. Against this background, general considerations on environmental protection (...) cannot be taken into account in the analysis and at the same time cannot justify unfair trade practices.[315]

The commitment to upholding the Union interest, on the other hand, implies a commitment to the interests of the Union as a whole, not to the interests of singular economic operators, and calls on the Commission to define this interest in a balanced way, and to adapt its definition of the Union interest to political and social changes.[316] Moreover, the EU's trade defence legislation and its application may not run counter to the remainder of the Union's policies, as provided for by Article 21 (3) subpara. 2 TEU.[317] This also extends to the Union's environmental policy. Consequently, the TEU mandates an application of the EU's trade defence instruments that does not contravene its internal environmental policy objectives.

Articles 3 (5), 21 (1), (2) TEU, listing the objectives to be pursued by the EU in its external relations, serve as further evidence of the Treaties mandating the integration of non-economic concerns in the EU's common commercial policy. The Treaties thus permit the Union institutions to have regard to the promotion of sustainable development objectives when assessing whether the imposition of anti-dumping or anti-subsidy measures would be in the interest of the EU.[318]

Over the last years, calls for the integration of non-economic concerns into the framework of the EU's trade defence instruments have become more frequent. Already in 2013, legal scholars noted the possibility of the imposition of trade

---

[315] Commission Regulation (EC) No 193/2009 of 11 March 2009 imposing a provisional anti-dumping duty on imports of biodiesel originating in the United States of America recital 158; cf. also Council Regulation (EC) No 1205/2007 of 15 October 2007 imposing anti-dumping duties on imports of integrated electronic compact fluorescent lamps (CFL-i) originating in the People's Republic of China following an expiry review pursuant to Article 11(2) of Council Regulation (EC) No 384/96 and extending to imports of the same product consigned from the Socialist Republic of Vietnam, the Islamic Republic of Pakistan and the Republic of the Philippines (n 230) recital 106: 'Anti dumping measures are aimed at addressing unfair competitive advantages resulting from practices of dumping of imports to the Community. The existence of other Community policies as such would therefore not preclude the imposition and continuation of duties should these be needed.'

[316] Tauschinsky and Weiß (2018), p. 4.

[317] Cf. further above p. 83 et seq.

[318] Cf. also Tauschinsky and Weiß (2018), p. 28. In more detail on taking the situation regarding the protection of the environment and workers' rights in the exporting country into account during the Union interest assessment cf. below p. 265 et seq.

defence measures on products related to the production of renewable energies, such as solar panels or biodiesel, having negative consequences for the production of renewable energy in the EU and, in the long term, for the environment. In order to avoid the EU's trade defence instruments operating to the detriment of the EU's climate policy goals and the environment in general, authors proposed to include environmental policy concerns into the EU interest test.[319] Up to now, scholarly contributions to the inclusion of environmental aspects into the Union interest test have been limited to the effect the (non-)imposition of measures would have on the internal environmental policy objectives of the EU. The Commission's more recent practice shows that it has responded to these calls by adopting a more inclusive approach towards environmental concerns, referencing them more frequently during the Union interest analysis. These changes in the Commission practice are not limited to investigations carried out under the reformed basic regulations; rather, one can observe environmental policy concerns being mentioned on a regular basis since the *Solar Panels* proceedings in 2013.[320]

The Commission does not appear to follow a stringent approach concerning the inclusion of environmental concerns in the Union interest analysis. In a number of investigations, it has addressed the environmental impact of the (non-)imposition of measures when evaluating the interests of one of the economic operators mentioned in Article 21 (1) BADR and Article 31 (1) BASR, as it for example did in *E-bikes*. Here, it concluded that the imposition of anti-dumping measures would

> contribute to the sustainable development of electric bicycles in Europe and its wider benefits to society in terms of protection of the environment and improved mobility

when elaborating upon the interests of consumers.[321]

In another another investigation, the Commission addressed objections that the imposition of measures would contradict the objectives set by the Union in its renewable energy policies when determining whether the imposition of measures would conflict with the interests of users.[322] In *GOES*, the Commission found

---

[319]Bungenberg (2015), pp. 226, 237–238; Kasteng (2013).

[320]Commission Regulation (EU) No 513/2013 of 4 June 2013 imposing a provisional anti-dumping duty on imports of crystalline silicon photovoltaic modules and key components (i.e. cells and wafers) originating in or consigned from the People's Republic of China and amending Regulation (EU) No 182/2013 making these imports originating in or consigned from the People's Republic of China subject to registration (Chap. 6, n 86) recitals 247 et seq.

[321]Commission Implementing Regulation (EU) 2018/1012 of 17 July 2018 imposing a provisional anti-dumping duty on imports of electric bicycles originating in the People's Republic of China and amending Implementing Regulation (EU) 2018/671 (n 6) recital 252.

[322]Commission Implementing Regulation (EU) 2020/776 of 12 June 2020 imposing definitive countervailing duties on imports of certain woven and/or stitched glass fibre fabrics originating in the People's Republic of China and Egypt and amending Commission Implementing Regulation (EU) 2020/492 imposing definitive anti-dumping duties on imports of certain woven and/or stitched glass fibre fabrics originating in the People's Republic of China and Egypt (n 44) recitals 503–507. Cf. further Commission Implementing Regulation (EU) 2021/546 of 29 March 2021 imposing a definitive anti-dumping duty and definitively collecting the provisional duty imposed on imports of

that the imposition of measures would allow the Union industry to return to profitability and (. . .) meet the efficiency targets of the EcoDesign Regulation,[323]

combining environmental concerns with the interests of the Union industry regarding the imposition of anti-dumping duties. Pursuing yet another approach, the Commission has sometimes opted for a separate evaluation of environmental concerns as 'other interests'.[324] The *GOES* proceedings are one of the instances where the Union interest test had an impact on the form of measures imposed. When deciding on the imposition of definitive duties, the Commission concluded that maintaining the measures in their current form would cause the users to be harmed disproportionally, which would in turn negatively impact their competitiveness *vis-à-vis* their competitors outside the Union. The Commission then continued to elaborate that

[i]n addition, the objective set out in the EcoDesign Regulation (. . .) would be undermined by the imposition of measures in the form of an *ad valorem* duty.[325]

Accordingly, the type of duty imposed was changed.[326]

---

aluminium extrusions originating in the People's Republic of China (n 48) recitals 314, 344, 351, where the Commission included environmental policy concerns when elaborating on the interests of the Union industry, suppliers and users, respectively, and Commission Implementing Regulation (EU) 2021/1266 of 29 July 2021 imposing a definitive anti-dumping duty on imports of biodiesel originating in the United States of America following an expiry review pursuant to Article 11(2) of Regulation (EU) 2016/1036 of the European Parliament and of the Council recitals 137–139.

[323] Commission Implementing Regulation (EU) 2015/763 of 12 May 2015 imposing a provisional anti-dumping duty on imports of certain grain-oriented flat-rolled products of silicon-electrical steel originating in the People's Republic of China, Japan, the Republic of Korea, the Russian Federation and the United States of America (n 266) recital 235.

[324] Cf. e.g. Commission Implementing Regulation (EU) 2021/582 of of 9 April 2021 imposing a provisional anti-dumping duty on imports of aluminium flat-rolled products originating in the People's Republic of China (n 216), recitals 450 et seq, where the Commission argued that the imposition of duties would contribute to the EU lowering its CO_2 emissions; Commission Regulation (EU) 2018/683 of 4 May 2018 imposing a provisional anti-dumping duty on imports of certain pneumatic tyres, new or retreaded, of rubber, of a kind used for buses or lorries, with a load index exceeding 121 originating in the People's Republic of China, and amending Implementing Regulation (EU) 2018/163 (Chap. 5, n 14) recitals 243 et seq; Commission Implementing Regulation (EU) 2017/366 of 1 March 2017 imposing definitive countervailing duties on imports of crystalline silicon photovoltaic modules and key components (i.e. cells) originating in or consigned from the People's Republic of China following an expiry review pursuant to Article 18(2) of Regulation (EU) 2016/1037 of the European Parliament and of the Council and terminating the partial interim review investigation pursuant to Article 19(3) of Regulation (EU) 2016/1037 (n 258) recitals 725 et seq.

[325] Commission Implementing Regulation (EU) 2015/1953 of 29 October 2015 imposing a definitive anti-dumping duty on imports of certain grain-oriented flat-rolled products of silicon-electrical steel originating in the People's Republic of China, Japan, the Republic of Korea, the Russian Federation and the United States of America recital 149.

[326] Ibid recital 169.

As can be inferred from the Commission practice presented above, environmental policy concerns may be relevant when it comes to the interests of each of the actors referred to in Article 21 (1) BADR and Article 31 (1) BASR as regards the imposition of measures. Additionally, environmental policy arguments were also advanced by the Commission when deciding upon the form of the measures. It furthermore becomes apparent that in the majority of cases, environmental considerations are advanced as an additional argument in support of the imposition of measures, with the Commission focussing on how the imposition of the anti-dumping or anti-subsidy measures would contribute to the Union's environmental policies.

On the other hand, the Commission will likewise address arguments regarding potential environmentally detrimental effects caused by the imposition of measures.[327] In *Solar Glass*, the Commission devoted an entire section named '*environmental aspects*' of the Union interest analysis to arguments brought forward by the users who had advanced that maintaining the measures on solar glass would not be in line with the Commission's goals regarding the use of clean energies. With the measures remaining in force, the Union solar module industry would be forced out of the market as it would not undertake planned new investments due to a lack of solar glass supply and would therefore not be competitive.[328] The Commission rejected these submissions, considering that the continuation of the measures was crucial to ensure the continued existence of a viable solar glass industry and enhance research and development in the EU, also from the perspective of environmental policy.[329] The Commission then continued to hold that, while its policy also supported the Union solar module industry, the analysis carried out by the Commission had concluded that the additional costs of the users were not significant enough to

---

[327] Cf. e.g. Commission Implementing Regulation (EU) 2021/546 of 29 March 2021 imposing a definitive anti-dumping duty and definitively collecting the provisional duty imposed on imports of aluminium extrusions originating in the People's Republic of China (n 48), recitals 344–345; Commission Implementing Regulation (EU) 2019/1688 of 8 October 2019 imposing a definitive anti-dumping duty and definitively collecting the provisional duty imposed on imports of mixtures of urea and ammonium nitrate originating in Russia, Trinidad and Tobago and the United States of America (Chap. 6, n 125) recital 268; Commission Implementing Regulation (EU) 2019/1379 of 28 August 2019 imposing a definitive anti-dumping duty on imports of bicycles originating in the People's Republic of China as extended to imports of bicycles consigned from Indonesia, Malaysia, Sri Lanka, Tunisia, Cambodia, Pakistan and the Philippines, whether declared as originating in these countries or not, following an expiry review pursuant to Article 11(2) of Regulation (EU) No 2016/1036 (n 78) recital 337; Commission Implementing Regulation (EU) 2019/576 of 10 April 2019 imposing a provisional anti-dumping duty on imports of mixtures of urea and ammonium nitrate originating in Russia, Trinidad and Tobago and the United States of America (n 127) recital 256.

[328] Commission Implementing Regulation (EU) 2020/1080 of 22 July 2020 imposing a definitive anti-dumping duty on imports of solar glass originating in the People's Republic of China following an expiry review pursuant to Article 11 (2) of Regulation (EU) 2016/1036 of the European Parliament and of the Council recital 242.

[329] Ibid recital 245.

prevent their operation or future expansion. Therefore, maintaining the measures would not harm the Union's environmental policies.[330]

Prima facie, the *Solar Glass* proceedings are a particularly clear example of environmental policy concerns being given more weight during the Union interest assessment. When examining the argumentative structure of the Commission in greater detail, however, it becomes apparent that the Commission's assessment in essence is still a conventional one, with the Commission weighing the detrimental economic effects the imposition of measures would entail for users against the beneficial effects for the Union industry. While the central role of renewable energies in realising the EU's environmental policy objectives is recognised, these environmental policy considerations are merely used to reinforce the Commission's conclusion that the Union industry's interest in having the measures continued must be accorded more weight than the users' interest in having them discontinued.

The approach adopted by the Commission in *Solar Glass* and the other proceedings presented above shows that whenever the environmental impact of the (non-)imposition of measures is debated during the Union interest test, this will only be done in connection with economic considerations. A truly independent analysis of the environmental impact of the imposition of anti-dumping or anti-subsidy measures during the Union interest analysis has yet to occur.

To conclude, while the Commission's more recent practice is reflective of the increasing relevance of environmental policy in the EU's policy priorities, the integration of environmental concerns has not led to a fundamental change of the character of the Union interest assessment. At its core, the Union interest test remains a balancing exercise used to weigh economic interests against each other, with environmental policy aspects not carrying any weight on their own. Instead, they only serve as an additional means of legitimising the Commission's decisions in the context of the Union interest test. Nor do they result in a fundamental reassessment of the relevance attached to the different economic operators' interests: as can be derived from the *Solar Glass* case, the Commission continues to favour the interests of the EU industry when carrying out the Union interest assessment.

The fact that the Commission does not attach particular importance to environmental policy concerns is not necessarily a cause for criticism. For one, environmental concerns will almost inevitably be interrelated with the (economic) interests of the parties mentioned in Article 21 (1) BADR and Article 31 (1) BASR, so that a truly independent assessment of environmental policy might not even be possible in an investigation. Moreover, there is merit to the '*Pandora's box*' argument presented above—a stand-alone consideration of the environmental aspects of imposing trade defence measures would extend the Commission's already substantial discretion in the area of trade defence even further, not least with regard to the inaccuracies associated with the integration of non-economic concerns in the balancing of interests. This in turn creates the danger of a greater politicisation of the use of the EU's trade defence instruments, with the legal uncertainty this ensues. Coming back

---

[330] Ibid recital 247.

to the *'Pandora's box'* argument once more, allowing for environmental policy to play a decisive role during the Union interest assessment would open up the possibility of incorporating further policy considerations not directly related to trade defence proceedings. Such an expansive approach is already visible in the new 'Union interest test' to be carried out under the legal instruments envisaged by the Commission in addressing the market-distorting effects of foreign subsidies. Here, wider public policy objectives such as the 'digital transformation' are to be taken into account.[331] If the Commission practice in applying the EU's trade defence instruments were to evolve in this direction, the EU's trade defence instruments would risk being alienated even further from economic rationales than it is already the case. This would ultimately harm the overall legitimacy of the EU's trade defence instruments, both within the EU and abroad.

7.2.4.3 The New Union Interest Test

As mentioned in the section on the modifications concerning the scope of application of the lesser duty rule, Regulation (EU) 2018/825 introduced a new Union interest test. Other than the regular Union interest test, the new test is explicitly intended to influence the level of duties. Based on the outcome of this additional analysis, the Commission will decide to limit the level of measures at the injury margin (in accordance with the lesser duty rule) or it will impose measures up to the full level of the margin of dumping or subsidisation. Opposed to anti-subsidy investigations, where the test will always come into play, its application in anti-dumping investigations is limited to instances where the Commission has found raw material distortions to exist.[332] This signifies that the Commission now has to carry out a two-step Union interest analysis in those instances: first when deciding whether or not to impose measures and second when examining whether it is in the Union interest or not to apply the lesser duty rule.[333] The introduction of this additional Union interest analysis is the correlate to the limitation of the scope of application of the lesser duty rule: while higher duty levels award a higher degree of protection to the complainant Union industry, these higher duty levels might place an unsustainable additional burden on users and supply chains dependent on the imported products.[334] Based on the objectives of the new Union interest test, environmental and competition concerns will not be of relevance here, as the test is exclusively concerned with the economic impact of the higher duty level on the various economic operators.

---

[331] European Commission, 'White Paper on levelling the playing field as regards foreign subsidies (COM(2020) 253 final)' (Chap. 1, n 4) 17.

[332] For details cf. above p. 192 et seq.

[333] van Bael and Bellis (2019) § 6.01.

[334] Müller (2018), p. 49.

Article 7 (2b) BADR is the relevant provision in anti-dumping investigations. In a difference to the Union interest test contained in Article 21 BADR, the new test is a positive one: only where the Commission can clearly conclude that it is in the Union's interest to levy duties up to the full dumping margin the lesser duty rule will not be applied. If the Commission does not have sufficient information proving that a higher duty is necessary, it has to go back to applying the lesser duty rule.[335] In carrying out this assessment, the Commission shall actively seek information from interested parties enabling it to determine whether the lesser duty rule shall apply or not.[336] Here, all EU producers and not just those producers submitting the complaint shall be heard.[337] Consequently, the relevance given to the interests of the various economic operators varies from the regular Union interest analysis to be carried out under Article 21 BADR: the emphasis on the interests of the Union industry is not as pronounced; instead, the interests of users are given more room.

However, one should also take note of the procedural default rule[338] set out in Article 7 (2b) BADR. In the absence of cooperation, the Commission may conclude that it is in accordance with the Union interest to impose a duty up to the full dumping margin.[339] Therefore, if users or other parties affected by the duties make no submissions, the Commission may assume that their interests would not be hurt disproportionally by the imposition of a higher duty. On the one hand, this is understandable in that it is primarily the economic interests of users that are to be protected by this additional Union interest analysis. Consequently, the Commission may take the absence of any information to the contrary as evidence that their interests would not be harmed by higher duty levels. On the other hand, just as it is the case under the regular Union interest analysis, it is again the users of the product who must proactively provide the Commission with sufficient information to prevent it from imposing a higher duty. A lack of cooperation will be to the detriment of their interests. Accordingly, the procedural design of the new Union interest test in the BADR is still advantageous to the Union industry.

As set out in the section on the lesser duty rule, the Commission practice concerning the application of the new rules is limited. So far, the Commission has had the chance to apply Article 7 (2b) BADR only in two investigations. Therefore, the impact of the new Union interest test cannot be assessed conclusively. In one of these two investigations, the Commission found that it could not conclude that the imposition of duties up to the dumping margin would be in the Union interest. The possible impact of a higher level of measures would be disproportionate in view of the possible strong negative effects on supply chains for certain Union companies and on users. Under such a scenario, the user industry—particularly those users which purchase significant volumes from China or Indonesia—might be unduly

---

[335] Hoffmeister (2020), p. 222.

[336] Article 7 (2b) second sentence BADR.

[337] Recital 22 of Regulation (EU) 2018/825 (Chap. 1, n 10).

[338] Hoffmeister (2020), p. 222.

[339] Article 7 (2b) fourth sentence BADR.

affected and could become as a result loss making.[340] Thus, the Commission chose to apply the lesser duty rule, and limit the level of measures at the injury margin. Another aspect to be taken into consideration in this second Union interest analysis is the competitive situation for raw materials on the exporting producer's home market. Up to now, the Commission has not carried out a meaningful assessment of the competitive situation on the market of the raw material concerned. Instead, it has effectively confined itself to re-stating the facts which previously led it to conclude that raw material distortions exist, this time holding that the same circumstances result in the EU industry being disadvantaged in the competion for raw materials.[341]

A different situation presents itself under the BASR. Here, the removal of the lesser duty rule is the norm and its application the exception: unless the Commission can clearly conclude that it is not in the Union's interest to do so, measures will be imposed at the total amount of countervailable subsidies.[342] The Commission thus has to carry out a separate Union interest analysis in every single anti-subsidy investigation. However, opposed to the modifications introduced in the BADR, the reformed BASR does not provide for any specific procedural rules to be adhered to when carrying out this separate Union interest analysis. Therefore, in line with the negative formulation of the Union interest test, the users of the product concerned need to provide the Commission with sufficient information for it to conclude that the negative impact of the higher duty level borne by them would manifestly outweigh any possible benefit enjoyed by the Union industry. So far, the Union interest analysis has not had an impact on the level of measures imposed in anti-subsidy investigations.

The reason for this more restrictive approach regarding users' interests in the Union interest analysis presumably lies in the rationale provided for the limitation of the scope of application of the lesser duty rule, namely that the subsidisation of their companies by foreign governments warrants a more principled response.[343] This reasoning however fails to take into account that the negative effects a higher level of measures has on users and supply chains are identical regardless of whether the measures imposed on the product they depend on are anti-dumping or anti-subsidy measures.

---

[340] Commission Implementing Regulation (EU) 2020/508 of 7 April 2020 imposing a provisional anti-dumping duty on imports of certain hot rolled stainless steel sheets and coils originating in Indonesia, the People's Republic of China and Taiwan (n 76) recitals 368–377.

[341] Cf. above p. 199 et seq.

[342] Cf. Article 12 (1) subparas. 3, 4 BASR. Identical provisions for the imposition of definitive duties and undertakings can be found in Article 15 (1) subparas. 3, 4 BADR and Article 13 (1) subparas. 3, 4 BASR.

[343] Cf. above p. 194 et seq.

7.2.4.4 Conclusions and Further Recommendations

Even though competition-related arguments are included during the Union interest assessment and during the injury analysis, an assessment of the instances where the parties put forward such claims shows that they are unlikely to prevail. This can be attributed to the Commission's practice of following a strict approach in deciding which arguments it considers relevant to the investigation at hand while at the same time only conducting a very superficial analysis of the competition-related arguments presented before it. This applies to the assessments carried out during the injury analysis as well as the Union interest test.

The evaluation of the Commission's practice further has revealed that the inclusion of environmental concerns in the Union interest assessment has not resulted in a fundamental re-orientation of the character of the Union interest test, which continues to be driven by economic considerations. As this serves to prevent a greater politicisation of the EU's trade defence instruments—which would ultimately harm their legitimacy—it is recommended that the Commission continues to restrict the considerations taken into account during the Union interest assessment to those intrinsically linked to the interests of the economic operators mentioned in Article 21 (1) BADR and Article 31 (1) BASR.

Conversely, there is significant room for improvement as regards the Commission practice of addressing competition-related arguments. This does not necessarily require legislative changes to be made to the provisions just mentioned. Instead, much would already be gained by DG TRADE addressing these concerns in greater detail and boosting competition law expertise in the Directorate-General: it should go without saying that its interpretation of the EU competition rules should be based on the interpretation provided by the CJEU and DG COMP. In its reply to the criticism voiced in the ECA report mentioned previously, the Commission held that

> it would like to recall that there is currently an internal contact channel between competent departments, which facilitates an exchange of information on competition related issues that may arise in respective investigations.[344]

It would appear prudent to further strengthen the cooperation between DG TRADE and DG COMP, given that the current level of cooperation does not seem sufficient to satisfactorily address such concerns during the Union interest assessment. Moreover, and in line with the criticism voiced by the ECA, the competition analysis should be adapted to encompass a more thorough analysis of the prospective effects the imposition of measures would have on the competitive situation within the EU.

Likewise, the way in which anti-competitive behaviour is taken into account during the injury assessment must be considered unsatisfactory. In particular, the Commission's 2013 pledge to initiate interim reviews in instances where it has found the Union industry to engage in anti-competitive practices is insufficient. The

---

[344]European Court of Auditors (Chap. 6, n 49), Commission reply to paragraph 49 and 50.

examples given above demonstrate that the review practice has to be improved. As the last years have shown that non-binding pledges did not have any impact on the Commission practice, this is best achieved in the form of legislative changes to the basic regulations. These should be amended to explicitly provide for the initiation of an interim review where the Commission or a national competition authority has found the complainant industry to engage in anti-competitive behaviour, and the temporal proximity between the investigation period and the anti-competitive behaviour is such that it cannot be excluded that the anti-competitive behaviour affected the injury assessment.

It is frequently advanced that the effectiveness of the Union interest test would be improved if its current formulation were changed to a positive one.[345] However, it must be called into doubt whether this would actually provide for any significant changes in the application of the basic regulations, unless one were to also change the special weight accorded to the interests of the Union industry in trade defence investigations and also during the Union interest assessment. The new Union interest test contained in Article 7 (2b) BADR illustrates this: even though it is formulated in a positive way, meaning that the Commission has to establish that the imposition of a higher level of duties is in the interest of the Union, its procedural set-up still favours the Union industry. As set out above, this prioritisation of the Union industry's interests in investigations is a direct consequence of the trade defence instruments' central immediate objective being the protection of the Union industry.[346] As questionable as this immediate objective may be from an economic and from a competition law perspective, this rationale is central to the EU's trade defence legislation and thus unlikely to undergo significant changes. Therefore, absent a fundamental policy re-orientation of the EU's trade defence instruments, it is improbable that a revision of the formulation of the Union interest test is to strengthen its effectiveness. Instead, modifying the Commission practice as presented above will be more appropriate to better integrate competition-related arguments during the Union interest test analysis.

7.3   Chapter Conclusions

Analysing the changes to the basic regulations introduced by the Trade Defence Modernisation Package, it has become apparent that the EU legislature not only does not award a great deal of attention to the issue of anti-competitive effects brought about by the application of the EU's trade defence instruments, but that the modifications introduced alienate competition and trade defence even further. In order to better integrate competition-related concerns in the design and the application of the

---

[345] Cf. e.g. Reymond (2015), p. 71; Sinnaeve (2007), p. 176.

[346] Cf. above p. 234 et seq.

basic regulations, further legislative changes as well as changes to the Commission practice are required.

First, it should be noted that parts of the amendments to the basic regulations entail the risk of an increasingly politicised use of the EU's trade defence instruments, such as the focus on *ex officio* initiations of investigations as expressed in recital 6 of Regulation (EU) 2018/825 or the assessment regarding the existence of State-induced raw material distortions under Article 7 (2a) BADR.

Another trend that can be observed in the modifications introduced by the Trade Defence Modernisation Practice is that the Commission is being awarded even more discretion under the modernised trade defence rules. This is visible, *inter alia*, in the new methodology contained in Article 2 (6a) BADR or the additional Union interest test to be carried out when deciding upon the application of the lesser duty rule in the event of raw material distortions in anti-dumping investigations and under the provisions of the BASR.

Most important, however, also with regard to the relationship between trade and competition, is the observation that numerous amendments to the basic regulations favour the interests of the EU industry, and correspondingly disadvantage those of the exporting producers and users. This concerns the new methodology of Article 2 (6a) BADR. The list of criteria used to establish the existence of significant distortions extends to factors which go beyond the methodology's declared objective of addressing interventions of the exporting producer's home State in the economy, and which cover aspects where the competitors of the EU industry enjoy genuine comparative advantages, such as a lower level of environmental protection. The inclusion of social and environmental aspects in the choice of the appropriate representative country is another aspect which is likely to increase duty levels, thereby favouring the interests of the EU industry. An analysis of the Commission practice has further revealed that it applies different standards in what it considers a sufficient level of social and environmental protection when determining the existence of significant distortions and when choosing a representative country. Thus, in order to ensure coherency at different stages of the investigation, the basic regulations need to be amended to clarify which degree of protection is considered sufficient when addressing the existence of significant distortions and when selecting a representative country.

The procedural burden placed upon the EU industry to reach the evidentiary threshold necessary for the Commission to apply Article 2 (6a) BADR is alleviated by the Commission itself publishing reports on the existence of significant distortions, upon which it relies heavily in investigations. Overall, the procedural set-up as well as the substantive law of the new methodology is highly advantageous to the EU industry: with only little extra effort on part of the EU industry required, its application is guaranteed to result in higher levels of measures, awarding an extra degree of protection to the EU industry.

Likewise, the calculation of the injury margin under the reformed basic regulations favours the interests of the EU industry, in particular the inclusion of a minimum target profit and basing the target price on a price that is sufficient to recover 'full costs and investments'. These amendments must be deemed incompatible with the *EFMA* standard according to which the target profit must be limited to the level of profitability to be expected under normal conditions of competition.[347] Basing the target profit *inter alia* on the level of profitability before an increase of imports from the country under investigation in general must be objected to as well. All of the above amendments are likely to result in higher injury margins, and hence in higher levels of measures in investigations where the lesser duty rule still applies. Moreover, while the inclusion of costs borne by the EU industry in complying with social and environmental legislation in the profit margin calculation is justified in principle, additional legislative changes to the basic regulations are warranted in order to clearly define the *ratione materiae* of these provisions and to address those instances where the EU industry is already receiving compensation for these costs, either from an EU Member State or a third State.

As a result of the limitations to the scope of application of the lesser duty rule by Regulation (EU) 2018/825, the average level of measures is likely to increase. Instead of serving as a corrective to competitive imbalances, the imposition of anti-dumping and anti-subsidy measures up to the full margin of dumping or subsidisation will increasingly act as a deterrent, foreclosing the Union market against foreign imports to a higher degree. This upsets the balance between the competing interests of the EU industry, users and the exporting producers as struck by the lesser duty rule in favour of the interests of the EU industry.

Unaffected by the changes introduced by the Trade Defence Modernisation Package, the Union interest analysis of Article 21 BADR and Article 31 BASR can be expected to follow the same considerations as before the entry into force of the amendments. This holds true despite the Commission's more frequent inclusion of environmental policy concerns and the overall increased visibility of questions of social and environmental protection in the reformed basic regulations. At its core, the Union interest test remains focussed on weighing economic interests against each other, with environmental concerns not being of any relevance of their own.

There is significant room for improvement with regard to the Commission's practice in addressing competition-related arguments in its Union interest analysis. This does not necessarily require changes to the basic regulations. Instead, much would already be gained by DG TRADE addressing these concerns in greater detail and boosting competition law expertise in the Directorate-General in order to avoid conflicting interpretations of competition law concepts by DG TRADE on the one side and DG COMP and the CJEU on the other side. This would also entail for DG TRADE to assess competition-related arguments in greater detail. As a re-formulation of the Union interest test from a negative to a positive one is unlikely to significantly enhance its effectiveness, modifying the Commission practice within the existing framework appears more appropriate to better integrate competition-related arguments in the Union interest analysis and to overall enhance the effectiveness of the Union interest test.

---

[347] *European Fertilizer Manufacturers' Association (EFMA) v Council* (n 101) 60.

Conversely, as regards competition-related arguments during the injury analysis, legislative changes are required as non-binding pledges have not had an impact on the Commission practice. Accordingly, the basic regulations should be amended to explicitly provide for the initiation of an interim review where the Commission or a national competition authority has found the complainant industry to engage in anti-competitive behaviour, and the temporal proximity between the investigation period and the anti-competitive behaviour is such that it cannot be excluded that the anti-competitive behaviour affected the injury assessment.

References[348]

Akritidis V, Sneij F (2018) The shake-up of the EU institutions' dumping calculation methodology and the compatibility of a market-oriented concept of normal value with WTO law. Global Trade Cust J 13(4):129

Baetge D (1998) Das Verhältnis zwischen Antidumpingrecht und Wettbewerbsrecht im Recht der Europäischen Gemeinschaft. Rabels Zeitschrift für ausländisches und internationales Privatrecht 62(4):648

Bierwagen RM (1990) GATT Article VI and the protectionist bias in anti-dumping laws. Springer, Netherlands

Bungenberg M (2015) Umweltschutz als Thema der unionalen Gemeinsamen Handelspolitik. In: Nowak C (ed) Konsolidierung und Entwicklungsperspektiven des Europäischen Umweltrechts. Nomos

Cornelis J (2018) The EU's modernization regulation: stronger and more effective trade defence instruments? Global Trade Cust J 13(11):539

Giannakopoulos TK (2011) Safeguarding companies' rights in competition and anti-dumping/anti-subsidies proceedings, 2nd edn. Kluwer Law International

Hartmann B (2018) Artikel 21 AD-GVO. In: Krenzler HG, Herrmann C, Niestedt M (eds) EU-Außenwirtschafts- und Zollrecht. C.H. Beck

Hoffmeister F (2013) The deep and comprehensive free trade agreements of the European Union – concept and challenges. In: Cremona M, Takács T (eds) Trade liberalisation and standardisation – new directions in the 'low politics' of EU foreign policy. T.M.C. Asser Press

Hoffmeister F (2015) Modernising the EU's trade defence instruments: mission impossible? In: Herrmann C, Streinz R, Simma B (eds) Trade policy between law, diplomacy and scholarship: liber Amicorum in Memoriam Horst G. Krenzler. Springer

Hoffmeister F (2020) The devil is in the detail: a first guide on the EU's new trade defence rules. In: Weiß W, Furculita C (eds) Global politics and EU trade policy: facing the challenges to a multilateral approach. Springer

Horlick G, Vermulst E (2007) Problems with dumping and injury margin calculations in ten user countries. Global Trade Cust J 2(1):1

Huyghebaert K (2019) Changing the rules mid-game: the compliance of the amended EU basic anti-dumping regulation with WTO law. J World Trade 53(3):417

Kasteng J (2013) Targeting the environment: exploring a new trade in the EU's trade defence investigations. Available at <https://papers.ssrn.com/sol3/papers.cfm?abstract_id=2310564>

Kulms R (1990) Competition, trade policy and competition policy in the EEC: the example of antidumping. Common Mark Law Rev 27(2):285

---

[348] All online sources were last accessed on 8 September 2021.

Kuplewatzky N (2018) Defining anti-dumping duties under European Union law. Trade Law Dev 10(2):448

Laprévote FC (2015) Antitrust in wonderland: trade defense through the competition looking-glass. Concurrences 1

Loets A (2018) Die neue Verzerrungsregelung im EU-Antidumpingzollrecht. Zeitschrift für europäisches Wirtschaftsrecht (EuZW) 309

Luo Y (2010) Anti-dumping in the WTO, the EU and China: the rise of legalization in the trade regime and its consequences. Wolters Kluwer

Matsushita M and others (2015) The World Trade Organization: law, practice, and policy, 3rd edn. Oxford University Press

Mavroidis PC (2016) The regulation of international trade: vol II: the WTO Agreements on trade in goods. MIT Press

Mueller W, Khan N, Scharf T (2009) EC and WTO anti-dumping Law: a handbook, 2nd edn. Oxford University Press

Müller W (2017) The EU's trade defence instruments: recent judicial and policy developments. In: Bungenberg M and others (eds) European yearbook of international economic law 2017. Springer

Müller W (2018) The EU's new trade defence laws: a two steps approach. In: Bungenberg M and others (eds) The future of trade defence instruments – global policy trends and legal challenges. Springer

Müller-Ibold T (2018) Antidumping and competition law – common origin, a life of their own and peaceful coexistence?. In: Kokott J, Pohlmann P, Polley R (eds) Europäisches, Deutsches und Internationales Kartellrecht: Festschrift für Dirk Schroeder zum 65. Geburtstag. Dr. Otto Schmidt

Pachmann R (2005) Das Verhältnis von Antidumping zum internationalen Wettbewerbsrecht. Dissertation, Universität Hamburg

Prost O (2014) Modernisation of the EU's trade defence instruments: more effective and transparent rules to resist protectionism: workshop on the modernisation of the EU's trade defence instruments (TDIs)', Organized by the European Parliament, Available at <https://www.europarl. europa.eu/RegData/etudes/workshop/join/2014/433842/EXPO-INTA_AT(2014)433842_EN. pdf>

Rados N (2018) Artikel 4 AD-GVO. In: Krenzler HG, Herrmann C, Niestedt M (eds) EU-Außenwirtschafts- und Zollrecht. C.H. Beck

Reinhold P, Van Vaerenberg P (2021) Significant distortions under Article 2(6a) BADR: three years of commission practice. Global Trade Cust J 16(5):193

Reymond D (2015) Antidumping et concurrence à l'aune de la modernisation des Instruments de Défense Commerciale. Concurrences 64

Rovegno L, Vandenbussche H (2012) Anti-dumping practices in the EU. In: Gaines SE, Olsen BE, Sørensen KE (eds) Liberalising trade in the EU and the WTO: a legal comparison. Cambridge University Press

Scharf T, Kuplewatzky N (2019) Artikel 9 AD-GVO. In: Krenzler HG, Herrmann C, Niestedt M (eds) EU-Außenwirtschafts- und Zollrecht. C.H. Beck

Shadikhodjaev S (2018) Non-market economies, significant market distortions, and the 2017 EU anti-dumping amendment. J Int Econ Law 21(4):885

Sinnaeve A (2007) The 'community interest test' in anti-dumping investigations: time for reform? Global Trade Cust J 2(4):157

Tauschinsky E, Weiß W (2018) Unionsinteresse und Bürgernähe in der Handelspolitik. Europarecht:3

Tharakan PKM, Greenway D, Kerstens B (2006) Anti-dumping and excess injury margins in the European Union: a counterfactual analysis. Eur J Polit Econ 22(3):653

van Bael I, Bellis J-F (2019) EU anti-dumping and other trade defence instruments, 6th edn. Kluwer Law International

Vandenbussche H, Wauthy X (2001) Inflicting injury through product quality: how European antidumping policy disadvantages European producers. Eur J Polit Econ 17(1):101

Vermulst E (2005) The 10 major problems with the anti-dumping instrument in the European Community. J World Trade 39(1):105

Vermulst E (2014) Modernization of the EU's trade defence instruments: throwing out the baby with the bath water?: Workshop on the modernisation of the EU's trade defence instruments (TDIs). Organized by the European Parliament , available at <https://www.europarl.europa.eu/RegData/etudes/workshop/join/2014/433842/EXPO-INTA_AT(2014)433842_EN.pdf>

Vermulst E, Dion Sud J (2018) The new rules adopted by the EU to address significant distortions in the anti-dumping context. In: Bungenberg M and others (eds) The future of trade defence instruments – global policy trends and legal challenges. Springer

Vermulst E, Graafsma F (2007) EC dumping and injury margin calculation methods: ten major problems. Global Trade Cust J 2(1):27

Vermulst E, Sud J (2013) Modernization of the EU's trade defence instruments and the law of unintended consequences. Global Trade Cust J 8(7/8):202

Vermulst E, Sud J (2018) Treatment of China in EU Anti-dumping Investigations Post-December 2017: Plus ça change, plus c'est la même chose. In: Nedumpara JJ, Zhou W (eds) Non-market economies in the global trading system: the special case of China. Springer, Singapore

Vermulst E, Waer P (1991) The calculation of injury margins in EC anti-dumping proceedings. J World Trade 25(6):5

Wenig F-H (1996) Public interest litigation in anti-dumping law. In: Micklitz H-W, Reich N (eds) Public interest litigation before European courts. Nomos

Chapter 8
The EU's Modernised Trade Defence Instruments: Promoting Sustainable Development in the EU's Trade Relations?

8.1 Introduction

The analysis of the amendments introduced by the Trade Defence Modernisation Package undertaken in the preceding chapters has revealed that the Package's detrimental effects to competition in the internal market can in part be attributed to the reformed basic regulations integrating social and environmental concerns. As elaborated upon in Chaps. 2 and 4, the Treaties provide that while the EU's trade defence legislation is intended to offset the distortions to competition caused by unfair trading practices, its use must be restricted to what is necessary to achieve this aim, and distortions to competition brought about by the imposition of trade defence measures are to be avoided. In today's Treaty framework, this can *inter alia* be inferred from Article 21 (3) subpara. 2 TEU, which mandates consistency between the EU's internal and external policies, and the hierarchy of norms: EU competition law is contained in primary law, whereas the EU's trade defence instruments are set out in secondary legislation.[1]

Traditionally, the objective of the trade defence instruments as being aimed at addressing unfair trading practices only extended to dumping and subsidisation. Flowing from the integration of the EU's common commercial policy into the wider framework of the EU's external relations particularly through Articles 3 (5), 21 (1), (2) TEU, the objective of ensuring fairness in international trade has to be adapted as also encompassing matters of ethical or equitable trade.[2] Thus, the Treaties provide an explicit basis for the inclusion of environmental and social concerns in the design and the application of the EU's trade defence instruments.

Yet, for the reasons just set out above, also under this novel, broader understanding of 'fair' trade, the use of trade defence instruments must be restricted to what is

---

[1] Cf. above p. 31 and 83.
[2] Cf. above Chap. 4, p. 83 et seq.

necessary to contribute to the attainment of this objective. In particular, Articles 3 (5), 21 (1), (2) TEU and their focus on non-commercial objectives cannot be used to legitimise purely protectionist measures. Instead, any inclusion of non-commercial considerations in the EU's trade defence legislation must show a strong link between the market foreclosure effects emanating from its application and the actual promotion of these non-commercial objectives, while respecting the principle of proportionality.[3] It follows that in order to establish whether the market foreclosure effects resulting from the inclusion of labour and environmental matters during trade defence investigations can be justified by having recourse to Articles 3 (5), 21 TEU, a proportionality assessment must be undertaken. The first step of such a proportionality assessment is to determine whether the amendments to the basic regulations in question actually promote compliance with international environmental and labour standards by the EU's trading partners. The second step would then be to balance the competing interests, in this case the interest in reducing the market foreclosure effects of the EU's trade defence instruments and the interest in promoting social and environmental protection through their design and application. As already stated, the EU institutions enjoy a wide margin of discretion in defining and prioritising the objectives of the common commercial policy.[4]

Thus, this chapter sets out to determine whether the changes to the basic regulations relating to the inclusion of social and environmental objectives actually result in the EU's modernised trade defence instruments contributing to the global promotion of sustainable development objectives, as would be necessary for them in order to be based on Articles 3 (5), 21 (1), (2) TEU. Following an overview of the approach pursued by the EU in integrating non-commercial concerns in its common commercial policy instruments, the chapter will dedicate itself to presenting the ways in which the amendments to the basic regulations relating to sustainable development concerns conflict with this approach. It will furthermore be argued that parts of the amendments find no basis in the Treaties. In particular, they cannot be based on Articles 3 (5), 21 (1), (2) TEU and the EU's obligation arising therefrom to foster a wide array of objectives, including non-commercial ones, in its CCP.

---

[3] Dimopoulos (2010), p. 167; also holding that Article 21 TEU may not be used to legitimise purely protectionist policies: Weiß (2014) para. 26. Cf. also the Opinion of Advocate General Léger in *Commission v NTN Corporation and Koyo Seiko* (Chap. 4, n 118) 9; *Anton Dürbeck v Hauptzollamt Frankfurt am Main-Flughafen* (Chap. 4, n 111) 44.

[4] Cremer (2016) para. 13; Vedder (2013), p. 143.

8.2 The Integration of Non-Economic Concerns in the EU's Common Commercial Policy

The integration of non-trade concerns in the EU's common commercial policy is not a recent phenomenon. Already the 1989 Lomé Convention concluded between the EU and the African Caribbean Pacific countries linked trade benefits with the adherence to human rights standards.[5] Starting in the 1990s, the EU began to systematically include 'human rights clauses' in the trade agreements it concluded.[6] In a more recent development, the EU's free trade agreements also comprise chapters on sustainable development matters, i.e. on environmental protection and the protection of workers' rights (trade and sustainable development or TSD chapters). To some extent, this development was prompted by the entry into force of the Treaty of Lisbon and the integration of the EU's CCP into the broader framework of its external relations.[7] However, already the 2006 *'Renewed EU Sustainable Development Strategy'* insisted on the Commission and the EU Member States increasing their efforts in using international trade as a means towards pursuing *'genuine global sustainable development'*.[8] The Council further called upon the EU to work

> together with its trading partners to improve environmental and social standards and to use the full potential of trade or cooperation agreements at regional or bilateral level to this end.[9]

In a similar vein, in its 2006 *'Global Europe'* strategy, the Commission stated its intention to strengthen sustainable development through the EU's bilateral relations by means of incorporating provisions relating to labour standards and environmental protection.[10] Against this backdrop, the Commission began to include TSD chapters in its priorities when negotiating trade agreements already before the entry into force of the Treaty of Lisbon.[11] The first agreement to encompass chapters explicitly dedicated to matters of sustainable development was the 2008 EU-Cariforum

---

[5] Donno and Neureiter (2018), p. 335, 336.

[6] Bartels (2015), p. 73.

[7] On trade policy in the Treaty of Lisbon cf. above p. 26 et seq.

[8] Council of the European Union, 'Review of the EU Sustainable Development Strategy (EU SDS) – Renewed Strategy (Document 10117/06)' (Brussels 26 June 2006) 21.

[9] Ibid.

[10] European Commission, 'Communication from the Commission to the Council, the European Parliament, the European Economic and Social Committee and the Committee of the Regions: Global Europe: Competing in the World: A Contribution to the EU's Growth and Jobs Strategy (COM(2006) 567 final)' (4 October 2006) 9.

[11] Gruni notes that besides the chapters explicitly dedicated to TSD matters, other parts of a trade agreement are relevant for the pursuit of sustainable development objectives, too, Gruni (2018), pp. 4, 8–10.

Economic Partnership Agreement,[12] and others agreements have followed since.[13] The provisions included in these chapters relate to labour and environmental standards that are primarily anchored in ILO conventions and multilateral environmental agreements.[14]

In addition to exporting social and environmental standards by way of bilateral conditional market access, the EU also provides its trading partners with incentives for adhering to such standards through its unilateral CCP instruments. In this respect, the GSP Regulation has been central, as it grants additional tariff preferences upon the ratification and effective implementation of a number of international human rights, labour, environmental and good governance instruments.[15]

8.2.1   Bilateral Trade Policy Instruments

The human rights clauses included in the EU's current trade agreements are usually formulated as 'essential elements' clauses,[16] making respect for democratic principles and fundamental human rights an essential part of the agreement. This classification allows the parties to impose sanctions or to withdraw themselves from the agreement pursuant to Article 60 (3) lit. b) of the Vienna Convention on the Law of Treaties (VCLT)[17] should the other party not comply with its human rights obligations as set out in the clause.[18] In accordance with this, the human rights clauses contained in the trade agreements concluded after the entry into force of the Treaty of Lisbon also encompass a 'non-execution' clause, which explicitly enables the parties to take appropriate measures in case the other party violates the 'essential elements' clause.[19] The parties are to give priority to those measures that least disrupt the functioning of the agreement, and the suspension of measures only would be a

---

[12]Bartels (2013), p. 73. Cf. Chaps. 4 (Environment) and 5 (Social aspects) of Part II, Title I (Trade in Goods) in 'Economic Partnership Agreement between the CARIFORUM States, of the one part, and the European Community and its Member States, of the other part (OJ 2008 L 289/3)' (30 October 2008).

[13]These include the EU agreements with Central America, Canada, Colombia, Georgia, Korea, Moldova, Peru, and Ukraine, Singapore and Vietnam. They are also included in draft negotiating texts in the Transatlantic Trade and Investment Partnership with the United States of America, the Comprehensive Economic Partnership Agreement with Indonesia, and the EU-MERCOSUR Association Agreement, Harrison et al. (2019), p. 635, 639.

[14]European Commission, 'Non-paper: Trade and Sustainable Development (TSD) chapters in EU Free Trade Agreements (FTAs)' (Brussels 11 July 2017) 2.

[15]Marx and others (2015), p. 6.

[16]This does not apply to all of the agreements concluded by the EU, though. For example, the EU-Vietnam FTA does not explicitly set out the suspension of the agreement in the event of human rights violations.

[17]Vienna Convention on the Law of Treaties (1155 U.N.T.S. 331) (23 May 1969).

[18]Borchert et al. (2018), p. 7.

[19]Ibid.

measure of last resort.[20] In general, the partial or entire suspension of the agreement will be preceded by dialogue and consultations between the parties to the agreement.[21] Overall, the Commission considers sanctions under the non-execution clause to be limited to the most extreme and flagrant violations of human rights.[22]

As indicated above, the trade agreements entered into by the EU after 2008 also comprise chapters dedicated to the subject matter of sustainable development. The chapters contain two main sets of obligations, namely a non-regression clause prohibiting the parties from reducing their existent levels of social and environmental protection, and a clause on minimum obligations regarding the effective enforcement of environmental and labour standards.[23] At the same time, the chapters usually include a clarification that environmental and labour standards should not be used for protectionist purposes and that their respective comparative advantages should in no way be called into question.[24] The chapters on sustainable development are excluded from the dispute settlement procedure established in the free trade agreements. Concerns related to the adherence to these chapters are to be resolved through a self-contained two-step dispute settlement system involving consultations followed by a referral to a panel of experts.[25] Thus, no party can bring an action under the regular dispute settlement provisions relating to the non-compliance with TSD chapters that would result in the suspension of trade preferences against the other party.[26] The effectiveness of TSD chapters is unclear, with studies yielding no definitive evidence that trade agreements with provisions on social and

---

[20] Bartels (2013), p. 78.

[21] European Parliament, *Briefing: Human rights in EU trade agreements: The human rights clause and its application* (2019) 8; Donno and Neureiter (2018), p. 348 specifically on the Lomé Convention.

[22] European Parliament, *Briefing: Human rights in EU trade agreements* (2019) 8; European Commission, 'Non-paper: Using EU Trade Policy to promote fundamental human rights' (2012) 3.

[23] Bartels (2013), p. 84. Cf e.g. Article 13.7 of the 'Free Trade Agreement between the European Union and its Member States, of the one part, and the Republic of Korea, of the other part (OJ 2011 L 127/6)' (14 May 2011) which reads: '(1) A Party shall not fail to effectively enforce its environmental and labour laws (...). (2) A Party shall not weaken or reduce the environmental or labour protections afforded in its laws to encourage trade or investment, by waiving or otherwise derogating from, or offering to waive or otherwise derogate from, its laws, regulations or standards.'

[24] Cf. e.g. Article 13.2 of the EU-Korea Free Trade Agreement (n 23): '(2) The Parties stress that environmental and labour standards should not be used for protectionist trade purposes. The Parties note that their comparative advantage should in no way be called into question.'

[25] Bartels (2013), p. 297, 310. Cf. e.g. Articles 23.9, 23.10 and Articles 24.15, 24.16 of the 'Comprehensive Economic and Trade Agreement (CETA) between Canada, of the one part, and the European Union and its Member States, of the other part (OJ 2017 L 11/23)' (14 January 2017).

[26] Harrison and others (2019), p. 640; Gruni (2018), p. 7. In this context, the dispute settlement procedure initiated by the EU under the trade and sustainable development chapter of the EU-Korea trade agreement should be mentioned. It constitutes the first instance where the dispute resolution process set out in the TSD chapters has been activated. For more information cf. European Commission, *EU-Korea dispute settlement over workers' rights in Korea enters next stage* (2019).

environmental provisions lead to increased protection standards.[27] Nonetheless, it can be argued that already the Commission's policy of including matters of sustainable development in its policy priorities when negotiating the conclusion of a trade agreement can incentivise the EU's trading partners to pre-emptively ratify international conventions in the hope of obtaining better market access conditions. The Vietnamese government's decision to ratify core ILO conventions[28] during the negotiation process leading up to the conclusion of the EU-Vietnam FTA[29] can be seen as an example in this respect.

Against the backdrop of the perceived lack of effectiveness of TSD chapters, reforms of the EU's TSD chapters have been initiated. One of the options for strengthening the impact of the TSD chapters that has been discussed is the adoption of a sanctions-based model, such as the one currently in practice in the United States and Canada. Both jurisdictions provide for sanctions in cases of non-compliance with standards relating to sustainable development matters. The United States withdraw trade concessions, Canada relies on fines.[30] This is done to ensure that domestic producers are not harmed by lower labour and environmental standards in the countries' trading partners,[31] i.e. primarily out of concerns for the domestic industry. Consequently, the sanctions are intended to compensate parties for economic damage resulting from a failure to comply with commitments under the agreement.[32] When evaluating this model, the Commission concluded that the practice under the U.S. and Canadian approach indicates that such a concept would narrow down the number of complaints that would qualify for dispute settlement under the rules of the trade agreement: under the model operated by the two jurisdictions, in order to qualify for sanctions, the alleged violations of labour or environmental provisions have to affect trade between the parties. By contrast, under the method currently followed by the EU, the majority of complaints concerns TSD violations that are relevant in the wider context of trade but do not have a direct impact on trade between the parties to the agreement.[33] The Commission further notes that such a restructuring of the TSD chapters would necessarily make them more confrontational, potentially jeopardising long-term links with trading partners

---

[27] For an overview on labour standards cf. e.g. Harrison and others (2019) and Marx and Soares (2015).

[28] European Commission, *EU set to sign trade and investment agreements with Vietnam on Sunday* (2019).

[29] 'Free Trade Agreement between the European Union and the Socialist Republic of Viet Nam' (OJ 2020 L 186/3) (12 June 2020).

[30] European Commission, 'Non-paper: Trade and Sustainable Development (TSD) chapters in EU Free Trade Agreements (FTAs)' (Brussels 11 July 2017) 7.

[31] Ibid 8.

[32] European Commission, 'Non-paper: Feedback and way forward on improving the implementation and enforcement of Trade and Sustainable Development chapters in EU Free Trade Agreements' (Brussels 26 February 2018) 3.

[33] European Commission, 'Non-paper: Trade and Sustainable Development (TSD) chapters in EU Free Trade Agreements (FTAs)' (Brussels 11 July 2017) 8.

to improve capacity and effect changes.[34] Consequently, the Commission has stated that it will not consider a sanctions-based approach to enhance the effectiveness of TSD chapters, but instead will work on improving their impact by means of a set of *'concrete and practicable actions to be taken to revamp the TSD chapters'*.[35] Overall, the Commission has chosen to adhere to what has been described as a 'promotional approach' to sustainable development, with dialogue- and cooperation-based solutions.[36] This includes attempts by the Commission directed at encouraging the early ratification of core international agreements during the negotiation of new trade agreements.[37] *Harrison et al.* notice parallels to the EU's approach towards GSP+ beneficiaries in this regard, which likewise requires the EU's trading partners to comply with international conventions on labour and environmental matters before they are granted additional tariff preferences.[38]

8.2.2 Unilateral Trade Policy Instruments

Before the EU adopted the policy of including TSD chapters in its trade agreements, its GSP scheme was the flagship policy in pursuing sustainable development objectives by means of trade policy instruments.[39] The GSP scheme is a mechanism through which the EU provides developing countries with preferential access to the internal market. Other unilateral measures aimed at advancing human rights and sustainable development objectives in the EU's commercial relations with other States include the Conflict Minerals Regulation[40] or the Dual-use Regulation.[41] The GSP scheme, however, remains at the core of the EU's unilateral efforts aimed at actively promoting sustainable development and human rights in partner nations.[42]

Today's GSP scheme is divided into three parts: the general GSP scheme which partially or entirely removes customs duties on imports from the beneficiary

---

[34] Ibid 9.

[35] European Commission, 'Non-paper: Feedback and way forward on improving the implementation and enforcement of Trade and Sustainable Development chapters in EU Free Trade Agreements' (Brussels 26 February 2018) 2.

[36] Borchert and others (2018), p. 11.

[37] European Commission, 'Non-paper: Feedback and way forward on improving the implementation and enforcement of Trade and Sustainable Development chapters in EU Free Trade Agreements' (Brussels 26 February 2018) 8.

[38] Harrison and others (2019), p. 649.

[39] Gruni (2018), p. 7.

[40] Regulation (EU) 2017/821 of the European Parliament and of the Council of 17 May 2017 laying down supply chain due diligence obligations for Union importers of tin, tantalum and tungsten, their ores, and gold originating from conflict-affected and high-risk areas.

[41] Council Regulation (EC) No 428/2009 of 5 May 2009 setting up a Community regime for the control of exports, transfer, brokering and transit of dual-use items.

[42] Curran and Eckhardt (2020), p. 151.

countries, the GSP+ scheme which provides for close to a full removal of duties on imports dependent on the implementation and ratification of certain international conventions and, lastly, the 'Everything but Arms' (EBA) scheme, which gives duty-free, quota-free access for all goods from least developed countries except for arms and ammunition.[43] The initial GSP itself was based upon the idea of granting developing countries non-reciprocal and non-discriminatory preferential market access, with the objective of increasing their export earnings, promoting their industrialisation and accelerating their rates of economic growth.[44] The current version of the EU GSP scheme allows for the temporary withdrawal of all preferential arrangements in the circumstances set out in Article 19 of the GSP Regulation. These include, *inter alia*, serious and systematic human rights violations, the export of goods made by prison labour as well as serious and systematic unfair trading practices including those affecting the supply of raw materials, which have an adverse effect on the Union industry.[45] The conditionality between compliance with international obligations and tariff preferences is strongest in the GSP+ scheme, as it makes additional tariff preferences dependent on the ratification and implementation of a list of 27 international conventions covering not only the subject matter of human rights but also labour rights, environment and good governance principles.[46] The special incentives arrangement under the GSP+ scheme can be regarded as an expression of the EU's obligation to promote respect for human rights and sustainable development in its external relations as prescribed by Article 21 (1), (2) lit. d) TEU.[47]

The conditionality employed by the GSP+ scheme can be described as 'positive conditionality' in that it rewards compliant countries with additional tariff preferences.[48] Conversely, just like the general GSP and the EBA scheme, the GSP+ scheme possesses a 'negative conditionality' aspect as the GSP+ preferences can be revoked in case of a failure of ratifying or effectively implementing the relevant conventions.[49] Pursuant to recital 11 of the GSP Regulation, the GSP+ scheme is

---

[43] European Commission, 'Commission Staff Working Document: Report on the implementation of the European Commission Communication on "Trade, Growth and Development" and follow-up to the Council Conclusions on "EU's approach to trade, growth and development in the next decade" (SWD(2016) 47 final)' (Brussels 25 February 2016) 4.

[44] Borchert and others (2018), p. 12. The principle of a GSP as a scheme linking trade to development was adopted in 1968 at the United Nations Conference on Trade and Development taking place in New Delhi, resolution 21 (II).

[45] Article 19 of Regulation (EU) No 978/2012 of the European Parliament and of the Council of 25 October 2012 applying a scheme of generalised tariff preferences (Chap. 7, n 69).

[46] Cf. Article 15 of Regulation (EU) No 978/2012 of the European Parliament and of the Council of 25 October 2012 applying a scheme of generalised tariff preferences (Chap. 7, n 69), which provides for the withdrawal of preferences under the GSP+ scheme where it is established that the beneficiary country does not respect its obligations arising out of the scheme.

[47] Eeckhout (2012), p. 452.

[48] Borchert and others (2018), pp. 14–16.

[49] Ibid 16, referring to Article 15 of Regulation (EU) No 978/2012 of the European Parliament and of the Council of 25 October 2012 applying a scheme of generalised tariff preferences (Chap. 6, n 39).

intended to promote sustainable development and good governance by helping developing countries assume the special burdens and responsibilities resulting from the ratification of the core conventions mentioned above.[50] Yet, similar to the TSD chapters in the EU's trade agreements, the effectivity of the EU's GSP scheme is frequently called into doubt. Critics remark that the element of negative conditionality—i.e. the withdrawal of trade preferences—is rarely being utilised.[51] To date, benefits have only been withdrawn on four occasions: against Myanmar and Belarus (withdrawal from the whole scheme), Sri Lanka[52] (withdrawal from GSP+) and Cambodia[53] (withdrawal from EBA). As acknowledged by the European Parliament, while Myanmar and Sri Lanka initiated political and economic reforms in the years following the withdrawal of the preferences,

> it is impossible to assess the relative importance of EU trade measures among a myriad of other factors driving regime change and (. . .) reforms.[54]

Parliament also considered, however, that

> [t]he system's most effective leverage is not primarily based on the real use of sanctions, but on its strength to act as a deterrent due to the consequences of a potential loss of trade preferences. (. . .) [I]ncentives, being more effective, are preferable to sanctions.[55]

Indeed, studies have confirmed that already the very existence of the GSP+ arrangement provides standard GSP beneficiaries with an incentive to ratify and effectively implement labour and human rights conventions in exchange for better access to the EU internal market. The same applies regarding the environmental impact of the GSP scheme.[56] Therefore, just as it is the case under the EU's bilateral trade policy instruments, the EU is privileging incentives-based cooperation and dialogue with its partners in trade over the use of sanctions.[57]

---

[50] Recital 11 of Regulation (EU) No 978/2012 of the European Parliament and of the Council of 25 October 2012 applying a scheme of generalised tariff preferences (Chap. 6, n 39).

[51] Cf. Borchert and others (2018), p. 18 et seq with further references.

[52] European Parliament, *Briefing: Human rights in EU Trade Policy – Unilateral Measures* (2017) 5.

[53] European Commission, *EU triggers procedure to temporarily suspend trade preferences for Cambodia* (2019).

[54] European Parliament, *Briefing: Human rights in EU Trade Policy – Unilateral Measures* (n 52) 8.

[55] Ibid 8–9.

[56] European Commission, 'Commission Staff Working Document: Midterm Evaluation of the Generalised Scheme of Preferences accompanying the document "Report from the European Commission to the European Parliament and the Council on the application of Regulation (EU) 978/2012 applying a Scheme of Generalised Tariff Preferences and repealing Council Regulation (EC) No 732/2008" (SWD(2018) 430 final)' (Chap. 4, n 104) 27–29.

[57] Cf. also European Commission, 'Trade for all – Towards a more responsible trade and investment policy (COM(2015) 497)' (Chap. 4, n 103) 23: '*The EU is also in the lead on using trade policy to promote the social and environmental pillars of sustainable development. This is done in a positive, incentive-based way, without any hidden protectionist agenda.*'

8.3   Trade Defence Instruments as a Novel Instrument for the Promotion of Sustainable Development Objectives

8.3.1   Legal Context

The growing number of calls relating to a social and environmental impact assessment of the imposition of trade defence measures during the Union interest test has been mentioned in the previous chapter.[58] Furthermore, integrating the concerns of the labour and the environmental movement into the framework of the EU's trade defence instruments is deemed necessary to counter the growing scepticism towards the benefits of international trade.[59] To the advocates of such an approach, the integration of labour and environmental concerns into the BADR and the BASR presents a welcome change, and aligns the regulations with the duty to foster non-commercial objectives expressed in Articles 3 (5), 21 TEU. However, for the amendments to find their legal basis in these provisions, it is first to be established whether the amendments to the basic regulations in question actually promote sustainable development in the EU's trading partners. A separate but related issue is the question of whether the changes introduced by the Trade Defence Modernisation Package can be reconciled with the EU's overarching strategy in promoting compliance with international standards of environmental protection and the protection of workers' rights by its trading partners as outlined above. This is called for by Article 21 (3) subpara. 2 TEU, which obliges the EU institutions to ensure consistency not only between the EU's internal and external policies, but also between the EU's various external policy measures.[60]

8.3.2   Compatibility with the EU's Approach for Promoting Sustainable Development in Its Trade Relations

In examining the inclusion of matters of sustainable development in the reformed basic regulations with regard to their compatibility with the EU's overall approach for promoting sustainable development in its CCP, one has to differentiate between two separate strands of the EU's modernised rules: the provisions taking costs stemming from compliance with social and environmental concerns into account when calculating the injury margin and those addressing compliance with international standards in the EU's trading partners during the investigation. The latter set of rules encompasses the new methodology of the BADR, the provisions relating to the

---

[58]Bungenberg (2015), pp. 226, 237–238; Bungenberg (2014) para. 82; Kasteng (2013).

[59]Curran and Eckhardt (2020), p. 157.

[60]In detail on the concept of coherence under the Treaty of Lisbon cf. Cremona (2008).

initiation of interim reviews, and the rejection of undertaking offers. The first set of rules, i.e. those related to the modifications of the injury margin calculation, is not intended to foster compliance with social and environmental standards by the EU's trading partners, but it is their declared objective to improve the accuracy of the injury margin calculation.[61] Consequently, they were integrated for economic reasons and do not address the environmental or social standards maintained by the EU's trading partners. Therefore, the criticism expressed in the previous chapter regarding these amendments cannot be countered by arguing that they might be viewed more positively from the perspective of promoting non-commercial objectives on the international plane.

For this reason, the following section will not address the changes to the calculation of the injury margin, but only the second set of rules, namely those concerned with issues of compliance with social and environmental standards in non-EU Member States. Finally, given its prominence in the debate surrounding the inclusion of sustainability aspects in the EU's trade defence framework, the options for including non-commercial considerations in the Union interest test with the objective of promoting compliance with international social and environmental standards by the EU's trading partners will be discussed, too.

8.3.2.1 Tenuous Link Between Market Access and Compliance with International Environmental and Labour Law Standards

Marx et al. note that governance through trade can be executed in two different forms of conditionality: either directly, by making access to the market dependent upon the adherence to specific standards, or indirectly, by providing additional preferences as an incentive to enhance one's trading partners' commitment to human rights, sustainable development and good governance.[62] As becomes apparent from the above observations, the EU has been combining these two methods in the formulation of its trade policy.

8.3.2.1.1 The Amendments to the Basic Regulations

A common feature of the trade policy instruments employed by the EU in contributing to international compliance with international environmental or labour law is that they are explicit in their conditionality: adherence to certain international standards is communicated as an element upon which access to the internal market is dependent.[63] The modernised trade defence instruments lack such a clear element of conditionality, linking a sufficient level of social and environmental protection to

---

[61] Cf. above p. 207.

[62] Marx and others (2015), p. 6.

[63] Cf. above p. 257 et seq.

the degree of market access awarded to the goods exported to the EU. This can be attributed, for one, to the fact that the EU's system of trade defence instruments is not designed to respond to violations of sustainable development standards, but to remedy the injury to the EU industry caused by the presence of dumped or subsidised imports on the internal market. Thus, the imposition of trade defence measures as such is not conditional upon compliance with international standards concerning the protection of the environment or workers' rights, but on the criteria just mentioned.

This also holds true after the Trade Defence Modernisation Package. The reformed basic regulations do connect compliance with international sustainable development standards to the use of trade defence instruments. However, the component of conditionality introduced by the reform is limited to the modalities of the application of the trade defence instruments, such as the acceptance of undertaking offers by the Commission. Further, while the application of the new methodology of Article 2 (6a) BADR is detrimental to exporting producers due to its effect of increasing the level of measures, the BADR does not acknowledge this. In addition, the social and environmental standards in the country of export are not the only criteria upon which the application of the new methodology is dependent. Instead, the new methodology can also be applied in instances where there are no concerns regarding the level of social and environmental protection in the country of export. The element of conditionality is visible more clearly in recital 12 of Regulation (EU) 2018/825, pertaining to the initiation of interim reviews in the event of changed circumstances in the country under measures relating to social and environmental standards,[64] and the provisions of the reformed regulations providing for the rejection of undertakings based on concerns relating to the principles and obligations arising out of multilateral environmental agreements and core ILO conventions.[65,66] Nonetheless, a clear provision—e.g. in the recitals of the reformed basic regulations—acknowledging the linkage between a sufficient level of social and environmental protection and the degree of market access awarded to dumped or subsidised goods, also with regard to the new methodology, is missing from the reformed basic regulations. However, without the conditionality being made explicit, the basic regulations lack clarity.

Overall, the impetus the reformed basic regulations provide to the EU's trading partners to step up their commitment to international environmental and labour law is thus likely to be negligible.

It should moreover be noted that selecting the country with a higher level of social and environmental protection as the appropriate representative country when

---

[64] Recital 12 of Regulation (EU) 2018/825 (Chap. 1, n 10).

[65] Article 8 (3) BADR and Article 13 (3) BASR.

[66] The ECA furthermore criticises the formalistic approach expressed in the basic regulations, as they only focus on ratification of certain conventions and not on their practical enforcement and the actual level of protection, European Court of Auditors (Chap. 6, n 49) 40, cf. also above p. 190.

determining normal value under the new methodology of Article 2 (6a) BADR[67] is another aspect which is not consistent with the approach taken by the EU in promoting non-trade objectives in its common commercial policy. While liable to foreclose the EU market to the exporting producers to a greater extent,[68] the application of the norm is not conditional upon non-compliance with international labour or environmental standards by the exporting producer's home State. The decision to include such considerations in selecting the representative country thus remains entirely extraneous to the trade conditionality approach otherwise followed by the EU which, in accordance with the requirements set by Articles 3 (5), 21 TEU, makes the degree of access to the internal market conditional upon compliance with international conventions relating to human rights or sustainable development matters in the country of export, but not in a third country.

8.3.2.1.2 Possible Changes to the Interests Considered During the Union Interest Test

8.3.2.1.2.1 Legal Basis

The environmental situation in the exporting producer's country has not yet played a role during the Union interest analysis. Where the Commission has had recourse to environmental policy arguments in carrying out the Union interest analysis, it limited its comments to the effect the (non-)imposition of measures would have on the realisation of the EU's own, internal environmental policy objectives.[69] This aspect must be separated from the question of whether the EU Treaties permit the Commission to take the level of environmental protection and respect for workers' rights in its trading partners into account when carrying out the Union interest analysis.[70] While the first question focuses on the EU's own internal environmental policy objectives, the second question relates to the EU's external policy. Concerning the latter, their inclusion can likewise be based on Articles 3 (5), 21 (1), (2) TEU.[71] Therefore, in principle, the Treaties would permit the Union institutions to have regard to non-commercial aspects such as the EU's trading partners' track record with regard to compliance with labour and environmental standards when assessing whether the imposition of anti-dumping or anti-subsidy measures would be in the interest of the EU.[72]

---

[67] Article 2 (6a) lit. a) BADR.

[68] Cf. above p. 174 et seq.

[69] Cf. above p. 238 et seq.

[70] This question has already been addressed in the previous chapter, p. 237 et seq.

[71] Cf. above p. 255.

[72] Cf. above p. 240. Cf. also Bungenberg (2015), pp. 237–238.

8.3.2.1.2.2   Contribution to the International Promotion of Sustainable Development

Thus, in theory, the Commission could integrate the degree of respect for international environmental and labour law shown by its trading partners in the Union interest assessment. In order to do so, the Commission would have to argue, in accordance with Articles 3 (5), 21 (2) TEU, that the imposition of trade defence measures fosters compliance with international standards relating to the protection of workers' rights or the environment by its trading partners.[73]

This reasoning requires the imposition of trade defence measures to have a positive effect on the protection of the environment and workers' rights in these countries. Accordingly, the imposition of measures would have to operate as a sanctioning mechanism for not adhering to international environmental and labour law standards, exerting pressure on the EU's partners in trade to comply with such standards. However, under the present system of the basic regulations, measures will be imposed regardless of the exporting producer's home country's compliance with international labour and environmental law. This also extends to the duration of the measures: even if the exporting producer's home country were to improve the level of protection awarded to workers or the environment, the measures would not be repealed. This relates to the lack of conditionality between the imposition of measures and compliance with labour and environmental standards as outlined above.[74] Therefore, the current basic regulations do not provide effective incentives for the EU's trading partners to change their policy with regard to compliance with international environmental and labour law.[75] Consequently, the argument that the imposition of anti-dumping or anti-subsidy measures *in itself* would promote adherence to the standards set by international environmental and labour law by its trading partners cannot be accepted. In the absence of any real promotion of environmental or labour policy concerns through the imposition of trade defence measures as such, any attempt at utilising the Union interest test to make the decision on whether to impose measures or not dependent on the level of social and environmental

---

[73] The opposite argument, namely that the non-imposition of measures would be beneficial for compliance with standards relating to the protection of workers' rights and the environment, would run counter to the mechanism of negative conditionality employed by the basic regulations, i.e. making the imposition of trade defence measures dependent upon (non-)compliance with rules on 'fair' trade. This line of argument was employed by parties in recital 228 in the *Ceramics* case, Commission Regulation (EU) No 1072/2012 of 14 November 2012 imposing a provisional anti-dumping duty on imports of ceramic tableware and kitchenware originating in the People's Republic of China. The argument was not taken up by the Commission.

[74] This must be differentiated from the form and the level of measures being dependent upon compliance with international environmental and labour law, cf. above p. 254. Likewise, the criticism put forward by Curran and Eckhardt (2020) should be recalled.

[75] In theory, the basic regulations could be reformed to make the imposition of measures dependent upon (non-)compliance with TSD standards. This would, however, constitute a fundamental change and do away with the currently existing system of the basic regulations.

protection in the country under measures cannot be based on Articles 3 (5), 21 TEU. It must thus be rejected.

8.3.2.2   No Clear Focus on the Promotion of Sustainable Development in the EU's Trading Partners in Applying the EU's Trade Defence Instruments

It should furthermore be recalled that in the instances where the EU withdraws trade preferences in response to the violation of human rights or sustainability standards, it does not do so with the primary objective of providing compensation to the EU industry. Instead, this form of sanctions is used to exert pressure on the EU's trading partners to comply with their obligations in these policy areas.[76] With regard to a reform of the functioning of the TSD chapters in the trade agreements concluded by the EU, the Commission likewise argued that a sanctions-based approach would not ensure that the TSD chapters actually would contribute to '*effective, sustainable and lasting improvement of key social and environmental standards on the ground*'.[77] Consequently, where the EU uses trade policy instruments to foreclose its market in response to the violation of human rights, labour or environmental standards, the instruments must be used in a way that focuses on improving the situation in the addressee country.[78] Although it cannot be excluded that some aspects of the EU's reformed trade defence instruments could to some extent contribute to the promotion of sustainable development in the exporting countries, this is not their primary objective. Rather, their aim is to protect the EU industry by offsetting the injury caused by 'unfair' trading practices by the exporting producers.[79] Thus, where the EU's trade defence legislation has regard to insufficient labour or environmental standards when calculating the dumping margin and when deciding upon the form of measures or the initiation of an interim review, this is not done with the primary aim of exerting pressure on the EU's trading partners to live up to their commitments under international law. Instead, the legislation is centred on delineating the circumstances under which the EU industry requires additional protection against the competitive pressure exerted by dumped or subsidised goods which were produced

---

[76]Cf. the statement made by the European Parliament already referenced on p. 251: '*The system's most effective leverage is not primarily based on the real use of sanctions, but on its strength to act as a deterrent due to the consequences of a potential loss of trade preferences. (. . .) [I]ncentives, being more effective, are preferable to sanctions.*' European Parliament, *Briefing: Human rights in EU Trade Policy – Unilateral Measures* (n 52) 8.

[77]European Commission, 'Non-paper: Feedback and way forward on improving the implementation and enforcement of Trade and Sustainable Development chapters in EU Free Trade Agreements' (Brussels 26 February 2018) 3.

[78]Furthermore, the existence of a link between the protectionist effects of a trade policy measure and the promotion of non-economic objectives is necessary so that the EU institutions can rely on Articles 3 (5), 21 TEU in adopting these measures, cf. above p. 253 et seq.

[79]Cf. above p. 256.

in disregard of international environmental and labour law standards. This emphasis on protecting the EU industry from the detrimental effects of the presence of dumped or subsidised imports, which follows from the systematics and the *telos* of the basic regulations, is another central difference to the usual justifications provided for the restriction of access to the internal market prompted by the violation of sustainable development objectives.

8.3.2.3   No Dialogue Between the EU and Its Trading Partners

With a view to promoting non-commercial objectives through its trade defence instruments, the EU adheres to a sanctions-based approach, as it responds to concerns about environmental or social standards in the exporting country by imposing higher duties, rejecting undertaking offers or initiating interim reviews. This use of sanctions without any prior attempts at resolving the issue in cooperation with the government of the exporting country stands in stark contrast to the incentives-based approach taken by the EU in the other parts of its common commercial policy. Where the EU legislation provides for the imposition of sanctions, it requires the EU institutions to enter into a dialogue with the other party before sanctions can be imposed: in trade agreements, concerns regarding compliance with the chapter on sustainable development are to be addressed through a two-step mechanism, the first step of which are consultations between the parties to the agreement. The same applies regarding possible violations of human rights committed by one of the EU's partners in trade. Here, too, consultations between the parties to the agreement have to take place before the EU can decide to terminate the agreement as the *ultima ratio*.[80] Under the GSP Regulation, the beneficiary country likewise is given the opportunity to comment on its status regarding the ratification and implementation of international conventions before the Commission can withdraw tariff preferences.[81] The Commission itself describes the EU's approach of promoting human rights and sustainable development objectives in trade relations as being

> characterised by cooperation and dialogue. Where the EU adopts unilateral measures aimed at fostering its trading partners' commitment to international conventions, it does so in an incentives-based manner.[82]

---

[80]Cf. above p. 258 et seq.

[81]Article 15 (4) lit. b), (5) and Article 19 (5), (7) of Regulation (EU) No 978/2012 of the European Parliament and of the Council of 25 October 2012 applying a scheme of generalised tariff preferences (Chap. 6, n 39).

[82]European Commission, 'Commission Staff Working Document: Midterm Evaluation of the Generalised Scheme of Preferences accompanying the document "Report from the European Commission to the European Parliament and the Council on the application of Regulation (EU) 978/2012 applying a Scheme of Generalised Tariff Preferences and repealing Council Regulation (EC) No 732/2008" (SWD(2018) 430 final)' (Chap. 4, n 104), pp. 27–28.

While the exporting producer's home government may comment on the Commission's findings during an anti-dumping or an anti-subsidy investigation,[83] this is not comparable with the spirit of inter-governmental cooperation and eye-level dialogue visible in the other instruments of the EU's trade policy intended to foster human rights or sustainable development objectives. The approach adopted in the reformed trade defence instruments must therefore be regarded as quite confrontational, lacking any elements intended to address concerns related to the adherence to environmental or labour rights standards by means of dialogue and mutual cooperation. Moreover, the fact that the findings relating to non-compliance with international labour or environmental law will immediately result in sanctions is at odds with the general policy pursued by the EU of imposing sanctions only as a means of a last resort and only to address the most flagrant violations of international law.[84]

It should further be mentioned that scholars and EU institutions alike have cautioned against unilateral attempts by the EU at promoting human rights and sustainable development objectives on the international plane. *Simoes et al.* remark that any unilateral approach may not be advisable due to its lack of consideration of the positions of trading partners, the support of which the EU needs where it intends to advocate for reforms at the bilateral, plurilateral and multilateral level.[85] In the past, the Commission has voiced similar concerns with regard to the implementation of TSD chapters, noting that close cooperation with the relevant international bodies is necessary to avoid any risk of introducing parallel labour and environmental standards and being seen as undermining the multilateral governance in these areas.[86] These considerations also apply with regard to the EU's trade defence instruments. Unilateral decisions by EU institutions whether the labour standards in another country are satisfactory or whether its level of environmental protection is adequate—as it happened in *Organic Coated Steel*[87]—risk alienating the EU's trading partners and endanger the success of the EU's efforts on a multilateral level, and ultimately also the work carried out by international organisations. The ambition to impose one's own level of environmental protection on one's trading partners is also visible in recital 12 of Regulation EU 2018/825. With regard to the initiation of interim reviews in cases of changed circumstances in exporting countries relating to social and environmental standards, the provision states that the withdrawal of a country under measures from a multilateral environmental

---

[83] Article 6 (6), (7) and Article 11 (2) subpara. 3 BADR; Article 11 (6), (7) and Article 18 (3) BASR.

[84] Cf. above p. 259, 263 et seq.

[85] Simoes and Dolle (2017), p. 484, 488.

[86] European Commission, 'Non-paper: Feedback and way forward on improving the implementation and enforcement of Trade and Sustainable Development chapters in EU Free Trade Agreements' (Brussels 26 February 2018) 4.

[87] Commission Implementing Regulation (EU) 2019/687 of 2 May 2019 imposing a definitive anti-dumping duty on imports of certain organic coated steel products originating in the People's Republic of China following an expiry review pursuant to Article 11 (2) of Regulation (EU) 2016/1036 of the European Parliament and of the Council (Chap. 7, n 39) recitals 51–52. This investigation is covered in more detail in the preceding chapter.

agreement to which the Union is a party can be taken into account. Hereby, the EU is effectively equating an adequate level of environmental protection in its trading partners with the level of environmental protection prevailing within the EU.[88]

At the same time, partly because of the confrontational nature of the basic regulations, it is far from clear whether the method chosen by the EU will induce any real policy change in its partners in trade. As analysed by *Curran/Eckhardt*,

> indicating that trading partners which do not respect [international] standards will be treated differently in trade defence cases is a rather blunt instrument in effecting real policy change in those partner countries.[89]

8.3.2.4   Difference in Standards

Another noteworthy aspect is that the modernised basic regulations do not consider the general human rights situation in the exporting country to be relevant. The only references in the basic regulations to non-economic objectives concern matters of labour rights and environmental protection. It can be assumed that the reason for their inclusion is that international conventions on these subjects are particularly relevant to the production process of goods that are later exported to the EU. Ultimately, however, the lack of consideration given to core human rights conventions would result in exporting producers receiving less favourable treatment under the EU trade defence legislation if their home government decides to withdraw, for example, from the Paris Agreement of 2015,[90] but not if the government were to commit grave violations of human rights, such as torture or capital punishment. This stands in contrast to the fundamental importance of respect for human rights in shaping EU external relations as expressed in the Treaties, which consider respect for human rights a founding value of the EU (Article 3 (5) TEU), a guiding principle (Article 21 (1) TEU) as well as an objective (Article 21 (2) lit. b) TEU).[91]

Lastly, attention should again be drawn to the fact that the list of ILO conventions considered relevant under the reformed basic regulations only comprises eight core conventions,[92] whereas the GSP Regulation provides for a withdrawal of trade preferences under all of the schemes provided for in the regulation in the event of violations of the fifteen ILO conventions referred to in Annex VIII of the GSP

---

[88] This tendency to equate an 'adequate level of protection' with the one prescribed in one's own legislation is also evident in *Organic Coated Steel*, where the Commission accepted the complainants' arguments that a lower level of environmental protection contributed to the existence of significant distortions under Article 2 (6a) BADR, cf. above p. 178 et seq.

[89] Curran and Eckhardt (2020), pp. 157–158.

[90] Paris Agreement (FCCC/CP/2015/L.9/Rev.1) (Chap. 7, n 70); cf. also above p. 185.

[91] Cf. also European Commission, 'Trade for all – Towards a more responsible trade and investment policy (COM(2015) 497)' (Chap. 4, n 103) 25 et seq.

[92] Annex Ia to the BADR and Annex Ia to the BASR.

Regulation.[93] Thus, GSP beneficiaries are held to a higher standard in the protection of workers' rights than the EU's trading partners when it comes to the imposition of trade defence instruments.

8.4   Chapter Conclusions

At the outset, it should be noted that the elements of the reformed basic regulations pertaining to the inclusion of social and environmental standards which do not foster compliance with labour and environmental standards in the exporting countries cannot be based on Articles 3 (5), 21 (1), (2) TEU. This concerns the inclusion of social and environmental aspects when selecting the appropriate representative country as well as any attempts at including the situation in the exporting country regarding labour and environmental standards when deciding on whether to impose trade defence measures during the Union interest assessment. The above-mentioned TEU provisions and the interpretation of fair trade as equitable or ethical trade cannot serve as grounds for such changes to EU trade defence law and practice since they, as mentioned, presuppose that the EU's measures are intended to foster non-economic objectives in the EU's trading partners.[94] Lacking any contribution to this effect, market foreclosure effects emanating from their inclusion cannot be counterbalanced by the global promotion of sustainable development objectives. A vague commitment to '*high social and environmental standards*' as expressed by the Commission[95] is not sufficient to justify the market foreclosure effects arising from their inclusion absent any contribution to the promotion of compliance with said standards.

The remainder of the reforms to the basic regulations relating to the promotion of sustainable development objectives may be based on Articles 3 (5), 21 (1), (2) TEU. Nevertheless, opposite to what is mandated by Article 21 (3) subpara. 2 TEU, the above analysis has revealed a significant number of divergences between the approach generally adopted by the EU in promoting non-economic objectives through its common commercial policy and the way in which these matters are integrated in the reformed basic regulations. This criticism extends to the amendments relating to the initiation of interim reviews, the rejection of undertakings and considering the level of environmental or social protection in the country of export when establishing the existence of significant distortions. The first central difference lies in the only tenuous link between compliance with international obligations on part of the exporting producer's home country and the imposition of measures under the basic regulations. While the type or the level of measures may be influenced by

---

[93] Article 19 (1) of Regulation (EU) 2012/978 of the European Parliament and of the Council of 25 October 2012 applying a scheme of generalised tariff preferences (Chap. 6, n 39).

[94] Dimopoulos (2010), p. 167.

[95] European Commission, 'Factsheet: Europe's Trade Defence Instruments' (Chap. 7, n 124) 4.

compliance with international standards, this is not the case for the imposition of measures themselves. Furthermore, the basic regulations do not always communicate the connection between a sufficient level of social and environmental protection and the degree of market access awarded to the dumped or subsidised products clearly. In addition, as can also be taken from the above, the reformed basic regulations do not place a focus on promoting sustainable development among the EU's partners in trade. Instead, the imposition of measures under the basic regulations continues to be primarily targeted at neutralising the injury caused to the EU industry by the presence of dumped or subsidised imports on the internal market.

A second difference is the confrontational nature of the reformed basic regulations, as they do not foresee any inter-governmental dialogue intended to improve TSD compliance by means of cooperation and dialogue. As detailed above, this risks alienating the EU's trading partners and potentially undermines the EU's efforts at addressing these issues through multilateral solutions.

Third, the lack of relevance attached to the general human rights situation in the exporting country contradicts the central importance attributed to them by the Treaties, Articles 3 (5), 21 (1), (2) lit. b) TEU.

Finally, it is acknowledged that the EU institutions enjoy a wide margin of discretion in balancing the competing objectives of avoiding market foreclosure effects emanating from the imposition of trade defence measures and the EU's trade defence legislation being used to foster sustainable development objectives. Nonetheless, the efficiency of these amendments to the basic regulations in terms of actually promoting compliance with international environmental and labour standards must be questioned as a whole. The main reasons for this lie in the confrontational nature of the reformed provisions of the basic regulations and the limited incentives they offer to the EU's trading partners to change their national policies. Therefore, the inclusion of social and environmental standards in the basic regulation might do more harm than good, especially in view of the higher degree of market foreclosure emanating from the application of the reformed provisions.

Moreover, even if one were to assume that it constitutes a legitimate objective of the EU's trade defence instruments to protect the EU industry against social and environmental dumping,[96] the amendments cannot effectively contribute to the attainment of this objective, as the standards referred to in the basic regulations (in particular with regard to the protection of workers' rights) are significantly lower than the level of protection prevailing within the EU.[97] In order to promote compliance with international standards in an efficient manner and to protect the EU industry against price competition arising from the presence of imports that were

---

[96] A standpoint which must be rejected, cf. above p. 255.

[97] For example, several EU Member States have ratified more than 100 ILO Conventions. Spain, the country with the highest number of ratifications, has ratified 133 ILO conventions. Even Estonia, the country with the lowest ratification record, has ratified 39, International Labour Organization, 'Ratifications by Country', available at <https://www.ilo.org/dyn/normlex/en/f?p=NORMLEXPUB:11001:0::NO:::>. By contrast, the reformed basic regulations only require compliance with eight core ILO conventions.

produced in violation of international labour or environmental standards, a more fundamental retooling of the EU's trade defence instruments would be needed.[98] This, however, would still risk alienating the EU's trading partners and undermining the EU's efforts at the multilateral level as set out above.

References[99]

Bartels L (2013) Human rights and sustainable development obligations in EU Free Trade Agreements. Legal Issues Econ Integr 40(4):297

Bartels L (2015) Human rights and sustainable development obligations. In: Wouters J et al (eds) Global governance through trade – EU policies and approaches. Edward Elgar Publishing Ltd

Borchert I et al (2018) Trade Conditionality in the EU and WTO legal regimes. Respect Working Papers (December 2018), available at <http://respect.eui.eu/wp-content/uploads/sites/6/2019/02/EU_conditionality_D2.2.pdf>

Bungenberg M (2014) Autonome Handelspolitik. In: von Arnauld A (ed) Europäische Außenbeziehungen. Nomos, Baden-Baden

Bungenberg M (2015) Umweltschutz als Thema der unionalen Gemeinsamen Handelspolitik. In: Nowak C (ed) Konsolidierung und Entwicklungsperspektiven des Europäischen Umweltrechts. Nomos

Cremer W (2016) Art. 21 EUV. In: Calliess C, Ruffert M (eds) Das Verfassungsrecht der Europäischen Union mit Europäischer Grundrechtecharta (EUV/AEUV), 5th edn. C.H. Beck

Cremona M (2008) Coherence through Law: what difference will the Treaty of Lisbon make? Hamburg Rev Soc Sci 3(1):11

Curran L, Eckhardt J (2020) EU Trade Policy in a trade-sceptic context. In: Weiß W, Furculita C (eds) Global politics and EU trade policy: facing the challenges to a multilateral approach. Springer

Dimopoulos A (2010) The effects of the Lisbon Treaty on the principles and objectives of the common commercial policy. Eur Foreign Aff Rev 15(2):153

Donno D, Neureiter M (2018) Can human rights conditionality reduce repression? Examining the European Union's economic agreements. Rev Int Organ 13(3):335

Eeckhout P (2012) EU external relations law, 2nd edn. Oxford University Press

Gruni G (2018) Towards a sustainable world trade law? The commercial policy of the European Union after Opinion 2/15. Global Trade Cust J 13(1):4

Harrison J and others (2019) Labour standards provisions in EU Free Trade Agreements: reflections on the European Commission's reform Agenda. World Trade Rev 18(4):635

Kasteng J (2013) Targeting the environment: exploring a new trade in the EU's trade defence investigations. Available at <https://papers.ssrn.com/sol3/papers.cfm?abstract_id=2310564>

Marx A and others (2015) Global governance through trade: an introduction. In: Wouters J and others (eds) Global governance through trade – EU policies and approaches. Edward Elgar Publishing Ltd

Marx A, Soares J (2015) Does integrating labour provisions in free trade agreements make a difference? An exploratory analysis of freedom of association and collective bargaining rights in 13 EU trade partners. In: Wouters J, and others (eds) Global governance through trade – EU policies and approaches. Edward Elgar Publishing Ltd

---

[98] On this cf. Shaffer (2019), p. 1, 33 et seq. The WTO compatibility of such an approach would, however, be questionable.

[99] All online sources were last accessed on 8 September 2021.

Shaffer G (2019) Retooling trade agreements for social inclusion. Ill Law Rev 1
Simoes B, Dolle T (2017) How to properly account for sustainable production. Global Trade Cust J 12(11):484
Vedder C (2013) Linkage of the common commercial policy to the general objectives for the Union's external action. In: Bungenberg M, Herrmann C (eds) Common commercial policy after Lisbon. Springer, Hiedelberg
Weiß W (2014) Vertragliche Handelspolitik der EU. In: von Arnauld A (ed) Europäische Außenbeziehungen. Nomos

Chapter 9
Compatibility of the Reformed Basic Regulations with WTO Law

9.1 Introduction

It has already been mentioned that, since the EU is a member to the WTO, its trade defence instruments have to be WTO compliant.[1] Consequently, also its reformed trade defence instruments have to conform to the obligations stemming from WTO law. The compatibility of the basic regulations with WTO law is not the central issue of this thesis and it would go beyond the scope of this chapter—and this work—to examine the criticism directed against the two regulations in detail. Nonetheless, given the paramount importance of WTO law regarding the design and application of the EU's trade defence instruments, the following chapter will again be dedicated to examining the amendments addressed above—however this time with a focus on their compatibility with WTO law. Here, the obligations assumed under the ADA, the ASCM and the GATT 1994 are of central importance.

Before embarking upon a more detailed analysis of the reformed basic regulations, it is worth noting already at the outset of this section that trade law experts such as *Van Bael/Bellis* consider it '*highly unlikely that the new rules could survive WTO dispute settlement proceedings*'[2]—and with good reasons, it appears.

---

[1] Herrmann et al. (2007) para. 130; cf. also above p. 89 et seq.
[2] van Bael and Bellis (2019) § 3.11 [F].

© The Author(s), under exclusive license to Springer Nature Switzerland AG 2022
P. Trapp, *The European Union's Trade Defence Modernisation Package*, EYIEL
Monographs - Studies in European and International Economic Law 23,
https://doi.org/10.1007/978-3-030-91363-2_9

9.2   Issues Relating to the New Non-Standard Methodology for Constructing Normal Value in Anti-Dumping Investigations

9.2.1   Dumping Margin Calculation

When examining the WTO compatibility of the price comparison methodologies contained in the BADR, two separate sets of issues have to be distinguished from each other. First, even though the deadline set out in Article 15 lit. d) of the Chinese Accession Protocol to the WTO[3] elapsed in December 2016 and with it arguably the possibility of applying the analogue country method contained in the old Article 2 (7) BADR,[4] the new methodology as introduced by Regulation (EU) 2017/2321 did not enter into force until December 2017. Unsurprisingly, China initiated proceedings against the EU's continued application of the old analogue country methodology before the WTO DSB.[5] The second question is whether the new methodology now contained in Article 2 (6a) BADR conforms to WTO law. The request for consultations the Chinese authorities sent to the Chairperson of the DSB encompassed both aspects.[6] Even though proceedings before the DSB were suspended in May 2019, the compliance of the new methodology with WTO law remains highly contested, with a number of scholars disputing its compatibility with the WTO legal order.

9.2.1.1   Rejection of Domestic Prices Pursuant to Article 2.2 ADA

To begin with, it is argued that the rejection of an exporting producer's prices or costs due to a finding of country-wide or sector wide distortions—as it is the case under the new methodology—stands in contrast to the concept of 'dumping', which concerns the pricing behaviour of individual exporting producers.[7] Furthermore, Article 2.2 ADA contains an exhaustive list[8] of circumstances under which the normal value of a product is not to be determined on the basis of the prices paid or

---

[3] World Trade Organization, 'Accession of the People's Republic of China (WT/L/432)' (Chap. 3, n 164).

[4] On this cf. e.g. Tietje and Sacher (2018), pp. 90–93; Zhou and Peng (2018), p. 505; Herrmann and Müller (2017), p. 500; Suse (2017), pp. 951, 956–963; Vermulst et al. (2016), p. 212.

[5] European Union – Measures Related to Price Comparison Methodologies (2016) WT/DS516 (proceedings were suspended in June 2019; accordingly, the authority for the establishment of the panel lapsed in June 2020).

[6] European Union – Measures Related to Price Comparison Methodologies: Request for Consultations by China (WT/DS516/1 – G/L/1170 – G/ADP/D116/1) (2016) WT/DS516.

[7] European Union – Anti-Dumping Measures on Certain Footwear from China (Chap. 7, n 98) para. 7.88.

[8] Vermulst and Dion Sud (2018), p. 79.

payable in the exporter's home country. These include the absence of sales of the like product in the ordinary course of trade or the existence of a particular market situation, which does not permit a proper comparison to be made between domestic and the export prices, in the domestic market of the exporting country.

It has been argued that the 'significant distortions'-criterion of Article 2 (6a) BADR cannot be subsumed under any of the situations included in Article 2.2 ADA. There seems to be little debate that the circumstances described in Article 2 (6a) BADR do not suggest that a sale is not conducted 'in the ordinary course of trade' within the meaning of Article 2.2 ADA.[9]

Neither can Article 2 (6a) BADR be reconciled with the conditions under which a particular market situation, which does not permit a proper comparison to be made between domestic and export prices, can be assumed to exist.[10] In *Australia—A4 Copy Paper,* the Panel found that the 'existence of a particular market situation' is to be read separately from the question whether this particular market situation precludes a proper comparison between the domestic price and the export price.[11] According to the Panel, State-induced distortions to the economy might justify a finding of the existence of what is considered a 'particular market situation' within the sense of Article 2.2. ADA.[12] The mere existence of such distortions however does not enable the investigating authority to reject domestic costs in the dumping margin calculation. Instead, it still has to conduct a separate assessment whether the cost distortions arising from a 'particular market situation' would in fact make a comparison between the domestic and the export price misleading.[13] At this point, regard should be had to the emphasis the Panel placed on the 'proper comparison'-criterion. The focus on the issue of whether the State measures preclude a proper comparison between domestic and export prices seems to suggest that the Panel adopted an *'approach of even-handedness'*:[14] only if the situation concerned does not affect the domestic and the export price to the same extent, then the comparability of the domestic price would be impacted, which therefore must not be used for the determination of dumping margins. Conversely, where the State measures in question equally affect domestic and export prices, a proper comparison between the two prices is still possible.[15]

Article 2 (6a) BADR and the criteria upon which the Commission may base its findings regarding the existence of significant distortions do not make such a distinction. For example, a finding of significant distortions may be based on

---

[9]Tietje and Sacher (2018), pp. 97–98; Vermulst and Dion Sud (2018), p. 79.

[10]Huyghebaert (2019), p. 425; Vermulst and Dion Sud (2018), p. 78.

[11]*Australia – Anti-Dumping Measures on A4 Copy Paper* (4 December 2019) WT/DS529/R para. 7.27 (Panel Report).

[12]Ibid paras. 7.53–7.57.

[13]Ibid paras. 7.86–7.89.

[14]Zhou and Peng (2021), pp. 94, 99.

[15]Ibid. Cf. already to this respect Zhou and Percival (2016), p. 863, 869, 881 et seq.

distorted wage costs.[16] However, wage costs will usually be identical for products destined for the domestic market and for the like products designed for the export market. Even where they are distorted, this will not affect price comparability.[17] In line with the Panel's findings in *Australia—A4 Copy Paper*, while it cannot be excluded that distorted wage costs might enable an investigating authority to arrive at a finding regarding the existence of a particular market situation within the sense of Article 2.2 ADA, it is more than unlikely that these distortions to wage costs preclude a proper comparison between the domestic price and the export price.[18] The same reasoning applies with regard to the lack, discriminatory application or inadequate enforcement of bankruptcy, corporate or property laws.[19] It is not apparent why a company being able to acquire land for its production site at prices below market value[20] would affect domestic and export prices to a different extent.[21] Consequently, at least some of the State measures listed in Article 2 (6a) BADR are not of such a nature as to allow the conclusion that their existence does not permit a proper comparison between domestic and export costs. For identical reasons, an insufficient level of environmental protection prevailing in the country of export[22] may not be used to discard domestic prices under Article 2.2 ADA.

9.2.1.2   Calculation of Normal Value Pursuant to Article 2.2.1.1 ADA

Even if some of the factors listed in Article 2 (6a) lit. b) BADR would permit the Commission to disregard domestic prices in calculating the dumping margin, a series of recent rulings in WTO disputes casts further doubt on the WTO compatibility of the methodology for computing normal value under Article 2 (6a) BADR.

Pursuant to Article 2.2.1.1 ADA, when constructing the normal value, this shall normally be done on the basis of the records kept by the exporter or producer under investigation. The investigating authorities may only use other sources if the records

---

[16] Article 2 (6a) lit. b) BADR, fifth indent.

[17] Huyghebaert (2019), p. 425.

[18] Specifically with regard to decreased cost for an input *Australia – Anti-Dumping Measures on A4 Copy Paper* (n 11) paras. 7.90–7.91.

[19] Article 2 (6a) lit. b) BADR, fourth indent.

[20] Cf. Commission Implementing Regulation (EU) 2019/1267 of 26 July 2019 imposing a definitive anti-dumping duty on imports of tungsten electrodes originating in the People's Republic of China following an expiry review under Article 11(2) of Regulation (EU) 2016/1036 (Chap. 6, n 93) recital 75; European Commission, 'Commission Staff Working Document on Significant Distortions in the Economy of the People's Republic of China for the Purposes of Trade Defence Investigations (SWD(2017) 483 final/2)' (Chap. 7, n 21) 210, 213–215.

[21] Huyghebaert (2019), p. 425.

[22] Cf. recital 4 of Regulation (EU) 2017/2321 (Chap. 1, n 9): '*When assessing the existence of significant distortions, relevant international standards, including core conventions of the International Labour Organisation (ILO) and relevant multilateral environmental conventions, should be taken into account, where appropriate.*'

are not in accordance with generally accepted accounting principles or do not reasonably reflect the costs incurred when producing and selling the product.

According to the Appellate Body in *European Union—Biodiesel (Argentina)* on the interpretation of Article 2.2.1.1 ADA, as long as the exporters' records are accurate and as long as they reflect the costs incurred in producing and selling the product under consideration, it does not matter whether these costs were distorted e.g. by the tax system in the exporters' home country.[23] The object of the comparison should be whether the records reasonably reflect the actual costs incurred by the producers, not costs that investigating authorities consider to be more reasonable under a different set of conditions or circumstances.[24] This view was reiterated by the Appellate Body in *Ukraine—Ammonium Nitrate*, where it held that there is no standard of reasonableness that governs the meaning of costs under Article 2.2.1.1 ADA which would allow the investigating authorities to disregard domestic input prices.[25] The Panel in *European Union—Cost Adjustment Methodologies (Russia)* followed an identical approach in its interpretation of Article 2.2.1.1 ADA.[26] These rulings do not sit well with Article 2 (6a) lit. a) BADR, which mandates the automatic rejection of the actual production costs of investigated exporting producers where the Commission concludes that significant distortions exist.[27]

Furthermore, the Appellate Body in *European Union—Biodiesel (Argentina)* held that, when constructing normal value based on out-of-country-information, an investigating authority cannot simply substitute producers' costs by reference to international prices or other information. Instead, these sources must be used in order to arrive at the cost of production in the country of origin.[28] Consequently, an investigation authority needs to 'adapt' any collected information from external sources.[29] The Panel's findings in *European Union—Cost Adjustment Methodologies (Russia)* affirm this. Even though the Panel report does not address the compatibility of the new methodology with WTO law,[30] it nonetheless clarifies that where an investigating authority uses out-of-country costs in establishing normal value, it must provide a

---

[23] *European Union – Anti-Dumping Measures on Biodiesel from Argentina* (6 October 2016) WT/DS473/AB/R para. 6.30 (Appellate Body Report).

[24] Wüstenberg (2019), p. 407, 413. Suse puts it his way: '*[I]t is the reflection of the costs that must be reasonable and not the costs themselves*', Suse (2017), p. 971.

[25] *Ukraine – Anti-Dumping Measures on Ammonium Nitrate* (12 September 2019) WT/DS493/AB/R para. 6.88 (Appellate Body Report).

[26] *European Union – Cost Adjustment Methodologies and Certain Anti-Dumping Measures on Imports from Russia (second complaint)* (24 July 2020) WT/DS494/R para. 7.102 (Panel Report).

[27] On the *European Union – Biodiesel* decision cf. Vermulst and Dion Sud (2018), p. 81; also noted by Antonini (2018), p. 79, 91 and by Furculita (2017), p. 360, 365.

[28] *European Union – Anti-Dumping Measures on Biodiesel from Argentina* (n 23) para. 6.73.

[29] Tietje and Sacher (2018), p. 101; Suse (2017), p. 973.

[30] *European Union – Cost Adjustment Methodologies and Certain Anti-Dumping Measures on Imports from Russia (second complaint)* (n 26) paras. 7.79–7.81.

reasoned and adequate explanation of how the information used in its calculations was adapted to ensure that it represented the cost of production in the country of origin.[31]

Consequently, the Panel emphasised that the alternative sources used in constructing normal value need to be reflective of the costs in the country of origin. These findings of the Appellate Body and the Panel respectively appear to be another point where Article 2 (6a) BADR is in conflict with the requirements of the ADA, as the provision provides for the construction of normal value on the basis of international benchmarks or third country costs in Article 2 (6a) lit. a) BADR. However, these certainly do not represent costs in the country of origin.[32]

At this point, it should be disclosed that the Panel in *Australia—A4 Copy Paper* followed a different approach, both with regard to the circumstances under which an investigating authority may disregard the producer's costs, and the alternative sources used in constructing normal value. First, the Panel argued that the term 'normally' in Article 2.2.1.1 ADA may provide some flexibility to investigating authorities in determining whether the costs contained in the producer's records are 'reasonable', and to replace them if they find that they are distorted, even if the two conditions set out in Article 2.2.1.1 ADA are fulfilled.[33] Such an interpretation of Article 2.2.1.1 ADA creates significant caveats for the use of surrogate costs where government-induced price distortions are present. It further deviates from the spirit of the Appellate Body's findings in *European Union—Biodiesel (Argentina)* and the Panel's findings in *European Union—Cost Adjustment Methodologies (Russia)*, where the adjudicative bodies' reasoning expressed the desire to limit such flexibility on part of the investigating authorities.[34] As concerns the sources used in constructing normal value, both the Panel report in *European Union—Cost Adjustment Methodologies (Russia)* and the Appellate Body report in *European Union—Biodiesel (Argentina)* clearly require the investigating authorities to adapt, where necessary, out-of-country sources to arrive at the cost of production in the country of origin. Here, too, the Panel's reasoning in *Australia—A4 Copy Paper* points in a different direction, holding that Article 2.2 ADA only requires investigating authorities

to consider available alternatives for replacing recorded costs as to use the costs that are unaffected by the distortion to the extent possible.[35]

Hereby, the Panel appears to limit the required adjustments to benchmarks to those components of the producer's costs that are not affected by government-

---

[31] Ibid paras. 7.129, 7.131.

[32] It is precisely for this reason that these alternative benchmarks are chosen, cf. Wüstenberg (2019), p. 414; Vermulst and Dion Sud (2018), p. 81; Suse (2017), p. 973.

[33] *Australia – Anti-Dumping Measures on A4 Copy Paper* (n 11) paras. 7.110–7.117.

[34] On the Panel's findings in *European Union – Biodiesel* cf. Zhou and Peng, 'Australia – Anti-Dumping Measures on A4 Copy Paper' (n 14) 99; cf. also the Panel's findings in *European Union – Cost Adjustment Methodologies and Certain Anti-Dumping Measures on Imports from Russia (second complaint)* (n 26) paras. 7.103–7.106.

[35] *Australia – Anti-Dumping Measures on A4 Copy Paper* (n 11) para. 7.162.

caused distortions.[36] By contrast, the *European Union—Biodiesel (Argentina)* report required such adjustments to include all conditions in the exporter's home market, including State-induced distortions.[37] In times of a dysfunctional Appellate Body it cannot be expected that the question of the correct interpretation of the provisions of the ADA will be resolved in the immediate future. Nonetheless, all three reports leave the WTO compatibility of the new methodology in doubt.

9.2.2 The EU's Contentious Approach to 'Input Dumping'

Additionally, parts of the amendments to the BADR raise questions concerning the EU's approach towards what is commonly referred to as 'input dumping'. This notion describes a situation where it is not the final product that is being dumped on export markets, but rather an input to that final product—such as raw materials, including energy—which is later being sold in the domestic market or international market.[38] Neither the GATT 1994 nor the ADA or the ASCM contain provisions that would curtail the members' right to input dumping, and the WTO members never reached a consensus on how to deal with this topic.[39] In the past, the WTO adjudicative organs have proven reluctant in permitting the members to address situations of input dumping through the imposition of anti-dumping or anti-subsidy measures. Already in *United States—Softwood Lumber IV*, the Appellate Body held that

> [w]here the producer of the input is not the same entity as the producer of the processed product, it cannot be presumed that the subsidy bestowed on the input passes through on the processed product. In such case, it is necessary to analyse to what extent subsidies on inputs may be included in the determination of the total amount of subsidies bestowed upon the processed products.[40]

Against this backdrop, the WTO compatibility of the BADR provisions on significant distortions in Article 2 (6a) BADR and on the (non-)application of the lesser duty rule in cases of raw material distortions pursuant to Article 7 (2a) BADR is unclear. Both situations—significant distortions and raw material distortions—address situations of input dumping as described above. Recent WTO jurisprudence has failed to provide clarity as regards members' options for addressing situations of input subsidisation in their anti-dumping legislation. While the Panel report in *Australia—A4 Copy Paper* contends that subsidisation by the State for input

---

[36] Zhou and Peng (2021), p. 100.

[37] Ibid.

[38] Bierwagen and Hailbronner (1988), p. 27, 29.

[39] Tietje et al. (2011), pp. 1071, 1090–1091.

[40] *United States – Final Countervailing Duty Determination with respect to certain Softwood Lumber from Canada (Softwood Lumber IV)* (19 January 2004) WT/DS257/AB/R 140 (Appellate Body Report).

materials may be addressed under Article 2.2 ADA as constituting a 'particular market situation',[41] so far, this constitutes a singular judgment. Conversely, members' options for discarding the producers' costs under Article 2.2.1.1 ADA because of input subsidisation by their home State appear to remain limited in light of the reports in *European Union—Biodiesel (Argentina)* and *European Union—Cost Adjustment Methodologies (Russia)*. It is thus unclear whether the EU's approach taking into account input dumping in calculating the dumping margin is permissible under the provisions of the ADA. Further, when deciding whether the lesser duty rule applies, the existence of raw material distortions such as dual pricing schemes or export taxes plays a decisive role.[42] As the application of the lesser duty rule is only discretionary under WTO law,[43] these amendments are unlikely to be challenged successfully under the ADA.[44] Yet, the conclusion remains that there are numerous uncertainties surrounding the legality of tackling the issue of input dumping under the framework of the ADA and the GATT 1994.

The Commission's practice in *Urea and Ammonium Nitrate* points at further issues related to the EU's approach towards input dumping under the reformed BADR. In determining whether Article 7 (2a) BADR was applicable to the situation at hand, the Commission had recourse to its findings in establishing normal value.[45] Here, the Commission had disregarded the costs contained in the exporting producer's records pursuant to Article 2 (5) BADR, as it did not consider them reflective of the costs associated with the production and sale of the product under consideration due to State-induced distortions regarding prices for natural gas, a key raw material in producing the product under investigation.[46] As just noted, this approach possibly conflicts with the judgments handed down in *European Union—Biodiesel (Argentina)* and *European Union—Cost Adjustment Methodologies (Russia)*, where the WTO adjudicative bodies held that the object of the comparison should be whether the records reasonably reflect the actual costs incurred by the producers, not costs that investigating authorities consider to be more reasonable under a different set of conditions or circumstances. While the cases concerned the determination of dumping, and not the issue of raw material distortions, this could

---

[41] *Australia – Anti-Dumping Measures on A4 Copy Paper* (n 11) paras. 7.29–7.32.

[42] Cf. Article 7 (2a) BADR.

[43] *European Union – Anti-Dumping Measures on Certain Footwear from China* (Chap. 7, n 98) para. 7.924; *United States – Anti-Dumping and Countervailing Measures on Steel Plate from India* (Chap. 7, n 98) para. 7.116.

[44] Authors have nonetheless remarked that this practice constitutes a *de facto* sanctioning of the countries in which such raw material distortions are found to exist, possibly conflicting with the general non-discrimination rules of the GATT 1994, cf. Wüstenberg (2019), p. 414. On the question of whether a measure that has been found to comply with the ADA or the ASCM may nonetheless be challenged under Article I:1 GATT 1994 cf. below p. 286 et seq.

[45] Commission Implementing Regulation (EU) 2019/576 of 10 April 2019 imposing a provisional anti-dumping duty on imports of mixtures of urea and ammonium nitrate originating in Russia, Trinidad and Tobago and the United States of America (Chap. 7, n 127) recital 210.

[46] Ibid recitals 52–58.

nonetheless result in the rather awkward situation that the exporting producer's records could not be discarded as not being reflective of the actual costs incurred when calculating the normal value, but when establishing whether the 17%-threshold has been met under Article 7 (2a) BADR.

Given the uncertainties surrounding the issue of input dumping in anti-dumping investigations, some scholars hold that the matter should preferably be addressed over the ASCM, in particular in the case of dual pricing or taxation schemes such as the one in the *European Union—Biodiesel (Argentina)* case.[47] However, in light of the Appellate Body's jurisprudence in *United States—Softwood Lumber IV*, it is far from clear whether the issue would be caught by the ASCM either.

9.2.3   The Issue of 'Double Counting'

While the ADA and the ASCM deem the application of the lesser duty rule desirable,[48] a member is not obliged to have the possibility of a lesser duty in its domestic legislation.[49] The EU has nonetheless chosen to incorporate the rule in its trade defence instruments, with its application preventing that the duty imposed goes beyond what is necessary to remove the injury caused by the dumped imports.[50] Due to the optional character of the rule under WTO law, the EU enjoys a wide margin of discretion regarding the modalities of application of the lesser duty rule.[51] Regulation (EU) 2018/825 has introduced significant changes in this regard, as it removes the mandatory application of the lesser duty rule in the case of all anti-subsidy investigations[52] as well as in the case of anti-dumping investigations where raw material distortions are found to exist.[53]

Despite the discretion enjoyed by the EU in deciding on whether or not to apply the lesser duty rule, the reformed basic regulations raise the issue of what is referred to as 'double remedies' or 'double counting'. In *United States—Anti-Dumping and Countervailing Duties (China)*, the Appellate Body defined 'double remedies' as a situation where the simultaneous application of anti-dumping and countervailing duties on the same imported products results, at least to some extent, in the offsetting

---

[47] Furculita (2017), p. 362.

[48] Article 9.1 ADA and Article 19.2 ASCM. For this reason, the 'lesser duty rule' sometimes is referred to as being a 'WTO plus'-feature of the EU trade defense regime, cf. e.g. Luo (2010), p. 127.

[49] *European Union – Anti-Dumping Measures on Certain Footwear from China* (Chap. 7, n 98) para. 7.924; *United States – Anti-Dumping and Countervailing Measures on Steel Plate from India* (Chap. 7, n 98) para. 7.116.

[50] *Crown Equipment (Suzhou) Co. Ltd. and Crown Gabelstapler GmbH & Co. KG v Council* (Chap. 3, n 141) 49.

[51] Vermulst (2005), pp. 171–172.

[52] Article 12 (1) subparas. 3, 4 BASR.

[53] Article 7 (2b) BADR.

of the same subsidisation twice.[54] This practice was found to be inconsistent with WTO law.[55] The WTO judicial organs held that 'double remedies' are likely to occur in cases where the products concerned originate in a non-market economy, because a dumping margin calculated under a non-market economy methodology reflects not only the price discrimination by the investigated producer between the domestic and export markets, but also economic distortions affecting the producer's costs of production, including subsidies. An anti-dumping duty calculated by using a non-market economy methodology may therefore remedy the existence of domestic subsidies to a certain extent.[56] The Appellate Body further noted explicitly that the issue is not restricted to dumping margin calculations concerning non-market economies, but that it may also arise in the context of domestic subsidies granted within market economies when anti-dumping and countervailing duties are concurrently imposed on the same products and an unsubsidised, constructed or third country normal value is used in the anti-dumping investigation.[57]

Under the modernised BADR and BASR, the issue of 'double remedies' arises from multiple angles. For one, in the event of parallel anti-dumping and anti-subsidy investigations, the existence of significant distortions on account of subsidisation would lead to the subsidisation to be taken into account twice, namely when establishing the existence of significant distortions under Article 2 (6a) BADR,[58] and again in calculating the subsidy margin.[59] As noted by the Appellate Body, the use of constructed normal values in determining the dumping margin and the concurrent imposition of countervailing duties too might constitute a situation where the issue of double remedies arises. Just as it is the case for the use of the non-market economy methodology, the use of international benchmarks or representative country data under the new methodology will not only address the price discrimination between the exporter's home market and the exporting market, but equally the alleged subsidies that contributed to lowering the producer's cost of production.[60]

In the past, the EU avoided the issue of 'double remedies' by applying the lesser duty rule, ensuring that the duties did not exceed the injury margin and thereby

---

[54] *United States – Definitive Anti-Dumping and Countervailing Duties on Certain Products from China* (11 March 2011) WT/DS379/AB/R para. 541 (Appellate Body Report). The Appellate Body further clarified that this issue is not confined to non-market economies, para. 543.

[55] *United States – Definitive Anti-Dumping and Countervailing Duties on Certain Products from China* (n 54) para. 583.

[56] Ibid paras. 541–543.

[57] Ibid para. 543.

[58] Leading to the use of a constructed normal value, which consequently results in a higher dumping margin.

[59] Vermulst and Dion Sud (2018), p. 85.

[60] Ibid.

preventing the same subsidisation from being addressed twice.[61] Consequently, the abolition of the lesser duty rule under the new BASR and its optional use under the reformed BADR in the event of raw material distortions create potential conflicts with the prohibition of 'double remedies' as established by the Appellate Body ruling in *US—Anti-Dumping and Countervailing Duties (China)*. In those instances, the lesser duty rule will no longer serve as a limiting factor, preventing the duty level to go beyond what is necessary to offset the injury suffered by the EU industry. The Commission has taken note of this issue: in *Glass Fibre Fabrics*, the Commission chose to deduct the full amount of the countervailing duty from the dumping rate. Thereby, it avoided the same subsidisation being taken into account during the anti-dumping investigation (through the application of the new methodology) and the anti-subsidy investigation, despite the lesser duty rule not applying in the latter investigation.[62]

A situation of 'double remedies' further has to be avoided in cases where anti-dumping duties are already in place, the margin of which was calculated in application of the old Article 2 (7) BADR. If a countervailing investigation against the same product and same country is initiated under the reformed BASR at a later point in time, the lesser duty rule will usually not be applicable.[63] This too runs the risk of offsetting the same subsidisation twice, once through the anti-subsidy duty and once through the anti-dumping duty based on the old non-market economy methodology.[64]

9.3   Issues Relating to the Inclusion of Social and Environmental Standards

Moreover, the WTO compatibility of the amendments to the basic regulations relating to the inclusion of social and environmental concerns must be discussed. At the outset, it is expedient to remark that the GATT 1994 signatories agreed that neither Article VI GATT 1994 nor the ADA cover exchange dumping, social

---

[61] Cornelis (2018), 541; Furculita (2017), p. 365. Vermulst and Dion Sud (2020), p. 240 argue, however, that the lesser duty rule does not resolve the issue entirely, because already the use of an alternative anti-dumping methodology inflates the injury margin.

[62] Commission Implementing Regulation (EU) 2020/776 of 12 June 2020 imposing definitive countervailing duties on imports of certain woven and/or stitched glass fibre fabrics originating in the People's Republic of China and Egypt and amending Commission Implementing Regulation (EU) 2020/492 imposing definitive anti-dumping duties on imports of certain woven and/or stitched glass fibre fabrics originating in the People's Republic of China and Egypt (Chap. 7, n 44) recitals 1117–1118, 1122, 1136 and Article 2.

[63] Article 12 (1) subparas. 3, 4 BASR and Article 15 (1) subparas. 3, 4 BASR.

[64] Cornelis (2018), p. 542. In addition, Cornelis notes what he calls the danger of an *'uneven'* application of the lesser duty rule, as it might not be applied in anti-subsidy proceedings relating to a certain product, but in parallel anti-dumping proceedings, Cornelis (2018), p. 541.

dumping, environmental dumping or freight dumping.[65] Consequently, Article VI GATT 1994 and the ADA only authorise members to take action against the exports of producers that practice dumping as a form of international price discrimination by selling at a lower price abroad than in their respective home markets.[66] It must thus be assessed whether, despite WTO law not permitting action against environmental or social dumping, a WTO member may take into account aspects of social and environmental protection in its anti-dumping legislation.[67] Similarly, the amendments to the BASR incorporating aspects of social and environmental protection must be examined with a view to their compatibility with WTO law.

9.3.1   Compatibility with the Anti-dumping-Agreement

In application of the principle of *lex specialis* as recalled by the Appellate Body in *European Communities—Bananas III*, when applying a body of norms to a given situation, one should evaluate that situation under the norm which most specifically addresses it.[68] Consequently, when assessing whether a WTO member's anti-dumping legislation or the application thereof conforms to WTO law, it is first to be determined whether it complies with the provisions of the ADA.[69]

The issues relating to the WTO compatibility of the new methodology of Article 2 (6a) BADR, also with regard to the incorporation of aspects of social and environmental protection, have already been presented. Accordingly, reference is made to the above observations.[70]

Given that the Union interest test is what is commonly referred to as a 'WTO plus'-obligation,[71] changes to its conceptualisation or application cannot be objected to under the Anti-Dumping Agreement. For similar reasons, challenges to the

---

[65] Adamantopoulos (2008) para. 4, citing Preparatory Committee of the International Conference on Trade and Employment, 'Summary Record of Technical Sub-Committee: U.N. Doc. E/PC/T/C.II/ 48' (11 November 1946).

[66] Vermulst (2005), p. 1.

[67] On the 'trade and environment' intersection in general cf. Espa (2019), p. 979; Krämer-Hoppe (2019); Mavroidis (2015).

[68] *European Communities – Regime for the Importation, Sale and Distribution of Bananas* (9 September 1997) WT/DS27/AB/R para. 204 (Appellate Body Report), confirmed *inter alia* in *United States – Anti-Dumping Act of 1916 (European Communities)* (31 March 2000) WT/DS136/ R para. 6.76 (Panel Report).

[69] Mavroidis (2016), p. 75.

[70] It should be recalled that including the level of social and environmental protection in selecting the appropriate representative country is not objectionable under the ADA *per se*, but for the lack of adaption of these out-of-country costs to arrive at the costs in the country of origin required by Article 2 (6a) lit. a) BADR. Similarly, it is unclear why a lack of social or environmental protection should enable the investigating authority to conclude that a proper comparison between domestic and export prices is not possible, cf. above p. 276 et seq.

[71] Cf. above p. 226 et seq.

methodology adopted by the EU in calculating the injury margin when applying the lesser duty rule are unlikely to succeed.[72] As noted by *Vermulst*,

> [t]hus far, the calculation of injury margins has not given rise to WTO litigation. This is probably not surprising as Article 9.1 ADA leaves the authorities complete discretion.[73]

While a patently incorrect or arbitrary application of the lesser duty rule might be in conflict with Article 17.6 lit. i) ADA,[74] it is unlikely that the modified criteria relating to the calculation of the injury margin would result in the EU's application of the lesser duty rule to successfully be challenged under Article 17.6 lit. i) ADA.

This leaves the modifications to the BADR relating to the rejection of undertakings for reasons of general policy, which comprise in particular the principles and obligations set out in multilateral environmental agreements and protocols thereunder, and of certain ILO conventions, for closer examination. Article 8.3 ADA holds that the investigating authorities may reject undertakings for reasons of general policy. As stated by the Panel in *United States—Offset Act (Byrd Amendment)*, the members' investigating authorities enjoy a significant amount of discretion in deciding whether to accept or reject price undertakings. Thus, an investigating authority is not required to examine a proposed price undertaking in an objective manner.[75] Given the nearly unbridled discretion of the investigating authorities in deciding whether to accept an undertaking offer, the rejection of undertaking offers due to concerns relating to the standard of environmental protection or respect for workers' rights in the country under investigation does not stand in conflict with Article 8.3 ADA.

While recital 12 of Regulation (EU) 2018/825 holds that the Commission should initiate interim reviews *inter alia* in cases of changed circumstances in exporting countries relating to social and environmental standards, with the review potentially resulting in the withdrawal of undertakings, the recital itself is not legally binding. Nonetheless, the recital might inform the application of the provision in the BADR governing the initiation of interim reviews, Article 11 (3) BADR. The corresponding rule of the ADA, Article 11.2 ADA, grants the investigating authorities significant discretion in deciding whether to initiate an interim review: indeed, authorities may self-initiate an interim review any time and for any reason.[76] Therefore, the initiation of an interim review based on a change in the level of social or environmental protection in the exporting country would be permissible under Article 11.2 ADA.

---

[72] The application of the lesser duty rule likewise is only optional under the WTO anti-dumping rules, cf. above p. 192 and n 57.

[73] Vermulst (2005), p. 173.

[74] Ibid.

[75] *United States – Continued Dumping and Subsidy Offset Act of 2000 (Byrd Amendment)* (Chap. 6, n 144) para. 7.81. Due to the parallel language of Article 8.3 ADA and Article 18.3 ASCM, the Panel's findings apply *mutatis mutandis* to undertakings in anti-dumping proceedings.

[76] Vermulst (2005), p. 191.

The objective of interim reviews is cited as being the tailoring of the application of anti-dumping duties to a change in circumstances.[77] Consequently, in responding to a change in circumstances, the review may also result in the form of the measures to be modified. This also encompasses the withdrawal of an undertaking.[78] Examples from the EU's recent practice where this was the case include the *Solar Panels* proceedings, where the Commission decided to replace the existing price undertaking with variable duties in the form of a minimum import price.[79] This move was prompted *inter alia* by concerns that a variable duty minimum import price would be more transparent, predictable and enforceable.[80] Moreover, the review investigation had revealed that the mechanism through which the minimum import price agreed upon in the undertaking was to be adjusted to global price developments did not function properly. Indeed, the Commission had become aware that throughout most of 2016 the undertaking minimum import price adjustment mechanism did not follow global price decreases, and hence did not reflect the non-injurious price.[81] Consequently, the EU chose to change the form of the measures.

Accordingly, a change in circumstances must prompt the investigating authorities carrying out the interim review to conclude that the measures in their current form are not appropriate to counteract the injurious effect of the dumping. It must be questioned whether a change in the level of social or environmental protection in the country of export may actually affect the viability of the undertaking in offsetting the injurious effect of the presence of the dumped products, warranting its withdrawal. Depending on the circumstances of the individual case, withdrawing an undertaking following an interim review solely due to a change in the level of social or environmental protection in the country of export might thus be inconsistent with Article 11.2 ADA.

To conclude, with the exception of the new methodology, challenges to the amendments to the BADR relating to the inclusion of social and environmental aspects stand little chance of success under the ADA.

---

[77] Bellis (2008) para. 7.

[78] Ibid para. 8.

[79] Commission Implementing Regulation (EU) 2017/1570 of 15 September 2017 amending Implementing Regulation (EU) 2017/366 and Implementing Regulation (EU) 2017/367 imposing definitive countervailing and anti-dumping duties on imports of crystalline silicon photovoltaic modules and key components (i.e. cells) originating in or consigned from the People's Republic of China and repealing Implementing Decision 2013/707/EU confirming the acceptance of an undertaking offered in connection with the anti-dumping and anti-subsidy proceedings concerning imports of crystalline silicon photovoltaic modules and key components (i.e. cells) originating in or consigned from the People's Republic of China for the period of application of definitive measures.

[80] Ibid recital 16.

[81] Ibid recital 24.

9.3.2 Compatibility with the Agreement on Subsidies and Countervailing Measures

As regards the changes to the provisions regulating the initiation of interim reviews or the rejection or withdrawal of undertakings in proceedings carried out under the reformed BASR, the ASCM is the standard against which the amendments are to be measured. Undertakings are governed by Article 18 ASCM; interim reviews may be initiated and carried out pursuant to Article 21.2 ASCM. Just as it is the case under Article 8.1 ADA, undertakings are discretionary and need not be accepted by the authorities.[82] Article 18.3 ASCM likewise enables authorities to reject undertakings for reasons of general policy. Consequently, the rejection of undertaking offers due to concerns relating to the standard of environmental protection or respect for workers' rights in the country under investigation is permissible under Article 18 ASCM. Given the parallels in the wording of Article 11.2 ADA and Article 21.2 ASCM, the initiation of an interim review for reasons of social and environmental protection does not present an issue under the ASCM. Nonetheless, depending on the circumstances of the case, the withdrawal of an undertaking following an interim review as a result of a decrease in the level of social and environmental protection might conflict with Article 21.2 ASCM. All in all, however, the chances of a challenge to the modified rules of the BASR concerning undertakings and interim reviews under the ASCM being successful are as slim as they are for a challenge of the BADR under the ADA.

9.4 Compatibility with Article I:1 GATT 1994

In a next step, it must be assessed whether the amendments to the BADR and BASR presented above violate the most-favoured nation (MFN) principle contained in Article I:1 GATT 1994. Article I:1 GATT 1994, which has been described as a *'cornerstone of the GATT'*,[83] lays out a rule of unconditional non-discrimination among WTO members. It prescribes that any advantage granted by a contracting party to a product originating in or destined for another contracting party must be accorded immediately and unconditionally to the like products originating in or destined for the territories of all other contracting parties.[84] The term advantage is to be interpreted broadly.[85] It could thus be argued that, although compliant with the

---

[82] Durling (2008) para. 16; cf. also *United States – Continued Dumping and Subsidy Offset Act of 2000 (Byrd Amendment)* (Chap. 6, n 144).

[83] *European Communities – Conditions for the Granting of Tariff Preferences to Developing Countries* (7 April 2004) WT/DS246/AB/R para. 101 (Appellate Body Report).

[84] Article I:1 GATT 1994.

[85] Mavroidis (2016), p. 201; *European Communities – Regime for the Importation, Sale and Distribution of Bananas* (n 68) para. 206, citing *United States – Denial of Most-Favoured Nation*

provisions of the ADA and the ASCM, denying the exporting producers from a country with a lower level of environmental and social protection the option of having an undertaking offer accepted or subjecting them to additional scrutiny through interim reviews amounts to a violation of the MFN principle of Article I:1 GATT 1994.[86] A similar reasoning could be put forward with regard to the non-application of the lesser duty rule in the event of raw material distortions pursuant to Article 7 (2a) BADR.

This raises the issue of the relationship between the ADA or the ASCM and the provisions of the GATT 1994. Article VI GATT 1994 constitutes an exception to the MFN principle of Article I:1 GATT 1994.[87] Therefore, if a measure complies with Article VI GATT 1994, it cannot be found in violation of Article I:1 GATT 1994.[88] The same must apply, *a fortiori*, to the relationship between the Anti-Dumping Agreement[89] and Article I:1 GATT 1994. This is confirmed by the General Interpretative Note to Annex 1A of the WTO Agreement, which provides that in the event of a conflict between a provision of the GATT 1994 and a provision of another agreement in Annex 1A to the WTO Agreement, the provision of the other agreement shall prevail to the extent of the conflict. This rule not only covers instances of mutually exclusive commands. Instead, it must also be applied to situations where a certain behaviour is permitted under the ADA or the ASCM, but would be prohibited under the GATT 1994.

This interpretation, however, is contested, with some authors arguing in favour of the application of the MFN principle to anti-dumping measures.[90] Those advocating

---

Treatment as to Non-Rubber Footwear from Brazil (19 June 1992) DS18/R para. 6.9 (Panel Report).

[86] The rules and formalities applied in anti-dumping investigations can be considered '*rules and formalities in connection with importation*' as referred to in Article I:1 GATT 1994, *United States – Definitive Anti-Dumping and Countervailing Duties on Certain Products from China* (22 October 2010) WT/DS379/R para. 14.167 (Panel Report).

[87] Müller-Ibold (2018), p. 204; Adamantopoulos (2008) para. 31.

[88] Müller-Ibold (2018), p. 206; Adamantopoulos (2008) para. 31; cf. also *European Communities – Definitive Anti-Dumping Measures on Certain Iron or Steel Fasteners from China* (Chap. 3, n 124) para. 392, holding that in order for an anti-dumping measure to be measured against Article I:1 GATT 1994, it has first to be established that it violates Article VI GATT 1994 and *Brazil – Desiccated Coconut* (21 February 1997) WT/DS22/AB/R 21–22 (Appellate Body Report), confirming the Panel's findings that because Article VI GATT 1994 did not constitute applicable law for the purposes of the dispute, the claims made under Articles I and II of the GATT 1994, which were derived from claims of inconsistency with Article VI of the GATT 1994, could not succeed. The issue of whether provisions of a WTO member's trade defence framework may discriminate among products originating in the territory of different WTO members must be differentiated from the question of whether it would be permissible to specifically target singular members under one's trade defence legislation or, *vice versa*, exempt other members from falling within its scope of application altogether, e.g. by means of a Regional Trade Agreement. On this subject cf. Müller-Ibold (2018), p. 206 et seq.

[89] The full title of which is 'Agreement on Implementation of Article VI of the General Agreement on Tariffs and Trade 1994'.

[90] cf. Bickel (2021), pp. 108–110; Mahncke (2014a), p. 169; Mahncke (2014b).

the application of the principle to anti-dumping measures draw support from the Panel report in *EU—Footwear*. Adopting a narrow definition of the term 'conflict', the Panel considered it possible that a member might act inconsistently with Article I:1 GATT 1994 in the application of its anti-dumping regulations without a specific violation of the Antidumping-Agreement.[91]

That said, other Panel and Appellate Body decisions have followed a different approach in defining the relationship between the ADA and the general provisions of the GATT 1994. In *United States—Shrimp (Thailand)* and *United States—Customs Bond Directive*, the Panel considered itself

> unable to accept that a measure which constitutes specific action against dumping in accordance with the provisions of the Ad Note, can nevertheless be found inconsistent with other provisions of the GATT 1994. For example, if we were to find that the [measure at issue] violates the MFN provision of Article I:1 of the GATT 1994, such a finding would, as a consequence, render inutile the provision (...) of the AD-Agreement, and by reference, Article VI of the GATT 1994.[92]

The Panel based its argumentation on the conflict rule contained in the General Interpretative Note. It thus considered that its findings concerning the legality of a measure under the Anti-Dumping Agreement must prevail over any potential finding of violation under Article I:1 of the GATT 1994.[93]

In applying the General Interpretative Note to the situation at hand, the Panel adopted a wider understanding of the concept of 'conflict' than the Panel in *European Union—Footwear*. Pursuant to this wider understanding, a conflict not only exists where obligations in different agreements cannot be complied with simultaneously,[94] but also where there is an incompatibility of contents, i.e. situations where an agreement prohibits what another one permits.[95] Likewise, the Panel in *European Communities—Bananas*, when tasked with interpreting the notion of 'conflict' contained in the General Interpretative Note, found that the term includes situations where a rule in one agreement prohibits what a rule in another agreement explicitly permits.[96]

---

[91] *European Union – Anti-Dumping Measures on Certain Footwear from China* (Chap. 7, n 98) paras. 7.103–7.105 and footnote 309 to para. 7.104.

[92] *United States – Measures Relating to Shrimp from Thailand* (29 February 2008) WT/DS343/R para. 7.159 (Panel Report) and *United States – Customs Bond Directive for Merchandise Subject to Anti-Dumping/Countervailing Duties* (29 February 2008) WT/DS345/R para. 7.168 (Panel Report).

[93] *United States – Measures Relating to Shrimp from Thailand* (n 92) para. 7.159 and *United States – Customs Bond Directive for Merchandise Subject to Anti-Dumping/Countervailing Duties* (n 92) para. 7.169.

[94] Cf. Chap. 3, footnote 165 in *European Union – Anti-Dumping Measures on Certain Footwear from China* (Chap. 7, n 98) para. 7.104.

[95] Arguing in favour for such a wide understanding of the concept of 'conflict' Pauwelyn (2003), p. 187, 190.

[96] *European Communities – Regime for the Importation, Sale and Distribution of Bananas* (1997) WT/DS27/R para. 7.159 (Panel Report).

The question that presents itself is thus whether the Panels' understanding of the notion of 'conflict' in *European Communities—Bananas* and *United States— Shrimps* or whether the one adopted *inter alia* in *European Union—Footwear* should be followed, as the interpretation of this notion is decisive in deciding whether claims under the general provisions of the GATT 1994 are precluded once a member's measure has been found to comply with the more specific provisions of the ADA or the ASCM. *Pauwelyn* argues that adhering to a strict definition—as other Panels have done on occasion[97]—would systematically elevate the obligations of WTO members over the rights of WTO members. However, under the WTO regime, rights and obligations of the members are of equal importance: the WTO must ensure the members' compliance with their obligations to achieve the desired liberalisation of trade, while at the same time respecting the rights of members to restrict trade where they can demonstrate a legitimate interest in doing so.[98] This balance between the WTO members' rights and obligations would be upset if one were to adopt a strict understanding of the concept of 'conflict' as laid out in the General Interpretative Note. As a consequence of such an understanding, the rights awarded to the GATT 1994 signatories under the Anti-Dumping Agreement would be hollowed out, effectively rendering parts of the Anti-Dumping Agreement meaningless. This reasoning also applies with regard to countervailing measures adopted by the WTO members. Therefore, where a measure has been found to comply with the provisions of the ADA or the ASCM, it cannot be challenged under the general rules of the GATT 1994.

9.5   Chapter Conclusions

Overall, the changes introduced by Regulation (EU) 2018/825 regarding the consideration of environmental and social standards in trade defence investigations do not give rise to any major concerns pertaining to their compatibility with the ADA or the ASCM. The only exception hereto are the provisions permitting the withdrawal of undertakings in the event of a decrease in the level of social and environmental protection in the country of export, in which case the compatibility with Article 11.2 ADA and Article 21.2 ASCM depends largely on the circumstances of the individual case. It should however be noted that WTO disputes on the subject of undertakings are extremely scarce. As far as the author is aware, the above-mentioned proceedings

---

[97] *Indonesia – Certain Measures Affecting the Automobile Industry* (2 July 1998) WT/DS54/R; WT/DS59/R; WT/DS64/R para. 14.99 (Panel Report); cf. also the references in the footnote in *European Union – Anti-Dumping Measures on Certain Footwear from China* (Chap. 7, n 98) to para. 7.104.

[98] Pauwelyn (2003), p. 198.

in *United States—Offset Act (Byrd Amendment)* constitute the only jurisprudence on the matter.[99]

A review of an amendment against Article 1:1 GATT 1994—or other provisions of the GATT 1994—is not possible where said amendment is found to comply with the requirements of the ADA or the ASCM. Any other interpretation would render meaningless numerous rights accorded to the members under the ADA and the ASCM and would interfere with the overall package of members' rights and obligations as set out in the agreements annexed to the Marrakesh Agreement. Consequently, the changes to the EU's trade defence legislation pertaining to the inclusion of social and environmental standards or the non-application of the lesser duty rule in the event of raw-material distortions pursuant to Article 7 (2a) BADR cannot be challenged under Article 1:1 GATT 1994.

The new methodology introduced by Regulation (EU) 2017/2321, however, appears to violate several provisions of the ADA. This relates both to the circumstances under which the BADR provides for the rejection of domestic prices and the sources used in calculating normal value. In particular Article 2.2 ADA and Article 2.2.1.1 ADA should be mentioned here. The recent case law of the Panels in *Australia—A4 Copy Paper* and *European Union—Cost Adjustment Methodologies (Russia)* has further reinforced concerns in this regard.

Lastly, the Commission must be careful to avoid instances of 'double counting' in the application of the reformed trade defence instruments.

References[100]

Adamantopoulos K (2008) Article VI GATT. In: Wolfrum R, Stoll P-T, Koebele M (eds) WTO – trade remedies. Martinus Nijhoff Publishers

Antonini R (2018) A "MES" to be adjusted: past and future treatment of Chinese imports in EU anti-dumping investigations. Global Trade Cust J 13(3):79

Bellis J-F (2008) Article 11 ADA. In: Wolfrum R, Stoll P-T, Koebele M (eds) WTO – trade remedies. Martinus Nijhoff Publishers

Bickel F (2021) Customs unions within the WTO: problems with anti-dumping. Springer

Bierwagen RM, Hailbronner K (1988) Input, downstream, upstream, secondary, diversionary and components or subassembly dumping. J World Trade 22(3):27

Cornelis J (2018) The EU's modernization regulation: stronger and more effective trade defence instruments? Global Trade Cust J 13(11):539

Durling JP (2008) Article 18 ASCM. In: Wolfrum R, Stoll P-T, Koebele M (eds) WTO – trade remedies. Martinus Nijhoff Publishers

Espa I (2019) New features of green industrial policy and the limits of WTO rules: what options for the twenty-first century? J World Trade 53(6):979

Furculita C (2017) Cost of production calculation in EU anti-dumping law: WTO consistent 'As Such' after EU—Biodiesel. Global Trade Cust J 12(9):360

---

[99] *United States – Continued Dumping and Subsidy Offset Act of 2000 (Byrd Amendment)* (Chap. 6, n 144).

[100] All online sources were last accessed on 8 September 2021.

Herrmann C, Müller S (2017) Die Gewährung des "Marktwirtschaftsstatus" gegenüber China im Antidumpingrecht: Ein Belastungstest für die europäische Wirtschaftsverfassung. Zeitschrift für europäisches Wirtschaftsrecht (EuZW) 500

Herrmann C, Weiß W, Ohler C (2007) Welthandelsrecht, 2nd edn. C.H. Beck

Huyghebaert K (2019) Changing the rules mid-game: the compliance of the amended EU basic anti-dumping regulation with WTO law. J World Trade 53(3):417

Krämer-Hoppe R (ed) (2019) Positive integration – EU and WTO approaches towards the "trade and" debate. Springer

Luo Y (2010) Anti-dumping in the WTO, the EU and China: the rise of legalization in the trade regime and its consequences. Wolters Kluwer

Mahncke H (2014a) Applying the MFN principle to WTO anti-dumping law: an opportunity for curbing the use of anti-dumping measures. Legal Issues Econ Integr 41(2):169

Mahncke H (2014b) The relationship between WTO anti-dumping law and GATT non-discrimination principles. Schulthess Juristische Medien AG

Mavroidis PC (2015) Reaching out for green policies – national environmental policies in the WTO legal order. In: Wouters J and others (eds) Global governance through trade – EU policies and approaches. Edward Elgar Publishing Ltd

Mavroidis PC (2016) The regulation of international trade: vol I. GATT MIT Press

Müller-Ibold T (2018) EU trade defence instruments and free trade agreements. In: Bungenberg M and others (eds) The future of trade defence instruments – global policy trends and legal challenges. Springer

Pauwelyn J (2003) Conflict of norms in public international law: how WTO law relates to other rules of international law. Cambridge University Press

Suse A (2017) Old wine in a new bottle: the EU's response to the expiry of Section 15(a)(ii) of China's WTO Protocol of Accession. J Int Econ Law 20(4):951

Tietje C, Sacher V (2018) The new anti-dumping methodology of the EU: a breach of WTO law?. In: Bungenberg M others (eds) The future of trade defence instruments – global policy trends and legal challenges. Springer

Tietje C, Kluttig B, Franke M (2011) Cost of production adjustments in anti-dumping proceedings: challenging raw material inputs dual pricing systems in EU anti-dumping law and practice. J World Trade 45(5):1071

van Bael I, Bellis J-F (2019) EU anti-dumping and other trade defence instruments, 6th edn. Kluwer Law International

Vermulst E (2005) The WTO anti-dumping agreement: a commentary. Oxford University Press

Vermulst E, Dion Sud J (2018) The new rules adopted by the EU to address significant distortions in the anti-dumping context. In: Bungenberg M and others (eds) The future of trade defence instruments – global policy trends and legal challenges. Springer

Vermulst E, Dion Sud J (2020) Are the EU's trade defence instruments WTO compliant?. In: Weiß W, Furculita C (eds) Global politics and EU trade policy: facing the challenges to a multilateral approach. Springer

Vermulst E, Dion Sud J, Evenett SJ (2016) Normal value in anti-dumping proceedings against China post-2016: are some animals less equal than others? Global Trade Cust J 11(5):212

Wüstenberg M (2019) Anti-dumping off the rails: the European Union's practice to alleged input dumping. Global Trade Cust J 14(9):407

Zhou W, Peng D (2018) Price comparison methodologies (DS516): challenging the non-market economy methodology in light of the negotiating history of Article 15 of China's WTO Accession Protocol. J World Trade 52(3):505

Zhou W, Peng D (2021) Anti-dumping measures on A4 Copy Paper. Am J Int Law 115(1):95

Zhou W, Percival A (2016) Debunking the myth of 'particular market situation'. In: WTO antidumping law. J Int Econ Law 19(4):863

Chapter 10
Conclusions

This study first traced the ways in which competition and commercial policy have interacted throughout the European integration process, and how the Treaties intended for conflicts between the two policy fields to be resolved. Even at the very beginning of the integration process, the Treaties' drafters recognised the potential impact the Community's trade policy towards third States would have on competition within the common market. Uniformity in the formulation of the commercial policy was deemed essential to avoid trade deflections and hence distortions of competition within the Community created by commercial policy measures. Thus, even in the early days of European integration, there was a consensus that the Community's external policy measures should not contradict its internal policies, impeding the success of the common market project. Today, this consistency between the EU's external and internal policies is explicitly mandated by Article 21 (3) subpara. 2 TEU. This also extends to the European Union's trade defence instruments, which must not be utilised in a manner that gives rise to distortions of competition within the internal market. The elevated importance attached to a system of undistorted competition within the EU as opposed to granting the EU industry the maximum degree of protection possible further flows from the hierarchy of norms, with trade defence legislation being contained in secondary legislation, whereas the EU's competition provisions form part of EU primary law, namely Articles 101 and 102 TFEU. Lastly, proponents of trade defence instruments traditionally advance that trade defence measures are aimed at re-establishing fair competition between the EU industry and their foreign counterparts. It already follows from this that the design and application of the EU's trade defence instruments must be restricted to what is necessary to achieve this aim and not unduly favour the interests of the EU industry, as this would constitute a distortion of competition in itself.

The short overview of the role the two policies have played during the European integration process has highlighted the relevance accorded to both trade policy and competition policy during the European integration process. These common

© The Author(s), under exclusive license to Springer Nature Switzerland AG 2022
P. Trapp, *The European Union's Trade Defence Modernisation Package*, EYIEL
Monographs - Studies in European and International Economic Law 23,
https://doi.org/10.1007/978-3-030-91363-2_10

historical roots result in trade defence policy and competition policy sharing some of their objectives, such as anti-dumping's original concern being the predatory behaviour of foreign competitors. Nowadays, the similarities in the objectives pursued by the respective policy field are much more limited. Nominally, competition and trade defence law are intended to foster long-term societal welfare by ensuring that markets remain open and competitive. However, they pursue this objective in different ways and exhibit a different understanding as to how competition within the internal market is to be protected. Owing to the history of EU integration, the market integration objective is a central objective of EU competition law, preventing private actors from re-erecting barriers to inter-State trade and ensuring the continued success of the internal market. For this reason, competition law is dedicated to a certain extent to the protection of a competitive market structure as such. Conversely, while the EU's trade defence regime must not hamper the objectives competition policy is set to achieve, it must not contribute to their attainment either. In particular, as the market integration objective is irrelevant to trade defence law, the application of the EU's trade defence instruments does not seek to protect a certain degree of competition within a given market. Instead, their primary aim is to ensure horizontal fairness in competition as equality of opportunities between the EU industry and their non-EU counterparts by offsetting competitive advantages an exporting producer enjoys which are not based on genuine comparative advantages. In the case of anti-dumping, the unfairness of the exporting producer's behaviour is inferred from the fact that he is able to practice dumping. Opposed to this, the role fairness considerations play in EU competition law is a much narrower one. In a central difference to trade defence law, where competition law intends to ensure fairness between competitors, the protection awarded is limited to equally efficient market operators only. This is once more an expression of competition law being concerned with safeguarding a competitive market structure as such and not with the protection of individual economic operators, and the absence of any such concerns in trade defence law. For identical reasons, in contrast to trade defence law, the application of the EU's competition provisions does not depend on the EU industry suffering some degree of injury, but on competition itself being distorted.

The *prima facie* commonalities between trade defence law and competition law extend to a number of concepts employed by both of them, such as market definition, price discrimination or predatory pricing. Yet, the content of these concepts differs significantly, as do the requirements regarding the authors of a practice possibly conflicting with trade defence or competition law. Other than trade defence law, competition law requires for the authors of a potentially anti-competitive practice to either collude or to possess a certain degree of market power. These requirements can be explained by competition law's concern being the protection of the competitive process as such. This objective is only endangered by practices which are either detrimental to the competitive process themselves or where resorted to by undertakings the market power of which is such is that they are able to unilaterally influence the competitive process. A parallel reasoning can be employed for the market integration objective of competition law. Instead, as trade defence law is primarily focussed on protecting the EU industry from harm caused by trading practices which are regarded unfair, it does not require for the exporting producers to act jointly or for them to possess a certain degree of market power: as long as the exporting producers are all resorting to an unfair trading practice, whether they are acting together or the degree of market power they possess is irrelevant. The same applies with regard to the differences in the concepts of predatory pricing: other than competition law, anti-dumping law compares price levels instead of cost levels, considers below-cost pricing objectionable *per se* and does not provide for grounds of justification. By limiting the circumstances under which a company's behaviour is found to violate Article 102 TFEU, competition law ensures that only pricing practices that are detrimental to the competitive structure on a given market—by excluding equally efficient competitors—fall within the scope of Article 102 TFEU. Such a limitation is not made in anti-dumping law, again due to anti-dumping law not being concerned with the protection of the competitive structure. Moreover, the concept of price discrimination is ascribed a completely distinct meaning in competition and trade defence law. In one central difference, and in line with the objectives pursued by the respective area of law, anti-dumping legislation aims to prevent price discrimination to the competitive disadvantage of the exporters' direct competitors, resulting in it addressing 'primary line' injury—and hereby contributing to the objective of re-establishing fair competition on the internal market. Conversely, Article 102 lit. c) TFEU seeks to prevent 'secondary line' injury. Lastly, the differences in market definition can be explained by the different functions of market definition in trade defence and competition law: regarding the latter, the central objective of delineating the market concerned lies in the identification of the competitive constraints an undertaking faces, whereas in trade defence law, market definition is undertaken to outline the scope of the investigation, regarding the products concerned and their origin.

While both originally intended to safeguard competition, the objectives and consequently also the legislative framework governing the application of EU competition and trade defence law have diverged significantly. This inevitably results in conflicts between the two areas of law. Yet, the analysis undertaken in this thesis has revealed that this appears not to have been a matter of concern for the EU legislators in reforming the BADR and the BASR. In particular in light of the Commission's attempts at facilitating SMEs' access to the EU's trade defence instruments, it would be advisable for the Commission to extend its support for SMEs by adapting its publications and guidelines on how to submit an anti-dumping or anti-subsidy complaint to include information on the extent of coordination permitted in doing so. This would minimise the risk of undertakings violating Article 101 (1) TFEU when compiling the information necessary for a complaint, especially in instances where the complainant industry is less acquainted with the EU's trade defence system. The significance of price undertakings in the Commission's practice has decreased over the last years. It is recommended that the Commission maintain its restrictive stance in that regard and, in particular, refrain from accepting joint undertaking offers and offers in oligopolistic markets, as the risk of undertakings being mis-used for price coordination practices infringing Article 101 (1) TFEU is particularly high in these two situations. Moreover, where the Commission discerns that an undertaking is used in a manner that conflicts with Article 101 (1) TFEU, it should be able to withdraw its acceptance of the undertaking. Hence, Articles 8 (9) BADR and 13 (9) BASR should be amended accordingly.

As detailed above, the re-establishment of fair competition within the European Union is the core policy rationale provided for the use of trade defence instruments. Yet, instead of levelling the playing field between the EU industry and exporting producers, various provisions of the reformed basic regulations favour the interests of the EU industry. This applies both with regard to procedural aspects of the investigations, such as the preparation of a report on significant distortions by the Commission under the new methodology as foreseen by Article 2 (6a) lit. c) BADR, and multiple of the amendments the Trade Defence Modernisation Package made to the substantive rules of the BADR and the BASR. Particularly the new methodology of Article 2 (6a) BADR must be criticised in this regard. The criteria included under Article 2 (6a) lit. b) BADR used to establish the existence of significant distortions go beyond the methodology's declared objective of addressing interventions of the exporting producer's home State in the economy, instead covering aspects where the competitors of the EU industry enjoy genuine comparative advantages. As the construction of normal value under the new methodology results in higher duty levels, extending its scope of application through an expansive interpretation of the criteria listed in Article 2 (6a) lit. b) is beneficial to the EU industry. Moreover, the level of measures in investigations where Article 2 (6a) BADR is applied will further be driven up by basing the choice of the representative country on the level of social and environmental protection prevailing in the potential representative countries, as foreseen by Article 2 (6a) lit. a) BADR. Foreclosing the EU market against foreign exports to a greater extent through a higher level of measures, the limitations to the scope of application of the lesser duty rule in the event of raw material distortions in anti-dumping investigations pursuant to Article 7 (2a) BADR and its general non-application in anti-subsidy investigations (Article 12 (1) subpara. 3 BASR and Article 15 (1) subpara. 3 BASR) likewise grant a higher level of protection to the EU industry. The reasoning presented to justify these changes to the scope of application of the lesser duty rule lacks merit, given that the lesser duty rule is considered an expression of the principle of proportionality: it strikes a balance between the interests of the EU industry and those of other economic operators, including the users of the product concerned. This balance is upset by limiting its scope of application. Moreover, even where the lesser duty rule still applies, the amended rules on the calculation of the target profit operate to the benefit of the EU industry, ensuring for a higher level of measures also in investigations where the duty level is based on the injury margin. The amended rules on target profit calculation can be criticised for a number of reasons, such as the introduction of a fixed *de minimis* profit margin. Yet, perhaps the most worrisome amendment is the inclusion of social and environmental costs incurred by the EU industry in calculating the target profit. Given the complete absence of guidance provided by the basic regulations on how to proceed in situations where an undertaking has already received State aid for such costs, it cannot be excluded that the EU industry receives double compensation for these costs where they are included in the reformed target profit calculation. Here, additional legislative changes to the basic regulations are required. It is proposed that Article 7 (2d) BADR and Article 12 (1b) BASR are amended accordingly to exclude such costs when calculating the target profit where the Commission is aware of compensation being granted during the investigation. Furthermore, Article 11 (3) BADR and Article 19 (2) BASR should be adapted to prescribe for the *ex officio* initiation of an interim review where DG COMP—or a national competition authority—adopts a decision regarding environmental subsidies affecting the accuracy of the target profit calculation only after the measures are imposed.

The Commission accords little weight to competition-related arguments, both during the injury analysis and the Union interest assessment. It is recommended that Articles 11 (3) BADR and Article 19 (2) BASR are further modified to explicitly provide for the initiation of an interim review where the complainant industry is found to engage in anti-competitive behaviour, and the temporal proximity between the time span during which the anti-competitive behaviour was practised and the period chosen for the injury assessment is such that it cannot be excluded that the anti-competitive behaviour affected the accuracy of the latter. Conversely, no legislative changes to the Union interest test are necessary. Instead, competition law expertise within DG TRADE should be strengthened and cooperation between DG COMP and DG TRADE expanded in order to allow for a more detailed assessment of competition-related arguments during the Union interest test. Finally, the analysis of the Trade Defence Modernisation Package has highlighted the potential for increasing the politicisation of the EU's trade defence instruments, a development further exacerbated by the significant discretionary powers granted to the Commission—*inter alia* visible in the second Union interest test to be carried out when deciding upon the application of the lesser duty rule in the event of raw material distortions under Article 7 (2b) BADR or when subsuming the criteria contained in Article 2 (6a) lit. b) BADR. This is noteworthy as, pursuant to recital 3 of Regulation (EU) 2018/825, it was a declared objective of the Trade Defence Modernisation Package to make the reformed basic regulations more transparent and their application more predictable. Yet, as can be inferred from the above, the changes do not necessarily appear conducive to these objectives. This unwelcome development could be countered to some degree by the Commission publishing guidelines on key aspects of a trade defence investigation, as it was envisaged during earlier attempts at reforming the EU's trade defence instruments. In this context, it should be mentioned that recital 13 of Regulation (EU) 2018/825 states that *'[i]t is possible for the Commission to adopt interpretative notices providing general guidance to possible interested parties on the application of the [BADR and the BASR]'*. That said, it appears unlikely that sufficient political impetus will develop for the Commission to do so in the foreseeable future.

Another novelty of the reformed basic regulations lies in the inclusion of questions of social and environmental protection. Whereas the inclusion of said aspects finds its legal basis in Articles 3 (5), 21 (1), (2) TEU and the interpretation of 'fair' trade as also covering aspects of sustainable development, it should be noted that Article 21 (3) subpara. 2 TEU mandates consistency between the EU's different external policy measures. Nevertheless, an analysis of the provisions integrating social and environmental concerns has revealed that the reformed trade defence instruments do not meet this requirement. Instead, and in stark contrast to the approach pursued by the EU in promoting sustainable development objectives in its commercial relations with the wider world, the trade defence instruments' approach must be characterised as confrontational, in particular due to the unilateral standard-setting by the EU as to which level of social and environmental protection it considers adequate. Moreover, the basic regulations do not possess a clear element of conditionality and do not accord any relevance to the general human rights situation in the exporting country. Overall, while contributing to the market fore-closure effects emanating from the reformed regulations, the efficacy of the amend-ments in question in inducing any real policy change in the EU's trading partners must be questioned. Likewise, as the minimum level of social and environmental protection mandated by the basic regulations still is significantly lower than the level of protection prevailing within the EU, the basic regulations are unlikely to effec-tively protect the EU industry against instances of social or environmental dumping.

Lastly, the inclusion of matters of social and environmental protection raises only limited concerns under WTO law. The only possible exception to this would be the withdrawal of undertakings following an interim review due to a change in the level of social and environmental protection existing in the country of export. However, here, the WTO compatibility depends on the circumstances of the individual case. By contrast, the new methodology appears to conflict with WTO law under multiple angles, in particular with Article 2.2 and Article 2.2.1.1 ADA. This concerns the criteria used in establishing the existence of significant distortions, the circumstances under which a producer's costs may be discarded in calculating normal value as well as the sources used in constructing normal value. It is further argued that, in accordance with the General Interpretative Note to Annex 1A of the WTO Agree-ment, a challenge of a WTO member's trade defence legislation under the general provisions of the GATT 1994 is precluded where the legislation has been found to comply with the provisions of the ADA or the ASCM.

The amendments to the basic regulations cannot be insulated from the EU's attempts to reposition itself in the changing environment of international trade and to achieve what is frequently referred to as the EU's 'open strategic autonomy'. In a speech delivered by European Council President *Charles Michel* in September 2020, he cited stability as one of the objectives the EU's strategic autonomy seeks to achieve. According to Mr. *Michel,*

> That calls for a favourable environment for investment and trade, both within our market and with the rest of the world. Upholding fair market conditions and reciprocity with our trading partners is one of our priorities. We advocate free and open economies, and we are opposed to protectionism. But access to our large market cannot be given away for free. The lower your compliance with standards, the more restricted your access. Whether you're leaving our Union, or building closer ties with it.[1]

---

[1] Charles Michel, *Strategic autonomy for Europe – the aim of our generation* (2020).

Naturally, this reference to compliance with standards encompasses matters of social and environmental protection. Yet, the search for common ground with one's trading partners is also relevant in another policy area shaping international trade, namely the issue of State subsidisation. Recently, the EU has sought to unilaterally address the increasingly pressing question of how to regulate economic activity within the internal market and imports into the EU benefitting from subsidisation by third States. This includes not only the Trade Defence Modernisation Package and the EU's more *'principled'* response to imports benefitting from State subsidisation,[2] but also the White Paper on foreign subsidies presented by the Commission in the summer of 2020[3] and the corresponding legislative proposal of May 2021. The relationship between the EU and the United Kingdom following the latter's withdrawal from the Union is also likely to depend on the subsidy regime the United Kingdom will operate in the future—as is well-known, the issue of the 'level playing field' was among the most contentious subjects in the negotiations leading to the conclusion of the Trade and Cooperation Agreement between the EU and the United Kingdom.[4] It thus comes as no surprise that the chapter addressing the issue of subsidisation is among the most extensive ones of the TCA.[5] It should further be mentioned that the EU-UK TCA explicitly affirms the possibility of imposing anti-dumping and anti-subsidy duties on products originating in the territory of the other party.[6] Such a step against a former Member State of the Union would certainly be historic. Yet, while there is arguably a need to rethink and reshape some of the EU's policies, it must be called into doubt whether the issue of distortions of international trade caused by State subsidisation can be effectively addressed by unilateral EU policy measures and without risking alienation from its trading partners. It is therefore recommended that the EU should not neglect its attempts at addressing the matter through multilateral solutions, such as promoting compliance with the WTO members' notification obligations set out in the ASCM—or any newfound autonomy might quickly turn into isolation.

---

[2] Cf. above p. 195.

[3] European Commission, 'White Paper on levelling the playing field as regards foreign subsidies (COM(2020) 253 final)' (Chap. 1, n 4).

[4] 'Trade and Cooperation Agreement between the European Union and the European Atomic Energy Community, of the one part, and the United Kingdom of Great Britain and Northern Ireland, of the other part' (OJ 2020 L 444/14) (31 December 2020) (EU-UK TCA).

[5] Title XI, Chapter 3: Subsidy control EU-UK TCA. For a first assessment of the provisions cf. Pablo Ibáñez Colomo, 'Subsidies in the EU-UK Trade Agreement: a codification of the EU acquis on State aid. How will the UK system work?' (28 December 2020), available at <https://chillingcompetition.com/2020/12/28/subsidies-in-the-eu-uk-trade-agreement-a-codification-of-the-eu-acquis-on-state-aid-how-will-the-uk-system-work/>.

[6] Article GOODS.17 EU-UK TCA.

Sources[1]

Table of Cases

Courts of the European Union

Accession of the European Union to the European Convention for the Protection of Human Rights and Fundamental Freedoms (18 December 2014) Opinion 2/13, ECLI:EU:C:2014:2454 (European Court of Justice).

Ajinomoto Co. Inc. and The NutraSweet Company v Council (18 December 1997) joined cases T-159/94 and T-160/94, ECLI:EU:T:1997:209, ECR 1997 II-02461 (Court of First Instance).

AKZO Chemie BV v Commission (3 July 1991) C-62/86, ECLI:EU:C:1991:286, ECR 1991 I-03359 (European Court of Justice).

Albany International BV v Stichting Bedrijfspensioenfonds Textielindustrie (21 September 1999) C-67/96, ECLI:EU:C:1999:430, ECR 1999 I-05751 (European Court of Justice).

Allianz Hungária and others (14 March 2013) C-32/11, ECLI:EU:C:2013:160 (European Court of Justice).

Anton Dürbeck v Hauptzollamt Frankfurt am Main-Flughafen (5 May 1981) C-112/80, ECLI:EU:C:1981:94, ECR 1981-01095 (European Court of Justice).

Alsthom Atlantique SA v Compagnie de Construction Mécanique Sulzer SA (24 January 1991) C-339/89, ECLI:ECLI:EU:C:1991:28, ECR 1991 I-00107 (European Court of Justice).

AstraZeneca v Commission (1 July 2010) T-321/05, ECLI:EU:T:2010:266, ECR 2010 II-02805 (General Court).

Banque Indosuez (16 October 1997) C-177/96, ECLI:EU:C:1997:494, ECR 1997 I-05659 (European Court of Justice).

---

[1] All online sources were last accessed on 8 September 2021.

© The Author(s), under exclusive license to Springer Nature Switzerland AG 2022
P. Trapp, *The European Union's Trade Defence Modernisation Package*, EYIEL
Monographs - Studies in European and International Economic Law 23,
https://doi.org/10.1007/978-3-030-91363-2

Beef Industry Development Society (20 November 2008) C-209/07, ECLI:EU: C:2008:643, ECR 2008 I-08637 (European Court of Justice).

Béguelin Import Co. v S.A.G.L. Import Export (25 November 1971) C-22/71, ECLI: EU:C:1971:113, ECR 1971 00949 (European Court of Justice).

BPB Industries and British Gypsum v Commission (1 April 1993) T-65/89, ECLI: EU:T:1993:31, ECR 1993 II-00389 (Court of First Instance).

British Airways v Commission (15 March 2007) C-95/04 P, ECLI:EU:C:2007:166, ECR 2007 I-02331 (European Court of Justice).

Brosmann Footwear (HK) Ltd. and others v Council (4 March 2010) T-401/ 06, ECLI:EU:T:2010:67, ECR 2010 II-00671 (General Court).

Canadian Solar Emea GmbH and others v Council (28 February 2017) T-162/ 14, ECLI:EU:T:2017:124 (General Court).

Canadian Solar Emea GmbH and others v Council (27 March 2019) C-236/ 17 P, ECLI:EU:C:2019:258 (European Court of Justice).

Canon Inc. and others v Council (5 October 1988) joined cases 277 and 300/85, ECLI:EU:C:1988:467, ECR 1988 05731 (European Court of Justice).

Cartorobica SpA v Ministero delle Finanze dello Stato (27 March 1990) C-189/ 88, ECLI:EU:C:1990:137, ECR 1990 I-01269 (European Court of Justice).

Caviro Distillerie and others v Commission (15 March 2018) T-211/16, ECLI:EU: T:2018:148 (General Court).

Commission v Council (Energy Star Agreement) (12 December 2002) C-281/ 01, ECLI:EU:C:2002:761, ECR 2002 I-12049 (European Court of Justice).

Commission v Fresh Marine (24 October 2000) T-178/98, ECLI:EU:T:2000:240, ECR 2000 II-03331 (Court of First Instance).

Commission v Italian Republic (17 November 2011) C-496/09, ECLI:EU:C:2011: 740, ECR 2011 I-11483 (European Court of Justice).

Committee of Polyethylene Terephthalate (PET) Manufacturers in Europe (CPME) v Council (5 April 2017) T-422/13, ECLI:EU:T:2017:251 (General Court).

Compagnie Maritime Belge Transports and others v Commission (16 March 2000) C-395/96 P, ECLI:EU:C:2000:132, ECR 2000 I-01365 (European Court of Justice).

Confédération européenne des associations d'horlogers-réparateurs (CEAHR) v Commission (15 December 2010) T-427/08, ECLI:EU:T:2010:517, ECR 2010 II-05865 (General Court).

Connect Austria Gesellschaft für Telekommunikation GmbH (22 May 2003) C-462/ 99, ECLI:EU:C:2003:297, ECR 2003 I-05197 (European Court of Justice).

Corsica Ferries (17 May 1994) C-18/93, ECLI:EU:C:1994:195, ECR 1994 I-01783 (European Court of Justice).

Consten and Grundig v Commission (13 July 1966) joined cases C-56 and 58/64, ECLI:EU:C:1966:41, ECR 1966 00429 (European Court of Justice).

Council v Alumina d.o.o. (1 October 2014) C-393/13 P, ECLI:EU:C:2014:2245 (European Court of Justice).

Crown Equipment (Suzhou) Co. Ltd. and Crown Gabelstapler GmbH & Co. KG v Council (18 October 2016) T-351/13, ECLI:EU:T:2016:616 (General Court).

Deutsche Telekom AG v Commission (14 October 2010) C-280/08 P, ECLI:EU: C:2010:603, ECR 2010 I-09555 (European Court of Justice).

Donckerwolcke (15 December 1976) C-41/76, ECLI:EU:C:1976:182, ECR 1976-01921 (European Court of Justice).

Easyjet v Commission (4 July 2006) T-177/04, ECLI:EU:T:2006:187, ECR 2006 II-01931 (Court of First Instance).

Échirolles Distribution SA v Association du Dauphiné and others (3 October 2000) C-9/99, ECLI:EU:C:2000:532, ECR 2000 I-08207 (European Court of Justice).

Éduard Leclerc v Au blé vert (10 January 1985) C-229/83, ECLI:EU:C:1985:1, ECR 1985-00001 (European Court of Justice).

EEC Seed Crushers' and Oil Processors' Federation (FEDIOL) v Commission (22 June 1989) C-70/87, ECLI:EU:C:1989:254, ECR 1989-01781 (European Court of Justice).

EMI Records Limited v CBS United Kingdom Limited (15 June 1976) C-51/ 75, ECLI:EU:C:1976:85, ECR 1976-00811 (European Court of Justice).

Euroalliages and others v Commission (8 July 2003) T-132/01, ECLI:EU:T:2003: 189, ECR 2003 II-02359 (Court of First Instance).

European Commission v Kingdom of Spain (11 December 2012) C-610/10, ECLI: EU:C:2012:781 (European Court of Justice).

European Fertilizer Manufacturers' Association (EFMA) v Council (28 October 1999) T-210/95, ECLI:EU:T:1999:273, ECR 1999 II-03291 (Court of First Instance).

Europemballage Corporation and Continental Can Company Inc. v Commission of the European Communities (21 February 1973) C-6/72, ECLI:EU:C:1973:22, ECR 1972-00215 (European Court of Justice).

Expedia Inc. v Autorité de la concurrence and others (13 December 2012) C-226/ 11, ECLI:EU:C:2012:795 (European Court of Justice).

Extramet Industrie v Council (11 June 1992) C-358/89, ECLI:EU:C:1991:214, ECR 1992 I-03813 (European Court of Justice).

Faust v Commission of the European Communities (28 October 1982) C-52/ 81, ECLI:EU:C:1982:369, ECR 1982 03745 (European Court of Justice).

France Télécom SA v Commission (Wanadoo) (2 April 2009) C-202/07 P, ECLI:EU: C:2009:214, ECR 2009 I-02369 (European Court of Justice).

Free Trade Agreement with Singapore (16 May 2017) Opinion 2/15, ECLI:EU: C:2017:376 (European Court of Justice).

French Republic and Société commerciale des potasses et de l'azote (SCPA) and Entreprise minière et chimique (EMC) v Commission of the European Communities (Kali and Salz) (31 March 1998) joined cases C-68/94 and C-30/95, ECLI: EU:C:1998:148, ECR 1998 I-01375 (European Court of Justice).

French Republic v Commission (19 March 1991) C-202/88, ECLI:EU:C:1991:120, ECR 1991 I-01223 (European Court of Justice).

Generics (UK) Ltd. and others (30 January 2020) C-307/18, ECLI:EU:C:2020:52 (European Court of Justice).

GlaxoSmithKline Services Unlimited v Commission (27 September 2006) T-168/ 01, ECLI:EU:T:2006:265, ECR 2006 II-02969 (Court of First Instance).

GlaxoSmithKline Services Unlimited v Commission (6 October 2009) joined cases C-501/06 P, C-513/06 P, C-515/06 P and C-519/06 P, ECLI:EU:C:2009:610, ECR 2009 I-09291 (European Court of Justice).

Gold East Paper (Jiangsu) Co. Ltd. and others v Council (11 September 2014) T-443/11, ECLI:EU:T:2014:773 (General Court).

Gold East Paper (Jiangsu) Co. Ltd. and others v Council (11 September 2014) T-444/11, ECLI:EU:T:2014:773 (General Court).

Hangzhou Duralamp Electronics Co. Ltd. v Council (11 July 2013) T-459/07, ECLI: EU:T:2013:369 (General Court).

Hilti AG v Commission (12 December 1991) T-30/89 1991, ECLI:EU:T:1991:70, ECR II-01439 (Court of First Instance).

Hoffmann-La Roche v Commission (13 February 1979) C-85/76, ECLI:EU:C:1979: 36, ECR 1979 00461 (European Court of Justice).

Ikea Wholesale Ltd. v Commissioners of Customs and Excise (27 September 2007) C-351/04, ECLI:EU:C:2007:547, ECR 2007 I-07723 (European Court of Justice).

Industrie des poudres sphériques v Commission (30 November 2000) T-5/97, ECLI: EU:T:2000:278, ECR 2000 II-03755 (Court of First Instance).

Industrie des poudres sphériques v Commission and others (3 October 2000) C-458/ 98 P, ECLI:EU:C:2000:531, ECR 2000 I-08147 (European Court of Justice).

Industrie des poudres sphériques v Council (15 October 1998) T-2/95, ECLI:EU: T:1998:242, ECR 1998 II-03939 (Court of First Instance).

InnoLux Corp. v Commission (27 February 2014) T-91/11, ECLI:EU:T:2014:92 (General Court).

Intel Corporation Inc. v Commission (6 September 2017) C-413/14 P, ECLI:EU: C:2017:632 (European Court of Justice).

International Agreement on Natural Rubber (4 October 1979) Opinion 1/78, ECLI: EU:C:1979:224, ECR 1979-02871 (European Court of Justice).

International Fruit Company NV and others v Produktschap voor Groenten en Fruit (12 December 1972) joined cases 21 to 24/72, ECLI:EU:C:1972:115, ECR 1972 01219 (European Court of Justice).

Irish Sugar plc v Commission (7 October 1999) T-228/97, ECLI:EU:T:1999:246, ECR 1999 II-02969 (Court of First Instance).

ITT Promedia v Commission (17 July 1998) T-111/96, ECLI:EU:T:1998:183, ECR 1998 II-02937 (Court of First Instance).

Javico International v Yves Saint Laurent Parfums (28 April 1998) C-306/96, ECLI: EU:C:1998:173, ECR 1998 I-01983 (European Court of Justice).

Jiangsu Seraphim Solar System Co. Ltd. v Commission (8 July 2020) T-110/ 17, ECLI:EU:T:2020:315 (General Court).

Jinan Meide Casting Co. Ltd. v Council (30 June 2016) T-424/13, ECLI:EU:T:2016: 378 (General Court).

John Deere v Commission (28 May 1998) C-7/95 P, ECLI:EU:C:1998:256, ECR 1998 I-03111 (European Court of Justice).

Kaufhof AG v Commission of the European Communities (8 April 1976) C-29/ 75, ECLI:EU:C:1976:55, ECR 1976 00431 (European Court of Justice).

Kingdom of Belgium v Commission of the European Communities (21 March 1990) C-142/87, ECLI:EU:C:1990:125, ECR 1990 I-00959 (European Court of Justice).

Klaus Höfner and Fritz Elser v Macrotron GmbH (23 April 1991) C-41/90, ECLI: EU:C:1991:161, ECR 1991 I-01979 (European Court of Justice).

Koninklijke Wegenbouw Stevin BV v Commission (27 September 2012) T-357/06, ECLI:EU:T:2012:488 (General Court).

Konkurrensverket v TeliaSonera Sverige AB (17 February 2011) C-52/09, ECLI:EU: C:2011:83, ECR 2011 I-00527 (European Court of Justice).

Local Cost Standard (11 November 1975) Opinion 1/75, ECLI:EU:C:1975:145, ECR 1975 01355 (European Court of Justice).

Marine Harvest Norway v Council (21 March 2012) T-113/06, ECLI:EU:T:2012: 135 (General Court).

MasterCard Inc. v European Commission (11 September 2014) C-382/12, ECLI: EU:C:2014:2201 (European Court of Justice).

Masterfoods Ltd. and others (14 December 2000) C-344/98, ECLI:EU:C:2000:689, ECR 2000 I-11369 (European Court of Justice).

MEO – Serviços de Comunicações e Multimédia SA v Autoridade da Concorrência (19 April 2018) C-525/16, ECLI:EU:C:2018:270 (European Court of Justice).

Metro SB-Großmärkte GmbH & Co. KG v Commission (25 October 1977) 26/76, ECLI:EU:C:1977:167, ECR 1977 01875 (European Court of Justice).

Motosykletistiki Omospondia Ellados NPID (MOTOE) (1 July 2008) C-49/07, ECLI:EU:C:2008:376, ECR 2008 I-04863 (European Court of Justice).

Nachi Fujikoshi Corporation v Council and others (7 May 1987) C-255/84, ECLI: EU:C:1987:203, ECR 1987 01861 (European Court of Justice).

NTN Corporation and Koyo Seiko Co. Ltd. v Council (2 May 1995) joined cases T-163/94 and T-165/94, ECLI:EU:T:1995:83, ECR 1995 II-01381 (Court of First Instance).

NTN Toyo Bearing Co. Ltd. and others v Council (7 May 1987) C-240/84, ECLI: EU:C:1987:202, ECR 1987 01809 (European Court of Justice).

NV Nederlandsche Banden Industrie Michelin v Commission (Michelin I) (9 November 1983) C-322/81, ECLI:EU:C:1983:313, ECR 1983 03461 (European Court of Justice).

O2 (Germany) v Commission (2 May 2006) T-328/03, ECLI:EU:T:2006:116, ECR 2006 II-01231 (Court of First Instance).

Pavel Pavlov and others v Stichting Pensioenfonds Medische Specialisten (12 September 2000) C-180/98 to C-184/98, ECLI:EU:C:2000:428, ECR 2000 I-06451 (European Court of Justice).

Photo USA Electronic Graphic, Inc. v Council (18 November 2014) T-394/13, ECLI:EU:T:2014:964 (General Court).

Piau v Commission (26 January 2005) T-193/02, ECLI:EU:T:2005:22, ECR 2005 II-00209 (Court of First Instance).

Portmeirion Group UK Ltd. v Commissioners for Her Majesty's Revenue & Customs (17 March 2016) C-232/14, ECLI:EU:C:2016:180 (European Court of Justice).

Portuguese Republic v Commission (Portuguese Airports) (29 March 2001) C-163/ 99, ECLI:EU:C:2001:189, ECR 2001 I-02613 (European Court of Justice).

Post Danmark AS v Konkurrencerådet (27 March 2012) C-209/10, ECLI:EU: C:2012:172 (European Court of Justice).

Protégé International Ltd. v Commission (13 September 2012) T-119/09, ECLI:EU: T:2012:421 (General Court).

R. & V. Haegeman v Belgian State (30 April 1974) C-181/73, ECLI:EU:C:1974:41, ECR 1974-00449 (European Court of Justice).

Raiffeisen Zentralbank Österreich AG and others v Commission of the European Communities (14 December 2006) joined cases T-259/02 to T-264/02 and T-271/ 02, ECLI:EU:T:2006:396, ECR 2006 II-05169 (European Court of Justice).

Rewe-Zentral AG v Bundesmonopolverwaltung für Branntwein (20 February 1979) C-120/78, ECLI:EU:C:1979:42, ECR 1979-00649 (European Court of Justice).

SA Roquette Frères v Commission (22 October 2002) C-94/00, ECLI:EU:C:2002: 603, ECR 1980 03333 (European Court of Justice).

Sanyo Electric v Council (10 March 1992) C-177/87, ECLI:EU:C:1992:111, ECR 1992 I-01535 (European Court of Justice).

SAT Fluggesellschaft mbH v Eurocontrol (19 January 1994) C-364/92, ECLI:EU: C:1994:7, ECR 1994 I-00043 (European Court of Justice).

Showa Denko KK v Commission of the European Communities (29 June 2006) C-289/04 P, ECLI:EU:C:2006:431, ECR 2006 I-05859 (European Court of Justice).

Since Hardware (Guangzhou) Co. Ltd. v Council (18 September 2012) T-156/ 11, ECLI:EU:T:2012:431 (General Court).

Slovak Telekom a.s. v European Commission (22 March 2012) joined cases T-458/ 09 and T-171/10, ECLI:EU:T:2012:145 (European Court of Justice).

Slovenská sporiteľňa (7 February 2013) C-68/12, ECLI:EU:C:2013:71 (European Court of Justice).

Società Italiana Vetro SpA and others v Commission (Italian Flat Glass) (10 March 1992) T-68/89, ECLI:EU:T:1992:38, ECR 1992 II-01403 (Court of First Instance).

Société alsacienne et lorraine de télécommunications et d'électronique (Alsatel) v SA Novasam (5 October 1988) C-247/86, ECLI:EU:C:1988:469, ECR 1988 05987 (European Court of Justice).

Société Technique Minière (STM) (30 June 1966) C-56/65, ECLI:EU:C:1966:38, ECR 1966 00337 (European Court of Justice).

SolarWorld AG and others v Council (1 February 2016) T-141/14, ECLI:EU: T:2016:67 (General Court).

SolarWorld and others v Commission (9 November 2017) C-204/16 P, ECLI:EU: C:2017:838 (European Court of Justice).

Sot. Lélos kai Sia EE and others v GlaxoSmithKline AEVE Farmakeftikon Proïonton (16 September 2008) joined cases C-468/06 to C-478/06, ECLI:EU:C:2008:504, ECR 2008 I-07139 (European Court of Justice).

Steinel Vertrieb GmbH v Hauptzollamt Bielefeld (18 April 2013) C-595/11, ECLI: EU:C:2013:251 (European Court of Justice).

Stergios Delimitis v Henninger Bräu AG (28 February 1991) C-234/89, ECLI:EU: C:1991:91, ECR 1991 I-00935 (European Court of Justice).

Suiker Unie and others v Commission (16 December 1975) joined cases C-40/73 etc., ECLI:EU:C:1975:174, ECR 1975 01663 (European Court of Justice).

Tetra Pak International SA v Commission (6 October 1994) T-83/91, ECLI:EU: T:1994:246, ECR 1994 II-00755 (Court of First Instance).

Tetra Pak International SA v Commission (Tetra Pak II) (14 November 1996) C-333/94 P, ECLI:EU:C:1996:436, ECR 1996 I-05951 (European Court of Justice).

Tetra Pak Rausing SA v Commission (10 July 1990) T-51/89, ECLI:EU:T:1990:41, ECR 1990 II-00309 (Court of First Instance).

Thyssen Stahl AG v Commission (11 March 1999) T-141/94, ECLI:EU:T:1999:48, ECR 1999 II-00347 (Court of First Instance).

Timab Industries and CFPR v European Commission (20 May 2015) T-456/ 10, ECLI:EU:T:2015:296 (European Court of Justice).

T-Mobile Netherlands and others (4 June 2009) C-8/08, ECLI:EU:C:2009:343, ECR 2009 I-04529 (European Court of Justice).

Tomra Systems ASA and others v Commission (19 April 2012) C-549/10 P, ECLI: EU:C:2012:221 (European Court of Justice).

Transnational Company 'Kazchrome' AO and ENRC Marketing AG v Council (30 November 2011) T-107/08, ECLI:EU:T:2011:704, ECR 2011 II-08051 (General Court).

United Brands Company v Commission (14 February 1978) C-27/76, ECLI:EU: C:1978:22, ECR 1978 00207 (European Court of Justice).

United Kingdom and Northern Ireland v Council of the European Union (19 November 1998) C-150/94, ECLI:EU:C:1998:547, ECR 1998 I-07235 (European Court of Justice).

Usha Martin Ltd. v Council and Commission (22 November 2012) C-552/ 10 P, ECLI:EU:C:2012:736 (European Court of Justice).

Voelk v Verwaecke (9 July 1969) C-5/69, ECLI:EU:C:1969:35, ECR 1969 00295 (European Court of Justice).

Walt Wilhelm (13 February 1969) 14/68, ECLI:EU:C:1969:4, ECR 1969 00001 (European Court of Justice).

Whirlpool Europe Srl v Council (13 September 2010) T-314/06, ECLI:EU:T:2010: 390, ECR 2010 II-05005 (General Court).

Yassin Abdullah Kadi and others v Council (3 September 2008) joined cases C-402/ 05 P and 415/05 P, ECLI:EU:C:2008:461, ECR 2008 I-06351 (European Court of Justice).

Yuanping Changyuan Chemicals Co. Ltd. v Council (20 May 2015) T-310/ 12, ECLI:EU:T:2015:295 (General Court).

Advocate General Opinions

British Airways v Commission (23 February 2006) C-95/04 P, ECLI:EU:C:2006:
133, ECR 2007 I-02331 (Opinion of Advocate General Kokott).

Canon Inc. and others v Council (8 March 1988) joined cases 277 and
300/85, ECLI:EU:C:1988:116, ECR 1988 05731 (Opinion of Advocate General
Slynn).

Commission v NTN Corporation and Koyo Seiko (16 September 1997) C-245/
95, ECLI:EU:C:1997:400, ECR 1998 I-00401 (Opinion of Advocate General
Léger).

Council v Gul Ahmed Textile Mills Ltd. (25 March 2013) C-638/11 P, ECLI:EU:
C:2013:277 (Opinion of Advocate General Sharpston).

Distillerie Bonollo v Commission (23 April 2020), C-461/18 P, ECLI:EU:C:2020:
298 (Opinion of Advocate General Tanchev).

Extramet Industrie v Council (21 March 1991) C-358/89, ECLI:EU:C:1991:144,
ECR 1991 I-02501 (Opinion of Advocate General Jacobs).

Generics (UK) Ltd. and others v Competition and Markets Authority (22 January
2020) C-307/18, ECLI:EU:C:2020:28 (Opinion of Advocate General Kokott).

MEO — Serviços de Comunicações e Multimédia SA v Autoridade da Concorrência
(20 December 2017) C-525/16, ECLI:EU:C:2017:1020 (Opinion of Advocate
General Wahl).

Moser Baer India Ltd. v Council (2 October 2008) C-535/06 P, ECLI:EU:C:2008:
532, ECR 2009 I-07051 (Opinion of Advocate General Trstenjak).

Nölle v Hauptzollamt Bremen-Freihafen (22 October 1991) C-16/90, ECLI:EU:
C:1991:402, ECR 1991 I-05163 (Opinion of Advocate General Van Gerven).

Reyners v Belgium (28 May 1974) C-2/74, ECLI:EU:C:1974:59, ECR 1974-00631
(Opinion of Advocate General Mayras).

WTO Adjudicative Bodies

Australia – Anti-Dumping Measures on A4 Copy Paper (4 December 2019)
WT/DS529/R (Panel Report).

Brazil – Desiccated Coconut (21 February 1997) WT/DS22/AB/R (Appellate Body
Report).

*European Communities – Anti-Dumping Duties on Malleable Cast Iron Tube or
Pipe Fittings from Brazil* (22 July 2003) WT/DS219/AB/R (Appellate Body
Report).

*European Communities – Conditions for the Granting of Tariff Preferences to
Developing Countries* (7 April 2004) WT/DS246/AB/R (Appellate Body
Report).

*European Communities – Countervailing Measures on Dynamic Random Access
Memory Chips from Korea* (17 June 2005) WT/DS299/R (Panel Report).

European Communities – Definitive Anti-Dumping Measures on Certain Iron or Steel Fasteners from China (15 July 2011) WT/DS397/AB/R (Appellate Body Report).

European Communities – Regime for the Importation, Sale and Distribution of Bananas (22 May 1997) WT/DS27/R (Panel Report).

European Communities – Regime for the Importation, Sale and Distribution of Bananas (9 September 1997) WT/DS27/AB/R (Appellate Body Report).

European Union – Anti-Dumping Measures on Biodiesel from Argentina (29 March 2016) WT/DS473/R (Panel Report).

European Union – Anti-Dumping Measures on Biodiesel from Argentina (6 October 2016) WT/DS473/AB/R (Appellate Body Report).

European Union – Anti-Dumping Measures on Certain Footwear from China (28 October 2011) WT/DS405/R (Panel Report).

European Union – Cost Adjustment Methodologies and Certain Anti-Dumping Measures on Imports from Russia (second complaint) (24 July 2020) WT/DS494/R (Panel Report).

Indonesia – Certain Measures Affecting the Automobile Industry (2 July 1998) WT/DS54/R; WT/DS55/R; WT/DS59/R; WT/DS64/R (Panel Report).

Mexico – Beef and Rice (29 November 2005) WT/DS295/AB/R (Appellate Body Report).

Ukraine – Anti-Dumping Measures on Ammonium Nitrate (12 September 2019) WT/DS493/AB/R (Appellate Body Report).

United States – Anti-Dumping Act of 1916 (European Communities) (31 March 2000) WT/DS136/R (Panel Report).

United States – Anti-Dumping Act of 1916 (European Communities) (26 September 2000) WT/DS136/AB/R; WT/DS162/AB/R (Appellate Body Report).

United States – Anti-Dumping and Countervailing Measures on Steel Plate from India (28 June 2002) WT/DS206/R (Panel Report).

United States – Continued Dumping and Subsidy Offset Act of 2000 (Byrd Amendment) (16 September 2002) WT/DS217/R (Panel Report).

United States – Customs Bond Directive for Merchandise Subject to Anti-Dumping/ Countervailing Duties (29 February 2008) WT/DS345/R (Panel Report).

United States – Definitive Anti-Dumping and Countervailing Duties on Certain Products from China (22 October 2010) WT/DS379/R (Panel Report).

United States – Denial of Most-Favoured Nation Treatment as to Non-Rubber Footwear from Brazil (19 June 1992) DS18/R (Panel Report).

United States – Measures Relating to Shrimp from Thailand (29 February 2008) WT/DS343/R (Panel Report).

United States – Definitive Anti-Dumping and Countervailing Duties on Certain Products from China (11 March 2011) WT/DS379/AB/R (Appellate Body Report).

United States – Final Countervailing Duty Determination with respect to certain Softwood Lumber from Canada (Softwood Lumber IV) (19 January 2004) WT/DS257/AB/R (Appellate Body Report).

International Treaties

International

Vienna Convention on the Law of Treaties (1155 U.N.T.S. 331) (23 May 1969).
Paris Agreement (U.N. Doc. FCCC/CP/2015/10/Add, 1) (13 December 2015).

World Trade Organization

Marrakesh Agreement Establishing the World Trade Organization (Uruguay Round Agreement) (1867 U.N.T.S. 154, Marrakesh 15 April 1994).
General Agreement on Tariffs and Trade 1994: Agreement Establishing the World Trade Organization, Annex 1A (1867 U.N.T.S. 190).
Agreement on Implementation of Article VI of the General Agreement on Tariffs and Trade 1994: Marrakesh Agreement Establishing the World Trade Organization, Annex 1A (1868 U.N.T.S. 201).
Agreement on Subsidies and Countervailing Measures: Marrakesh Agreement Establishing the World Trade Organization, Annex 1A (1869 U.N.T.S. 14).
Protocol on the Accession of the People's Republic of China (WT/L/432) (23 November 2001).

European Union

Treaty of Paris establishing the European Coal and Steel Community (18 April 1951).
Treaty of Rome establishing the European Economic Community (25 March 1957).
Single European Act (OJ 1987 L 169/1) (29 June 1987).
Treaty on European Union (Treaty of Maastricht) (OJ 1992 C 191/1) (29 July 1992).
Treaty of Amsterdam amending the Treaty on European Union, the Treaties establishing the European Communities and certain related acts (OJ 1997 C 340/01) (2 October 1997).
Treaty of Nice amending the Treaty on European Union, the Treaties establishing the European Communities and certain related acts (OJ 2001 C 80/1) (10 March 2001).
Treaty of Lisbon amending the Treaty on European Union and the Treaty establishing the European Community (OJ 2007 C 306/1) (13 December 2007).
Protocol No. 27 on the Internal Market and Competition (12008M/PRO/27).
Economic Partnership Agreement between the CARIFORUM States, of the one part, and the European Community and its Member States, of the other part (OJ 2008 L 289/3) (30 October 2008).

Comprehensive Economic and Trade Agreement (CETA) between Canada, of the one part, and the European Union and its Member States, of the other part (OJ 2017 L 11/23) (14 January 2017).

Free Trade Agreement between the European Union and its Member States, of the one part, and the Republic of Korea, of the other part (OJ 2011 L 127/6) (14 May 2011).

Free Trade Agreement between the European Union and the Socialist Republic of Viet Nam (OJ 2020 L 186/3) (12 June 2020).

Trade and Cooperation Agreement between the European Union and the European Atomic Energy Community, of the one part, and the United Kingdom of Great Britain and Northern Ireland, of the other part (OJ 2020 L 444/14) (31 December 2020).

European Union Legislation

Regulation (EEC) No 459/68 of the Council of 5 April 1968 on protection against dumping or the granting of bounties or subsidies by countries which are not members of the European Economic Community, OJ 1968 L 093/1.

Commission Decision of 15 July 1975 relating to a proceeding under Article 85 of the EEC Treaty (IV/27.000 – IFTRA rules for producers of virgin aluminium) (75/497/EEC), OJ 1975 L 228/3.

Commission Decision of 19 April 1977 relating to a proceeding under Article 86 of the EEC Treaty (ABG Oil Companies) (77/327/EEC), OJ 1977 L 117/1.

Commission Decision of 4 July 1984 relating to a proceeding under Article 85 of the EEC Treaty (Synthetic Fibres) (84/380/EEC), OJ 1984 L 207/17.

Commission Decision of 6 August 1984 relating to a proceeding under Article 85 of the EEC Treaty (IV/30.350 – zinc producer group) (84/405/EEC), OJ 1984 L 220/27.

Commission Decision of 19 December 1984 relating to a proceeding under Article 85 of the EEC Treaty (IV.26.870 – Aluminium imports from eastern Europe) (85/206/EEC), OJ 1985 L 92/1.

Commission Regulation (EEC) No 997/85 of 18 April 1985 imposing a provisional anti-dumping duty on imports of glycine originating in Japan, OJ 1985 L 107/8.

Council Regulation (EEC) No 2322/85 of 12 August 1985 imposing a definitive anti-dumping duty on imports of glycine originating in Japan, OJ 1985 L 218/1.

Commission Decision of 18 December 1985 relating to a proceeding pursuant to Article 85 of the EEC Treaty (IV/30.739 – Siemens/Fanuc) (85/618/EEC), OJ 1985 L 376/29.

Commission Regulation (EEC) No 3019/86 of 30 September 1986 imposing a provisional anti-dumping duty on imports of standardized multi-phase electric motors having an output of more than 0,75 kW but not more than 75 kW, originating in Bulgaria, Czechoslovakia, the German Democratic Republic, Hungary, Poland, Romania and the USSR, OJ 1986 L 280/68.

Commission Regulation (EEC) No 1361/87 of 18 May 1987 imposing a provisional anti-dumping duty on imports of ferro-silico-calcium/calcium silicide originating in Brazil, OJ 1987 L 129/5.

Council Regulation (EEC) No 3339/87 of 4 November 1987 imposing a definitive anti-dumping duty on imports of urea originating in Libya and Saudi Arabia and accepting undertakings given in connection with imports of urea originating in Czechoslovakia, the German Democratic Republic, Kuwait, the USSR, Trinidad and Tobago and Yugoslavia and terminating these investigations, OJ 1987 L 317/1.

Commission Decision of 22 December 1987 relating to a proceeding under Article 85 of EEC (IV/32.306 – Olivetti/Canon) (88/88/EEC), OJ 1988 L 52/51.

Commission Decision of 26 July 1988 relating to a proceeding under Articles 85 and 86 of the EEC Treaty (Tetra Pak I) (88/501/EEC), OJ 1988 L 272/27.

Commission Regulation (EEC) No 2140/89 of 12 July 1989 imposing a provisional anti-dumping duty on imports of certain compact disc players originating in Japan and South Korea, OJ 1989 L 205/5.

Commission Regulation (EEC) No 165/90 of 23 January 1990 imposing a provisional anti-dumping duty on imports of certain types of electronic microcircuits known as DRAMs (dynamic random access memories) originating in Japan, OJ 1990 L 20/5.

Commission Decision of 22 May 1990 accepting undertakings given in connection with the anti-dumping proceeding concerning imports of photo albums originating in South Korea and Hong Kong, and terminating the investigation (90/241/EEC), OJ 1990 L 138/48.

Council Regulation (EEC) No 541/91 of 4 March 1991 imposing a definitive anti-dumping duty on imports of barium chloride originating in the People's Republic of China, OJ 1991 L 60/1.

Commission Decision of 23 December 1992 relating to a proceeding pursuant to Article 85 of the EEEC Treaty (Ford/Volkswagen) (93/49/EEC), OJ 1993 L 20/14.

Commission Regulation (EEC) No 550/93 of 5 March 1993 imposing a provisional anti-dumping duty on imports of bicycles originating in the People's Republic of China, OJ 1993 L 58/12.

Commission Regulation (EEC) No 920/93 of 15 April 1993 imposing a provisional anti-dumping duty on imports of certain magnetic disks (3, 5 microdisks) originating in Japan, Taiwan and the People' s Republic of China, OJ L 1993 95/5.

Commission Decision of 29 April 1993 authorizing the French Republic to apply safeguard measures to the importation of bananas originating in the African, Caribbean and Pacific (ACP) States (92/236/EEC), OJ 1993 L 105/37.

Council Regulation (EC) No 3283/94 of 22 December 1994 on protection against dumped imports from countries not members of the European Community, OJ 1994 L 349/1.

Council Regulation (EC) 2557/94 of 19 October 1994 imposing a definitive anti-dumping duty on imports of calcium metal originating in the People's Republic of China and Russia, OJ 1994 L 207/27.

Commission Decision of 30 November 1994 relating to a proceeding under Article 85 of the EC Treaty (Cases IV/33.126 and 33.322 – Cement) (94/815/EC), OJ 1994 L 343/1.

Commission Regulation (EC) No 1748/95 of 17 July 1995 imposing a provisional anti-dumping duty on imports of peroxodisulphates (persulphates), originating in the People's Republic of China, OJ 1995 L 169/15.

Council Regulation (EC) 2962/95 of 18 December 1995 repealing Regulations (EEC) No 868/90 and (EEC) No 898/91 imposing definitive anti-dumping duties on imports of certain welded tubes, of iron or non-alloy steel, originating in Yugoslavia except Serbia and Montenegro and Romania, and in Turkey and Venezuela respectively, OJ 1995 L 308/65.

Council Regulation (EC) No 384/96 of 22 December 1995 on protection against dumped imports from countries not members of the European Community, OJ 1996 L 56/1.

Commission Regulation (EC) No 940/96 of 23 May 1996 imposing a provisional anti-dumping duty on imports of polyester textured filament yarn originating in Indonesia and Thailand, OJ 1996 L 128/3.

Commission Regulation (EC) No 18/98 of 7 January 1998 imposing a provisional anti-dumping duty on imports of synthetic fibre ropes originating in India, OJ 1998 L 4/28.

Council Regulation (EC) No 1965/98 of 9 September 1998 imposing a definitive anti-dumping duty on imports of polysulphide polymers originating in the United States of America and collecting definitively the provisional duty imposed, OJ 1998 L 255/1.

Commission Decision of 24 January 1999 relating to a proceeding under Article 81 of the EC Treaty and Article 53 of the EEA Agreement (CECED) (2000/475/EC), OJ 2000 L 187/47.

Commission Decision of 25 July 2001 relating to a proceeding under Article 82 of the EC Treaty: COMP/C-1/36.915 – Deutsche Post AG – Interception of cross-border mail (2001/892/EC), OJ 2001 L 331/40.

Council Regulation (EC) No 1/2003 of 16 December 2002 on the implementation of the rules on competition laid down in Articles 81 and 82 of the Treaty (Council of the European Union), OJ 2003 L 1/1.

Commission Regulation (EC) No 781/2003 of 7 May 2003 imposing a provisional anti-dumping duty on imports of furfuryl alcohol originating in the People's Republic of China, OJ 2003 L 114/16.

Council Regulation (EC) No 930/2003 of 26 May 2003 terminating the anti-dumping and anti-subsidy proceedings concerning imports of farmed Atlantic salmon originating in Norway and the anti-dumping proceeding concerning imports of farmed Atlantic salmon originating in Chile and the Faeroe Islands, OJ 2003 L 133/1.

Directive 2003/87/EC of the European Parliament and of the Council of 13 October 2003 establishing a system for greenhouse gas emission allowance trading within the Union and amending Council Directive 96/61/EC, OJ 2003 L 275/32.

Council Regulation (EC) No 74/2004 of 13 January 2004 imposing a definitive countervailing duty on imports of cotton-type bedlinen originating in India, OJ 2004 L 12/1.

Council Regulation (EC) No 139/2004 of 20 January 2004 on the control of concentrations between undertakings, OJ 2004 L 24/1

Council Regulation (EC) No 435/2004 of 8 March 2004 imposing a definitive anti-dumping duty and collecting definitively the provisional duty imposed on imports of sodium cyclamate originating in the People's Republic of China and Indonesia, OJ 2004 L 72/1.

Council Regulation (EC) No 437/2004 of 8 March 2004 imposing definitive anti-dumping duty and collecting definitively the provisional duty imposed on imports of large rainbow trout originating in Norway and the Faeroe Islands, OJ 2004 L 72/23.

Commission Regulation (EC) No 1009/2004 of 19 May 2004 imposing a provisional anti-dumping duty on imports of certain graphite electrode systems originating in India, OJ 2004 L 183/61.

Commission Decision of 24 May 2004 relating to a proceeding under Article 82 of the EC Treaty (Case COMP/C-3/37.792 Microsoft) (C(2004)900 final), OJ 2007 L 32/23.

Council Regulation (EC) No 1942/2004 of 2 November 2004 imposing a definitive anti-dumping duty and collecting definitively the provisional duty imposed on imports of okoumé plywood originating in the People's Republic of China, OJ 2004 L 336/4.

Commission Decision of 15 June 2005 relating to a proceeding under Article 82 of the EC Treaty and Article 54 of the EEA Agreement (Case COMP/A.37.507/F3 – AstraZeneca) (C(2005) 1757), OJ 2006 L 332/24.

Commission Regulation (EC) No 1259/2005 of 27 July 2005 imposing a provisional anti-dumping duty on imports of tartaric acid originating in the People's Republic of China, OJ 2005 L 200/73.

Council Regulation (EC) No 954/2006 of 27 June 2006 imposing definitive anti-dumping duty on imports of certain seamless pipes and tubes, of iron or steel originating in Croatia, Romania, Russia and Ukraine, OJ 2006 L 175/4.

Commission Regulation (EC) 2005/2006 of 22 December 2006 imposing provisional anti-dumping duties on imports of synthetic staple fibres of polyesters (PSF) originating in Malaysia and Taiwan, OJ 2006 L 379/65.

Commission Regulation (EC) No 1350/2006 of 13 September 2006 imposing a provisional anti-dumping duty on imports of certain tungsten electrodes originating in the People's Republic of China, OJ 2006 L 250/10.

Council Regulation (EC) No 1472/2006 of 5 October 2006 imposing a definitive anti-dumping duty and collecting definitively the provisional duty imposed on imports of certain footwear with uppers of leather originating in the People's Republic of China and Vietnam, OJ 2006 L 275/1.

Commission Decision of 19 June 2007 terminating the anti-dumping proceeding concerning imports of synthetic staple fibres of polyesters (PSF) originating in

Malaysia and Taiwan releasing the amounts secured by way of the provisional duties imposed (2007/430/EC), OJ 2007 L 160/30.

Commission Regulation (EC) No 994/2007 of 28 August 2007 imposing a provisional anti-dumping duty on imports of ferro-silicon originating in the People's Republic of China, Egypt, Kazakhstan, the former Yugoslav Republic of Macedonia and Russia, OJ 2007 L 223/1.

Commission Regulation (EC) No 1071/2007 of 18 September 2007 imposing a provisional anti-dumping duty on imports of coke of coal in pieces with a diameter of more than 80 mm (Coke 80+) originating in the People's Republic of China, OJ 2007 L 244/3.

Council Regulation (EC) No 1205/2007 of 15 October 2007 imposing anti-dumping duties on imports of integrated electronic compact fluorescent lamps (CFL-i) originating in the People's Republic of China following an expiry review pursuant to Article 11(2) of Council Regulation (EC) No 384/96 and extending to imports of the same product consigned from the Socialist Republic of Vietnam, the Islamic Republic of Pakistan and the Republic of the Philippines, OJ 2007 L 272/1.

Council Regulation (EC) No 1279/2007 of 30 October 2007 imposing a definitive anti-dumping duty on certain iron or steel ropes and cables originating in the Russian Federation, and repealing the anti-dumping measures on imports of certain iron or steel ropes and cables originating in Thailand and Turkey, OJ 2007 L 285/1.

Council Regulation (EC) No 1331/2007 of 13 November 2007 imposing a definitive anti-dumping duty on imports of dicyandiamide originating in the People's Republic of China, OJ 2007 L 296/1.

Council Regulation (EC) No 1420/2007 of 4 December 2007 imposing a definitive anti-dumping duty on imports of silico-manganese originating in the People's Republic of China and Kazakhstan and terminating the proceeding on imports of silico-manganese originating in Ukraine, OJ 2007 L 317/5.

Council Regulation (EC) No 221/2008 of 10 March 2008 imposing a definitive anti-dumping duty and collecting definitively the provisional duty imposed on imports of certain manganese dioxides originating in South Africa, OJ 2008 L 69/1.

Council Regulation (EC) No 1193/2008 of 1 December 2008 imposing a definitive anti-dumping duty and collecting definitively the provisional duties imposed on imports of citric acid originating in the People's Republic of China, OJ 2008 L 323/1.

Commission Regulation (EC) No 112/2009 of 6 February 2009 imposing a provisional anti-dumping duty on imports of wire rod originating in the People's Republic of China and the Republic of Moldova, OJ 2009 L 38/3.

Commission Regulation (EC) No 193/2009 of 11 March 2009 imposing a provisional anti-dumping duty on imports of biodiesel originating in the United States of America, OJ 2009 L 67/22.

Council Regulation (EC) No 383/2009 of 5 May 2009 imposing a definitive anti-dumping duty and collecting definitively the provisional duty imposed on imports of certain pre- and post-stressing wires and wire strands of non-alloy steel (PSC wires and strands) originating in the People's Republic of China, OJ 2009 L 118/1.

Council Regulation (EC) No 428/2009 of 5 May 2009 setting up a Community regime for the control of exports, transfer, brokering and transit of dual-use items, OJ 2009 L 134/1.

Council Regulation (EC) No 393/2009 of 11 May 2009 imposing a definitive anti-dumping duty and collecting definitively the provisional duty imposed on imports of certain candles, tapers and the like originating in the People's Republic of China, OJ 2009 L 119/1.

Commission Decision of 5 October 2009 accepting an undertaking offered in connection with the anti-dumping proceeding concerning imports of certain aluminium foil originating, inter alia, in Brazil (2009/736/EC), OJ 2009 L 262/50.

Commission Decision (EU) 177/2010 of 23 March 2010 amending Decision 2006/109/EC by accepting three offers to join the joint price undertaking accepted in connection with the anti-dumping proceeding concerning imports of certain castings originating in the People's Republic of China, OJ 2010 L 77/55.

Commission Regulation (EU) 330/2010 of 20 April 2010 on the application of Article 101(3) of the Treaty on the Functioning of the European Union to categories of vertical agreements and concerted practices, OJ 2010 L 102/1.

Commission Decision of 30 June 2010 relating to a proceeding under Article 101 TFEU and Article 53 EEA Agreement (COMP/38.344 – Prestressing Steel) (C(2010) 4387 final), OJ 2011 C 339/7.

Commission Regulation (EU) 1217/2010 of 14 December 2010 on the application of Article 101(3) of the Treaty on the Functioning of the European Union to certain categories of research and development agreements, OJ 2010 L 335/36.

Regulation (EU) No 182/2011 of the European Parliament and of the Council of 16 February 2011 laying down the rules and general principles concerning mechanisms for control by Member States of the Commission's exercise of implementing powers, OJ L 2011 55/13.

Council Implementing Regulation (EU) No 451/2011 of 6 May 2011 imposing a definitive anti-dumping duty and collecting definitively the provisional duty imposed on imports of coated fine paper originating in the People's Republic of China, OJ 2011 L 128/1.

Commission Decision (EU) 279/2011 of 13 May 2011 accepting an undertaking offered in connection with the anti-dumping proceeding concerning imports of zeolite A powder originating in Bosnia and Herzegovina, OJ 2011 L 125/26.

Council Implementing Regulation (EU) No 792/2011 of 5 August 2011 imposing a definitive anti-dumping duty and collecting definitively the provisional duty imposed on imports of certain ring binder mechanisms originating in Thailand, OJ 2011 L 204/11.

Regulation (EU) No 978/2012 of the European Parliament and of the Council of 25 October 2012 applying a scheme of generalised tariff preferences, OJ 2012 L 303/1.

Commission Regulation (EU) No 1072/2012 of 14 November 2012 imposing a provisional anti-dumping duty on imports of ceramic tableware and kitchenware originating in the People's Republic of China, OJ 2012 L 318/28.

Commission Decision (EU) 81/2013 of 13 February 2013 terminating the anti-dumping proceeding concerning imports of white phosphorus, also called elemental or yellow phosphorus, originating in the Republic of Kazakhstan, OJ 2013 L 43/38.

Council Implementing Regulation (EU) 412/2013 of 13 May 2013 imposing a definitive anti-dumping duty and collecting definitively the provisional duty imposed on imports of ceramic tableware and kitchenware originating in the People's Republic of China, OJ 2013 L 131/1.

Commission Regulation (EU) No 513/2013 of 4 June 2013 imposing a provisional anti-dumping duty on imports of crystalline silicon photovoltaic modules and key components (i.e. cells and wafers) originating in or consigned from the People's Republic of China and amending Regulation (EU) No 182/2013 making these imports originating in or consigned from the People's Republic of China subject to registration, OJ 2013 L 152/5.

Commission Regulation (EU) No 1205/2013 of 26 November 2013 imposing a provisional anti-dumping duty on imports of solar glass from the People's Republic of China, OJ 2013 L 316/8.

Council Implementing Regulation (EU) 1238/2013 of 2 December 2013 imposing a definitive anti-dumping duty and collecting definitively the provisional duty imposed on imports of crystalline silicon photovoltaic modules and key components (i.e. cells) originating in or consigned from the People's Republic of China, OJ 2013 L 325/1.

Commission Implementing Decision (EU) 707/2013 of 4 December 2013 confirming the acceptance of an undertaking offered in connection with the anti-dumping and anti-subsidy proceedings concerning imports of crystalline silicon photovoltaic modules and key components (i.e. cells) originating in or consigned from the People's Republic of China for the period of application of definitive measures, OJ 2013 L 325/214.

Commission Implementing Regulation (EU) 2015/82 of 21 January 2015 imposing a definitive anti-dumping duty on imports of citric acid originating in the People's Republic of China following an expiry review pursuant to Article 11(2) of Council Regulation (EC) No 1225/2009 and of partial interim reviews pursuant to Article 11(3) of Regulation (EC) No 1225/2009, OJ 2015 L 15/8.

Regulation (EU) 2015/478 of the European Parliament and of the Council of 11 March 2015 on common rules for imports, OJ 2015 L 83/16.

Regulation (EU) 2015/755 of the European Parliament and of the Council of 29 April 2015 on common rules for imports from certain third countries, OJ 2015 L 123/33.

Commission Implementing Regulation (EU) 2015/763 of 12 May 2015 imposing a provisional anti-dumping duty on imports of certain grain-oriented flat-rolled products of silicon-electrical steel originating in the People's Republic of

China, Japan, the Republic of Korea, the Russian Federation and the United States of America, OJ 2015 L 120/10.

Commission Implementing Regulation (EU) 2015/787 of 19 May 2015 imposing a provisional anti-dumping duty on imports of acesulfame potassium originating in the People's Republic of China as well as acesulfame potassium originating in the People's Republic of China contained in certain preparations and/or mixtures, OJ 2015 L 125/15.

Commission Implementing Regulation (EU) 2015/1429 of 26 August 2015 imposing a definitive anti-dumping duty on imports of stainless steel cold-rolled flat products originating in the People's Republic of China and Taiwan, OJ 2015 L 224/10.

Council Regulation (EU) 2015/1589 of 13 July 2015 laying down detailed rules for the application of Article 108 of the Treaty on the Functioning of the European Union, OJ 2015 L 248/9.

Regulation (EU) 2015/1843 of the European Parliament and of the Council of 6 October 2015 laying down Union procedures in the field of the common commercial policy in order to ensure the exercise of the Union's rights under international trade rules, in particular those established under the auspices of the World Trade Organization, OJ 2015 L 272/1.

Commission Implementing Regulation (EU) 2015/1953 of 29 October 2015 imposing a definitive anti-dumping duty on imports of certain grain-oriented flat-rolled products of silicon-electrical steel originating in the People's Republic of China, Japan, the Republic of Korea, the Russian Federation and the United States of America, OJ 2015 L 284/109.

Commission Implementing Regulation (EU) 2016/388 of 17 March 2016 imposing a definitive anti-dumping duty on imports of tubes and pipes of ductile cast iron (also known as spheroidal graphite cast iron) originating in India, OJ 2016 L 73/53.

Regulation (EU) 2016/1036 of the European Parliament and of the Council of 8 June 2016 on protection against dumped imports from countries not members of the European Union, OJ 2016 L 176/21.

Regulation (EU) 2016/1037 of the European Parliament and of the Council of 8 June 2016 on protection against subsidised imports from countries not members of the European Union, OJ 2016 L 176/55.

Commission Implementing Regulation (EU) 2016/1247 of 28 July 2016 imposing a definitive anti-dumping duty and collecting definitively the provisional duty imposed on imports of aspartame originating in the People's Republic of China, OJ 2016 L 204/92.

Commission Implementing Regulation (EU) 2016/1778 of 6 October 2016 imposing a provisional anti-dumping duty on imports of certain hot-rolled flat products of iron, non-alloy or other alloy steel originating in the People's Republic of China, OJ 2016 L 272/33.

Commission Implementing Regulation (EU) 2016/2005 of 16 November 2016 imposing a provisional anti-dumping duty on imports of certain lightweight thermal paper originating in the Republic of Korea, OJ 2016 L 310/1.

Commission Implementing Regulation (EU) 2017/141 of 26 January 2017 imposing definitive anti-dumping duties on imports of certain stainless steel tube and pipe butt-welding fittings, whether or not finished, originating in the People's Republic of China and Taiwan, OJ 2017 L 22/14.

Commission Implementing Regulation (EU) 2017/336 of 27 February 2017 imposing a definitive anti-dumping duty and collecting definitively the provisional duty imposed on imports of certain heavy plate of non-alloy or other alloy steel originating in the People's Republic of China, OJ 2017 L 50/18.

Commission Implementing Regulation (EU) 2017/366 of 1 March 2017 imposing definitive countervailing duties on imports of crystalline silicon photovoltaic modules and key components (i.e. cells) originating in or consigned from the People's Republic of China following an expiry review pursuant to Article 18(2) of Regulation (EU) 2016/1037 of the European Parliament and of the Council and terminating the partial interim review investigation pursuant to Article 19(3) of Regulation (EU) 2016/1037, OJ 2017 L 56/1.

Regulation (EU) 2017/821 of the European Parliament and of the Council of 17 May 2017 laying down supply chain due diligence obligations for Union importers of tin, tantalum and tungsten, their ores, and gold originating from conflict-affected and high-risk areas, OJ 2017 L 130/1.

Commission Implementing Regulation (EU) 2017/1570 of 15 September 2017 amending Implementing Regulation (EU) 2017/366 and Implementing Regulation (EU) 2017/367 imposing definitive countervailing and anti-dumping duties on imports of crystalline silicon photovoltaic modules and key components (i.e. cells) originating in or consigned from the People's Republic of China and repealing Implementing Decision 2013/707/EU confirming the acceptance of an undertaking offered in connection with the anti-dumping and anti-subsidy proceedings concerning imports of crystalline silicon photovoltaic modules and key components (i.e. cells) originating in or consigned from the People's Republic of China for the period of application of definitive measures, OJ 2017 L 238/22.

Regulation (EU) 2017/2321 of the European Parliament and of the Council of 12 December 2017 amending Regulation (EU) 2016/1036 on protection against dumped imports from countries not members of the European Union and Regulation (EU) 2016/1037 on protection against subsidised imports from countries not members of the European Union, OJ 2017 L 338/1.

Commission Regulation (EU) 2018/683 of 4 May 2018 imposing a provisional anti-dumping duty on imports of certain pneumatic tyres, new or retreaded, of rubber, of a kind used for buses or lorries, with a load index exceeding 121 originating in the People's Republic of China, and amending Implementing Regulation (EU) 2018/163, OJ 2018 L 116/8.

Regulation (EU) 2018/825 of the European Parliament and of the Council of 30 May 2018 amending Regulation (EU) 2016/1036 on protection against dumped imports from countries not members of the European Union and Regulation (EU) 2016/1037 on protection against subsidised imports from countries not members of the European Union, OJ 2018 L 143/1.

Commission Implementing Regulation (EU) 2018/1012 of 17 July 2018 imposing a provisional anti-dumping duty on imports of electric bicycles originating in the People's Republic of China and amending Implementing Regulation (EU) 2018/ 671, OJ 2018 L 181/7.

Commission Implementing Regulation (EU) 2019/73 of 17 January 2019 imposing a definitive anti-dumping duty and definitively collecting the provisional duty imposed on imports of electric bicycles originating in the People's Republic of China, OJ 2019 L 16/108.

Commission Decision of 6 February 2019 declaring a concentration to be incompatible with the internal market and the functioning of the EEA agreement (Case M.8677 Siemens/Alstom) (C(2019) 921 final), OJ 2019 C 300/14.

Commission Implementing Decision (EU) 2019/245 of 11 February 2019 accepting undertaking offers following the imposition of definitive countervailing duties on imports of biodiesel originating in Argentina, OJ 2019 L 40/71.

Commission Implementing Regulation (EU) 2019/244 of 11 February 2019 imposing a definitive countervailing duty on imports of biodiesel originating in Argentina, OJ 2019 L 40/1.

Commission Implementing Regulation (EU) 2019/576 of 10 April 2019 imposing a provisional anti-dumping duty on imports of mixtures of urea and ammonium nitrate originating in Russia, Trinidad and Tobago and the United States of America, OJ 2019 L 100/7.

Commission Implementing Regulation (EU) 2019/687 of 2 May 2019 imposing a definitive anti-dumping duty on imports of certain organic coated steel products originating in the People's Republic of China following an expiry review pursuant to Article 11 (2) of Regulation (EU) 2016/1036 of the European Parliament and of the Council, OJ 2019 L 116/5.

Commission Implementing Regulation (EU) 2019/915 of 4 June 2019 imposing a definitive anti-dumping duty on imports of certain aluminium foil in rolls originating in the People's Republic of China following an expiry review under Article 11(2) of Regulation (EU) 2016/1036 of the European Parliament and of the Council, OJ 2019 L 146/63.

Commission Implementing Regulation (EU) 2019/1198 of 12 July 2019 imposing a definitive anti-dumping duty on imports of ceramic tableware and kitchenware originating in the People's Republic of China following an expiry review pursuant to Article 11(2) of Regulation (EU) No 2016/1036, OJ 2019 L 189/8.

Commission Implementing Regulation (EU) 2019/1259 of 24 July 2019 imposing a definitive anti-dumping duty on imports of threaded tube or pipe cast fittings, of malleable cast iron and spheroidal graphite cast iron, originating in the People's Republic of China and Thailand, following an expiry review pursuant to Article 11(2) of Regulation (EU) 2016/1036 of the European Parliament and of the Council, OJ 2019 L 197/2.

Commission Implementing Regulation (EU) 2019/1267 of 26 July 2019 imposing a definitive anti-dumping duty on imports of tungsten electrodes originating in the People's Republic of China following an expiry review under Article 11(2) of Regulation (EU) 2016/1036, OJ 2019 L 200/4.

Commission Implementing Regulation (EU) 2019/1344 of 12 August 2019 imposing a provisional countervailing duty on imports of biodiesel originating in Indonesia, OJ 2019 L 212/1.

Commission Implementing Regulation (EU) 2019/1379 of 28 August 2019 imposing a definitive anti-dumping duty on imports of bicycles originating in the People's Republic of China as extended to imports of bicycles consigned from Indonesia, Malaysia, Sri Lanka, Tunisia, Cambodia, Pakistan and the Philippines, whether declared as originating in these countries or not, following an expiry review pursuant to Article 11(2) of Regulation (EU) No 2016/1036, OJ 2019 L 225/1.

Commission Implementing Regulation (EU) 2019/1662 of 1 October 2019 imposing a definitive anti-dumping duty on imports of ironing boards originating in the People's Republic of China following an expiry review pursuant to Article 11(2) of Regulation (EU) 2016/1036 of the European Parliament and of the Council, OJ 2019 L 252/1.

Commission Implementing Regulation (EU) 2019/1688 of 8 October 2019 imposing a definitive anti-dumping duty and definitively collecting the provisional duty imposed on imports of mixtures of urea and ammonium nitrate originating in Russia, Trinidad and Tobago and the United States of America, OJ 2019 L 258/21.

Commission Implementing Regulation (EU) 2019/1693 of 9 October 2019 imposing a provisional anti-dumping duty on imports of steel road wheels originating in the People's Republic of China, OJ 2019 L 259/15.

Commission Implementing Regulation (EU) 2019/2092 of 28 November 2019 imposing a definitive countervailing duty on imports of biodiesel originating in Indonesia, OJ 2019 L 317/92.

Commission Implementing Regulation (EU) 2020/39 of 16 January 2020 imposing a definitive anti-dumping duty on imports of peroxosulphates (persulphates) originating in the People's Republic of China following an expiry review pursuant to Article 11(2) of Regulation (EU) 2016/1036 of the European Parliament and of the Council, OJ 2020 L 13/18.

Commission Implementing Regulation (EU) 2020/353 of 3 March 2020 imposing a definitive anti-dumping duty and definitively collecting the provisional duty imposed on imports of steel road wheels originating in the People's Republic of China, OJ 2020 L 65/9.

Commission Implementing Regulation (EU) 2020/379 of 5 March 2020 imposing a provisional countervailing duty on imports of continuous filament glass fibre products originating in Egypt, OJ 2020 L 69/14.

Commission Implementing Regulation (EU) 2020/492 of 1 April 2020 imposing definitive anti-dumping duties on imports of certain woven and/or stitched glass fibre fabrics originating in the People's Republic of China and Egypt, OJ 2020 L 108/1.

Commission Implementing Regulation (EU) 2020/508 of 7 April 2020 imposing a provisional anti-dumping duty on imports of certain hot rolled stainless steel sheets and coils originating in Indonesia, the People's Republic of China and Taiwan, OJ 2020 L 110/3.

Commission Implementing Regulation (EU) 2020/705 of 26 May 2020 imposing a provisional anti-dumping duty on imports of certain heavyweight thermal paper originating in the Republic of Korea, OJ 2020 L 164/28.

Commission Implementing Regulation (EU) 2020/776 of 12 June 2020 imposing definitive countervailing duties on imports of certain woven and/or stitched glass fibre fabrics originating in the People's Republic of China and Egypt and amending Commission Implementing Regulation (EU) 2020/492 imposing definitive anti-dumping duties on imports of certain woven and/or stitched glass fibre fabrics originating in the People's Republic of China and Egypt, OJ 2020 L 189/1.

Commission Implementing Regulation (EU) 2020/870 of 24 June 2020 imposing a definitive countervailing duty and definitively collecting the provisional countervailing duty imposed on imports of continuous filament glass fibre products originating in Egypt, and levying the definitive countervailing duty on the registered imports of continuous filament glass fibre products originating in Egypt, OJ 2020 L 201/10.

Commission Implementing Regulation (EU) 2020/909 of 30 June 2020 imposing a definitive anti-dumping duty on imports of ferro-silicon originating in Russia and the People's Republic of China, following an expiry review pursuant to Article 11(2) of Regulation (EU) 2016/1036, OJ 2020 L 208/2.

Commission Implementing Regulation (EU) 2020/1080 of 22 July 2020 imposing a definitive anti-dumping duty on imports of solar glass originating in the People's Republic of China following an expiry review pursuant to Article 11 (2) of Regulation (EU) 2016/1036 of the European Parliament and of the Council, OJ 2020 L 238/1.

Commission Implementing Decision (EU) 2020/1202 of 14 August 2020 terminating the anti-dumping proceeding concerning imports of pins and staples originating in the People's Republic of China and subjecting imports of pins and staples originating in the People's Republic of China to surveillance, OJ 2020 L 269/40.

Commission Implementing Regulation (EU) 2020/1336 of 25 September 2020 imposing definitive anti-dumping duties on imports of certain polyvinyl alcohols originating in the People's Republic of China, OJ 2020 L 315/1.

Commission Implementing Regulation (EU) 2020/1408 of 6 October 2020 imposing a definitive anti-dumping duty and definitively collecting the provisional duty on imports of certain hot rolled stainless steel sheets and coils originating in Indonesia, the People's Republic of China and Taiwan, OJ 2020 L 325/26.

Commission Implementing Regulation (EU) 2020/1428 of 12 October 2020 imposing a provisional anti-dumping duty on imports of aluminium extrusions originating in the People's Republic of China, OJ 2020 L 336/8.

Commission Implementing Regulation (EU) 2020/1524 of 19 October 2020 imposing a definitive anti-dumping duty and definitively collecting the provisional duty imposed on imports of certain heavyweight thermal paper originating in the Republic of Korea, OJ 2020 L 346/19.

Commission Implementing Regulation (EU) 2020/1534 of 21 October 2020 imposing a definitive anti-dumping duty on imports of certain prepared or preserved citrus fruits (namely mandarins, etc.) originating in the People's Republic of China following an expiry review pursuant to Article 11(2) of Regulation (EU) 2016/1036 of the European Parliament and of the Council, OJ 2020 L 351/2.

Commission Implementing Regulation (EU) 2021/9 of 6 January 2021 imposing a provisional anti-dumping duty on imports of certain hot-rolled flat products of iron, non-alloy or other alloy steel originating in Turkey, OJ 2021 L 3/4.

Commission Implementing Regulation (EU) 2021/546 of 29 March 2021 imposing a definitive anti-dumping duty and definitively collecting the provisional duty imposed on imports of aluminium extrusions originating in the People's Republic of China, OJ 2021 L 109/1.

Commission Implementing Regulation (EU) 2021/582 of of 9 April 2021 imposing a provisional anti-dumping duty on imports of aluminium flat-rolled products originating in the People's Republic of China, OJ 2021 L 124/40.

Commission Implementing Regulation (EU) 2021/854 of 27 May 2021 imposing a provisional anti-dumping duty on imports of stainless steel cold-rolled flat products originating in India and Indonesia, OJ 2021 L 188/61.

Commission Implementing Regulation (EU) 2021/939 of 10 June 2021 imposing a provisional anti-dumping duty on imports of mono ethylene glycol originating in the United States of America and the Kingdom of Saudi Arabia, OJ 2021 L 205/4.

Commission Implementing Regulation (EU) 2021/940 of 10 June 2021 imposing a provisional anti-dumping duty on imports of birch plywood originating in Russia, OJ 2021 L 205/47.

Commission Implementing Reglation (EU) 2021/983 of 17 June 2021 imposing a provisional anti-dumping duty on imports of aluminium converter foil originating in the People's Republic of China, OJ 2021 L 216/142.

Commission Implementing Regulation (EU) 2021/1100 of 5 July 2021 imposing a definitive anti-dumping duty and definitively collecting the provisional duty imposed on imports of certain hot-rolled flat products or iron, non-alloy or other allow steel originating in Turkey, OJ 2021 L 238/32.

Commission Implementing Regulation (EU) 2021/1266 of 29 July imposing a definitive anti-dumping duty on imports of biodiesel originating in the United States of America following an expiry review pursuant to Article 11(2) of Regulation (EU) 2016/1036 of the European Parliament and of the Council, OJ 2021 L 277/34.

Publications by the EU Institutions

European Commission

'First Report on Competition Policy' (Brussels, Luxembourg April 1972), available
at <https://op.europa.eu/en/publication-detail/-/publication/418817dc-c69b-42
b1-a787-013fd545017d>.

'Commission Notice on the definition of relevant market for the purposes of
Community competition law (97/C 372/03)', OJ 1997 C 372/5.

'White Paper on Modernisation of the Rules implementing Articles 85 and 86 of the
EC Treaty (1999/C 132/01)', OJ 1999 C 132/1.

Speech by Commissioner for Competition Mario Monti, '*The Future for Competition Policy in the European Union (SPEECH/01/340)*' (London 9 July 2001),
available at <https://ec.europa.eu/commission/presscorner/detail/en/
SPEECH_01_340>.

'Eighteenth annual report from the Commission to the European Parliament on the
Community's anti-dumping and anti-subsidy activities (1999) (COM/2000/0440
final)' (Brussels 11 July 2000).

Speech by Commissioner for Competition Mario Monti, '*Competition in a Social
Market Economy: Speech at the Conference of the European Parliament and the
European Commission on "Reform of European Competition Law"*' (Freiburg
9 November 2000), available at
<https://ec.europa.eu/competition/speeches/text/sp2000_022_en.pdf>.

'Guidelines on the assessment of horizontal mergers under the Council Regulation
on the control of concentrations between undertakings (2004/C 31/03)', OJ 2004
C 31/5.

'Guidelines on the effect on trade concept contained in Articles 81 and 82 of the
Treaty (2004/C 101/07)', OJ 2004 C 101/81.

'Guidelines on the application of Article 81(3) of the Treaty (2004/C 101/08)', OJ
2004 C 101/97.

Speech by Commissioner for Competition Neelie Kroes, '*European Competition
Policy – Delivering Better Markets and Better Choices (SPEECH/05/512)*'
(London 15 September 2005), available at <https://ec.europa.eu/commission/
presscorner/detail/en/SPEECH_05_512>.

'Communication from the Commission to the Council, the European Parliament, the
European Economic and Social Committee and the Committee of the Regions:
Global Europe: Competing in the World: A Contribution to the EU's Growth and
Jobs Strategy (COM(2006) 567 final)' (4 October 2006).

'Communication from the Commission: Global Europe – Europe's trade defence
instruments in a changing global economy: A green paper for public consultation
(COM (2006) 763 final)' (6 December 2006), available at <https://eur-lex.
europa.eu/legal-content/EN/TXT/?uri=celex%3A52006DC0763>.

'Communication from the Commission: Guidance on the Commission's enforcement priorities in applying Article 82 of the Treaty to abusive exclusionary conduct by dominant undertakings (2009/C 45/02)', OJ 2009 C 45/7.

Speech by Commissioner for Competition Joaquín Almunia, *Competition – what's in it for consumers? (SPEECH/11/803)*' (Poznan 24 November 2011), available at <https://ec.europa.eu/commission/presscorner/detail/en/SPEECH_11_803>.

Notice of initiation of an anti-dumping proceeding concerning imports of crystalline silicon photovoltaic modules and key components (i.e. cells and wafers) originating in the People's Republic of China, OJ 2012 C 269/5 (6 September 2012).

'Non-paper: Using EU Trade Policy to promote fundamental human rights' (2012), available at <http://trade.ec.europa.eu/doclib/docs/2012/february/tradoc_149064.pdf>.

'Commission Staff Working Document – Impact Assessment accompanying the document "proposal for a regulation of the European Parliament and of the Council on the modernisation of trade defence instruments" (COM(2013) 192 final) (SWD(2013) 106 final)' (Brussels 10 April 2013).

'Proposal for a Regulation of the European Parliament and of the Council amending Council Regulation (EC) No 1225/2009 on protection against dumped imports from countries not members of the European Community and Council Regulation (EC) No 597/2009 on protection against subsidised imports from countries not members of the European Community (COM(2013) 192 final)' (Brussels 10 April 2013).

'Statement by Commissioner for Trade Karel de Gucht on mobile telecommunications networks from China' (Brussels 15 May 2013), available at <https://ec.europa.eu/commission/presscorner/detail/en/MEMO_13_439>.

'Communication by the European Commission to the Council and the European Parliament on Modernisation of Trade Defence Instruments (COM(2013) 191 final)' (Brussels 10 April 2013).

'DG Trade Working Document: Draft Guidelines on Union Interest' (Brussels 2013), available at <http://trade.ec.europa.eu/doclib/docs/2013/april/tradoc_150839.pdf>.

'DG Trade Working Document: Draft Guidelines on the Determination of the Profit Margin Used in Establishing the Injury Margin' (Brussels 2013), available at <https://trade.ec.europa.eu/doclib/docs/2013/april/tradoc_150840.pdf>.

'Notice on agreements of minor importance which do not appreciably restrict competition under Article 101(1) of the Treaty on the Functioning of the European Union: De Minimis Notice', OJ 2014 C 291/1.

Speech by Director-General of the Directorate-General for Competition Johannes Laitenberger, *EU competition law in innovation and digital markets: fairness and the consumer welfare perspective*' (Brussels 10 October 2017), available at <https://ec.europa.eu/competition/speeches/text/sp2017_15_en.pdf>.

'Trade for all – Towards a more responsible trade and investment policy (COM (2015) 497)' (14 October 2015).

'EU ETS Handbook' (2015), available at <https://ec.europa.eu/clima/system/files/2017-03/ets_handbook_en.pdf>.

'Commission Staff Working Document: Report on the implementation of the European Commission Communication on "Trade, Growth and Development" and follow-up to the Council Conclusions on "EU's approach to trade, growth and development in the next decade" (SWD(2016) 47 final)' (Brussels 25 February 2016).

'Commission Staff Working Document Impact Assessment: Possible change in the calculation methodology of dumping regarding the People's Republic of China (and other non-market economies) (SWD(2016) 370 final)' (Brussels 9 November 2016).

'Annual Activity Report of DG Competition 2016' (7 December 2016), available at <https://ec.europa.eu/info/sites/info/files/file_import/aar-comp-2016_en_0.pdf>.

'Non-paper: Trade and Sustainable Development (TSD) chapters in EU Free Trade Agreements (FTAs)' (Brussels 11 July 2017), available at <https://trade.ec.europa.eu/doclib/docs/2017/july/tradoc_155686.pdf>.

Press release: *The EU is changing its anti-dumping and anti-subsidy legislation to address state induced market distortions* (5 October 2017), available at <http://trade.ec.europa.eu/doclib/press/index.cfm?id=1736>.

'Commission Staff Working Document on Significant Distortions in the Economy of the People's Republic of China for the Purposes of Trade Defence Investigations (SWD(2017) 483 final/2)' (Brussels 20 December 2017).

Speech by Commissioner for Competition Margrethe Vestager, *'Fairness and competition'* (Brussels 25 January 2018), available at <https://wayback.archive-it.org/12090/20191129212136/https://ec.europa.eu/commission/commissioners/2014-2019/vestager/announcements/fairness-and-competition_en>.

'Non-paper: Feedback and way forward on improving the implementation and enforcement of Trade and Sustainable Development chapters in EU Free Trade Agreements' (Brussels 26 February 2018), available at <https://trade.ec.europa.eu/doclib/docs/2018/february/tradoc_156618.pdf>.

'36th Annual Report from the Commission to the Council and the European Parliament on the EU's Anti-Dumping, Anti-Subsidy and Safeguard activities (2017) (COM(2018) 516 final)' (Brussels 31 July 2018).

'Factsheet: Europe's Trade Defence Instruments: Now Stronger and More Effective' (7 June 2018), available at <http://trade.ec.europa.eu/doclib/docs/2018/june/tradoc_156921.pdf>.

Press release: *EU trade defence: stronger and more effective rules enter into force* (7 June 2018), available at <http://trade.ec.europa.eu/doclib/press/index.cfm?id=1859>.

'Concept Paper on WTO Reform' (July 2018), available at <https://trade.ec.europa.eu/doclib/docs/2018/september/tradoc_157331.pdf>.

'Commission Staff Working Document: Midterm Evaluation of the Generalised Scheme of Preferences accompanying the document "Report from the European Commission to the European Parliament and the Council on the application of Regulation (EU) 978/2012 applying a Scheme of Generalised

Tariff Preferences and repealing Council Regulation (EC) No 732/2008" (SWD (2018) 430 final)' (Brussels 4 October 2018).

'Commission Staff Working Document accompanying the 37th Annual Report from the Commission to the Council and the European Parliament on the EU's Anti-Dumping, Anti-Subsidy and Safeguard Activities and the Use of Trade Defence Instruments by Third Countries (COM(2019) 158 final) (SWD(2019) 141 final)' (Brussels 27 March 2019).

'37th Annual Report from the Commission to the Council and the European Parliament on the EU's Anti-Dumping, Anti-Subsidy and Safeguard activities and the Use of trade defence instruments by Third Countries targeting the EU in 2018 (COM(2019) 158 final)' (Brussels 27 March 2019).

'Anti-Dumping, Anti-Subsidy, Safeguard Statistics covering 2018' (Brussels December 2018), available at <https://trade.ec.europa.eu/doclib/docs/2019/march/tradoc_157773.pdf>.

Press release: *EU triggers procedure to temporarily suspend trade preferences for Cambodia* (11 February 2019), available at <https://ec.europa.eu/commission/presscorner/detail/en/MEMO_19_988>.

Notice of initiation of an anti-dumping proceeding concerning imports of pins and staples originating in the People's Republic of China, OJ 2019 C 425/8 (18 December 2019).

Notice of initiation of an anti-dumping proceeding concerning imports of steel road wheels originating in the People's Republic of China, OJ 2019 C 60/7 (15 February 2019).

'2018 Annual Activity Report of the Directorate-General for Trade' (Brussels 15 July 2019), available at <https://ec.europa.eu/info/sites/info/files/trade_aar_2018_final.pdf>.

Press release: *EU set to sign trade and investment agreements with Vietnam on Sunday* (25 June 2019), available at <http://trade.ec.europa.eu/doclib/press/index.cfm?id=2036&title=EU-set-to-sign-trade-and-investment-agreements-with-Vietnam-on-Sunday>.

Speech by Commissioner Margrethe Vestager, '*Global markets and a fair deal for consumers*' (Bergen 4 September 2019), available at <https://wayback.archive-it.org/12090/20191130061303/https://ec.europa.eu/commission/commissioners/2014-2019/vestager/announcements/global-markets-and-fair-deal-con sumers_en>.

Candidate for President of the European Commission Ursula von der Leyen, 'Political Guidelines for the Next European Commission 2019-2024: A Union that strives for more – my agenda for Europe' (10 September 2019), available at <https://ec.europa.eu/info/sites/default/files/political-guidelines-next-commis sion_en_0.pdf>.

Press release: *EU-South Korea dispute settlement over workers' rights in Korea enters next stage* (19 December 2019), available at <https://trade.ec.europa.eu/doclib/press/index.cfm?id=2095>.

'Commission Staff Working Document Accompanying the 38th Annual Report from the Commission to the Council and the European Parliament on the EU's

Anti-Dumping, Anti-Subsidy and Safeguard activities and the Use of trade defence instruments by Third Countries targeting the EU in 2019 (COM(2020) final) (SWD(2020) 71 final)' (Brussels 30 April 2020).

Press release: *Trade defence report: restoring the level playing field for European producers* (4 May 2020), available at <https://trade.ec.europa.eu/doclib/press/index.cfm?id=2144>.

'White Paper on levelling the playing field as regards foreign subsidies (COM(2020) 253 final)' (Brussels 17 June 2020).

'Commission Staff Working Document on Significant Distortions in the Economy of the Russian Federation for the Purposes of Trade Defence Investigations (SWD (2020) 242 final)' (Brussels 22 October 2020).

'39th Annual Report from the Commission to the Council and the European Parliament on the EU's Anti-Dumping, Anti-Subsidy and Safeguard activities and the Use of trade defence instruments by Third Countries targeting the EU in 2020 (COM(2021) 496 final)' (Brussels 30 August 2021).

'Commission Staff Working Document Accompanying the 39th Annual Report from the Commission to the Council and the European Parliament on the EU's Anti-Dumping, Anti-Subsidy and Safeguard activities and the Use of trade defence instruments by Third Countries targeting the EU in 2020 (COM(2021) 496 final) (SWD(2021) 234 final)' (Brussels 30 August 2021).

'Anti-Dumping Questionnaire for Producers in the Analogue Country', available at <https://trade.ec.europa.eu/doclib/docs/2013/december/tradoc_151941.pdf>.

'Questionnaire for the Union producers in case AD659 – Thermal Paper (Certain Heavyweight)', available at <http://trade.ec.europa.eu/tdi/case_details.cfm?id=2419>.

'Trade defence: Help for SMEs', available at <https://ec.europa.eu/trade/policy/accessing-markets/trade-defence/actions-against-imports-into-the-eu/help-for-smes/>.

'How to Make an Anti-Dumping Complaint: A Guide', available at <https://trade.ec.europa.eu/doclib/docs/2006/december/tradoc_112295.2.20.pdf>.

European Parliament

'Amendments adopted by the European Parliament on 5 February 2014 on the proposal for a regulation of the European Parliament and of the Council amending Council Regulation (EC) No 1225/2009 on protection against dumped imports from countries not members of the European Community and Council Regulation (EC) No 597/2009 on protection against subsidised imports from countries not members of the European Community (COM(2013)0192)', OJ 2017 C 93/261.

Briefing: *'Human rights in EU Trade Policy – Unilateral Measures'* (January 2017), available at <https://www.europarl.europa.eu/RegData/etudes/BRIE/2017/595878/EPRS_BRI(2017)595878_EN.pdf>.

Committee on International Trade (INTA) of the European Parliament, 'Joost Koorte at the Public Hearing on EU Trade Defence Instruments' (28 February 2017), available at <http://www.europarl.europa.eu/news/en/news-room/20170223 IPR63789/committee-on-international-trade-28022017-(pm)>.

Briefing: *Human rights in EU trade agreements: The human rights clause and its application* (July 2019), available at <https://www.europarl.europa.eu/RegData/etudes/BRIE/2019/637975/EPRS_BRI(2019)637975_EN.pdf>.

Briefing: *'EU international procurement instrument'* (March 2020), available at <https://www.europarl.europa.eu/RegData/etudes/BRIE/2020/649403/EPRS_BRI(2020)649403_EN.pdf>.

European Council

European Council, 'Essen Declaration on a Strategy for Central and Eastern Europe (Bulletin of the European Communities No. 12/1994)' (9 December 1994).

Office for Official Publications of the European Communities, 'Presidency Conclusions of the Laeken European Council: Laeken Declaration on the future of the European Union' (Luxembourg 15 December 2001).

Speech by European Council President Charles Michel, *Strategic autonomy for Europe – the aim of our generation* (Brussels 28 September 2020), available at <https://www.consilium.europa.eu/de/press/press-releases/2020/09/28/l-autonomie-strategique-europeenne-est-l-objectif-de-notre-generation-discours-du-president-charles-michel-au-groupe-de-reflexion-bruegel/>.

Council of the European Union

'Review of the EU Sustainable Development Strategy (EU SDS) – Renewed Strategy (Document 10117/06)' (Brussels 26 June 2006).

'Note from the Presidency to the Permanent Representatives Committee on the subject of the proposal for a Regulation of the European Parliament and of the Council amending Regulation (EU) No 2016/1036 on protection against dumped imports from countries not members of the European Union and Regulation (EU) No 2016/1037 on protection against subsidised imports from countries not members of the European Union (15530/17): Analysis of the final compromise text with a view to agreement' (Interinstitutional file 2013/0103 (COD), Brussels 15 December 2017).

European Court of Auditors

'Special Report: Trade defence instruments: system for protecting EU businesses from dumped and subsidised imports functions well' (Luxembourg 2020) 17/2020, available at <https://www.eca.europa.eu/lists/ecadocuments/sr20_17/ sr_trade_defence_instruments_en.pdf>.

Printed by Printforce, the Netherlands